THE MAN OF
THE PEOPLE

THE MAN OF
THE PEOPLE

Political Dissent and the Making
of the American Presidency

Nathaniel C. Green

University Press of Kansas

Published by the University Press of Kansas (Lawrence, Kansas 66045),
which was organized by the Kansas Board of Regents and is operated
and funded by Emporia State University, Fort Hays State University,
Kansas State University, Pittsburg State University, the University of
Kansas, and Wichita State University.

Library of Congress Cataloging-in-Publication Data
Names: Green, Nathaniel C., author.
Title: The man of the people : political dissent and the making of the
American presidency / Nathaniel C. Green.
Description: Lawrence : University Press of Kansas, 2020. | Includes
bibliographical references and index. |
Identifiers: LCCN 2020008280 | ISBN 9780700629954 (cloth) |
ISBN 9780700629961 (epub)
Subjects: LCSH: Presidents—United States—History—18th century. |
Presidents—United States—History—19th century. | Political
culture—United States—History—18th century. | Political culture—
United States—History—19th century. | Opposition (Political
science)—United States—History—18th century. | Opposition
(Political science)—United States—History—19th century. | National
characteristics, American—Political aspects. | United States—
Politics and government—1789–1815. | United States—Politics and
government—1815–1861.
Classification: LCC E302.1 .G838 2020 | DDC 973.933092 [B]—dc23
LC record available at https://lccn.loc.gov/2020008280.

British Library Cataloguing-in-Publication Data is available.

Printed in the United States of America

10 9 8 7 6 5 4 3 2 1

The paper used in this publication is recycled and contains 30 percent
postconsumer waste. It is acid free and meets the minimum
requirements of the American National Standard for Permanence
of Paper for Printed Library Materials Z39.48-1992.

TO MY PARENTS,
who taught me to love questions
as much as answers.

AND TO JANE,
who always asks the best questions.

CONTENTS

ACKNOWLEDGMENTS

It is customary for authors to relegate their family to the final paragraph or two of their acknowledgements section. That has never made much sense to me. My family is the reason I exist, and thus the reason this book exists.

My parents, Bill and Diane Green, did not raise me to be a historian. But as a philosophy major and an English major, respectively, they did instill in me a love of reading, a love of discussing, and a love of writing. They also modeled for me each and every day what a loving marriage looks like. The joy I experience with Jane Fiegen Green, to whom I've been married for a decade, began with my parents' daily lessons on how to be a responsible, caring partner.

I met Jane in graduate school at Washington University in St. Louis, where this project began under the direction of David Konig (who was Jane's adviser, too), and Peter Kastor. Both Peter and David have left an indelible mark on my development as a scholar, and both have followed my career after graduate school. Peter went above and beyond his duties as a second reader of my dissertation, writing letters of recommendation for me, even after I graduated, and offering sage advice and encouragement.

Other scholars heard various iterations of this project and offered helpful insights and encouragement along the way, including Peter Onuf, Frank Cogliano, Andrew Robertson, and Aziz Rana. I had the great fortune of meeting Pauline Maier at a conference on the 225th anniversary of the Constitution in March, 2013, just six months before she passed away. I will always remember her tough but completely valid criticism of the paper I gave at that conference, on the role of the presidency in the public ratification debate, because it helped me refine my ideas into this book's first chapter.

While I was in graduate school, my parents, aunts, uncles, and cousins asked for updates on this project, and never lost faith that I would finish it. One of those cousins, Lee Casebolt, is the closest thing I have to a brother. He and his wife, Jen, provided a place for me to stay while conducting research at the University of Iowa libraries. But more than that, Lee has been a kind of kindred spirit to me. Growing up, we shared a love of intelligent conversation laced with juvenile humor. Lee is still the best natural storyteller I've ever met. He and Jen are two of the kindest, smartest, most caring people I know.

Beyond Washington University, this project benefited enormously from the insights and encouragement of Jeffrey L. Pasley, one of the foremost historians of early United States politics. Jeff was working on his outstanding study of the presidential election of 1796, *The First Presidential Contest: 1796 and the Founding of American Democracy* (also published by the University Press of Kansas) while I was in graduate school, and he graciously agreed to provide feedback on a seminar paper that eventually became chapter 4 of this book. He also agreed to serve as an outside reader on my thesis committee. That chapter, and this project as a whole, have been deeply influenced by Jeff's work, and I thank him for the time he gave.

As a graduate student, I received funding from Washington University in St. Louis, the White House Historical Association, and the International Center for Jefferson Studies. I remain grateful to them all for the financial assistance they provided, which allowed me to conduct research at the Library of Congress, the New-York Historical Society, Columbia University, the American Antiquarian Society, the Library of Virginia, and the Albert and Shirley Small Special Collections Library at the University of Virginia, all of which have staff who were generous with their time and expertise. This project also benefited greatly from the wealth of primary sources available in published collections, especially the *Documentary History of the Ratification of the Constitution*, and the Papers of the first four presidents and other national political figures. Rotunda has made the published volumes of these collections available digitally through the University of Virginia Press, which came in handy for me when a physical copy of a particular volume was not immediately available. I also made extensive use of databases such as Early American Imprints and Early American Newspapers, which not only make early newspapers and pamphlets available electronically but also preserve the originals in archives such as those named above. I am grateful to NewsBank, Inc., and the American Antiquarian Society, which maintain these databases, for the vast amount of materials they have made available. Without the ability to quote from these sources, this project would have taken even longer to complete, and the finished product would be far less rich.

I could not have completed this book without further assistance from the Fred W. Smith National Library for the Study of George Washington at Mount Vernon, which awarded me a fellowship in the spring of

2015, and the American Antiquarian Society, which awarded me a Jay and Deborah Last fellowship in 2019. I would like to thank both the Library (and the Mount Vernon Ladies Association) and the American Antiquarian Society for their support for my work and for the ease with which they granted permission to use their wealth of resources in this project. At Mount Vernon I met Holly Mayer and Dana Stefanelli, and my conversations with them, to my delight, did not end with my fellowship. At the American Antiquarian Society I met and learned from Ittai Orr and his partner, Jason Fitzgerald, as well as Whitney Stewart, Greg Childs, Kimberly Takahata, Rachel Walker, and Zachary Bennett. The staff at the American Antiquarian Society was especially helpful in tracking down materials. I would particularly like to thank Nan Wolverton, Elizabeth Pope, and Vincent Golden for their help throughout my time at AAS. Philip Lampi demonstrated his astounding knowledge of AAS's immense holdings when he tracked down one of the Andrew Jackson images featured in this book—without consulting the catalog—after discussing my project with me for only a matter of minutes.

Living in the Washington, DC, area has made research at the Library of Congress and the Fred W. Smith National Library for the Study of George Washington convenient, and the staff at both institutions were an immense help. Eric Frazier in the Library of Congress's Rare Book and Special Collections Division helped me locate the image that appears on the cover, and Julie Miller answered all my questions when I did research in the Manuscript Division. At Mount Vernon, Samantha Snyder graciously agreed to look up specific newspaper sources when the spread of the coronavirus made it impossible for me to visit the Library.

Beyond the financial support and the assistance from library staff, this work also required time, which Jane provided, time and again. All books require time to write. All authors with families depend on partners, spouses, and often extended family members to help them create that time. Far too many authors, especially men, simply assume that time will be given as a matter of course. Those of us who are fortunate to have partners and spouses who carve out time because they believe in our work—believe in *us*—owe it to them to be more conscientious, to never take the time they have given us for granted, and to say as much when the project is complete, knowing full well that no words of appreciation can do justice to their generosity.

Research from this project informed my contributions to the *American Yawp*, a free, online American history textbook now published by Stanford University Press. I served as a content contributor—writing material on political partisanship, Jeffersonian democracy, the "Revolution of 1800," and other subjects—as well as the editor for chapter 7: The Early Republic. In some cases I liked the way I had used a primary source or phrased a particular point so well that I decided I might want to use it verbatim, or modified, in this book. I thank Stanford University Press for permission to do so. Likewise, research conducted at Mount Vernon in 2015 resulted in an article, "'The Focus of the Wills of Converging Millions': Public Opposition to the Jay Treaty and the Origins of the People's Presidency," in the Fall 2017 issue of the *Journal of the Early Republic.* That article is essentially a stand-alone version of chapter 3 of this book, though small passages from the article also appear elsewhere in the pages that follow. I thank the University of Pennsylvania Press for permission to republish material from this article.

I was thrilled when David Congdon, editor at the University Press of Kansas, expressed interest in this project and again when Brian Steele and Todd Estes revealed themselves as the peer reviewers for this book. Both Brian and Todd offered insightful comments that only careful, thoughtful attention to a manuscript can produce. The standard scholarly caveat applies: if this book has succeeded as a scholarly contribution, it is due in no small part to their comments at the final stages. If it has not, the fault is mine alone.

Our four-year-old son has been mostly indifferent to this project, preferring instead to play with his little brother. But I love them both dearly. That I get to be their dad is but the latest of my life's good fortunes, beginning with my parents, whose encouragement and support made it possible for me to go to graduate school and begin this project in the first place, and continuing with my marriage to Jane, who let me know every day that she believed I was capable of finishing it. To them this book is dedicated, with all my love.

PROLOGUE

ON JANUARY 20, 1808, loyal Jeffersonian Republicans Aaron Haynes, Abner Grandel, Thomas Osborn, John Mattison, and John Palmer, braving the winter cold, gathered in their hometown of Hoosick, in upstate New York, to draft a letter to the president of the United States, Thomas Jefferson. Feeling their nation besieged by attacks from foreign governments, from Federalists, and even from discontented Republican groups critical of the actions of Jefferson's administration, the five men sought to assure their leader that they had not lost faith in his leadership.

They began with the salutation "To his Excellency Thomas Jefferson Esquire president of the United States." But at this, they paused. Someone zeroed in on that appellation, "Esquire": now used by lawyers, in the colonial era it was a term of distinction held by gentlemen, elites—men who stood above other men. Likely whoever wielded the pen simply wrote the word by habit. After all, Jefferson was both a lawyer and a wealthy planter. But now Jefferson was the president of the United States. That meant that he was *their* president, not a man who stood above them, commanding their deference, but the man who represented their voice. "Esquire" simply would not do. So they crossed it out (see figure 0.1).[1]

The slash marks obscuring the word "Esquire" in this letter to Jefferson offer a small but substantial clue about how much had changed over the

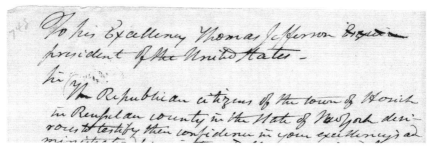

Figure 0.1: "Hosick, NY: Letter to Thomas Jefferson from Hoosick Republicans, 1807–08." Dated January 20, 1808. Detail. MSS Collection, Hoosick (NY) Collection, 1771–1842, AHMC-Hoosick (NY) (copy), New-York Historical Society.

first two decades of the presidency's existence and how these five citizens grappled with that change. In the colonial era it was common for lower- and middle-class persons to acknowledge the higher status of their social betters. This expectation continued even beyond the Revolution. But times were changing. Non-elites, from free women and men to enslaved people,[2] increasingly chafed at traditional expectations that they simply accept the superior status, power, and political influence of those above them. The Republican Party had coalesced in the 1790s around a shared criticism of the Federalists and an insistence that the president embody the egalitarian values of the new nation. The party had risen to prominence and elevated its champion to the presidency in 1801. Soon after, Republicans made Federalists a minority party in Congress as well. True, even in 1808 a group of New York Jeffersonian Republicans had reflexively bestowed gentlemanly status on Jefferson. Old habits die hard. But then they took it away from him, perhaps after discussing what that title implied about Jefferson's office and its proper relationship to the American citizenry.

These five New York Republicans were convinced that the president and all true, patriotic Americans shared an intimate and profound bond that had to be defended at all costs. The letter they produced said as much, assuring Jefferson of their "confidence in your excellency's administration" and of their "readiness to contribute their aid in carrying into execution such measures as have been or shall be adopted by your excellency for the Defence of our common country and the vindication of the national Honor." Their country was under siege by "the insidious attempts of a traitorous faction in this section of . . . our country who seek to acquire an undeserved confidence from that government which they are ever ready to oppose and to load with the vilest censures." To oppose such subversive forces, these five New Yorkers made it clear to Jefferson that they were prepared to go to any length, even engaging in armed combat with such foes in order to ensure the young republic's survival—just as "their fathers and their brothers in arms" and even they "Themselves" had done during the American Revolution, "when the hallowed cause of Freedom called them to battle." Referencing a pivotal battle near Hoosick that ended in a resounding American victory, the men assured Jefferson that they and their compatriots in that Revolutionary cause "anticipate future triumphs under republican leaders when your excellency shall deem it expedient to direct their Republican ardor against the enemies of their country." Closing their letter "With sentiments of esteem & respect," the five declared themselves to be the president's "devoted friends."[3]

As these five Hoosick Republicans saw it, they owed who they were as Americans to the bravery of patriots who had chosen to dissent against monarchical tyranny, insisting on the right to be their own sovereigns by choosing war and even the possibility of death over a lifetime as subjects to any king. As they and other patriots in the War for Independence had done, these five New Yorkers were determined to defend their free, republican society from all foreign and domestic threats. They saw Jefferson as one of them: a free citizen chosen not to stand above them but to exemplify and promote the indomitable desire for freedom that all Americans shared. For these five New York Republicans, the pledge they made to their president was an affirmation of who they were as Americans.

The sentiment was widely shared, not only by their fellow Republicans around the country, but ironically by the Federalists—the very political opponents these Hoosick Republicans ominously referenced. "The popular mistake, that their power is their liberty, and the jealousy, that ever grows out of excessive love, and which produces hatred and a thirst for revenge, augmented the jacobin faction in all the states," Federalist congressman Fisher Ames scoffed in an essay published in the *Boston Gazette* in 1804 under the pseudonym The Republican. "The flatterers, who stick at nothing, had an easy access to the affections and confidence of the multitude. They called themselves the people's friends—champions for their rights and power." As a testament to their political views, Ames continued, "Mr. Jefferson's adherents very early tried to stick upon his name the mountebank, impostor title of *The Man of the People*." With Jefferson now the president, Ames predicted that rabid chants of radical democracy would radiate out into all of American society, a "rage of party" that, ironically, "drowned every voice, but its own."[4]

A loyal Jeffersonian, writing in an angry scrawl under the pseudonym Esculapius, produced a "receipt"—in other words, a recipe—to describe the ingredients that comprised traitorous Federalists like Ames, and even Republican critics of Jefferson, derisively dubbed *tertium quids* (Latin for "third thing"), or just "Quids." To the author of the "Receipt to Make a Modern Federalist," Federalists and Quids alike were enemies to the nation—and the writer made that point by associating them both with black and mixed-race people. Ingredients to make a modern Federalist could be purchased "at wholesale of the quid council at the moderate price of the suffrages of the purchasers and at retail of all the haberdashers in federal row at . . . negro village," the author informed readers, "and of the guardians of the federal interest . . . at Mullattoe square."[5]

Republicans, Federalists, and Quids disagreed vehemently on the direction the country was heading under Jefferson's presidential leadership,
but they agreed on one crucial thing: the president was "the man of the
people," the symbol and servant of a vision of the American nation that
Americans widely shared. Divided over whether a bright future or irrevocable national decline awaited, Americans across partisan lines nonetheless agreed that over two decades of bitter partisan politics had made
the presidential office the cultural touchstone of a shared vision of what
it meant to be American. Popular debate over presidents' words and actions—taking place in taverns and street corners, in halls of government
and in private houses, in private letters, political cartoons, and printed
materials—had shaped the contours of a contentious and even violent debate over what America stood for, who counted as an American, and what
constituted a threat to the nation's future. Far more than debates over
what the occupant of a particular governmental office should or should
not do, these contentious disagreements over what presidents did and said
were really arguments over what the values, the beliefs—participants often called them the "character"—of the American people were, or should
be. For better or for worse, the presidency had become the site where
fundamentally incompatible visions of America waged an ongoing battle.[6]

This book traces the origin of that battle and tells the story of how
the presidency came to stand at its center. In essence, this book traces the
origins of a story that twenty-first-century Americans experience every
day. No American alive today personally experienced a time when the
presidency did not stand at the center of American politics. The office is
not only the institutional center of the national government; it is also the
most prominent and powerful symbol of a singular, unified America that
millions of citizens imagine. That no one person can humanly embody the
aspirations, ideals, priorities, and cultural attitudes of millions of different
people does not make this standard any less powerful or politically significant. To the contrary, it is precisely the impossibility of this political
standard that gives the presidential office its unparalleled political luster.
For just as the presidency represents the dream of national unity, it acts
as a forum for fierce disagreement over which direction the nation should
be headed, where it is actually headed, who counts as a member of the
American nation, and who constitutes a threat.

These themes are especially dominant now, in the aftermath of Donald
Trump's 2016 victory and his ascent to the presidency. Defying nearly
every prediction, Trump won the presidency by appealing to a vaguely
defined "great" American past, boasting that he would reinvigorate an

emasculated American nation beleaguered by dangerous foreigners, duplicitous Washington elites, and an entrenched liberal establishment promoting gender equality and religious, racial, and ethnic diversity. He characterized most migrants from Mexico as "rapists," vowing to build a wall on the southern border of the United States to keep out dangerous "illegals" and make Mexico pay for it. He called for a complete ban on the entry of Muslims into the United States, characterizing them as an inherent threat to America. He dismissed with impunity comments he had made about sexually assaulting women as harmless "locker-room talk." He peddled the racist "birther" conspiracy that the first black president of the United States, Barack Obama, was born in Kenya, even after Obama released his birth certificate from the state of Hawaii.

Trump's election shocked the world because it was viewed as far more than simply an electoral victory for an individual; it was a profound and, to many, ominous statement about what America stood for. For those of us who recoil at Trump's nativism and racism (and I say "us," because I make no pretense at neutrality when it comes to Trump, and no apology for asserting that I am appalled by him and the prejudices he promotes), it is tempting to view him as the relic of a bygone age: the promoter of a bigotry that reflects the nation's regrettable history of racism and nativism, rather than the promise of America's national values. It is also tempting to blame Trump alone for the toxic politics before us and easy to view acts of political dissent, other than simply voting for a different candidate in the next presidential election, as pointless at best and divisive at worst.

But as this work demonstrates, these positions are only tenable if we ignore how integral widespread and contentious political commentary on the presidency has been to making it what it remains today. To more fully understand our present political landscape, and the presidency's place at its center, we must examine more closely the first several decades of our country's history under the Constitution: the so-called "founding era," when the presidency and the American nation were new. We must look beyond the mythology of this fabled era and beyond the elite political leaders and presidential incumbents that so often dominate the story.

It is commonplace to view the current occupant of the presidency—whomever that might be at a given moment—as a bellwether for the state of the nation as a whole. And invariably, the "founding era" acts as a natural point of comparison or, more typically, contrast, with the state of politics today. Early presidents like George Washington, Thomas Jefferson, and Andrew Jackson act as avatars for early national values in all their splendor or their rapid decline into the cacophony of partisan division that are now the hallmark of American politics. Who a president is before he is president, and what a president does while in office, matter tremendously, of course. But fixating on specific presidents to this degree ignores or minimizes the crucial political context within which presidential incumbents operate. The result is often a political narrative that credits—or more typically blames—individual presidents for what the American nation was, what it is currently, and how it got to be that way.[7]

In particular, twenty-first-century political commentary has been attuned to the profound connection between the presidential office and American nationalism. During his campaign and after his electoral victory, Trump's conservative and progressive critics alike pointed out the myriad ways he deviated from presidential norms. Not only did his braggadocio, his personal attacks on those who questioned or criticized him, and (more recently) his claims that the Constitution granted him all but absolute power fall far short of "presidential" behavior, but Trump also employed virulently racist rhetoric, stoking fears among whites that black and Hispanic people—citizens as well as immigrants and asylum-seekers—constituted a vicious horde that had to be repulsed in order to save American jobs and American lives. Trump demonstrated a staggering ignorance of the nation's founding ideals, while at the same time conjuring a vile nationalism indicative of the worst prejudices of his predecessors. Comprised of equal parts bigotry and violence that generations of Americans, led by valiant and patriotic civil-rights leaders, had worked assiduously to undo, Trump's nation was a vision that, to millions of his critics across the political spectrum, bore no resemblance to the nation they knew.

This interpretation fails to account for the historical foundations of American nationalism, its intimate connection with the office of the presidency, or the role that early public commentary on the presidency, by political leaders as well as citizens "out of doors"—that is, outside of government—in the nation's earliest decades, played in defining the relationship between the two. Presidential incumbents were not the sole, or even the primary, authors of either "the American nation" or the presidency's unique role as its most prominent political symbol. Though occupied only by elite white men, the office of the presidency was a collaborative project between elite, middling, and plebeian Americans—young and old, women and men—whose words and actions added up to a swirl of public commentary that presidential incumbents could never fully control. Though dominated by whites, this commentary also included black voices, whose claims to full membership in the American nation whites in the North and the South would strive to silence. In the first two decades of the country's history under the Constitution, it would be this extended debate among political participants across partisan, regional, and even racial lines, responding to what presidents did and said—not the actions of presidential incumbents alone—that vested the presidency with the essential symbolic role that Americans recognize today: "the man of the people," tasked with promoting, protecting, and exhibiting the character that united Americans and distinguished them as one people.

This approach is heavily indebted to, but is situated within the seams between, the history of the early presidency and the history of early American nationalism. Both of these subjects boast a voluminous literature that has traced parts of this story before, but never the whole. Presidential studies is a crowded field dominated by biographies of individual incumbents, studies of specific presidential elections, and analyses of the office's institutional role and Constitutional powers.[8] Recent works have ably shown how the country's earliest presidents, particularly George Washington and Thomas Jefferson, were among the first nationalists; their ideas about American nationhood would resonate in their lifetimes and beyond.[9] Yet most studies of the presidency do not stray far beyond presidential incumbents and their closest allies in government. Existing literature has ably examined the roots of early American nationalism in our country's most pervasive prejudices and has even traced its expression by a broader American public beyond the halls of government—in print and in writing, in celebrations and "street theater," in public acts of protests, in music and even in material goods. Yet rarely if ever do these studies examine the impact of this popular nationalism on the nascent institutions of government.[10] Indeed, more recent studies of nationalism emphasize that the very notion of a single, cohesive, universally adopted vision of "the American nation" was a fiction from the very beginning. The vast majority of citizens in the early United States identified far more closely with their home states than with "the American nation." Even into the nineteenth century, when citizens did begin to proclaim their primary identity as "Americans," local, state, and sectional politics informed what they meant by that. Being an American meant something far different to a white Southerner in the aftermath of the War of 1812 than it did to someone in New England. As president, Andrew Jackson understood the American nation very differently than the proponents of "nullification," even though they were Southerners just like Old Hickory. Thus, these studies show, the national was always reflective of the local; what ostensibly united all Americans across regional, state, political, and sectional lines actually exacerbated bitter division.[11]

Taken together, studies of the presidency and American nationalism do not do justice to the presidency's vital role as a locus where abstract and amorphous ideas about American nationhood could be contemplated and defined more explicitly. This omission reduces people outside of elite positions of political power to the role of relatively minor players in the story of the presidency and can lead to the erroneous assumption that people outside elite circles cared little about the presidency except during presidential elections and exerted little influence over the office, while individual incumbents—especially Jefferson and Jackson—transformed the office more or less single-handedly.[12] In sum, studies of the presidency and early American nationalism fail to capture the essential role a broad array of political commentators out-of-doors played in defining the presidency as a cultural symbol of an imagined bond all true Americans shared—and the ongoing debate over the meaning of that bond that would divide the country along regional, sectional, political, and racial lines.

Far from uninterested or passive, citizens out-of-doors commented on the presidency constantly, not just for brief spans every four years. Presidential incumbents were unnerved by the intensity of debate and disagreement that surrounded the decisions they made, and each sought to one degree or another to maintain a distance from the public and the partisanship they saw developing around them. When not striving to act the part of a "patriot king" by remaining "above party," early presidents sought to stymie political dissent by questioning the legitimacy of their opponents to criticize them, or by taking steps to silence them completely.[13] Yet despite their efforts to prevent it, the presidency was pulled into the middle of the partisan conflict that soon came to define the early national political landscape. This was because partisan commentators on the presidency considered their capacity to voice opposition to the actions of their government—to dissent—essential to their claim as sovereign citizens.

To be sure, in the immediate aftermath of the American Revolution, the notion of what made someone an "American" was ill-defined at best. The young nation's first plan of government, the Articles of Confederation, reflected both the primacy of states and a deep suspicion of concentrated and aloof government power, especially executive power. Under the Articles of Confederation, the Continental Congress possessed no real taxation authority, and its "president" was empowered to do little more than attend sessions of Congress. With no way to amend the Articles if even a single state objected, the Continental Congress had little formal power to compel a stable national union. Instead, it adopted public rituals, bestowed awards, and printed money, among other conspicuous acts, in an

Figure 0.2: Benjamin Franklin, Continental Currency
"Linked Rings" design. Courtesy of the Eric P. Newman
Numismatic Education Society, Washington University in
St. Louis.

anemic attempt to cultivate a national bond with itself at its center. Benjamin Franklin's "Linked Rings" design, one of many designs adorning the currency printed by the Continental Congress, literally illustrates the that body's aspiration to embody the young nation's confederated union (see figure 0.2).[14]

Nonetheless, this very fear of concentrated government power, a resolve to define Americans as citizens rather than subjects by opposing such power, and ultimately defining the terms of citizenship by racial exclusion, were core themes in early patriotic rituals from New England to the Deep South during and after the war. As historian Len Travers has shown, whether seeking to inspire public support during the war or to commemorate it in the years immediately afterward, Fourth of July celebrations from Boston to Philadelphia to Charleston, South Carolina, re-appropriated colonial (and even monarchical) rituals to communicate a shared antimonarchy, republican identity. These rituals, though varying some from region to region, all adhered to a basic formula that was designed to communicate to participants and observers that the American Revolution was a measured, deliberate act of resistance of oppression. Praise for "order" and calls for adequate education for future generations reflected the view of many in the 1780s that citizens would have to be brought up with a thorough understanding of republican virtue in order to ensure that the country became neither a monarchy nor an ochlocracy.[15] More recently, Robert G. Parkinson has documented how war narratives "propagated" by the press during the American Revolution cast nonwhites—Native Americans, as well as free and enslaved black people—as "traitors" to the American "common cause," in league with America's British adversary, and thus ineligible for inclusion in the emerging republican nation. The ability to choose who counted within the nation, who counted among the collective sovereigns to whom the nation's government would be accountable, was a key mark of citizenship: one that whites, both during the war and for years after, reserved for themselves alone.[16] Ironically, it would be the creation of a plan for a stronger national government—the Constitution—with a single executive with broad and vaguely defined powers that would provoke ferocious debate over whether such a thing as a unified America existed (or could exist) and whether the proposed government represented the culmination or the betrayal of the spirit of dissent that had fueled the Revolution.

Though commentators criticized leaders in Congress and the Supreme Court as well, public debate over the actions of presidents took on unique political significance. Popular memory cast the War for Independence as a war against monarchy, and partisans characterized the ability to dissent against a sitting president as a vital test of how much their status as citizens differed from that of monarchical subjects. Adding to this obvious comparison was the singularity of the presidency itself—and the reputation of the man who was first to occupy it. Though delegates to the Constitutional Convention debated the idea of a plural executive, ultimately the office consisted of a single person, and the overwhelming choice among delegates and citizens throughout the country was George Washington, the leader of the country's War for Independence, who had already proven himself capable of resisting the lure of power when he freely resigned his commission and returned to Mount Vernon after the war had been won.

Washington's virtue was not enough to ease widespread concerns about the national government from "antifederalists" during the public ratification debate of 1787 and 1788. But, as chapter 1 demonstrates, those who advocated for ratification—who called themselves "federalists," a more flattering term than the pejorative term "antifederalist" that they gave to the Constitution's critics—used the presidency to assure the public that the national government described in the Constitution would indeed possess more authority than the Articles of Confederation.[17] Contrary to antifederalist fears, however, federalists claimed the government would always remain accountable to the public at large. It would not be an aloof, tyrannical aristocracy or monarchy; it would be a truly representative system, drawing its considerable but necessary power from the people, using that power to promote their interests and ultimately strengthen the bond between them. In short, federalists during the public ratification debate looked to the presidency—the office that most closely resembled the British monarchy—to promise the public that the proposed government would reflect the republican principles that had animated the War for Independence.

As chapters 2 and 3 explain, during Washington's presidency critics took that promise seriously, insisting that no matter how illustrious Washington's reputation, no matter how singular his contributions to American liberty, Washington was obligated as president to listen to the voices of dissent emerging from the public. These critics of Washington, who would coalesce into the Republican Party, argued that their opposition was in keeping with America's Revolutionary dissenting spirit. They were not attempting to undermine public faith in the government or sow anarchy. They were trying to salvage the government's republican essence by holding to account a president who acted beyond their sanction.

Washington and his supporters, who formed the Federalist Party, did not see it that way. To them, these voices of dissent were illegitimate, the work of un-American "factions" who harbored dangerous "foreign"—by which they meant French—ideas. They claimed that America's founding act of dissent against the monarchy had culminated in the adoption of a republican plan of government that vested sovereignty in the people and resulted in the election of a presidential father figure, a "man of the people," tasked with acting on behalf of all Americans. Dissent against *that*, they countered, showed that the president's critics were not full members of the American nation. Instead, they were a threat to it.

This contentious dynamic between Federalists and Republicans illustrates a crucial component of "dissent" as discussed in the story this book tells. Those out of power invoked the memory of the Revolution to justify their opposition to the policies and principles of sitting presidents; presidential incumbents and their supporters invoked it to justify measures meant to silence that opposition. For those out of power, sustained opposition to presidential actions was a testament to the enduring spirit of the Revolution: a commitment of true Americans never to capitulate to government authority that betrayed their identity as independent, liberty-loving citizens. But presidential incumbents who held power, and their supporters, invoked the spirit of dissent as well. They argued that public opposition to the sitting president was an unpatriotic act, a betrayal of the dissenting spirit that culminated in their man's ascent to the presidency. To describe how commentators in the early decades of United States history drew upon the memory of the Revolution, I borrow a phrase from the historian Saul Cornell—"the dissenting tradition in America"—though my definition differs from Cornell's. Cornell describes the "dissenting tradition in America" as a set of limited-government principles that animated the political thought of antifederalists. Those principles, Cornell convincingly argues, would inform Jeffersonian Republican and Jacksonian Democratic constitutional thought even decades after the Constitution was ratified. When I refer to the "dissenting tradition in America," I refer to a suspicion of government power that critics of those in power—and, crucially, those in power, as well—would invoke to justify their respective political positions on a president's given actions and their predicted impact on the future of "the nation" as a whole.[18]

For Federalists and Republicans alike, the ability to dissent from governmental authority—to express displeasure with, or even outright opposition to, the actions or policies of those in formal positions of power—determined the extent to which the public was truly sovereign over, or subordinate to, the government. Casting their attacks and their defenses of the president as reflective of the republican spirit of the young nation, partisans engaged in a contentious and even bloody back-and-forth that made the presidential office foundational to their competing visions of who counted as an American (and who did not), and what the proper relationship between the American people and the national government should be. In so doing, they made the presidency the possession of the American people, the young democracy's most powerful national symbol, its most coveted political prize.

Chapter 4 examines the contentious election of 1796, "the first presidential contest" that commenced after Washington announced his retirement from the presidency in 1796.[19] Unable to silence Republican

criticism and fearful of national decline if Thomas Jefferson should succeed Washington, Federalists in the election attacked Jefferson personally,
accusing him of a "want of firmness," an accusation that attacked his
status as a man, a leader, and an American by calling into question his
bravery, his decisiveness, and even his commitment to white supremacy.
Republican dissenters' insistence that the president listen to and engage
with the American public pushed Federalists to posit an even more personal connection between the president and the people, one that made
explicit the racial basis of American national identity and linked it directly
to the presidential office.

The assumption that independence was reserved for whites predated
the American presidency. Indeed, recent scholarship has demonstrated
that the American Revolution acted as a crucible for the formation of a
nascent American national identity rooted in racial distinctions and fear
of anything deemed "foreign." Commentators who ascribed to the American people a civilized, sovereign, and free character defined those concepts
by exclusion. Being "civilized" had little meaning apart from "savages,"
especially Indians, whose perceived barbarity provided a contrast with
white society. Being "sovereign" distinguished Americans from "foreign"
subjects of monarchs and emperors, especially those of Britain or France,
even as early national political parties divided over *which* foreign power
and its people posed a greater threat. And being free was inseparable from
the condition of slavery that, by the late eighteenth century, had come to
be synonymous with black people.[20] To be black—even if one was free—
was to belong to the race that most whites deemed destined for perpetual
slavery. It was to be the target of what the black intellectual Benjamin
Banneker called "the almost general prejudice and prepossession which is
so prevailent [sic] in the world against those of my complexion."[21] And
crucially, the converse held true as well: to be subordinated to the will of
another—even if one were white—was to share a detested common status with black people. None less than George Washington himself noted
this during the American Revolution when he remarked in 1774 that it
was imperative to resist the "Measures" the British government "hath
for sometime been, and now are, most violently pursuing . . . or Submit
to every Imposition that can be heap'd upon us; till custom and use, will
make us as tame, & abject Slaves, as the Blacks we Rule over with such
arbitrary Sway."[22]

The racial basis for membership in the American nation was so widely
assumed that early in the presidency's history commentators rarely thought
it necessary to make that basis explicit. By the mid-1790s, however, the

stubborn presence of the dissenting Republican Party—which dominated the South, a region whose slave population gave it a profound advantage in the national government due to the three-fifths clause—provoked Federalist fears of potentially irreversible national decline if the Republicans' champion, Thomas Jefferson, should ascend to the presidency. During the election of 1796 and even after Jefferson won the presidency in 1800, whites across partisan lines made more explicit the racial basis of their national visions and of their evaluation of the president's conduct in promoting or threatening them. Though bitterly divided, white Federalists and Republicans expected the president to exemplify and promote a national character that applied to whites alone. Drawing upon racialized language to denigrate their political opponents, political commentators revealed how foundational was white supremacy to the competing nationalisms that whites across partisan lines projected onto the presidency.[23]

Chapter 5 examines the presidency of John Adams, a president who, though known as a brilliant but long-winded and didactic political theorist, understood his role as president in more than just terms of abstract political theory. The second president also saw himself as the guardian and promoter of a "character" that all Americans, from the chief executive on down, held in common.[24] Adams, his Federalist supporters, and his Republican (and Federalist) critics, connected the health of the nation to a set of cultural values that connected the president and the people, casting that relationship in moral and familial terms. As tensions between the United States and France mounted, Adams reveled in pledges by supporters, young and old, to take up arms at President Adams's say-so and endorsed measures by the Federalist-controlled Congress to vest in the presidency broad powers to arrest and prosecute people whom the administration deemed threatening to the nation—the infamous Alien and Sedition Acts. Efforts to silence political dissent backfired, however, as Republicans pushed back against the acts by claiming that the powers they vested in the president constituted an assault on the American "family"; they undermined public "affection" for the president and, by extension, the government as a whole because they sought to make sovereign citizens into "slaves" to the executive. They were a betrayal of not only constitutional principles but the moral bond linking the president to the Americans he represented. By the time Jefferson ascended the presidency, commentators across partisan lines agreed that the health of the nation depended on an intimate connection between the president and the people. Federalists' attempts to silence political dissent faltered as the party itself fractured under Adams's leadership. Republicans' claims that their acts of dissent were necessary to salvage the nation from Federalist "monarchists" would determine how they justified Jefferson's actions once he ascended to the presidency.

During the presidencies of Thomas Jefferson and James Madison (the focus of chapters 6 and 7), Federalists and Republicans continued to claim that they were the legitimate heirs to the nation's dissenting tradition, that that tradition was the key to promoting the intimate bond between the president and "the people" that ensured the health of the nation, and that their opponents posed an existential threat to the nation, alongside dangerous "foreign" forces, Indian "savages" on the frontier, and free and enslaved black "internal enemies" in their midst. Once out of power, Federalists continued this argument, claiming that their predictions of dangerous national decline into racial equality was coming to pass and that Southern slave-holding Republicans were abusing the government's power in order to render Northern states, especially the Federalist stronghold of New England, "slaves" to the government that Jeffersonian Republicans now controlled. For their part, Republicans denigrated critics of Jefferson and Madison as enemies of the nation by associating them with black people, Indians, and British monarchists—tactics that would come to be foundational to Republicans' pro-war propaganda during the War of 1812. These tactics linked the office of the presidency directly to the integrity of the nation, making the racial basis for the national vision that whites expected the presidency to symbolize more explicit than ever.[25]

As chapter 8 demonstrates, by the end of the War of 1812, commentators across political lines agreed that the president and the people were bound together in a relationship made possible by Americans' capacity to dissent, a relationship that defined the democratic character of the nation itself. Whites had dominated political commentary on the presidency for its entire existence and demonstrated their commitment to maintaining their vision of a nation governed by and for whites through their commitment to ignore, silence, and ridicule the claims to membership in the American nation made by both free and enslaved black persons. Some black people answered President Madison's call to arms in the War of 1812—taking up arms in defense of the nation against British tyranny, in keeping with the nation's Revolutionary dissenting tradition—just as Republican propaganda claimed all true patriotic Americans must. Others, like Lemuel Haynes, spoke out against the war itself—expressing criticism of a presidency that whites for decades had held up as the defining feature of free, independent Americans. Such acts challenged whites to imagine an American democracy that included nonwhite voices, and whites responded by minimizing or denigrating black service in the war, or omitting it from their descriptions altogether, and by pantomiming black political participation through cruel caricature.[26]

The relationship between the people and the president, as defined by this decades-long public debate, consisted of multiple layers of irony. The presidency, Americans widely agreed, was the symbol of the people's independent spirit, demonstrated by their capacity to dissent against the government if it failed to serve and protect that independence. Despite Washington's fear that such open and relentless public criticism would undermine public confidence in the presidency (and, by extension, the government as a whole), that capacity for dissent actually *strengthened* the public's affection for the office and for the national government. The existence, and persistence, of political dissent fueled the perception that the government, led by the president, should listen to and engage with the American people, and ultimately led to the belief that the government should directly reflect who the people were, rather than act as a tyrannical force subordinating them to its arbitrary authority. This shared view of political dissent reflected a shared aspiration toward a nation whose people were united across state lines, political differences, and increasingly vast distances. But this shared aspiration for national unity—"a more perfect union"—of citizens who ensured the democratic character of that union by insisting that the president remained "the man of the people" also inspired continued conflict, and further political fracture, in the years following the War of 1812.

After the war, the Republican Party emerged triumphant, relegating the Federalists to a state of political oblivion at the national level from which they would never recover. Successive Republican administrations would seek to implement an ambitious series of internal improvements and impose a tariff meant to protect Northern industry. A financial panic hit the nation in 1819, and Missouri's petition for statehood exposed the widening divide between Southern slave states and Northern free states. In this politically polarized environment, Andrew Jackson emerged as the champion of ordinary (white) Americans against an entrenched Washington establishment. To be sure, Jackson was, in important respects, a new man for a new age. But he and his supporters offered an answer to a question that, for decades, Americans had looked to the presidency to answer: Who are the American people? The answer provided by Jacksonians was a familiar one: Americans were dissenters, who would not tolerate any political establishment stripping them of their rights. Jackson's critics and his supporters agreed that Jackson was a violent man for a violent age. But where Jackson's opponents cited his brutality toward Indians, his reckless use of military authority, and his participation in slavery as evidence that he was erratic and power-hungry—and thus wholly unfit for presidential leadership—Jackson's supporters celebrated his violence as itself an expression of dissent against the political establishment. Present leaders in government were too weak and indecisive, present civic institutions too convoluted and controlled by the elite. What was needed was another revolution that put government back in the hands of Americans. Jackson was just the man to lead the way.[27]

Thus, this book diverges from many traditional studies of the presidency. Presidential incumbents are vital to this story, but this is not primarily a narrative of their actions. Nor is it a rehash of early legal debates about executive power. In choosing this approach, I hope to demonstrate how the history of the presidency is more than simply the sum of presidential actions and legal debates taking place among elected officials and a small cadre of well-connected political elites, important though these are. By tracing the origin of a phenomenon that, in the twenty-first century, is commonplace—the tendency of a broad mass of people to vest profound cultural meaning in the presidency as the symbol of who "we" are, and what "we" stand for as a people—I hope to demonstrate how popular politics cultivated not only early partisan division but also the early nation-state. A broad American public, not merely elite white men cloistered in halls of government power, made increasingly explicit the racial basis for "the people" and projected onto the presidency the widely held expectation that the country's nascent institutions of government would reflect and enforce that vision of "the people" through the exercise of its authority.

In an age before modern media, commentary on the presidency took place in a variety of forms: through word of mouth, through private letters and diaries, and especially through printed materials, particularly newspapers. As such, these materials form the evidentiary basis for this book. Together, they attest that Americans talked about, read about, and wrote about the presidency constantly—not just during elections—arguing simultaneously over what the president did and said, and who the American people were, and in the process establishing a relationship between the two that would define the contours of national politics for generations to come.

Avid readers and prolific publishers, Americans read accounts of presidential actions on a daily basis in newspapers, which published presidential speeches, citizens' petitions, rumors about presidential decisions and personal behavior, open letters to the president on pressing political issues, and accounts of events like meetings, marches, and even holiday celebrations that functioned as a means of political expression. Most of these newspaper accounts were written by newspaper editors or political insiders, often under a pseudonym or with no attribution at all. The pseudonymous authors of these critical essays—some of whose identities are still unknown—made up an admittedly slim portion of the population. Most, if not all, of them were middling or elite men; some were hired pens or political operatives with their own axes to grind. Yet the partisan nature of the message, and the disproportionately large role that a select few individuals played in crafting it, does not change how profoundly this message reimagined the presidency's relationship to everyday citizens or the fact that the message circulated widely alongside accounts of political participation by non-elites. Newspapers cannot provide a wholly faithful record of national politics as everyday people experienced it. No source can. But newspapers were the primary means by which political ideas and arguments circulated on a national scale. Americans read them voraciously. Some copies of newspapers from the era contain marginalia. Passages crossed out or marked up, commentary scribbled above or below printed text or in the margins, attest to readers' deep engagement with the news and the commentary they encountered (see figure 0.3). Political leaders recognized newspapers as the medium for disseminating political messages intended for a broad audience. Newspapers also contained accounts of the political involvement of non-elites, including public assemblies, written petitions, and even civil unrest, attesting to the fact that common citizens did not simply absorb these political ideas passively, but acted, and in doing so, demonstrated the power of these ideas to inspire political action. As such, newspapers are the historian's best source for examining the ideas that non-elites most likely encountered and the ideas that made up the common currency of a still-developing national political culture in the midst of profound change. They are proof that the presidency, an office frequently associated with only a handful of powerful, elite men, owes its rich cultural prestige to a vast array of political voices.[28]

Debates over who counted as an American, who did not, and how a president should represent all Americans, paid little mind to the tidy boundaries distinguishing the different theories of representation explored by present-day political theorists. While a more "democratic" notion of presidential representation supplanted the ideal of an aloof "patriot king" by Jefferson's presidency, what it meant for the president to embody, promote, and protect "the people" remained far from settled. At various

Figure 0.3: Detail of back page of *Pittsburgh Gazette* (October 23, 1812), "Address of the Democratic-Republican Committee of the Borough of Pittsburgh, and Its Vicinity, Favorable to the Election of De Witt Clinton, to the Presidency of the United States, at the Ensuing Election," with marginalia. One reader of this copy crossed out "Democratic" and wrote "Anti or Discontented." Courtesy of the American Antiquarian Society.

moments in time, commentators claimed the president represented the people by remaining separated from the public or by listening attentively to their voice. Some claimed that presidential elections proved the validity of particular political ideologies. Others argued that minority views were right even when the president and a majority of voters disagreed. These arguments coexisted at identical moments in time, even among members of the same political party. The diversity of views attests to the shifting political circumstances taking place, the rhetorical maneuvering necessary to cast one's partisan cause in a favorable light, and the political stakes involved in claiming the presidency: in so doing, one could claim legitimacy for one's vision of the American nation over one's adversaries.[29]

The nation's earliest public commentary on the presidency reveals that presidential incumbents were not the sole authors of the presidency's role as the exemplar of the "character" that bound all Americans together and defined them as one people. That role was a collaborative project among presidents, other political leaders, and private citizens, who projected onto the presidency their competing visions of nationhood, revealing the widespread prejudices, broadly held aspiration to national cohesion, and partisan division that constituted democracy in the early United States. In one sense this book tells the story of how ordinary Americans, through unrelenting and often violent disagreement, first made the presidential office their own. But in another sense the story of how the American public made the president of the United States "the man of the people" is the story of how the presidency came to stand at the center of a hotly contested, divisive fight over what it meant to be an American: a fight that continues to this day.

1

Ratification and the Promise of "the Man of the People"

"WE ARE ALL contending for popular applause," Archibald Stuart explained to John Breckenridge in late October, 1787, just over a month after the Constitution had first appeared in print. Its publication ignited debates that took place in taverns, meeting houses, convention halls, homes, and in the streets. Newspapers published commentaries written by the document's defenders as well as its critics. Though forged in a secret meeting of delegates whose original purpose had only been to revise the Articles of Confederation, the Constitution was now the talk of the young country. To ensure its ratification, the people would have to be convinced.[1]

The public debate over whether to ratify the US Constitution was, of course, also the initial public debut of the presidential office. Though its authority and position within the proposed government reminded many of the British monarchy, the presidency departed in fundamental ways from the British executive, as the people themselves had departed from their mother country in the War for Independence. So strange was the office that participants in the public ratification debate often used the term "president" and "executive" more or less interchangeably, seldom making the more contemporary distinction between the office, the powers it wields, or its position at the head of the executive branch of government. At a time when being an American held little tangible meaning for most citizens, whose identities tended to stem more strongly from their respective states, the presidency reflected both the American people's British heritage as well as their newly won but still amorphous status as an independent people.[2]

The presidency was only one component of an intricate plan of government debated fiercely by the delegates to the Constitutional Convention in the summer of 1787 and described throughout the seven-article constitution they produced. Yet the office was crucial to the way the Constitution's advocates, who styled themselves "federalists," defended the

proposed plan of government against its critics, whom federalists derisively dubbed "antifederalists." Both terms were misleading in ways that
benefited the Constitution's defenders. Advocating for a government that
would be truly national in scope—whose laws, as Article VI declared,
would be "supreme"—the so-called federalists were far more nationalist than their chosen name suggests. Similarly, the "antifederalists," who
raised concerns about the sovereignty of states and the autonomy of local
courts, were far more federal than the "federalists." The Constitution's
critics correctly understood the term "antifederalist" as a derogatory one,
directed at them to discredit them. Most never embraced it. Yet the names
stuck, not least because the Constitution's defenders held key advantages
in the press and in most state ratifying conventions.[3]

Both federalist friends of the Constitution and antifederalist critics invoked the American Revolution to justify their positions. They agreed
that the Revolution was a signal act of dissent against executive-centered
government authority that had proven the American people's commitment
to their rights and ultimately to a government that derived its power from
their freely given assent. This characterization stressed the relationship
between executive authority and public accountability, making that relationship indicative of the entire government's tendency to serve the people
or to threaten them. In the back-and-forth that ensued after the Constitution was published, the presidency was more than simply one component
of the proposed government that was worthy of discussion on its own. As
the only office that would represent citizens across the country—and one
that vested its sole occupant with broad and heretofore vaguely defined
powers—the presidency reflected what antifederalists viewed as the proposed government's tendency toward "consolidation" of power, making it
a threat to the liberties that citizens had fought to attain in the Revolution.
For federalists, the office's promise of "energetic" authority predicated on
public accountability made it indicative of the republican genius of the
government as a whole.[4]

Of course, one key component of the debate that forged the presidency
in the Constitutional Convention—and shaped the back-and-forth between federalists and antifederalists—was the man that everyone assumed
would fill the office if the Constitution were ratified. George Washington
cast a considerable shadow over the debate, shaping what was in essence a
game of competitive prediction about what the decision facing the nation
would mean for its future. Washington had been, of course, the leader of
the Continental Army, the champion of the Revolution, who had given

back his commission to the Continental Congress after winning the war. He thus exemplified the dissenting spirit that had animated the patriots during the Revolution and won them independence. His seeming imperviousness to the lure of power made him the obvious choice to fill the presidency.

Yet neither antifederalist criticism nor federalist defenses of the Constitution relied primarily on Washington to make their respective points. Both agreed that any plan of government worthy of the American people would have to outlast the life span of any one man, no matter how incorruptibly virtuous he might be. Both the Constitution's critics and its allies focused mostly on the indelible connections between the presidential office and every other component of the proposed national government. Ultimately, both looked to the presidency to explain what the relationship between this proposed government and the people themselves would look like.

That relationship was the crux of the matter. Would the country persist as a republic, its people their own sovereigns, with rights that superseded the power the government possessed? Or were they reverting back to a type of oligarchy, or perhaps even a monarchy like the one they had just won their freedom from a few years earlier? Antifederalists pondered what would happen after Washington departed the presidency, arguing that even if Washington could be trusted with the office's vaguely defined and potentially despotic power, the government was destined to pull power toward its center, "consolidating" authority at the expense of state autonomy and individual liberty. Antifederalists considered such consolidation a betrayal of the very ideals for which Americans had fought the Revolution. Federalists invoked the presidency to assure skeptics that the entire government would remain always accountable to the people. This accountability, exemplified by the promise of a presidential office distinct from Washington, bound the office to the people themselves. The president would be "the man of the people," federalists insisted, the agent of a nation of citizens who had dissented courageously from a tyrannical monarchy and who had now created a plan of government that would be powerful enough to ensure their perpetual union, but which drew its power from a public confidence that the people could withdraw at any moment. Through the presidency, federalists responded to antifederalist criticism by promising a government that would remain accountable at all times to the populace, a symbol of the revolutionary spirit of dissent that had won the people their independence.

A "MAN . . . OF CONTINENTAL REPUTATION"

The Constitution made its public debut in September 1787, having been devised by delegates from nearly every state, meeting in Philadelphia for the ostensible purpose of revising the existing plan of government, the Articles of Confederation. The deliberations were supposed to be secret, though word did get out and rumors did circulate during that summer that what the delegates actually were doing—jettisoning the Articles completely and creating a wholly new plan of government—was far different from the Convention's stated purpose.[5]

Historians' most reliable guide to the delegates' debates in the Constitutional convention remains James Madison's meticulous notes chronicling in detail the daily speeches and votes. Madison was not the only delegate to take notes during the Convention, but his are the most detailed, and it is for that reason that they are often the foundation for scholarship on the Convention. Madison's notes were not an objective transcript, however. Madison was also an active participant in the debate, and Constitutional scholar Mary Sarah Bilder has convincingly shown that Madison continued to revise his notes for years following the Convention's permanent adjournment in September 1787. This does not diminish the importance of Madison's notes, however. Indeed, as Bilder has argued, it makes the notes *more* valuable since they are first and foremost a window into Madison's mind: his priorities, his interests, and his own evolving political views, both during the Convention and after. Madison was a keen, though by no means impartial, observer of the events taking place. And though neither he nor anyone else in attendance could possibly know the full gravity of their actions at the time, his notes attest both to the herculean task before the Convention and to the frustrations endemic to any collaboration among passionate, talented individuals. Delegates all arrived with their own agendas and disagreed, sometimes strenuously. They took up particular issues and then dropped them, unresolved, only to resume them again later. They despaired at the glacial pace of the proceedings. Invariably, one subject would touch upon a variety of distinct but related issues. Few debates in the Convention were really about just one thing. The aspect of the completed Constitution that made it so remarkable is precisely what made it so immensely difficult to craft: everything was connected to everything else.[6]

Madison's top priority during the Convention was not the "executive," as he reports the delegates called the position for most of their time in Philadelphia. Indeed, Madison was far more concerned with ensuring that state authority would be firmly subordinated beneath a national government, and that within that national government, legislative representation would be determined by population. This led him to consistently misread the objections of colleagues from smaller states—especially in the North. Madison was convinced that their discomfort stemmed from a belief that such a government would erode the sovereignty and rights of individual states, perhaps dissolving them entirely. But what primarily worried Madison's Northern colleagues was not that the states would disappear, but that certain states—namely *Southern* states, chief among them Madison's home state of Virginia—would dominate the national government in perpetuity. For his part, Madison's attempts to ensure that slavery would be built into the system of representation did little to allay those fears.[7]

These tendencies to misread or misunderstand his colleagues and to pay particular attention to issues that interested him, while ignoring or glossing others, must inform how we view Madison's notes. Simply because Madison omitted a particular point, or only mentioned it in passing, does not mean it was insignificant. To take but one example: on June 11 Madison entirely omitted from his notes a speech made by Massachusetts delegate Elbridge Gerry against a precursor to what would become the three-fifths clause. Four other delegates—William Paterson of New Jersey, Pierce Butler of South Carolina, and New Yorkers John Lansing, Jr. and Robert Yates—all took notes on the speech, jotting down specific passages of remarkable similarity. Their notes attest to the intensity of debate surrounding the issue of slavery that Madison's subsequent revisions through the years sought to tamp down. "Slaves not to be put upon the Footing as freemen," Paterson recorded Gerry saying. "Freemen of Massts. not to be put upon a Footing with the Slaves of other States—Horses and Cattle ought to have the Right of Representat(io)n Negroes—Mules." Lansing heard something similar. "If Negroes represented why not Horses and Cows—Slaves not to be taken in under any Idea of Representation." According to Yates, Gerry said, "Blacks are property, and are used to the southward as horses and cattle to the northward; and why should their representation be increased to the southward on account of the number of slaves, than horses or oxen to the north?" The variation between "slave," "negro," and "black" in these notes is not insignificant; it suggests a clear tendency on the part of Gerry—or the notetakers, or both—to equate slavery and blackness, viewing the proposed representation as advantageous to the South and a kind of slippery slope toward a level of racial equality that threatened the citizenship of free white men. Madison actually responded to Gerry's speech and likely brought debate on the topic to a close (at least for the time being). But readers of his notes would never know it. The omission keeps us from peering into a heated moment where a delegate from a state that had already abolished slavery (Massachusetts) bristled at the thought of three-fifths of an enslaved population being counted for the purpose of legislative representation for two reasons at once. One was, of course, the sheer power it would give to a state like Virginia, which boasted nearly 300,000 slaves, more than any other state at the time. The other was its concession of personhood to slaves who were legally property. The debate captured the centrality of race-based slavery in the dual dilemma of power and representation at the heart of the Convention. At issue was not only the power that such a provision would grant to slave states. Delegates also wondered what message the incorporation of enslaved persons—and by extension all black people—into the system of representation said about their place in the nation.[8]

Madison did record other instances where this dilemma divided delegates, and his notes join those of his colleagues as evidence of the naked self-interest at the heart of Southerners' motivation to build slavery into the system of representation—and their Northern colleagues' willingness to call them out on it. George Mason, himself a Virginia slave-owner, captured the ambiguity in his own justification for holding fellow humans in bondage. "It was certain that slaves were valuable, as they raised the value of land, increased the exports & imports, and of course the revenue," he conceded on July 11—the day before the Convention agreed to the three-fifths clause. But they also "would supply the means of feeding & supporting an army, and might in cases of emergency become themselves soldiers." For these "important" reasons, Mason concluded (according to Madison's notes), "they were useful to the community at large, they ought not to be excluded from the estimate of Representation." But, of course, neither could he "regard them as equal to freemen," and thus they would have no direct voting power. They were a "peculiar species of property, over & above the other species of property common to all the states."[9] Nearly a month later, Gouvernor Morris of New York pushed back against the idea that slaves could be both people and property at the same time. "Upon what principle is it that the slaves shall be computed in the representation? Are they men? Then make them Citizens and let them vote," Morris asked his colleagues in a lengthy speech on August 8. "Are they property? Why then is no other property included?" Morris did not accept Mason's "peculiar species of property" position. Slaves were either people or property. Southerners could not have it both ways.[10]

Nothing the delegates did that summer, including the adoption of the three-fifths clause, removed the ambiguity surrounding the place of slaves, and black people more generally, in the new nation. On the one hand, slaves were human enough to count partially toward representation and to be thought of as unique among types of property, as even Mason conceded. On the other, black slaves *were* property, and representation for them could threaten the status of free whites by placing the latter on equal "footing" with the former.[11] The questions that really divided the delegates over the issue of slavery—Were slaves *persons*, to be counted alongside the citizenry of the young nation? If so, how to justify enslaving them? If not, why should they count toward representation at all—and *could* they ever be persons in the future?—were integral to an even more fundamental issue that the debate over the executive brought into particular relief: Were the people of the United States already one "people," or did they need a stronger national government to *make* them a single, united "people"?

By mid-July, little about the executive had been decided. Yet debates over ostensibly discrete subjects—whether the executive would be one person or multiple people, how much power the executive would possess, what the executive's relationship to the legislature would be, and, of course, how the executive would be chosen—revealed the fundamental questions dividing the delegates throughout the summer: how would the government relate to the people, who counted among "the people," and who did not? Delegates were cognizant that the executive would be vital for securing support from the public for the power the new government possessed. If the right person (once the Convention determined the executive would be singular) did not fill the office, the ability of the government to maintain the public confidence needed to create and maintain this strong national bond would be compromised. That was why, as Madison noted, Gouverneur Morris thought the people of the United States could be trusted to choose an executive who was a "man of distinguished character, or services; some man, if he might so speak, of continental reputation."[12]

That statement appeared straightforward, but it actually captured the uncertain nature of the entity for which the delegates were attempting to craft a government. The notion of a man with a "continental reputation" suggested something that bound all people across state, regional, and political lines, some preexisting standard all people shared that they agreed this "man of distinguished character" had met. Yet the need for such a man to cultivate this kind of universal esteem was so dire because at the moment it was so rare. Legislatures, the bodies that were supposed to represent the citizenry, could not be trusted to choose an executive, because they were natural places where "intrigues & sinister views," as Pennsylvanian James Wilson put it, were likely to spawn.[13] Morris made a similar point later in the Convention. "The Legislature is worthy of unbounded confidence in some respects," as when its interests "coincide precisely" with the populace it serves, "and liable to equal distrust in others." It was inevitable that at times legislative bodies would be motivated by "strong personal interest" that ran counter to "the general interest," and in these cases, the legislature was not to be trusted. Making the legislature in charge of choosing the executive was "the worst" method of election the convention could choose, Morris explained.[14]

Ironically, Madison's notes were a testament to the very political "interest" that Morris feared. Madison's own agenda to craft a government based on population, and to ensure that the population included slaves in some form or fashion, was a product of his own status as a wealthy Virginia plantation owner. Northerners knew it, and they objected that such a scheme would place the power of the proposed national government squarely and irrevocably in the hands of Virginians. Given that, it may seem surprising that Morris—a Northerner—voiced confidence in the people's ability to choose as their executive "a man of continental reputation." For such a man sat among them: a Virginian, no less.[15]

Washington was the president of the Convention, sitting mostly in silence throughout the entire summer. But Washington did not need to say much; his name was already legend. The leader of the Continental Army, Washington had won near universal acclaim for freely relinquishing command of the army to the Continental Congress in 1783. This defied the received wisdom of the day, which taught that humans were naturally corrupt and would never give up power unless compelled to do so by force. Washington's selfless act was hailed as all but superhuman, and though Washington had led the Continental Army to victory in battle, his true genius lay in his decision to retire peacefully to his Mount Vernon home. Around the country (and beyond), praise for Washington emphasized that he was a man of all but incomparable virtue and disinterestedness: that is, that he subordinated his own selfish desires in favor of the public good. He had resisted temptation to a degree few of his countrymen could have matched, as the superlatives often used in poems, songs, open letters, and dedications to him attested. Yet even as contemporaries characterized Washington as something akin to a deity (at times even calling him "godlike"), they also claimed him as exemplary of the revolutionary spirit of the American people—not only their capacity to oppose tyrannical forces that threatened their liberty, but the capacity of their revolution to radically transform the political thinking of the Western world. "Great without pomp, without ambition brave,/ Proud, not to conquer fellow-men, but to save," a poet trumpeted in a piece in the *New Hampshire Gazette* that appeared in newspapers from New England to South Carolina. Washington was

> Too wise to learn from *Machiavel's* false school,
> That truth and perfidy by turns should rule;
> Warm'd by *Religion's* sacred genuine ray,
> That points to future bliss th' unerring way;
> Yet ne'er controul'd by Superstition's laws,
> That worst of tyrants in the noblest cause.[16]

As breathless language like this attests, no one boasted a continental reputation that rivaled Washington's. It was a reputation that transcended even his status as a Virginian, and that was key. For if anyone could be trusted with considerable power—even power that had been devised by Southerners with a clear eye toward serving their own interests—it was Washington. That meant that the establishment of a stronger system of government, and the choice of Washington as the executive, would act as a kind of repudiation, rather than a confirmation, of the fears that Southern, especially Virginian, interests were destined to dominate. Establishing a stronger system of government, headed by the man who had laid aside the sword he had used to win the war, would be the Revolution's true crescendo—not with violent explosions or brutal bloodshed, but with a diverse confederation of people uniting in peace to express their shared confidence in the executive they had chosen, and the new government he led.

But before Washington could ascend to the presidency, the Constitution would have to be ratified by a minimum of nine states. The Constitution itself stipulated further that even if that threshold were met, the new government would only be implemented by the specific states that had ratified. Thus, even if nine states did ratify, the country could still be broken up geographically if particular states, particularly in the upper South or the mid-Atlantic, did not ratify. When the Constitution was first published in September 1787, a heated debate over ratification began, which would extend to the following summer. Every state called a convention for the express purpose of deliberating on the Constitution and rendering a decision. Antifederalist commentaries on the Constitution were detailed and disciplined; they picked apart every passage, pointing out ambiguities, omissions, and terms that supported their considerable apprehensions.

Though federalists exerted more control over the circulation of informa-tion—federalists dominated newspaper publishing, in some states all but quashing published antifederalist commentary completely—antifederalist voices were widespread and compelling enough, and federalist discomfort with public criticism of the Constitution and the illustrious "characters" who had created it was intense enough that federalists could not ignore them, nor could they simply rest on Washington's accolades. Great though Washington was, his virtue alone would not be enough to satisfy antifed-eralists' objections.[17]

"THE FOUNTAIN OF ALL HONORS IN THE UNITED STATES"

It is difficult to overstate the extent of public participation in the ratifica-tion debate. Across the country wealthy, middling, and poor Americans, women as well as men, followed the debate over the Constitution with rapt attention. To be sure, elites exerted a disproportionately large influ-ence over the ratification debate and authored the majority of the most influential commentaries the debate produced. Nonetheless, Stuart's ob-servation about "popular applause" held true. The literacy rate among white Americans was quite high (in New England, it was about 90 per-cent), as was the general public interest in politics. Non-elite citizens read the Constitution with great interest alongside their gentry counterparts. Many also participated in the debate, and were even encouraged to do so, as everyone—man and woman, young and old, wealthy and poor—would be affected by the decision the country made.[18]

The debate over the Constitution took place in state conventions—called, per the Constitution's requirements, for the express purpose of de-ciding whether to ratify—as well as in newspapers, which printed extended commentaries in favor of ratification or critical of the Constitution, and in spirited verbal exchanges with fellow citizens on streets, in taverns, and in public squares. To be sure, some state ratifying conventions commanded more attention, and caused more drama, than others. The state conven-tion of Pennsylvania, for instance, was especially contentious. It contained a sizable antifederalist contingent, including those who formally embraced the term. In the ratifying convention Pennsylvania federalist James Wilson infuriated antifederalists by moving that their objections to the Constitu-tion not be printed in the official proceedings, to save on printing costs. The incensed delegates instead published their objections as "The Address and Reasons of Dissent of the Minority of the Convention of Pennsylvania to Their Constituents," which became one of the most widely influential antifederalist texts of the ratification debate, reprinted in thirteen newspapers in five states by mid-March 1788; it appeared in pamphlet form in the North and in the South. The "Dissent of the Minority" was likely written by Samuel Bryan, who also published essays that spoke to the concerns of rural, plebeian antifederalists. His first letter under the pseudonym Centinel likewise went through dozens of reprints in Pennsylvania and beyond, communicating to the country that the concerns of non-elites were considerable, and not limited by state boundaries.[19]

Pennsylvania was also important because it was a geographically large state. Since Article VII specified that nine states were needed to ratify the Constitution but the new government would only be in effect for the states that ratified it, if Pennsylvania did not ratify, its sheer geographic size would substantially narrow the physical connection between New England and the Southern states—and the country would no longer contain Philadelphia, a city of immense political and economic significance to the country. Pennsylvania ratified the Constitution on December 22, 1787, but two other states, also large and politically and economically vital, would not ratify until June of 1788. One was New York, and the other was Virginia. If either or both had failed to ratify, the country would have been divided entirely, as both states extended from the Atlantic coast to what was at the time the western frontier.

Praise for Washington was part of the debate. Federalists published poems, toasts, essays, and even images extolling Washington's virtue. Some argued that the people should place their trust in the proposed national government simply because Washington endorsed it, and everyone assumed he would lead it.[20] In effect, public praise for Washington used the commander in chief of the Continental Army to connect the untested proposed system of government to the legacy of the Revolution. But there were limits to how far Washington could be used to make this connection. "You are too well informed to decide by the opinion of others, and too independent to need a caution against undue influence," a piece in the *New-Jersey Journal* assured readers.[21] Since the plan of government was meant to owe its power to all Americans, neither its opponents nor its supporters could rely mostly, let alone entirely, on Washington to make their respective arguments. Participants in the ratification debate urged the public to evaluate the plan of government on its own merits, distinct from any one man's celebrity endorsement, no matter how admirable or incorruptible he might be.

Washington recognized this, and strove to maintain a generally low profile during the ratification debate, though he took it upon himself to communicate with associates in his home state. He wrote private letters to his contacts and confidantes through the length of the debate and kept abreast of developments in other states. The letters he wrote on behalf of ratification were private correspondences to specific people, and he was surprised when one of his letters found its way into print.[22]

Washington's endorsement of the Constitution was an undeniable trump card for federalists. Nonetheless, participants on every side of the debate agreed that discussion of the Constitution—and the presidency—could not be confined to him alone. Critics refused to accept assurances by the Constitution's supporters that the proposed government could be trusted simply because Washington would be first to lead it. In the presidency they saw an entity that seemed to encapsulate the troubling tendency toward "consolidation" that characterized the government as a whole.

"[O]n the judicious organization of the executive power," James Monroe declared in the Virginia state ratifying convention, "the security of our interest and happiness greatly depended." His colleague George Mason concurred. "There is not a more important article in the Constitution" than Article II, Mason concluded. "The great fundamental principle of responsibility in republicanism is here sap[p]ed."[23]

The Constitution's opponents differed widely across region, class, and interest. Some were plebeian farmers who feared the Constitution would simply provide new ways for elites to wield power at a distance from everyone else. Others were wealthy leaders, concerned that the Constitution would draw power toward a central authority, thereby stripping them of their local authority. Some spoke for rural fears of a more powerful national government in a distant city. Still others dwelled in cities—particularly in the North—and worried how ratification would shift power further southward, due to the advantages it gave the slave-powered Southern economy. Yet for all these differences, the opponents launched a remarkably coherent and consistent public criticism of the proposed government. They feared oppressive taxation; senatorial aristocracy; judicial tyranny; inadequate representation in the House; the creation of a standing army; the absence of a bill of rights; and the "blending" of power among the legislature and an executive whom some feared would wield the same power as a king. All of these were expressions of a more fundamental grievance: that the Constitution represented a dangerous "consolidation" of government power into a national system that threatened the federal nature of the union and the rights of the people within it.[24]

The Constitution's critics subscribed to the received wisdom of the day, articulated most famously by Montesquieu, that only geographically small and demographically homogeneous countries were capable of drawing their power from the consent of the populace and could thus ever be truly republican. Neither of the requisite conditions for republics—small geographic size and limited demographic diversity—existed in the United States. In fact, the opposite was true. "Federal Farmer" and "John De-Witt" perhaps said it best when they argued that the United States was "so very extensive" and "the difference of interest, different manners, and different local prejudices, in the different parts of the United States" so great, that no singular, common interest existed for a powerful national government to legitimately represent.[25] Difference, not commonality, dominated the American landscape, both literally and figuratively, argued New York critic "Brutus" (likely Robert Yates, one of the state's three delegates to the Philadelphia Convention), since "the United States includes a variety of climates," and its people, in "their manners and habits differ as much as their climates and productions; and their sentiments are by no means coincident."[26] Antifederalists' contentions of the diversity that characterized the early national landscape dealt a powerful rebuke to the Constitution's bold declaration that a singular, collective "We, the People" had "ordained" the government with the powers the document described. Instead, antifederalists argued, national unity was a myth. The people of the United States were far more different than they were alike.

Given the physical extent of the country, antifederalists were convinced that this division was sure to continue and that a government that concentrated power as the Constitution appeared to would always be in tension with the diffuse interests, manners, and habits extant across the American geographic and demographic landscape.[27] The Constitution posited the fiction of a unified "We, the People" as an excuse to concentrate power for itself at the expense of the states, and thus, ultimately, to separate itself further from the people within those states, whose interests it claimed to represent.

This was what critics meant by "consolidation," a word that was ubiquitous in the most widely printed critiques of the Constitution. A consolidated government, as the critics understood it, was its own source of power—the precise source of oppression against which Americans had fought in the Revolution. To embrace consolidated government was to embrace the essential "despotic" government that Americans claimed to fundamentally oppose.[28] Yet even a critic like Elbridge Gerry acknowledged that the country needed a stronger system of government than its current one. "The question on this plan involves others of the highest importance[:] 1st Whether there shall be a dissolution of the *Foederal* government? 2dly Whether the several State Governments shall be so altered, as in effect to be dissolved? and 3dly Whether in lieu of the *Foederal & state* Governments, the *national* constitution now proposed shall be substituted without amendment?" Elbridge Gerry, a Massachusetts delegate to the Philadelphia Convention who refused to sign the Constitution, wrote his "Objections to the Constitution," one of the most widely reprinted critical pieces in the debate (it was reprinted thirty times). "[N]ever perhaps were a people called on to decide a question of greater magnitude—should the Citizens of America adopt the plan as it now stands, their liberties may be lost: or should they reject it altogether Anarchy may ensue."[29] Would ratification preserve the American experiment in representative government, born in dissent against government tyranny, or was it a betrayal of everything America stood for?

In his first letter, which went through twenty-seven reprintings, Pennsylvanian Samuel Bryant, writing as Centinel, predicted that the confederation would "be melted down into one empire," and implored readers "to consider, whether such a government, however constructed, would be eligible in so extended a territory; and whether it would be practicable, consistent with freedom?"[30] A group of dissenting delegates to the Pennsylvania state convention, in a piece reprinted twenty times, opposed the Constitution "first, because it is the opinion of the most celebrated writers on government, and confirmed by uniform experience, that a very extensive territory cannot be governed on the principles of freedom, otherwise than by a confederation of republics, possessing all the powers of internal government; but united in the management of their general, and foreign concerns." Second, they objected to the Constitution because, in their view, "the powers vested in Congress by this Constitution, must necessarily annihilate and absorb the legislative, executive, and judicial powers of the several states, and produce from their ruins one consolidated government."[31]

The Constitution's critics had seen this kind of accumulation of power before and knew full well its ultimate victim and its ultimate beneficiary. "Consolidation" of government power, they concluded, could only harm the majority of the people who would never have direct contact with their elected leaders, weakening the connection between members of the legislature tasked with representing state-level constituencies and strengthening the internal bond among "rulers" at a national level. This was what Gerry meant when he voiced his concern that "the Constitution proposed has few, if any *Foederal* features, but is rather a system of *national* government."[32] This concentration of power could be expressed in many despotic acts—through oppressive taxation, through the violation of the sovereignty of state courts, through the threat of coercion and violence by a standing army, to name but a few.[33] But the most conspicuous embodiment of this consolidation would be the executive.

The association of executive power with government abuses of all kinds, from oppressive taxation demanded by royal tax collectors to judges chosen by colonial governors to military abuses visited upon colonists by the crown's sanction, made executive power, and the traumatic experiences associated with it, a ubiquitous presence in critics' writings. If the nation's colonial past had taught anything, it was that the executive's powers were like tentacles, extending outward and grasping every conceivable corner of authority within reach. Prior to the Revolution, there was no branch, no body, no function of the colonial government that the authority of the king or the governors did not touch. The Constitution's critics saw nothing in the proposed government to make them believe that the nation's future under the Constitution would be any different.

Thus, even subjects like taxation, standing armies, and legislative representation were not entirely distinct from the critics' fear of executive power. Consolidation of power was what made taxation, representation, and diplomacy worth arguing about, and the executive appeared to be involved in every aspect of consolidation. As one critic, An Old Whig, remarked, the president was "the fountain of all honors in the United States, commander in chief of the army, navy and militia, with the power of making treaties and of granting pardons, and to be vested with an authority to put a negative upon all laws."[34] It was the execution of the laws—specifically by the "standing army" that would surely be "numerous," and the phalanx of "officers in every department: judges, collectors, tax-gatherers, excisemen and the whole host of revenue officers," all of them under the command of the president, "swarm[ing] over the land, devouring the hard earnings of the industrious[,] Like the locusts of old, impoverishing and desolating all before them"—that the authors of the "Dissent of the Minority" believed would bring "the supremacy of despotism" to fruition.[35] In the president, critics were reminded of everything America had fought against to become an independent country. The only real question that divided them was, who would control the power of the executive branch? Would the president alone wield that power like a king, or would he be a mere figurehead, a hollow shell through which a haughty senatorial aristocracy ruled supreme?[36]

An Old Whig made the comparison between the presidency and the British monarchy explicit, challenging readers "to look into the constitution of that country, and then tell me what important prerogative the King of Great-Britain is entitled to, which does not also belong to the president during his continuance in office." True, the president did not possess the power to "create nobility" as the British king did, "but our president will have the power of making all the *great men*, which comes to the same thing."[37] The New York critic Cato (possibly the pen name of either Abraham Yates, Jr., or George Clinton) agreed. The "powers, in both the president and the king [of Great Britain], are substantially the same: he is the generalissimo of the nation, and of course, has the command & controul of the army, navy and militia; he is the general conservator of the peace of the union—he may pardon all offences, except in cases of impeachment, and the principal fountain of all offices & employments."[38]

Those who accused the president of being a king in disguise conflated the two different types of eighteenth-century executive authority wielded by the British crown and the colonial governors. When critics attacked the president as a monarch by a different name, they at times ignored limitations on the powers expressly stated in the Constitution—so strongly did the memory of executive despotism by both the king and the colonial governors remain in their minds. The president did not possess all but absolute "controul over the army, militia, and navy," as Cato argued. Article I, Section 8 stated that Congress retained the power "to provide for calling forth the Militia." The president did not possess the sole power to make treaties, as An Old Whig suggested; he shared it with the Senate, as Article II, Section 2 specified. But such oversights only underscore the extent to which these critics considered the presidency to be the personification of the government's potential for dangerous and irreversible "consolidation" of power at the expense of state autonomy and individual rights.[39]

Other antifederalist critics predicted that the Senate would rule over the government by dominating the executive, pointing to the Senate's relationship to the executive through the Constitution's vaguely defined "advise and consent" role. While no less convinced of the national (and thus antifederal and despotic) nature of the proposed government than the fears of a king-like president, fears of senatorial supremacy over the executive emphasized the "aristocratic," rather than monarchical, tendencies of the proposed government and stressed the dominion by the Senate over the president through sheer force. As "John DeWitt" explained: "[T]he Senate excepting in nomination, have a negative upon the president, and if we but a moment attend to their situation and to his . . . we cannot hesitate to say, that he will be infinitely less apt to disoblige them, than they to refuse him. It is far easier for twenty to gain over one, than one twenty." The fear ultimately led back to an executive whose power could be wielded by a small minority in government over the states and the people. Antifederalists argued that the Senate possessed a disturbing "share in the executive," reflecting the belief that the executive remained the fundamental source of corruption, even if the Senate would be the body that controlled executive power in practice.[40]

In this way, antifederalists positioned the presidency as indicative of the Constitution's tendency toward what George Mason ominously called "a Monarchy, or a corrupt oppressive Aristocracy"—the very power structures that had provoked widespread colonial dissent and ultimately necessitated a bloody War for Independence.[41] Executive power, they all agreed, was the clearest expression of the consolidation of power that was the hallmark of this plan of government. Whether the executive himself— the president—or the Senate served as the source of this consolidation of power, antifederalists were convinced that the presidency would facilitate concentrated power that would serve the interest of the government over that of the states or the people, betraying the very reason that the Revolution had been fought and independence achieved in the first place.

Even the great virtue of George Washington was not enough to save the country from the government's tendency toward consolidation. An Old Whig asked readers to imagine that another man, sometime in the future, would become president, and unlike Washington, simply would not be able to stand to part with his power. Imagine further "this man to be a favorite with his army, and that they are unwilling to part with their beloved commander in chief," An Old Whig continued, before dropping the pretense, "or to make the thing familiar, let us suppose, a future president and commander in chief adored by his army and the militia to as great a degree as our late illustrious commander in chief; and we have only to suppose one thing more, that this man is without the virtue, the moderation and love of liberty which possessed the mind of our late general, and this country will be involved at once in war and tyranny." The writer predicted that the odds that the country would find another man of such incomparable virtue as Washington was "a chance of one hundred millions to one."[42]

An Old Whig's prediction that presidential power would corrupt lesser men than Washington and eventually lead to "war and tyranny" was one example of the antifederalists' claim that the Constitution failed to live up to its fundamental promise to promote peace—"domestic tranquility," as the Constitution's preamble put it—throughout the country.

To antifederalists, the presidency portended a violent future that nobody wanted, the result of the amount of concentrated power vested in the government. Washington might be virtuous enough to resist abusing the power of the presidency. But the best he could do was delay the inevitable.

The distinction between Washington and the presidency was so prominent that antifederalists hesitated to underscore Washington's complicity in another violent institution: slavery. Brutus echoed the frustrations of fellow Northerners when he complained about the advantages that the three-fifths clause conferred on Southerners. The House, Brutus argued, would apportion representatives unequally due to the this clause, privileging Southern states and making ownership of slaves a tangible political asset in national government. Slaves "have no share in government," Brutus noted, so "why is the number of members in the assembly, to be increased on their account? Is it because in some of the states, a considerable part of the property of the inhabitants consists in a number of their fellow men, who are held in bondage, in defiance of every idea of benevolence, justice, and religion, and contrary to all the principles of liberty, which have been publickly avowed in the late glorious revolution?" Yet Brutus did not mention that the great Washington was one of the practitioners of this institution and thus among those Southerners who stood directly to benefit from the three-fifths clause. In fact, in a later letter, Brutus praised Washington as "a patriot as well as a general," whose leadership had all but saved the United States from succumbing to the military dictatorship that befell so many republican armies of the past.[43]

Brutus's comments betray a widely shared cognitive dissonance regarding Washington's dual identities as the hero of the Revolution and as a Southern slave-owner. Like Brutus, participants in the public debate over ratification praised Washington for upholding American liberty in battle, yet sidestepped his complicity in an institution that critics—especially those in the North—decried as antithetical to liberty. Part of the answer lies in the participants' shared white supremacy. Here again, Brutus is instructive. To his credit, Brutus cast the issue of slavery as an immoral, violent institution, antithetical to the principles of independence and peace that the United States prized. The three-fifths clause was "evil," he wrote, made all the worse by the Constitution's stipulation "that these states are to be permitted to continue the inhuman traffic of importing slaves, until the year 1808—and for every cargo of these unhappy people, which unfeeling, unprincipled, barbarous, and avaricious wretches, may tear from their country, friends and tender connections, and bring into those states, they are to be rewarded by having an increase of members in the general assembly." Yet Brutus's sympathy for enslaved people extended only so far. He also complained that the government could "derive no additional strength, protection, nor defence from the slaves, but the contrary." Trafficking in widespread white fears of black violence, especially slave rebellions, Brutus decried the three-fifths clause by suggesting that it gave Southern whites an incentive to import more slaves, which in turn made whites less safe.[44]

Brutus's primary concern was the same as most Northern delegates to the Constitutional Convention: he cared less about the plight of enslaved persons than he did about the power that the three-fifths clause gave to the South. This set of priorities stemmed from the basic position that Brutus, along with most whites in the United States, held about race: however immoral and violent slavery was, most whites believed that black people were not, and never could be, sovereign citizens on an equal footing with whites. This shared white supremacy limited the outrage that most whites mustered over slavery—making the significance of Washington's participation in it, even when it directly related to the Constitution, easier to downplay or ignore.[45]

Moreover, because Washington's reputation as the virtuous hero of the Revolution so dominated how the public saw him, antifederalists opened themselves up to attack whenever they dared criticize him directly. Samuel Bryan crossed this line in his first Centinel essay. Singling out both Benjamin Franklin and George Washington, Bryan suggested that both men had been duped by federalists into supporting the Constitution. Bryan blamed the octogenarian Franklin's age ("the weakness and indecision attendant on old age"), while claiming that Washington lacked sufficient experience to assess the Constitution with clarity.[46]

Such arguments provided an opportunity for federalists to depict the Constitution as the fulfillment of America's proud, patriotic, and dissenting spirit through breathless praise for Washington and to condemn antifederalists as selfish partisans. One reply to Bryan's Centinel from a writer calling himself One of the Four Thousand implored readers to "turn your eyes to the illustrious American hero, whose name has ennobled human nature—I mean our beloved WASHINGTON." The superlatives did not stop there. "See him uniting and cementing an army, composed of the citizens of thirteen states, into a band of brothers." Was it possible, One of the Four Thousand asked readers, "that the deliverer of our country would have recommended an unsafe form of government for that liberty, for which he had for eight long years contended with such unexampled firmness, constancy and magnanimity[?]"[47]

With federalists so ready to pounce on any personal attack on Washington, antifederalists like Brutus had a strong incentive to steer clear of even mentioning Washington's status as a Virginia slave-owner. There was simply too high a price to pay for pointing out that Washington, like other white Virginians, stood to gain from an unjust, exploitative institution that ran counter to everything the Revolution stood for. In short, as antifederalists used the presidency to explain what fundamentally troubled them about the Constitution, Washington's illustrious reputation helped ensure that their discussion of the presidency would focus more on the office, and by extension the government as a whole, than on Washington himself.

The nature of the argument that antifederalists mounted shaped the rebuttal that federalists fashioned. Because their opponents used the presidency to support their fundamental objections to the plan of government, fixating on Washington had limited utility as a rebuttal strategy. Federalists thus mirrored their opponents' approach by making the office, more than the man who would be the first to occupy it, exemplary of their fundamental argument in favor of the Constitution: that the proposed government would always be accountable to the people and that that accountability would remain the cornerstone of the government, no matter who occupied the office.

"HE CAN EXERCISE NO POWER, BUT THAT WHICH WE CONFER UPON HIM"

"When the people established the powers of legislation under their separate governments," James Wilson told an audience of rapt listeners at the conclusion of a public speech in Philadelphia on October 6, 1787, "they invested their representatives with every right and authority which they did not in explicit terms reserve." The proposed Constitution, he argued, employed a different, unprecedented "criterion": "the congressional authority is to be collected, not from tacit implication, but from the positive grant expressed in the instrument of union. Hence it is evident, that in the former case every thing which is not reserved is given, but in the latter the reverse of the proposition prevails, and every thing which is not given, is reserved." Wilson led listeners through a systematic rebuttal to antifederalist objections. His speech would rank among the most influential defenses of the Constitution in the ratification debate; by the year's end, it had been reprinted over thirty times in a dozen different states. Fellow federalists cribbed from it, repeating his points in substance if not in precise wording. In convention speeches and in essays circulating in newspapers, federalists would follow Wilson's example of emphasizing the Constitution as an expression of the people's expressly delegated power. They would stress the necessity of the government's authority to cultivate and maintain a strong bond among the states, while respecting the states' autonomy. They would concede the Constitution's imperfection but would frequently assert that antifederalists criticized the Constitution because they were biased and self-interested partisans, who had a vested interest in maintaining a deeply flawed and ultimately untenable governmental status quo.[48]

Wilson knew his audience and he knew his objective. He had crafted his address to push back against antifederalist opposition with just the right blend of high political theory and patriotic theater. The proposed government's reliance on the people for its power made it wholly original, a testament to the love of liberty that bound together all Americans across states and regions. Enthusiastic applause interrupted him throughout his speech.[49]

Wilson's speech, and the larger federalist defense of the Constitution, contained a message that contemporary readers can easily misinterpret. It is easy to imagine Wilson extolling the virtues of America in the world, a brilliant, burning beacon of light to a world of oppressive, despotic darkness, from a twenty-first-century vantage point, when the United States stands as the perennial military and economic power in the world. Yet Wilson spoke at a time when the United States was young and weak, its survival far from assured, its status as a global superpower nothing more than a dream confined to an uncertain future. For Wilson, as for his compatriots, the Constitution contained the essential spark of the nation's revolutionary republican experiment, but the tiny flame flickered weakly amid the strong winds that threatened to snuff it out. On this point, he was far from alone.

The American nation was unlike any on the face of the earth, *"the favored of heaven,"* as one writer, A Democratic Federalist, put it.[50] Its success or failure, a pseudonymous writer who adopted the pen name Common Sense argued, depended upon the future "of this new and free world."[51] The loftiness of America's exceptional role in world history stood in stark contrast to its current, weak, and vulnerable state. "[W]e are the prey of every nation," Hugh Williamson stated bluntly in his "Remarks on the New Plan of Government," published serially in Pennsylvania, Massachusetts, New York, and his home state of North Carolina. The government had borrowed money from Spain and Holland with no way to repay the loan. No mechanism existed to compel the states to pay their fair share into the coffers of Congress. A paltry rabble "scattered along the Ohio" was the nation's only protection against hostile Indians and European colonists looking to disrupt trade, or worse, to invade the country from the west. In short, the dream of a peaceful, prosperous, and free American nation was just that: a dream—one that might die in its infancy, the victim of its own vulnerability in a merciless, violent world.[52]

Corrosive forces existed not merely outside the nation, John Jay noted, but within it as well. During the Revolution, Jay observed, the states had coalesced against their common British foe. But victory in the Revolution brought "ease, tranquility, and a sense of security" that "loosened the bands of union." This, in turn, brought about a selfishness that further stymied national cohesion. "The spirit of private gain expelled the spirit of public good, and men became more intent on the means of enriching and aggrandizing themselves, than of enriching and aggrandizing their country."[53]

This anemic quality permeated American society, federalists agreed, facilitated by a weak national government. The country wanted "energy," they often complained, the result of a decision to craft a plan of government, the Articles of Confederation, which lacked the power to replicate the tyranny that had provoked them to revolution against Britain. This was a complaint of some even during and immediately following the Revolution. Back in 1783, William Livingston had written that "we improvidently raised a battery against an attack that could never be made upon us, & accordingly constituted the Executive branch too weak and inefficatious to operate with proper energy & vigour."[54] The patriots' commitment to preserving their rights had sparked a momentous act of dissent against a tyrannical British government. But the very dissenting spirit that had fueled their revolution also made their government weak and their country vulnerable.

No one captured this point better than Benjamin Rush. "The confederation, together with most of our state constitutions, were formed under very unfavourable circumstances. We had just emerged from a corrupted monarchy. Although we understood perfectly the principles of liberty, yet most of us were ignorant of the forms and combinations of power in republics," Rush pointed out. "Add to this, the British army was in the heart of our country, spreading desolation wherever it went: our resentments, of course, were awakened. We detested the British name; and unfortunately refused to copy some things in the administration of justice and power, in the British government, which have made it the admiration and envy of the world." Specifically, the confederated system entrusted too little power to a national executive and too much power to state legislative bodies, who themselves were beholden to the diverse and self-interested desires of the masses. "In our opposition to monarchy, we forgot that the temple of tyranny has two doors. We bolted one of them by proper restraints; but we left the other open, by neglecting to guard against the effects of our own ignorance and licentiousness."[55]

On one level the federalists' lament actually echoed the antifederalists' point about the diversity that existed throughout the United States. Federalists actually agreed that the language "We, the People" in the Constitution's preamble was more aspiration than fact, that difference and division dominated the young country's political landscape. But federalists disagreed that the idea of a unified country of "We, the People" would *never* exist. They insisted instead that it was an aspiration that could become a reality because, for all their differences, Americans from Georgia to Massachusetts *did* hold something in common: their shared commitment to independence and a steadfast refusal to assent to any government that did not answer to them. To federalists neglecting to strengthen the government was tantamount to surrendering whatever hope of survival this fragile bond had left. It was to accede to the forces of violence. Their favorite example was Shays's Rebellion, the 1786 uprising of Massachusetts farmers, led by Revolutionary War veteran Daniel Shays. In a subsequent address given in December, Wilson made the connection explicit. "Do we wish a return of those insurrections and tumults to which a sister state was lately exposed or a government of such inefficiency as the present is found to be?" Wilson asked. "To the determination of Congress are submitted all disputes between states concerning boundary, jurisdiction, or right of soil." Even if a state were "to obtain a decree in her favor" against another state, what, Wilson asked, would happen next? The answer, of course, was nothing, Wilson explained, because "the Congress had no power to carry the decree into execution."[56] Agreeing with the antifederalists that the United States deserved a peaceful future, federalists refuted the antifederalists' contention that the power vested in the government fostered violent oppression. On the contrary, they countered, the violence that threatened the prospect of a prosperous, peaceful, united American nation was the direct result of a government that lacked the power to effectively make and execute laws.

Like Wilson, most federalist defenses also downplayed George Washington, or omitted him completely. Wilson, and the federalists more generally, agreed with the antifederalists that the proposed government had to stand on its own merits, not merely on the reputation of one man, however well deserved that reputation might be. Yet unlike Wilson's October 6 speech, which mentioned the presidential office only in passing, other federalist defenses would invoke the presidential office to make essentially the point that Wilson emphasized: far from a threat to their independence, the proposed government's considerable power would always exemplify the very sprit of independence that had fueled the Revolution and united all Americans, however tenuously, as one people.

For federalists around the country, "energy" provided a way to describe executive power—and by extension, government power as a whole—as a positive that the country needed, distinct from the despotism that antifederalists feared, because it was freely given by the people and its exercise would remain always subject to their scrutiny. Federalists frequently invoked "energy" as an attribute of the executive as a way of connecting the power of the executive described in the Constitution to what ailed the country as a whole. In the government described by the Constitution, "energy" in the executive combined with "stability" and "balance" within the legislature and an "intelligent[ly]" "organiz[ed]" judiciary, a writer in the *Poughkeepsie* (New York) *Country Journal* claimed. The Constitution's friends argued that the president supplied this needed "energy" within the proposed government, making the presidency reflective of the government's capacity for action on behalf of the people and of the force of the legislature and the judiciary in ensuring that "energy" never became oppression. The executive could facilitate government authority capable of "removing every *local* impediment to the harmony of the *whole*," "armed to be sure with all the customary powers of sovereignty, but . . . no more than necessary to the uniformity of the plan, and to give the system its proper balance and beautiful proportion." The result was government action in support of national interests that would nonetheless never threaten the autonomy of the states: a nation made stronger *and* more republican by vesting some select power in the hands of a national executive.[57]

From their bleak portrait of a beleaguered country teetering on the edge of oblivion and desperately in need of an "energy" that only a strong executive could truly provide, the Constitution's supporters made their case for the necessity of a robust national government, often by emphasizing the relationships among different government bodies to describe these essential traits at work in the Constitution. The House of Representatives, for instance, was useful for playing up the democratic character of the republican government that the Constitution created. As Tench Coxe, writing as An American Citizen, wrote: the House constituted "*the immediate delegates of the people*," a "truly popular assembly . . . chosen . . . *by the poor as well as the rich*."[58] But it was no good for emphasizing either consistency and stability in the government (its members only served two-year terms) or wisdom (its members, besides being popularly elected, could be as young as twenty-five years old). These were key elements of a firm national union, themes that the Constitution's friends believed they needed to stress, and the House's very democratic quality made it unfit for the job.

The Senate was better for highlighting these themes. Its members had to be older (a minimum of thirty years was specified in the Constitution) and chosen by the state legislatures, removed from the direct influence of the populace. It even had a share in the executive, providing advice and consent on treaties and appointments. Yet it too fell short if a particular writer wished to emphasize the need for more dynamic execution of the laws, or national unity, or public accountability, since senators were chosen by each state's legislature, not by direct popular vote. The judiciary was fine if one sought to stress the wisdom of entrusting power to evaluate laws to magistrates who were not subject to popular, legislative, or executive pressures. But it was not useful for emphasizing the government's continued reliance on the states, or to the people, as Supreme Court justices were appointed by the president (with the advice and consent of the Senate), and served for life. That left the executive—the president—which federalists used to connect every element of the government that supporters sought to promote and to assure the public that the government would derive its power from the people and would remain always accountable to their collective voice.

Ironically, the president's military power, which constituted the most disturbing similarity to the British monarchy, became in the federalists' telling a testament to the power that the people possessed to hold the government to account. Federalists argued that the plan of government, and the people's natural jealousy of their liberties, ensured that no president—not even Washington—could mire the country in unnecessary wars, turn troops against their fellow citizens, or violate the people's rights through force of arms. "The president is indeed to be a great man," Edmund Pendleton conceded, but he will have "no latent Prerogatives, nor any Powers but such as are defined and given him by law," which meant, among other things, that "he is to be Commander-in-Chief of the Army & Navy, but Congress are to raise & provide for them, & that not for above two years at a time."[59] The president was not "vested with all the powers of a monarch, as has been asserted," an anonymous writer named Cassius argued in the *Massachusetts Gazette*. Rather, "he is under the immediate controul of the constitution which if he should presume to deviate from he would be immediately arrested in his career, and summoned to answer for his conduct before a federal court, where strict justice and equity would undoubtedly preside."[60] Held in check by the laws, the executive's military command would only be as powerful as the people allowed it to be.

As easy as it would have been to invoke Washington to make this point, federalists instead emphasized the office's position within the government and the people's natural jealousy for their liberty. When they did gesture in Washington's direction, they often did so obliquely, and their point was to stress that even if a man who enjoyed the respect and admiration of the entire country—a man like Washington—ever were to attain the presidency and to be corrupted by the powers it vested, the people would oppose him with the same fiery spirit that had fueled their campaign for national independence. Thus, the federalists used Washington's celebrity in a way that twenty-first-century readers might find counterintuitive. Rather than assure readers not to worry about government tyranny because Washington was a virtuous man, federalists instead argued that even Washington's unparalleled reputation for virtue would not be enough to blind Americans into mindless assent to his authority. Their spirit of dissent was simply too strong.

This was Nicholas Collin's point when he noted that Americans were "allied by friendship and blood . . . bred in the principles of republican liberty" and would resist any would-be tyrant's despotic designs. The spirit of dissent, born from years of abuse by George III and brandished by Americans on the battlefields of the Revolution, had forged a national bond between "regular troops" and "other citizens" that would surely override a corrupt commander in chief's orders "to turn their arms against those with whom they have so long shared danger and glory; to enslave and murder their friends, and relations, brothers, sons and fathers—in all probability a great part of this army would take part with the nation."[61] The president attested to the people's capacity for self-government because "[w]e do not swear allegiance to him," and because "[h]e can exercise no power, but that which we confer upon him," Americanus observed. Thus, whoever occupied the office, the presidency would attest to the very principle that linked together Americans' War for Independence and the proposed system of government, that "no man can, in himself, claim a right over us."[62]

By making the president's military command a testament to the office's public accountability, federalists were able to counter a common antifederalist criticism that the government's tendency toward consolidation would coerce citizens into subjugation to its powers through the threat or actual use of force. The president's military authority was a vital means to accomplish what Oliver Ellsworth called "one of the prerequisites for national liberty": namely, "controling the whole [country], and bringing its force to a point."[63] But as a servant of the people, who lacked the power to declare war or make treaties on his own, the president, unlike the British king that critics were so fond of comparing him to, demonstrated the supremacy of the people of the several states over the actions of the general government, even in times of combat, through their representatives in Congress. He was bound to lead an army they supplied and funded, for a set time period that they specified. Moreover, he was always subject to resistance from the national populace should he attempt to use his military command against the country. These were not merely limitations on his power but boundaries within which he was expected to exercise power in concert with the people and the legislature, supplying "energetic" leadership in their common goal of security and unity.

Explaining military power as a potential positive good that would always operate within the boundaries of the public sanction was one way that supporters explained how the presidential office, in its relationship to the other bodies described in the Constitution, would always promote a peaceful, prosperous, republican nation that transcended regional, state, or political division. Supporters drew upon the president's relationship with Congress (especially the Senate) to highlight at different times the president's power as well as his accountability to the people. The president's veto power, in Ellsworth's estimation, even made him a potential instrument of public dissent. "Every bill that hath passed the Senate and Representatives must be presented to the president, and if he approve, it becomes law. If he disapproves, but makes no return within ten days, it still becomes law. If he returns the bill with his objections, the Senate and Representatives consider it a second time, and if two-thirds of them adhere to the first resolution, it becomes law notwithstanding the president's dissent." Thus, "we allow the president hath an influence, tho strictly speaking he hath not a legislative voice, and think such an influence must be salutary." Yet because "[i]n the president, all the executive departments meet," the president "will be a channel of communication between those who make and those who execute the laws," shaping laws with an eye to national interests and to the practical ability to execute laws, avoiding "a thousand absurd ordinances, which are solemnly made, only to be repealed and lessen the dignity of legislation in the eyes of mankind."

The result was a national system that was both energetic and perpetually accountable to the people.[64]

Some federalists even described the Electoral College as a reflection of this same principle, as Americanus did in an essay published in the *Virginia Independent Chronicle*: "The *president* is elected in an indirect manner by the citizens of the different states, and in such a mode as the respective legislatures may direct. He can continue in office no longer than four years, at the expiration of which time, he returns to the common mass of citizens and another election, conducted in every respect like the preceding one, will take place." Americanus buried the Electoral College in a single word—*indirect*—instead casting the president's electoral process as a basically democratic exercise. The point, though, was once again that the president was subject to the people, who could revoke their support at any time—in other words, dissent—and strip him of power. If the point were not clear enough, Americanus went on: "From the manner in which the *president* is elected, it must be acknowledged, that he is amenable to the people, and that they may have him removed from office, when he misapplies the powers, with which he is entrusted. It is a maxim universally true, that the power, which creates, can also annihilate."[65]

In the hands of John Dickinson, a Delaware delegate to the Philadelphia Convention writing as Fabius, even the Electoral College could be made reflective of the public will. "This president is to be chosen, not by the people at large," he conceded, "because it may not be possible, that all the freemen of the empire should always have the necessary information, for directing their choice of such an officer; nor by Congress, lest it should disturb the national councils; nor BY ANY ONE BODY WHATEVER, for fear of undue influence." Instead, the president was chosen by electors, designated by the states, according to procedures "the legislature thereof may direct." Yet Dickinson added that, "*if such be the pleasure of the people*" of a particular state, they may stipulate that the electors be chosen by popular vote. Thus, Dickinson implied, the choice of the president could be as democratic as the people in each state saw fit. In one stroke Dickinson used the Electoral College—an institution that is frequently (and justifiably) characterized as undemocratic—to attest to the proposed government's federalism and to argue that the people themselves determined how directly accountable the president would be.[66]

Thus federalists used the presidential office to make their essential promise to the American public: not only would the proposed government's power ultimately come from the people themselves, but also their jealousy of their independence ensured that they would actively oppose any abuse of the power they granted. Federalists stressed not only the Constitution's unprecedented ability to make power the servant of the people but also the "plain" nature of the Constitution's wording and the straightforward explanations that its defenders had offered.[67] Advocates for ratification echoed Wilson's claim that the Constitution was the best in the world. It was so, they claimed, because the Constitution was itself a statement of dissent against the worldwide received wisdom of politics. Because this was so, they went on to say, those who opposed it must be motivated by an ulterior motive. Sometimes they accused them of careless reading of the Constitution, but more often they claimed antifederalists were motivated by the advancement of their own selfish interest to poison public opinion against the document.

In this way federalists disparaged critics of the Constitution in a way that would have a lasting political impact. Because federalists characterized the Constitution as the culmination of the spirit of dissent that resided in the heart of every true American, dissent from the Constitution revealed one to be a self-interested subversive, an enemy to the very national unity, strength, and security that the people empowered the government to provide. As federalists looked to the presidency to issue their promise that the powers described in the Constitution ultimately derived from, and would be always subject to, the people, they condemned antifederalist criticism as fundamentally corrosive to the strong and lasting American nation they insisted the Constitution would bring about.

Foremost among the practitioners of this technique was Alexander Hamilton, who collaborated with John Jay and James Madison to produce eighty-five essays promoting the Constitution for "the People of the State of New York" that were later published together as *The Federalist*.[68] Hamilton is remembered as a leading advocate of executive authority, and his highly influential views are still regularly cited and quoted by jurists and legal scholars across the political spectrum. But Hamilton's defense of executive authority is usually tied closely to his elitism, and scholars of early US politics typically emphasize Hamilton's efforts to place the presidency above the public eye. There are understandable reasons for this, given the arguments Hamilton made in defense of Washington during Washington's two presidential terms. But this characterization overshadows the argument that Hamilton made as Publius during the public ratification debate.

Hamilton devoted eleven essays exclusively to the presidency (*Federalist* 67–77), more than Publius devoted to the House, the Senate, or the judiciary.[69] These eleven essays, like most *Federalist* essays, did not circulate very widely beyond New York during the ratification debate. Only later were they collected into a single volume, and only much later were specific essays, especially *Federalist* 10, widely read across much of the country.[70] Yet Hamilton's assault on the antifederalists was exemplary of the broader federalist campaign to discredit their antifederalist adversaries and cast those views of the Constitution as fundamentally dangerous to the country as a whole. An avowed proponent of expansive executive power, Hamilton, much like other federalists around the country, also understood the presidency's role as a powerful symbol of a people who were united by a shared commitment to remaining independent of and sovereign over their government.

As a delegate to the New York state ratifying convention, Hamilton had explained his views on the significance of the president's role in reflecting the American populace. "Besides, the president of the United States will be himself the representative of the people," Hamilton declared to his colleagues in the New York state convention. "From the competition that ever subsists between the branches of government, the president will be induced to protect their rights, whenever they are invaded by either branch." Crucially, the president's ability to fulfill this critical role depended on the public "confidence," "attachment," and "good will"—all of which the people could revoke at any time. In his most famous and sustained commentary on the presidency, *Federalist* 67–77, Hamilton advanced his vision of a strong, unified, republican nation exemplified by an "energetic" executive: one who was both empowered and limited by the people's capacity for dissent.[71]

The significance of the presidency, Hamilton noted at the beginning of *Federalist* 67, was precisely what made antifederalist assaults on it especially dangerous. "Here the writers against the Constitution seem to have taken pains to signalize their talents of misrepresentation," Hamilton remarked, "calculating upon the aversion of the people to monarchy, they have endeavoured to inlist all their jealousies and apprehensions in opposition to the intended president of the United States; not merely as the embryo but as the full grown progeny of that detested parent." The word "calculating" was crucial for Hamilton, for he sought to convince readers that antifederalist arguments were deliberate distortions, borne out of a conscious attempt to deceive. By attempting to manipulate public perceptions of the presidency, critics were in effect attempting to "insidiously" and "industriously" sabotage the people's rightful government. Such a tactic could only be the work of a self-interested cabal that was motivated by "an intention to deceive the people," not of the people themselves.[72]

Attempts to undermine public confidence in the president struck at the entire government's capacity for "energy," which Hamilton considered essential to "good government." "A feeble executive implies a feeble execution of the government," he wrote in *Federalist* 70. "A feeble execution is but another phrase for a bad execution: And a government ill executed, whatever it may be in theory, must be in practice a bad government."[73] "Energy" as Hamilton defined it was not power run amok. Instead, executive energy was a means to the ultimate end of "safety in the republican sense." (He remarked in *Federalist* 70 that the "ingredients which constitute . . . energy" had to "be combined with . . . other ingredients" before "safety in the republican sense" was achieved.) Ultimately, safety in the republican sense meant "a due dependence on the people" and "a due responsibility" *to* the people. That dependence and accountability required a people who were capable of distinguishing the necessary "energy" and power that elected leaders were required to exercise to promote order and good government from the despotism of kingly tyrants. This was what Hamilton meant by "an enlightened and reasonable people," and he flattered his readers by claiming they were the very people he meant—not "those who would persuade us" that the American presidency and the British monarchy was one and the same, and not "those who tell us, that a government, the whole power of which would be in the hands of the elective and periodical servants of the people, is an aristocracy, a monarchy, and a despotism." Note the use of "those" and "us," which Hamilton repeated twice for emphasis. For Hamilton, the sustained public criticism put forth by the "writers against the Constitution" demonstrated their unfitness for inclusion in the nation's body politic. It marked antifederalists as the duplicitous and self-interested "them," in contrast to the enlightened and reasonable Americans who demonstrated they were one of "us" through their support for the government, and especially for the chief magistrate at its center.[74]

Thus, alongside his commentary on the president's executive powers, which he listed and analyzed in exhaustive detail over his eleven essays, Hamilton described the president as the unique focal point of the people's "confidence" and scrutiny, and ultimately a testament to the government's accountability to them at all times. Key to this essential role was the president's duty as an antidote to the pervasive influence of "factions," "cabals" and political "parties," which Hamilton saw as particularly corrosive to national unity. In place of the self-interested schemes of divergent political parties, whose conspiracies pulled the nation in a multitude of directions, the president, by virtue of his singularity, his power, and ultimately his public accountability, would act as the focal point for the people's faith in and loyalty to the national government. Hamilton used many words to describe this loyalty—"confidence," "esteem," "approbation," "good will," "trust"—but ultimately he meant an acceptance of the government's power founded in a shared assurance that the entire government represented the people and acted in ways that promoted what was in their best interest, but always remained subject to their relentless scrutiny. The loyalty that the national government and its leaders commanded was what connected citizens across disparate states and regions as members of a single American nation. As he promoted his vision of a unified, peaceful, nonpartisan, president-centered American nation, Hamilton also warned that dangerous factions schemed to undermine this more perfect union and declared the critics of the Constitution to be examples of the alarming influence of these un-American cabals on the American political landscape.

For Hamilton "safety in the republican sense" was the product of national cohesion, not merely in governmental institutions but political sentiment. "Wherever two or more persons are engaged in any common enterprise or pursuit, there is always danger of difference of opinion. If it be a public trust or office in which they are cloathed with equal dignity and authority, there is peculiar danger of personal emulation and even animosity," Hamilton explained. "From either and especially from all these causes, the most bitter dissentions are apt to spring." Such dissentions posed the most serious threat to national cohesion because "they lessen the respectability, weaken the authority, and distract the plans and operations of those whom they divide." This was why a unitary—meaning single—presidency was paramount for the proper functioning of the government. If these dissentions "should unfortunately assail the supreme executive magistracy of a country, consisting of a plurality of persons, they might impede or frustrate the most important measures of the government, in the most critical emergencies of the state." But that was not the most important reason a single president was preferable to an executive council. What was "still worse" than the threat that dissentions posed to the government, was the possibility that "they might split the community into the most violent and irreconcilable factions, adhering differently to the different individuals who composed the magistracy."[75]

It was no accident that Hamilton listed "unity" first among the key "ingredients" to the energy that promoted republican safety. The unitary nature of the presidency made it a natural promoter of national cohesion and public "confidence," the enemies of faction and dissent. It also made the presidency the highest prize for "cabal, intrigue and corruption"—the "most deadly adversaries of republican government"—to claim. Factions arose "chiefly from the desire in foreign powers to gain an improper ascendant in our councils. How could they better gratify this, than by raising a creature of their own to the chief magistracy of the union?"[76]

Unlike in the executive, parties were inevitable in the legislature, where "promptitude of decision is oftener an evil than a benefit," Hamilton explained. "The differences of opinion, and the jarrings of parties in that department of the government, though they may sometimes obstruct salutary plans, yet often promote deliberation and circumspection; and serve to check excesses in the majority." But the very ability of factions to grind dynamic action to a halt by cultivating division among members hindered the executive's job of moving the nation swiftly and dynamically in a single direction. An executive council would "counteract those qualities in the executive, which are the most necessary ingredients in its composition, vigour and expedition, and this without any counterbalancing good." Executives in a council, like members of the legislature, could constantly point fingers at one another for errors or misdeeds, concealing from the public the true source of irresponsible government action. Everyone could be guilty, but no one would be blamed. The result would "deprive the people of the two greatest securities they can have for the faithful exercise of any delegated power": "the restraints of public opinion" and "the opportunity of discovering with facility and clearness the misconduct of the persons they trust."[77]

That word, "trust," was all important. Trust in the government was the lifeblood of the republic, for it indicated the public's awareness of the government's purpose and "the true means by which the public happiness may be promoted." "The republican principle demands, that the deliberate sense of the community should govern the conduct of those to whom they entrust the management of their affairs," Hamilton allowed, "but it does not require an unqualified complaisance to every sudden breese of passion, or to every transient impulse which the people may receive from the arts of men, who flatter their prejudices to betray their interests." The people mean to promote "the PUBLIC GOOD," but do not always "*reason right* about the *means* of promoting it." Perhaps to soften his criticism a bit, Hamilton qualified his observation that the people "sometimes err" by noting that "the wonder is, that they so seldom err as they do; beset as they continually are by the wiles of parasites and sycophants, by the snares of the ambitious, the avaricious, the desperate; by the artifices of men, who possess their confidence more than they deserve it, and of those who seek to possess, rather than to deserve it." Because this pressure from self-interested manipulators constantly blurred the boundaries between "the interests of the people" and "their inclinations," their elected leaders had a "duty . . . to be the guardians of those interests, to withstand the temporary delusion, in order to give them time and opportunity for more sedate and cool reflection." The opposite but equally important side of the equation was the duty of the people to show "gratitude to the men, who had courage and magnanimity enough to serve them at the peril of their displeasure."[78]

Legislative assemblies could not cultivate this gratitude alone, which Hamilton lamented was particularly a problem, given "[t]he tendency of the legislative authority to absorb every other" department, including inadequately protected executives. "In governments purely republican, this tendency is almost irresistable [*sic*]. The representatives of the people, in a popular assembly, seem sometimes to fancy that they are the people themselves; and betray strong symptoms of impatience and disgust at the least sign of opposition from any other quarter; as if the exercise of its rights by either the executive or judiciary, were a breach of their privilege and an outrage to their dignity." Specifically because legislatures were designed to reflect the diversity of the populace, and because "they commonly have the people on their side," legislatures also reflected the fractious political division that factions thrived on. As much as this might encourage deliberation in the legislature, it also made it "very difficult for the other members of the government to maintain a balance of the Constitution."[79]

This was why "duration" in office—the second ingredient in executive energy—was crucial. The concentration of executive authority in a single individual would inevitably make the presidency an attractive office for ambitious men, who without the proper inducements to act in the public interest might well do more harm with that power than good. An office that promised a potentially unlimited "duration"—in other words, one without term limits—provided a continual incentive for the incumbent to act responsibly, because he would always possess power that the people could continue or be taken away. Hamilton chose to frame this as a positive: a president without term limits could always be rewarded with re-election. As Hamilton succinctly put it: "His avarice might be a guard upon his avarice." Compare that to "[a]n ambitious man" who "found himself seated on the summit of his country's honors," facing "the time at which he must descend from the exalted eminence forever," and, due to a limit on the number of terms he could serve, facing the reality "that no exertion of merit on his part could save him from the unwelcome reverse."

"Such a man, in such a situation," Hamilton predicted, might attempt to hold on to power anyway, or use it while he still had it, to increase his comforts and wealth in anticipation of his inevitable descent.[80] Either way, the results would be potentially disastrous, because the people would have no way to reward meritorious leadership—and thus no real way to oppose corruption or abuse.

This was where a single executive of unlimited duration served a unique and vital function. While his power made him conspicuous to the public, his perpetual eligibility allowed him "opportunities . . . of establishing himself in the esteem and good will of his constituents." In Hamilton's estimation a four-year term, renewable for as long as the people's esteem and goodwill lasted, was long enough to "contribute to the firmness of the executive in a sufficient degree to render it a very valuable ingredient in the composition" but "not long enough to justify any alarm for the public liberty."[81]

Just how "valuable" was such an executive? Consider the scope of the executive's reach: "The administration of government," Hamilton wrote in *Federalist* 72, which, "in its largest sense, comprehends all the operations of the body politic, whether legislative, executive, or judiciary," was, "in its most usual and perhaps in its most precise signification . . . limited to executive details, and falls peculiarly within the province of the executive department."[82] Or consider the significance of the electoral process. Choosing the president, Hamilton argued, would be "an immediate act of the people of America, to be exerted in the choice of persons for the temporary and sole purpose of making the appointment." Hamilton was fudging his facts, of course. The Electoral College ensured that the election of the president was *not*, in fact, "an immediate act of the people," but an act of electors, most of whom were chosen by state legislatures.[83] His intention was to capture the significance of the executive, not only to the functioning of the government, but to "all the operations of the body politic." The "approbation and confidence" that the people conferred on the president reflected their more basic confidence in the government's responsiveness to the public interest. And that, in turn, was the truest gauge of the strength of the national union.[84]

Hamilton further emphasized the uniqueness of the presidency to the national union by stressing "adequate provision for support" and "competent powers." By adequate provision, Hamilton meant a compensation for the executive that Congress could not alter "till a new period of service by a new election commences."[85] The president's powers—the qualified veto, his command of the military, his pardoning power, and the treaty-making

and appointment powers he shared with the Senate—were all essential to
fostering the unity that the "spirit of faction" undermined by "sometimes
pervert[ing]" legislative "deliberations" and fostering public dissent to order and good government.[86] The veto "establishes a salutary check upon
the legislative body calculated to guard the community against the effects
faction, precipitancy, or of any impulse unfriendly to the public good,
which may happen to influence a majority of that body."[87]

The president's role as commander in chief "most peculiarly demands
those qualities which distinguish the exercise of power by a single hand,"
because "the direction of war implies the direction of the common
strength; and the power of directing and employing the common strength,
forms an usual and essential part in the definition of the executive authority." Of the multiple justifications for the president's pardoning power, the
"principal" one was that it had the potential to bring an end to "seasons
of insurrection or rebellion." During such times, "there are often critical
moments, when a well timed offer of pardon to the insurgents or rebels
may restore the tranquility of the commonwealth; and which, if suffered
to pass unimproved, it may never be possible afterwards to recall." Con-
vening the legislature to deliberate on such an act would be cumbersome
and time-consuming, and in such situations, "the loss of a week, a day, an
hour, may sometimes be fatal."[88]

Maintaining that the treaty power was "plainly neither" wholly executive or legislative in nature (a position he would change a few years later),
Hamilton praised the joint possession of the power by the president and
the Senate. Vesting the power entirely in the president would once again
provide too tempting an incentive to abuse the public trust. But placing
the power entirely in the Senate would "relinquish the benefits of the constitutional agency of the president, in the conduct of foreign relations,"
and expose such important decision-making to the influence of "pique
and cabal." Likewise entrusting the power to the House of Representatives would subject the decision-making to a "fluctuating, and taking its
future increase into account, . . . multitudinous" assembly. In addition
to "accurate and comprehensive knowledge of foreign politics," sound
foreign policy also required "a steady and systematic adherence to the
same views; a nice and uniform sensibility to national character, decision,
secrecy and dispatch," qualities that "are incompatible with the genius of
a body so variable and numerous."[89]

And the president's appointment power served a vital check on the partisan scheming that would dominate the proceedings if the power were
solely left up to Congress. The president's unique exposure to public

scrutiny ensured that appointments would not reflect "a spirit of favoritism, or an unbecoming pursuit of popularity." The president "would be both ashamed and afraid to bring forward for the most distinguished or lucrative stations, candidates who had no other merit, than that of coming from the same State to which he particularly belonged, or of being in some way or other personally allied to him, or of possessing the necessary insignificance and pliancy to render them the obsequious instruments of his pleasure."[90]

Notably absent from Hamilton's essays was George Washington. Here again, Hamilton's *Federalist* essays are reflective of a broader federalist trend. Like his fellow federalists around the country, Hamilton sought to present the Constitution as a plan of government that was worthy of public support on its own merits. The symbolic power of the presidency would thus not be supplied by Washington. The president would remain the natural focus of public accountability no matter who occupied the office. This ensured that whomever the people elected would always feel the pressure to conform to their interests, leading the president to stand as a testament to, and facilitator of, the government's "dependence" on and "responsibility" to the people. This he intended to describe not merely the government but society more broadly. For no matter who filled the office, the president alone would act as "a single object for the jealousy and watchfulness of the people," a testament to the public "responsibility" that was impossible in plural representative bodies. In this way, the president would be "the constitutional representative of the nation."[91]

"The president . . . will, under this Constitution, be placed in office as the President of the whole Union, and will be chosen in such a manner that he may be justly styled THE MAN OF THE PEOPLE," Wilson explained during the Pennsylvania state ratifying convention. "[B]eing elected by the different parts of the United States, he will consider himself as not particularly interested for any one of them, but will watch over the whole with paternal care and affection."[92] In the presidential office, federalists found the most effective vehicle for their essential promise to the American public. The government would not be a monarchy or an aristocracy, as antifederalists feared; it would neither annihilate the states nor run roughshod over the people's rights. Instead, it would derive its powers from the people themselves, and remain perpetually accountable to them. No other office exemplified this point as well as the presidency. Its power and its singularity, apart from the reputation of the man who would undoubtedly be the first to occupy it, would attract the watchful gaze of a vigilant people, serving as an agent for national unity and defense, and a conduit through which they governed themselves.

The ultimate testament to this argument's effectiveness is how long it endured after the ratification debate itself. Virginia and New York ratified in June of 1788, ensuring that the new "more perfect union" created by the Constitution would not be divided geographically and that it would include George Washington's home state. As anticipated, Washington would ascend to the presidency and devote himself as president to advancing what he considered the country's interests and to easing remaining doubts and apprehensions about the new government. He would leave an indelible mark on the presidency, but he would also encounter considerable criticism from citizens who faulted him for failing to live up to the presidency's lofty purpose. The promise of "the man of the people" would become the basis for a groundswell of public dissent that would forever transform the presidency and American national politics.

2

Washington's Ascent and the People's Assent

"WHEN *ally'd Armies* triumph'd in the field,/ And *full plum'd Victory* made Great-Britain yield," a poem declared in 1789. "When WASHING-TON commanded '*wars to cease*,'/ HE crown'd our triumphs, by a *glorious Peace.*/ For THESE, his country pours its honours down,/ And ranks him next—*her first, her darling Son.*" The poem, titled "Vice-President," was ostensibly about John Adams, the man who had finished second to Washington in the first-ever Electoral College vote. But so intense was public acclaim for Washington that it even annexed territory meant for others in the new national government.[1]

Though a military man, the Washington in this poem is the recipient of a unique and powerful public trust. This was a characterization that would be repeated countless times, in poems, songs, open letters, opinion pieces, and breathless accounts of Washington's election to the presidency and his subsequent actions while in office. Accounts like this one represented a sharp departure from the approach taken by the Constitution's advocates during the ratification debate. When trying to convince skeptics to endorse ratification, leaning too heavily on Washington posed a potential risk: it could possibly legitimate antifederalist fears that his endorsement would cloud the public's judgment, leading them to support a government that was fundamentally flawed simply because Washington supported it.

Yet once the requisite states had voted to ratify and elections were held across the country to fill the elected positions in the new national government, Washington's reputation became a precious asset. Federalist advocates for ratification could not simply point to Washington to reassure antifederalist skeptics that their fears were misplaced. But many around the country were convinced that Washington's successful election to the presidency would convince the populace that the new government's considerable power was in the right hands. Thus, public accounts of Washington's ascent to the presidency carried immense political significance.

It was not enough that Washington be chosen; his "unanimous" election was essential, because it suggested universal public support for the new government that Washington was to lead. Having no reputation of its own, the nascent government needed to lean on Washington's.

For those who celebrated Washington's election and subsequent presidency around the country, his elevation to the office would help legitimate the new government and more clearly define the collective national people it served. Celebrations of Washington's election suggested that something *did* unite all the people of the United States across vast distances and geographic, demographic, and political differences: a desire for liberty that had animated their efforts during the Revolution and an assent to the new national government that Washington now led.

In short, accounts of Washington's election characterized his ascent to the presidency, and the American people's "unanimous" assent to his leadership, as a further testament to the young nation's dissenting tradition. It was a testament to the people's ability to recognize virtuous leadership when they saw it. Songs, toasts, and accounts of public celebrations cast Washington's election as the culmination of the American people's successful transition from rebellion against a tyrannical form of government to their acceptance of a republican government in which they themselves were sovereign. Born out of a righteous act of dissent, the American nation had, through the election of Washington to the presidency, become an ordered republic, where the collective sovereignty of all Americans, expressed through the president's actions in executing the laws in accordance with their collective interests, would make dissent against the government unnecessary.

With so much riding on his performance, his duties understandably filled the first president with trepidation. In early January 1790, less than a year after his inauguration and in the interim between his two national tours, Washington explained the cause of his anxiety in a letter to Catharine Macaulay Graham. "In our progress toward political happiness my station is new; and, if I may use the expression, I walk on untrodden ground. There is scarcely any action, whose motives may not be subject to a double interpretation. There is scarcely any part of my conduct w[hi]ch may not hereafter be drawn into precedent." The office Washington occupied was not only new, it was captivating to the American public, whose unblinking eye was fixated on everything he did. His use of the passive voice—"be subject to a double interpretation," "be drawn into precedent"—suggests interpretation by a populace that Washington could neither succinctly name nor control. To Graham he asserted, "The establishment of our new Government . . . was to be done" through a combination of "*prudence . . . conciliation*," and "*firmness.*" He "always believed that an unequivocally free & equal Representation of the People in the Legislature; together with an efficient & responsable [*sic*] Executive were the great Pillars on which the preservation of American Freedom must depend." But his actions alone would not define the office, the government, or the republican union he sought to establish. The American public would be vital coauthors of the project, watching, interpreting, responding to his precedent-setting actions every step of the way. "Under such a view of the duties inherent to my arduous office, I could not but feel a diffidence in myself on the one hand; and an anxiety for the Community that every new arrangement should be made in the best possible manner on the other."[2]

Throughout his two presidential terms, Washington strove to maintain a strong, peaceful national union amid revolution in France and war between the United States' former Revolutionary ally and its former mother country. Yet everything he did drew attention, and with it, criticism.

The first president struggled to strike the proper balance between accessibility to and distance from the public in order to minimize partisan division. Yet the first two national political parties would ultimately form out of a sharp divide over a question that those who celebrated Washington's election sought to definitively answer. If the election of Washington to the presidency marked the fulfillment of the American people's dissenting campaign for independence and republican government, could those who dissented from the president be true "Americans"?

Washington's supporters, who would form the Federalist Party, dominated the argument during most of Washington's presidency. Federalists argued, and Washington agreed, that dissent against the president and his administration was a corrosive force, an affront to the principles of the revolution that had culminated in the new national government that Washington now led. Criticism of the president, the president and his Federalist allies maintained, undermined the authority of the government and potentially the peaceful society he was committed to maintaining.

Washington's earliest critics found themselves stymied by his stellar reputation, yet the argument they put forth posited a much more intimate and even directly confrontational relationship between the people and the president. These dissenters, who formed the Republican Party opposition, argued that criticism of the president was warranted to maintain public control over an office that was straying far beyond its Constitutional bounds. Not only could dissenters be true Americans, but all loyal

Americans expressed their willingness to dissent, peacefully and respectfully, in order to express views that the president needed to hear if he was
to act in accordance with their interests. Their willingness to criticize the
president did not make them violent partisans, but patriotic Americans.
And as president, they further claimed, he was obligated to hear them out.

Washington entered the presidency to great fanfare as a hero of the
Revolution and a peacemaker. Yet in striving to live up to that lofty expectation, Washington would find himself in the middle of a bitter and
increasingly contentious disagreement over the impact that public demonstrations of dissent against his administration had on the nation of Americans he was elected to represent. What, if anything, did the people of
the United States have in common? Was it a shared confidence in Washington and a commitment to assent to the laws he carried out on behalf
of the government he led? Or was it a collective obligation to speak out
against him if his actions strayed beyond the boundaries of the Constitution? Should the president expect more or less universal public deference
to his authority, or should he expect lively and even defiant engagement
from the populace when they disagreed with a decision he had made? Was
dissent against the president and his administration a betrayal of the Revolutionary character that Washington epitomized for so many—or was
it the ultimate expression of that dissenting spirit, a commitment to hold
one's leaders to public account, no matter how illustrious their name or
how exalted their position? The president, his allies, and his critics arrived
at profoundly different answers to these questions. But they all agreed that
the answers would determine the nation's future.

WASHINGTON'S "UNANIMOUS" ELECTION

Celebration of Washington as the leader of a new government that all patriotic Americans supported represented a considerable about-face from
the tactic employed by supporters of the Constitution during the ratification debate. No longer in the background of the debate, when he was
referenced occasionally and briefly, Washington was now front and center. Newspaper accounts and even private correspondence describing his
election to the presidency explicitly took his election to be a signifier of
the people's confidence in the new national government. Somewhat paradoxically, the key to this was Washington's status as a man of incomparable virtue. Accounts marveled at Washington's capacity to resist the
temptation to accrue power for himself, agreeing that virtually none of

his countrymen could have done the same.[3] Celebrations of Washington's election to the presidency, then, described the man simultaneously as of the people and above them; exemplary of their commitment to the liberty the government guaranteed to its citizens yet uniquely capable of wielding authority that would corrupt mere mortals. But this position above the people also reflected well on the American people as a whole. Few if any of them might be capable of Washington's disinterested virtue, but they knew that virtue when they saw it, and they rewarded it with their votes, their voices of approbation, and their pledges of obedience to the laws that Washington would be tasked with carrying out. That, Americans across the country agreed, was why Washington's "unanimous" election to the presidency mattered so much.

"The important DAY in the annals of AMERICA is past, which conferred on a single citizen those SOVEREIGN powers that require to be placed in one person, in order to render a NATION happy in peace and prosperous in war," a piece from Baltimore, reprinted in New York and Massachusetts, declared. "Perhaps that day has exhibited what has never happened before in any part of the globe; above *Three Millions* of people, scattered over a country of vast extent, of opposite habits and different manners, all fixing their hopes and wishes on the same man, and unanimously voting for him only, without the intervention of force, artifice, plan or concert. With what delight will the lover of mankind dwell on this period of history, and cherish the memory of a people who could thus feel and thus reward a life of great and virtuous actions!"[4] The piece is a perfect illustration of the significance that celebratory accounts placed on Washington's election to the presidency. At a time when "war and tumult at present extend their reign over the eastern and northern world," the election of a man who desired a peaceful retirement more than limitless power would be a signal to the world that the received wisdom about republics—and one of the fundamental fears of the antifederalists—was wrong. Sprawling republics were not doomed to decay into anarchy, confusion, and blood civil war. If the right leaders received enough support from the populace, even a de-mographically diverse and geographically diffuse country like the United States could survive and even thrive.[5]

Celebrations of Washington could not emphasize that point enough: a "unanimous" election for Washington signaled not only public support for him but for the new government as a whole. Given that the Constitu-tion had just emerged from a contentious national debate over whether to ratify it, two states (North Carolina and Rhode Island) had yet to ratify at all, and no one could be certain whether the new plan of government would last even for the states that had ratified, public confidence in the government was essential. Washington's election to the presidency could boost public confidence in the heretofore untried and untested national government. As another account put it: "The idea of the illustrious WASH-INGTON presiding as Chief over the Councils of that august assembly, heightens our joy—for in the language of the poet, *As great in battle, great is he in peace! He comes again to point our way to fame! The* FEDERAL PLAN *shall bid our evils cease, And stamp Columbia with a lasting name.*"[6] But getting Washington elected would not be enough. It was crucial that Washington's election be "unanimous."

Twenty-first-century Americans may assume that Washington's unanimous election was never in doubt, especially given that in the end every member of the Electoral College cast at least one of his two ballots for Washington. (To avoid the possibility that members of the Electoral College would each vote for his home state's favorite son, the Framers stipulated that every member of the Electoral College, chosen in the manner directed by his state, would cast two ballots, at least one of which had to be for a candidate outside his own state. Every elector cast at least one of his ballots for Washington, and John Adams, who tallied the second-greatest number of votes, became Washington's vice president). Yet Americans at the time considered Washington's unanimous election neither inevitable nor meaningless. Quite the opposite: commentators devoted a substantial amount of public fretting about whether the vote would be unanimous and an equal amount of political strategizing to make sure it came to pass.

The major threat to Washington's unanimous election, as most commentators saw it, was his eventual vice president, John Adams. Adams enjoyed considerable support for the vice presidency, but since the vice presidency went to the presidential candidate who won the second-greatest number of electoral votes, advocates for Adams had to strategize to ensure he got enough votes to surpass every other potential challenger, but not so many that he threatened Washington's unanimous election or ended up beating Washington for the presidency. That meant withholding some votes from him, to preserve Washington's unanimous victory. A Boston newspaper reported on a letter from New York concerning the votes of electors from Connecticut, New Jersey, and Pennsylvania, who had voted "unanimously" for Washington but not for Adams. Here, the explanation was that this was merely a strategic move to ensure that Washington gained the presidency and that Adams would come in second, thus securing him the vice presidency. "'Tis said these three States really wish to have Mr. ADAMS Vice-President; and would have been unanimous for him, had they not been fearful he might have been placed in the Chair, which they wish to have filled by the great WASHINGTON."[7]

Perhaps anticipating resentment from the notoriously easily offended Adams, a newspaper from New York sought to explain why the state's electors had voted "unanimously" for Washington but had withheld some votes from Adams: "We are told that the only reason why Mr. Adams had not an unanimous vote as Vice-President, was to prevent his being equal, or superior to General Washington in votes," the piece explained. "It is an honor, merited by few men, in being second to our beloved Washington in the affections and esteem of the people of the United States: Mr. Adams now enjoys this honor." That comment offers an important clue as to the significance of Washington's "unanimous" election: it was an expression of "the affections and esteem of the people of the United States." Not only did it imply that something did indeed unite the country's diffuse population as members of one nation—that "We, the People" in the Constitution's preamble existed, and not just as an aspiration—it also suggested that what held the American people together was their confidence in Washington's ability to govern. Washington's "unanimous" election would signify that the people of the United States had confidence also in the government Washington would lead.[8]

With this much at stake, it is no wonder that Washington's supporters feared the remaining antifederal influence, since prominent critics of the Constitution remained able to claim enough electoral votes to rob Washington of a unanimous victory. In New York the governor, George Clinton, was thought to command the unified support of electors who retained their antifederalist suspicions of the new government, and in Virginia, noted antifederalist firebrand Patrick Henry was a threat to steal some electoral votes from Washington (although by mid-January 1789, the *Pennsylvania Mercury* reported that "it seems the Anties have relinquished Patrick Henry, Esq; and have resolved not to deprive General WASHINGTON of an unanimous vote"). Of course, such maneuvering to ensure Washington's unanimous election involved acknowledging the very political and geographic division that that unanimity was meant to refute.[9]

Though today students learn that Washington was chosen unanimously by the Electoral College, reports from early 1789, when the election took place, went much farther. The Baltimore piece, and others throughout the country, described Washington's election as the "unanimous" choice of "millions" of people—not merely members of the Electoral College. In effect, reports from the time implied that most if not all of the people in the country had directly affirmed Washington as their choice for president. "The day—the long wished for day is arrived—and we hail it welcome," the *Massachusetts Centinel* breathlessly announced in February 1789, in a statement typical of the time. "Welcome, as again witnessing to the unanimous call of MILLIONS to the illustrious WASHINGTON, again to take under his direction, the welfare of that country, his valour so lately saved—and which has been since threatened with destruction."[10] Others specified an even more particular number: three million people— the approximate number of free citizens in the country. As they saw their native son off to New York to be sworn in, the people of Alexandria, Virginia, recounted the "unexampled honor" bestowed "by the spontaneous and unanimous suffrage of three millions of Freemen, in your election to the Supreme Magistracy."[11] "The fears of many honest, but scrupulous republicans, that the energy of the new government, might render it unfavorable to liberty, are at length subsided," the Philadelphia *Federal Gazette* announced. "All their apprehensions have been removed, by the election of their beloved WASHINGTON, to fill the office of the first Magistrate of the United States. . . . The *unanimous* vote of three millions of free Citizens, in favor of this distinguished Farmer, Hero and Statesman," ranked among "the greatest honors, that ever were conferred on man," and anticipated "the future greatness and respectability of our country." Two days later, the *Gazette of the United States* backpedaled slightly from this narrative, conceding that though millions had not directly cast a vote, if they had, they would all have voted for Washington anyway. The unanimity of the Electoral College vote, then, was for all intents and purposes a vote of millions around the country. "It is undoubtedly a new and astonishing thing under the sun, that the UNIVERSAL SUFFRAGES OF A GREAT AND VARIOUS PEOPLE, SHOULD CENTRE IN ONE AND THE SAME MAN," the *Gazette* piece marveled, "for it is evidently a fact, that was every individual *personally* consulted as to the man whom they would elect to fill the office of PRESIDENT of this rising empire, the only reply from *New-Hampshire* to *Georgia* would be WASHINGTON."[12]

The notion that the entire country had directly chosen Washington could also be found in the private correspondence between Washington and his aides. Washington had been "called not only by the unanimous votes of the Electors but by the voice of America," Washington's secretary, Charles Thomson, wrote on April 14, 1789, when he informed Washington of his victory. Washington replied "that the knowledge" of his "fellow citizens['] . . . unanimous suffrages having been given in my favor scarcely leaves me the alternative for an Option."[13]

Such rhetoric was not the result of public ignorance of the Electoral College or its members. The identities of electors was no secret, even across state lines. Newspaper editors and politicians understood that citizens wanted to know how electors across the country voted. Rather, the rhetoric was linked to the vision of national unity federalists sought to cultivate through Washington's election to the presidency. Once the votes of the electors from South Carolina and Georgia were known, the *Massachusetts Spy* reported in March, "it appears, that illustrious soldier and venerated citizen, GEORGE WASHINGTON, Esq; is unanimously elected first President of the United States." This election, the *Spy* explained, expressed "the full tide of *universal* approbation" for Washington.[14]

The characterization glossed over the fact that only electors cast a direct vote for the president, and it ignored the legal and political limitations on who could cast a vote for electors. White males under the age of sixteen, white women, enslaved persons, and non-property-owning white men were all counted alongside adult white male property-owners in the first census, conducted by Congress in 1790, the year following Washington's election. The 1790 census counted 3,893,635 persons across thirteen states. But the states of Rhode Island and North Carolina had yet to ratify the Constitution by March 1789, which meant that their combined population of 462,576 was ineligible to vote for any official in the new government, including the president. Enslaved people in the remaining eleven states also had no say in the matter, though they were included in the total population listed on the census, and three-fifths of their total did count toward determining how many members of Congress each state received. White women in the states that had ratified the Constitution by March, 1789 were barred from voting in every state except New Jersey, Connecticut, and Delaware, though the census included no age data for females. Even adopting the most generous voting eligibility criteria possible—labeling as eligible voters all white males aged sixteen and older in the eleven states that had ratified the Constitution as of March 1789 (721,087); all white women in New Jersey, Delaware, and Connecticut (223,119); and "all other free persons" in every state except Rhode Island and North Carolina, which had not yet ratified the Constitution, and Virginia, South Carolina, and Georgia, the three states that expressly barred free black men from voting (35,589)—one achieves a total of 979,795 people: a far cry from the "millions" of voices whom supporters claimed "unanimously" chose Washington.[15]

The claim that millions had unanimously chosen Washington clearly belied the reality of electoral politics in 1789. But Washington's trip from

Mount Vernon to New York for his inauguration, and subsequent tours throughout the country shortly after taking the oath of office, provided an opportunity for citizens to meet him personally and demonstrate their support for him and the new government he was to lead. Washington's own query on the matter to his vice president, John Adams, reveals Washington's astute understanding of the advantages to be gained by undertaking such a tour. Washington asked Adams, "whether, during the recess of Congress, it would not be advantageous to the interests of the Union for the President to make the tour of the United States," for the purpose of "becom[ing] better acquainted with their principal Characters & internal Circumstances, as well as to be more accessible to numbers of well-informed persons, who might give him useful informations and advices on political subjects?"[16] In fact, Washington made two ambitious tours, the first of the "Eastern" states, beginning in mid-October, 1789, and the second of the "Southern" states, beginning the following March.[17]

Washington planned his tours to maximize the political optics of his journey. Each day his carriage departed in the early morning for its next destination, passing hamlets and towns en route. Washington greeted the townspeople's cheers with a reserved gesture of thanks. His carriage often stopped outside his next intended stop, where the president would exit his carriage, mount his white horse, and enter the town, dressed in his full military uniform. Upon entering, he would be greeted by a crowd. Town officials peppered him with orations and addresses of praise. Children clamored to greet him. Sometimes a dinner followed with prominent men and women of the town, drinking and dancing long into the night. Washington would get a precious few hours of sleep, rise early the next morning, and do it all again.[18]

The historian T. H. Breen has chronicled Washington's early tours and demonstrated that Washington "performed" dual, symbolic roles: as the embodiment of both the new government and the nation of people who would govern it through their elected representatives and simultaneously the role of the nation itself, the foremost living example of the revolutionary ideals that bound all Americans to their new government and to one another. The people he met on these tours performed as well. The populace that greeted him performed an act of endorsement for him personally, and for the government more generally, that many of them could not do through the formal voting process. By celebrating Washington as *their* president, they affirmed Washington's status as the agent of the American people, and signaled that they were part of the "We, the People" that the president represented.[19]

This duet between people and president conveyed a powerful message that lent credence to the newspapers' insistence that the president truly was chosen "unanimously" by every American, not simply those who were empowered to cast a direct vote. From town to town, accounts of Washington's arrival included participation by adoring women, starry-eyed children, and even cooing babies, all of whom lacked the ability to vote but whose approval of Washington nonetheless joined the chorus of confidence in the president that the newspapers insisted the "unanimous" electoral vote represented. One observer wrote to his nephew that Washington's reception at the seat of government in late April was attended by "more than twenty thousand free citizens, who lined every fence, field and avenue between the bridge and city." This included "[t]he aged Sire, the venerable Matron, the blooming Virgin, and the ruddy Youth," who all expressed their support for the president-elect. Even "the lisping Infant did not withhold its innocent smile of praise and approbation."[20] The image of smiling women, middling and plebeian men, and adoring children continued during Washington's tours, as accounts emphasized the turnout by everyone in the town to see their champion.[21]

Washington's arrival was designed to work in tandem with the community's reception to break down divisions of all kinds: not just state and regional divisions, but also class, gender, and generational divides as well, and to reinforce a sense of collective unity around the man who had led their war for independence, and whom they had now empowered to lead the government of their future. It mattered little whether the gathering of celebrants were Bostonians or Richmonders, or whether they were young or old, wealthy or plebeian, man or woman. What mattered far more was that they were all Americans, something they demonstrated through their shared embrace of Washington's leadership, and by implication, their approval of the government authority he now commanded. "GREAT WASHINGTON the Hero's come,/ Each heart exulting hears the sound,/ Thousands to their Deliverer throng,/And shout him welcome all around!" a gathering of Bostonians sang in late October 1789, in the balcony of the Massachusetts state house, upon Washington's arrival. As if the picture of national unity around Washington was not clear enough, the gallery included a banner that read, "To the MAN who unites all Hearts."[22] "Strange is the impulse which is felt by almost every breast to see the face of a great good man—sensation better felt than expressed," an account from Charlotte County, Virginia, read.[23] "At his approach, party disappears; and every one runs a race in endeavouring who shall be foremost in paying him the tribute of grateful respect," exclaimed "An American" in the

Massachusetts Centinel. "Old and young—men and women—all, all are alike affected—and all alike endeavour to express their feelings by the most lively testimonials."[24]

Public adulation for Washington on his tours, capped by celebrations of his election, represented a major shift in emphasis from the promise made by federalists during the ratification debate. By late 1788 the anti-federalists had lost, and focus shifted to the country's future under the Constitution. Antifederal voices remained and would continue to agitate for a declaration of rights until the first ten amendments to the Consti-tution—now collectively called the Bill of Rights—would be ratified in 1791.[25] But most Americans who voiced an opinion on the matter were optimistic about the future under George Washington's presidential lead-ership. Relegated to the relative background of the ratification debate, Washington was now central to supporters' claim that the new national government was the fulfillment of the ideals for which the country's War for Independence had been fought—and that those ideals connected all Americans everywhere.

No less than the state legislature of Pennsylvania, and the state's su-preme court, agreed. Both bodies issued statements to Washington cele-brating his election and tracing a direct link between his past service in the war—including his willingness to resign his commission as commander in chief—and their predictions that his leadership would produce an era of unequalled peace and prosperity. "In reflecting upon the vicissitudes of the late war, in tracing its difficulties, and in contemplating its success, we are uniformly impressed with the extent and magnitude of the services which you have rendered to your country," the legislature wrote to Wash-ington, "and by that impression, we are taught to expect that the exercise of the same virtues and abilities, which have been thus happily employed in obtaining the prize of Liberty and Independence, must be effectually instrumental in securing to you fellow citizens and their posterity, the per-manent blessings of a free and efficient government."[26] The state supreme court concurred. "We are deeply sensible of what we owe to Almighty God, for the great deliverance he hath wrought for us by your Excellency, when General and commander in Chief of the armies of our country, and for having inspired the people with the wisdom of appointing you, by an unanimous suffrage, to the chair of the first Magistrate over them," read a statement signed by the four justices, including the chief justice, Thomas McKean. "The tender regard which heretofore you always paid to the laws and liberties of these states, when you possessed almost dictatorial power, gives us a certain prospect of a mild, legal and upright government in future."[27] Such celebrations of Washington fused the legacy and principles of the Revolution, the promise of the new national government, and the presidency, together through Washington. In him, the three joined together inseparably.

Connecting the promise of the new national government to the legacy of the Revolution through Washington allowed the president, along with his federalist allies (the supporters of ratification, not the political party, which had not yet formed), to cultivate trust in the power wielded by the new government by assuring the public that that power would always ultimately remain subject to the will of the people. Washington's ability to resist the temptations of power had distinguished him among most men. Yet that very ability also made him the ultimate public servant, perpetually beneath the people he served. His election to the presidency by "millions" was a testament to the people's ability to recognized Washington's greatness, even as it surpassed what most of them were capable of themselves. Once vested with that power, Washington could expect their confidence, their gratitude, and ultimately their obedience to the laws. Because the presidency was good enough for Washington, well-wishers reasoned, the new government was good enough for the people.

Such a cliché did it become that the people of the city of Alexandria, Virginia, in their prepared statement to Washington in late April, before he left Mount Vernon for New York, noted that what was foremost on their minds was not Washington's "glory as a Soldier." It was not their "gratitude for past services." They were not fixated on "the justice of the unexampled honor which has been conferred upon you, by the spontaneous and unanimous suffrage of three millions of Freemen, in your election to the Supreme Magistracy." Nor were they fixated on his incomparable patriotism. Rather, something "less splendid, but more endearing" mattered most to them: their neighbor, their hero, the "first and best of Citizens," the example to their children, was leaving. Yet they were willing to let him go, because they understood what it would mean for the entire country. "Farewell!—Go; and make a grateful people happy; a People who will be doubly grateful, when they contemplate this recent sacrifice for their interest."[28]

Thus, accounts of public adoration of Washington functioned to legitimate Washington's presidential role and the authority of the new national government, while also giving form and shape to the amorphous concept of "American" by defining it according to the "millions" of voices who lifted him to the presidency, whether by a formal vote or a conspicuous, public show of support for his leadership. As the US Senate put it in their statement to Washington: "[T]he office of President" was "an office highly important by the powers continuously annexed to it, and extremely honourable from the manner in which the appointment is made. The unanimous suffrage of the elective body in your favour is peculiarly expressive of the gratitude, confidence, and affection, of the citizens of America, and it is the highest testimonial at once of your merit and their esteem."[29] The point was to depict the choice as a universal expression of all citizens' love for their liberties and their willingness to follow his lead.

For his part, Washington's response to the accolades heaped upon him reinforced the message that "millions" of Americans "unanimously" looked to him, as president, to wield the ideals of the Revolution to realize the republican promise of the new government. When the justices of the supreme court of Pennsylvania cribbed from the Constitution's preamble in their letter to Washington, writing that "the great work . . . seems reserved for you . . . of establishing justice, insuring tranquility, promoting the general welfare, and securing the blessings of liberty and independence to the good people of your native country, and their latest posterity," Washington cribbed from them, repeating the line and noting that "I should find myself singularly happy in contributing to realize the glorious work."[30] When the faculty and trustees of the University of Pennsylvania distinguished Washington's achievement—becoming "the first magistrate of a great empire . . . by the UNANIMOUS voice of a FREE PEOPLE"—as "an event in the history of the world, as rare as those illustrious virtues, of which it is the just reward," Washington echoed the sentiment, noting that his decision to never again enter public life was no match for "the unanimous call of my country," revealed by the "honor" of his recent election, which served as "fresh and distinguished proof of its approbation."[31] To the people of Alexandria, mourning the loss of their most prominent neighbor, Washington also suggested that the "unanimity" of his election by the populace, along with "an ardent desire, on my own part, to be instrumental in conciliating the good will of my Countrymen towards each other, have induced an acceptance."[32]

To varying degrees, statements of praise for Washington all expressed the idea that public obedience to the government was essential to maintain the kind of nation that was now possible under Washington's virtuous leadership. Statements of confidence and affection for Washington posited that the people of the United States would follow the laws that the president would be tasked with executing, and as such, would act as vital assistants in maintaining an ordered, harmonious society. The Elders and Ministers of the German Reformed Congregations of the United States were among the most explicit on this point, professing their commitment "to impress the minds of the people entrusted to our care, with a due sense of the necessity of uniting reverence to such a government, and obedience to its laws, with the duties and exercise of religion." Pledging to do all they could to lighten "the burden of that weighty and important charge to which you have been called by the unanimous voice of your fellow-citizens, and which your love to your country has constrained you to take upon you," the Elders and Ministers emphasized Washington's piety among the long list of his praiseworthy traits—virtue, courage, morality, and patriotism among them. With Washington at the helm, those cultural values flowed from the president himself, down to local elites, and eventually to common citizens. Washington demonstrated what it meant to be patriotic, steadfast, selfless, and pious. Local elites assisted him by demonstrating these values after his example and modeling loyalty to the government by supporting his actions. This, in turn, communicated to ordinary citizens the importance of obedience to these local elites, and ultimately to the national government that Washington, as president, led. The top-down direction in which these cultural values flowed was as important as the values themselves. Ordinary citizens would learn how to be an American from their local elites, who in turn would take their cues from the ultimate American, occupying "the highest station in the national government." On this point, too, Washington enthusiastically concurred. Thus, the president noted in his reply, local elites could demonstrate proper obedience to the government by demonstrating their support for the president, and "by such conduct . . . [by] the virtuous: members of the community, . . . alleviate the burden of the important office which I have accepted."[33]

Ironically, townspeople along Washington's route expressed their approval of Washington and their commitment to obey the laws of the new government with celebrations that blended royalist and republican messages, borrowing from the songs and statements that Americans once used to celebrate the British crown, but reinforcing the stark difference between President Washington and King George III. As a virtuous servant of the people, Washington was the opposite of a king; appropriating royalist ritual to fete his leadership, then, was not to celebrate another King George but rather to celebrate the replacement of monarchy with the supremacy of the people, with Washington, the people's servant, as their symbol. In fact, because Washington embodied what separated the United States from its former mother country, his supporters could borrow from monarchical ceremonial ritual to celebrate his power. Washington the anti-monarch could be celebrated like a king because the sovereignty the people celebrated was not his but theirs.[34] Like a king, Washington was indeed chosen "by right divine," as an "ode" sung to the tune of "God Save the King" declared, but this divine right had been expressed through the public ratification of the Constitution, followed by the miraculous unanimity of votes in support of his executive leadership: "The Vox Populi, *in the unanimous choice of President* WASHINGTON, *has been as truly displayed, as on any event whatever, and nothing but a pure effort of divine Providence, could have produced such a union of sentiment.*"[35] Washington was a great and good man, but he neither possessed, nor needed, any artificial title but that which the people bestowed. In fact, a poem in the *New York Journal* declared, "HIS NAME alone strikes every Title dead."[36] His supremacy over the people, his command of their loyalty and assent was a testament to their collective freedom, not the president's tyrannical oppression. The Revolution, the American nation's signal act of dissent against tyranny, had culminated in the creation of the most innovative republican government the world had ever seen, headed by a man of incomparable virtue, chosen freely by his own fellow citizens. They would obey him because he represented their collective voice. As the *Gazette of the United States* succinctly put it, President Washington was the "representative of the Majesty of the United States."[37]

At the same time the breathless approbation of private citizens broke down local divisions to define every citizen's Americanness according to his or her support for the president, state assemblies voiced their approbation of his powerful, dynamic leadership and their unequivocal willingness to support his authority, reaffirming state political identities in order to bestow a federal character on the president's national authority. State assemblies around the country issued statements of support, painting vivid portraits of Washington's greatness and promising all but total devotion to his administration. Their statements, reprinted in newspapers outside their state's borders, complemented the sentiments voiced by the "millions" of private citizens out of doors by affirming the federal nature of the union alongside citizens' testaments to its national transcendence. Both houses of the Massachusetts state legislature, "cheerfully congratulate the citizens of these States, on the unanimous choice of a PRESIDENT, whose wisdom and virtues have long been an ornament and blessing to society; relying on his attachment to the liberties of his country, we rest assured, that he will be ever zealous to adopt such measures, as will advance our national dignity, and cement the affections of the people."[38] The New York state assembly assured Washington that it spoke for all "the freemen of this state, when we assure you of the regard they have for your person, of the confidence they repose in your wisdom, and of the firm expectation they entertain that your administration will, by the blessing of Almighty God, be glorious to yourself, and happy for your country."[39] Washington's "presence," the Connecticut general assembly proclaimed, "recalls to our admiration that assemblage of talents, which with impenetrable secrecy, and unvarying decision, under the smiles of Divine Providence, guided to victory and peace, the complicated events of the late long and arduous war," and they "beg[ged] liberty to assure" the president "of our zeal to support your public administrations."[40]

By voicing their approbation, the states asserted that not only did they continue to exist under the Constitution (in defiance of antifederalist critics' predictions) but that their support for the president's leadership of the general government further legitimated the new government's authority. Articulating their approbation of Washington's leadership and pledging to assist in its execution was the states' way of affirming their role as the gatekeepers of federalism that the advocates for ratification had promised they would be under the Constitution. While the people's endorsement of Washington broke down local and state political boundaries, the states' endorsement reaffirmed them. Combined, they attested to the general government's dual federal and national character. At the center of the pro-administration public vision of republican nationhood was executive power, surrounded by what historian David Waldstreicher has called a "union of sentiment" around the president that lauded the disintegration of kingly hierarchy while "recreat[ing] and ratify[ing] hierarchy" around the office and its incumbent.[41]

Together, the published approbation of private citizens and state assemblies presented Washington as the singular figure that Americans trusted completely to unite the people of the several states together, to govern according to their shared national interests, and, ultimately, to collaborate with them in the maintenance of a republic whose future would be defined by prosperity and peace. "The fears of many honest, but scrupulous republicans, that the energy of the new government, might render it unfavorable to liberty, are at length subsided," the Philadelphia *Federal Gazette* trumpeted. "All their apprehensions have been removed, by the election of their beloved WASHINGTON, to fill the office of first Magistrate of the United States." Washington's "firm" leadership had brought a "peace" and liberty, another poet, "Alexis," noted, that now "crowned," not Washington alone, but "thy native shore."[42]

Crucially, this early vision of the American nation appeared to be all inclusive, binding together all Americans from New England to the South:

Figure 2.1: "A Display of the United States of America," by Amos Doolittle
(1794). Courtesy of the Library of Congress Prints and Photographs Division.

men, women and children alike, from property-owning elites to commoners, from town elders to infants. Each could claim membership in the
nation's dissenting tradition by expressing their support for the president
who would direct the power that the new national government derived
from their freely given assent. Yet for all its appearance of inclusiveness,
this vision nonetheless excluded specific parties, most obviously, free and

enslaved black people. During Washington's presidency, the president's enslaved cook, a man named Hercules, and an enslaved woman named Ona
Judge, who served as Martha Washington's personal attendant, would
separately escape to freedom. Their attempts, and those of the nearly four
dozen other persons who attempted to escape the Washingtons' clutches
during the last thirty-nine years of George Washington's life, functioned as
acts of dissent from a power structure that denied them liberty, and served
as the ultimate negative endorsement of the first president's authority. Yet
the voices of black persons, enslaved or free, were not included among
the chorus of Americans who supposedly endorsed Washington with one
voice.[43]

This exclusion of black voices attested that, while not all people of
color were enslaved (and free people of color were included among the
free population), legal codes and social custom over more than a century
and a half had solidified the relationship between race and freedom in the
young nation. By the end of the eighteenth century, freedom in its fullest
sense was reserved for whites alone.[44] In his *Notes on the State of Virginia*,
Thomas Jefferson infamously declared that black people, not just slaves,
were inferior to whites "in the endowments both of body and mind."
The "difference" in skin pigment, "and perhaps" of intellect, Jefferson
mused, "is a powerful obstacle to the emancipation of these people." The
free black intellectual Benjamin Banneker rebutted Jefferson's racism in
a letter to the "Sage of Monticello" in 1791, observing that black people
had "long laboured under the abuse and censure of the world . . . and
that we have long been considered rather as brutish than human, and
Scarcely capable of mental endowments." Banneker's use of the collective
"we" emphasized that he himself was a member of this oppressed race,
even as he did not personally languish "under that State of tyrannical
thralldom, and inhuman captivity, to which too many of my brethren are
doomed."[45] Jefferson subscribed to the white supremacist status quo of
the late eighteenth century, while Banneker opposed it. Yet both in their
own way acknowledged the crucial truth behind the numbers of "free"
and "enslaved" that the census would record: to be white in the United
States meant to lay claim to a liberty that no black person was allowed,
fully, to share.

Some accounts of Washington's election in 1789 hinted at this connection
by invoking a more specific number of "millions" who had unanimously
chosen Washington, either directly or through the Electoral College. The
New York Daily Gazette declared in its April 27, 1789, issue that the
"power" of the presidency had been "conferred . . . by the unanimous and

free suffrages of the Representatives of near three millions of affectionate and grateful people."[46] Another account from a Philadelphia paper the very next day claimed Washington's election was "the spontaneous and unanimous suffrage of three millions of Freemen."[47] The "three million" number is noteworthy, in part, because it was a round number that approximated the total free population of the country—3,199,355.[48] The implication—so obvious to the celebrants of Washington's election to the presidency that no accounts elaborated on it—is nonetheless important for a thorough understanding of the presidency's earliest history. From the very beginning, those who celebrated Washington's ascent assumed that members of the enslaved race would not be a part of the "millions" of citizens whose collective voice granted power to the president and the government he led. In the coming years commentators would make the connection between the presidency and the racial politics of the young nation more explicit, specifying what celebrants in 1789 simply took as a given.

POLITICAL DISSENT AND THE "CHARACTER OF [THE] FIRST MAGISTRATE"

Washington's tours demonstrated the president's concern for, and considerable skill at, performing the role of national leader, unifier, and hero. But Washington's fixation with public perception was not limited to his tours. It encompassed every action he took. His fifth query to John Adams asked "[w]hether, when it shall have been understood that the President is not to give general entertainment in the manner the Presidents of Congress have formerly done, it will be practicable to draw such a line of discrimination in regard to" the number of "official characters" who "may be invited informally or otherwise to dine with him on the days fixed for receiving Company, without exciting clamours in the rest of the Community."[49] His sixth inquired "[w]hether it would be satisfactory to the Public" if he scheduled "four great entertainm[en]ts" annually, given how important it was for the president, "in his public character . . . to maintain the dignity of Office, without subjecting himself to the imputation of superciliousness or unnecessary reserve."[50]

Washington was right to anticipate that the public would take an interest in the frequency with which he would be available and to whom. The president's accountability to the public was what separated that office from that of a monarch. But Washington found it difficult to strike the right balance between privacy and accessibility. In a lengthy letter to David

Stuart, a clearly frustrated Washington explained why he was *"compelled . . .* to allot a day for the reception of idle and ceremonious visits." Before he set aside a specific day of the week to receive guests, guests came at all hours, morning, noon, and night. Feeling he could not simply turn them away, Washington was hard pressed to find time "to attend to any business *whatsoever.*" This left him with two choices: either "refuse them *altogether,* or to appropriate a time for the reception of them." Neither, he knew, was immune to criticism, nor would either "please every body." But it was the only way to combine the president's institutional role in the operation of the government with the office's equally crucial public accessibility. Besides that, Washington bristled at the suggestion that the weekly meetings were ostentatious. "These visits are optional," Washington explained. "They are made without invitation—Between the hours of three and four every Tuesday I am prepared to receive them—Gentlemen—often in great numbers—come and go—chat with each other—and act as they please." Upon arriving, they salute the president, who returns the gesture, and the rest of the time is spent in pleasant conversation, "what pomp there is in all this I am unable to discover." True, the guests generally stood the entire length of their visit, but that was only because the room was not large enough to accommodate enough chairs for the typical number of weekly visitors. Washington was sensitive to the accusation that the reason had anything to do with the desire to imitate some sort of courtly ceremony, insisting that *"no* supposition was ever more erroneous." His great desire was for retirement, not for a court, and his meetings were an expression of the esteem he held for "the propriety of giving to every one as free access, as consists with that respect which is due to the chair of government—and that respect I conceive is neither to be acquired or preserved but by observing a just medium between much state and too great familiarity." Tellingly, Washington concluded that criticism of his attempt to pull off this delicate balancing act could only be bred of the public ignorance about the government and fanned by "enemies to the Government."[51]

As this letter suggests, Washington was always concerned with cultivating just the right distance between himself and the citizens he represented, but he interpreted virtually any amount of public criticism of his actions as a dangerous threat to the government and the national union it was tasked with promoting. For Washington, promoting the "domestic tranquility" that the Constitution described meant minimizing public criticism, which Washington deemed the breeding ground for partisanship. But he knew he could not do that by remaining completely removed from the populace. That would betray the republican nature of his office and would likely backfire anyway, provoking more public backlash, and with it, more division. As he put it in his query to Adams, it all came down to "[w]hether a line of conduct, equally distant from an association with all kinds of company on the one hand and from a total seclusion from Society on the other, ought to be adopted by him? and, in that case, how is it to be done?" Even for Washington, it was not easy to remain aloof enough from the public to get work done, but not so aloof that he appeared out of touch.[52]

In retrospect, Adams was probably not the best person to consult on the subject. Adams was remarkably tone-deaf when it came to evoking public confidence that the people were the ultimate source of authority. Adams was committed, to an extent that bordered on obsession, with a grandiose title for the president that resembled the titles of royal rulers. While he was not the only advocate for a more robust presidential title than the one conferred by the Constitution, he seemed remarkably oblivious to the delicacy with which one needed to propose granting a near-regal title to the president of a newly formed republic and to the annoyance felt by his Senate colleagues whenever he brought the issue up. "[T]he President must be himself, something that includes all the dignities of the diplomatic Corps, and something greater still," Adams informed members of the Senate during a forty-minute "harrange" recorded by an irritated Pennsylvania senator, William Maclay. "[W]hat will the Common People of Foreign Countries, what will the Sailors and Soldiers say, George Washington President of the United States, they will despise him *to all eternity*."[53]

The idea was a tough sell even for many of the administration's staunchest supporters. Just days after Adams's "harrange," Fisher Ames, a Massachusetts congressman who would become one of the most passionate and eloquent members of the Federalist Party, insisted that no one in Congress was seriously advancing the idea. Ames accused the "antispeakers" in the House of Representatives of flying into an overreactive tizzy when the Senate rejected a committee report that "it is not proper to address the President by any other title than that in the Constitution" after the House had approved it "without debate." Their "zeal against titles" for the president, Ames insisted, was overblown. "Not a soul said a word *for* titles," Ames flatly asserted. "But the zeal of these folks could not have risen higher in case of contradiction." Any claim to the contrary must be either "addressed to the galleries, or intended to hurry the House to a resolve censuring the Senate, so as to set the two Houses at odds, and to nettle the

Senate to bestow a title in *their* address." Ames did not know which it was (though he suspected "the latter"), but he did know that the opposition to grandiose titles was little more than obnoxious and excessively dramatic grandstanding. The decision had already been made. The Senate, along with everyone else, "will call him President, &c., simply."[54]

Despite the unpopularity of the position, Adams pressed on, and his advocacy in favor of a more grandiose title for the president provided a bright target for Maclay's derision. Observing that presidential titles was the vice president's "favourite topick," that his unwanted address covered "old Ground," and that "he said fifty things more equally injudicious, which I do not think work minuting," Maclay displayed his naturally sour disposition and "wonderfully acid sense of humor," as historian Joanne B. Freeman puts it. Reading Maclay's words, one can practically see the saturnine senator roll his eyes in exasperation. He mocked the vice president as a man who was so out of touch with the principles of the American people, he could not even see how egregiously out of step his ideas actually were.[55]

Behind Maclay's sardonic commentary lay a crucial political point that Washington understood far better than Adams. Besides being unconstitutional (as Maclay pointed out, the Constitution forbade the granting of "*titles of nobility*"), Maclay also argued that "the appellations & Terms given to Nobility in the old World Are contraband language in The U.S." "[F]rom the English indeed we may borrow... Terms that would not be wholly Unintellig(ib)le to our own Citizens," Maclay conceded, "but will they thank Us for the Compliment[?]" After all, "would not the plagiarism be more likely to be attended with contempt, than respect, among all of them[?]" The subject of titles "must appear Bombastic nonsense in the Eye of every wise Man," but in politics, especially in a republican government, the title of one's elected leaders was supremely important. The labors of great minds "have been directed . . . to reduce the practice of [government] to the principles of common Sense, such as we see exemplified by the Merchant[,] the Mechanic and the farmer, when every Act or Operation tends to a productive or beneficial Effect," Maclay wrote. "And above all to illustrate this fact, That Government was instituted for the Benefit of the People and That no Act of Government is Justifiable That has not this for it's [*sic*] object."[56]

Maclay had succinctly explained the most crucial lesson in presidential leadership. Adams was advocating a position that would actually rile up the very populace that the president and the vice president sought to assure. The Pennsylvania senator's observation proved prescient. Throughout the next decade Adams's stubborn insistence on a near-regal chief executive would gain him a reputation as a monarchist—a charge that would earn him fierce rebukes from the opposition Republican Party in the years to come.

Indeed, to whatever extent Washington and his supporters had convinced themselves that there was one, single American people, united across sectional and state boundaries by a shared support for the president, the reality was far less harmonious. No longer relegated to the background, the office that Washington occupied was now the focal point of the public support and obedience that the president and his allies expected of all patriotic Americans. But as Washington made decisions as president, criticism accompanied every decision he made. One question would define the divide separating the emerging Federalist and Republican parties: were the president's critics acting in the spirit of the nation's Revolutionary dissenting tradition, or were they betraying it? Those who agreed with Washington that public acts of criticism and dissent were dangerous to the "order and good government" that maintained the peace would call themselves Federalists. Many of them—though not all—had been federalist supporters of ratification just a few short years earlier. Those who found fault with the actions of the executive—with Washington personally, or with other members of the executive branch under his leadership—and who claimed that by speaking out they were actually trying to salvage the republican character of the government from being compromised by the disturbing expanse of executive power, would call themselves Republicans.

In July of 1789, radicals in France stormed the Bastille, a prison holding, among others, political dissidents to the crown. This action would come to be the most iconic moment of the French Revolution, a radical revolt against the French monarchy that would result in the beheading of the king, Louis XVI, and his wife, Marie Antoinette, and the establishment of a representative Assembly. But it also spawned a violent persecution movement, called the Terror. Led by Maximilien Robespierre, the ultraradical Jacobins deemed anyone who lacked their full commitment to republican reform to be an enemy of the state. Executions by the Robespierre-led Committee of Public Safety were the prescribed remedy for rooting out traitors to radical French democracy.

The ripple effects of the French Revolution in the United States were profound. News of the Revolution filled statesmen with hope and dread. Some, like Washington's secretary of state, Thomas Jefferson, initially embraced the French Revolution as a continuation of the spirit of dissent that had fueled the American Revolution. Outside the halls of government, influential but short-lived political clubs, collectively called Democratic-Republican Societies, sprung up by the dozens in the early 1790s. These societies largely supported the French Revolution, referred to fellow members as "citizen," and drank toasts to Edmond Charles "Citizen" Genet, a flamboyant French diplomat sent to the United States in 1793 to solicit its help against Britain. Washington came to agree with Alexander Hamilton, his treasury secretary, that revolutionary France was proof that too much democracy was poison to an ordered society, ultimately leading to chaos and violence. Hamilton, often remembered for his ambitious financial plan and affinity for concentrated executive power, argued that Americans were a peaceful people and that Washington's declaration of American neutrality in France's war with Britain reflected America's commitment to peace, in contrast to the bloodshed that consumed the empires of Europe.[57]

In the fall of 1789, just months after the storming of the Bastille, the US Congress requested from Hamilton a plan for establishing public credit. Hamilton surpassed Congress's request, laying out a series of bold financial proposals that included a plan for the general government to assume the states' collective $25 million dollar war debts; a series of taxes on tea, coffee, and especially liquor to pay off those debts; and the most important recommendation: the establishment of a National Bank that would act as the nation's financial center, helping to procure revenue, offering credit, and providing available cash to the government in the event of emergencies. Currency from the Bank would be nationally recognized legal tender, simplifying economic exchanges, especially for the nation's businesses, whose growth Hamilton believed the government had a vested interest in promoting. Finally, the majority of the ten million dollars of total capital projected for the Bank would come from securities sold to private investors. Often interpreted as a testament to Hamilton's commitment to capitalism, the financial agenda that the treasury secretary proposed was actually meant to build up the power of the nascent national government. Hamilton recognized that the United States was vulnerable and that the government needed money, especially to beef up its paltry military forces, if it ever hoped to repel any potential invasion or other military threat.[58]

Washington could not be neutral when it came to either the French Revolution or Hamilton's financial plans. News about both divided Americans, and any action Washington took—even inaction—was doomed to anger some. Hamilton quickly emerged as the leading mind of the Federalist Party, and its members shared Washington's skepticism of the democratic promise of the French Revolution and held that the government needed to be less susceptible to the deleterious effects of widespread political dissent. For all their celebration of Washington's "unanimous" election by the American people, most political elites expected that voting would actually constrain citizens' ability to influence the government, as Benjamin Rush explained. "It is often said, that 'the sovereign and all other power is seated *in* the people,'" Rush wrote. "This idea is unhappily expressed. It should be—'all power is derived *from* the people.' They possess it only on the days of their elections. After this, it is the property of their rulers, nor can they exercise or resume it, unless it is abused. It is of importance to circulate this idea, as it leads to order and good government."[59]

Order and good government became the refrain of the Federalists as the democratic impulses of the French Revolution morphed into murderous rampage, widespread oppression, and eventually, the rise of Napoleon Bonaparte. Too much dissent, too much revolution, too much democracy too rapidly was poison to a society. No high-minded ideals could prevent that society from tearing itself apart. To translate the spirit of dissent that had fueled the American Revolution into a lasting republican nation—in short, to avoid the fate of France—the government had to be stronger and the people's assent to its authority, from the president on down, had to be all but absolute.

The emerging Republican Party (which Rush himself would eventually join) opposed nearly every syllable of the Federalists' political philosophy.[60] Made up of political leaders like Thomas Jefferson and James Madison, and most members of the Democratic-Republican Societies, the Republicans conceded that a certain amount of obedience to elected "rulers" was necessary to avoid perpetual revolution and anarchy. But they rejected the Federalists' insistence that that meant the populace ought to silently and passively accept all actions taken by a government that operated at a distance from them. Where Federalists saw the French Revolution as a cause for alarm and Hamilton's financial plan as a necessary set of measures to strengthen the government and ensure its ability to govern effectively, Republicans generally viewed the French Revolution more optimistically and perceived Hamilton's financial schemes with deep suspicion. Hamilton wanted to establish the Treasury as the most powerful executive department and situate himself as a minister in the mold of Robert Walpole, the influential British prime minister and first lord of the treasury, who sought to make himself the center of the national administration. Though he was ostensibly merely issuing a report to Congress,

Hamilton proved an effective lobbyist, operating on behalf of his plan "in the Stile of a british Minister," William Maclay remarked, drawing his own comparison between Hamilton and Walpole.[61]

On one issue, however, both Republicans and Federalists agreed: the country's future depended on Washington's presidential performance. More than any other person occupying any other office, Washington, in his words and actions, would dictate the course the country took, for better or for worse. Washington certainly recognized that fact from the moment he agreed to stand for election, and the citizens he met on his tours were certainly convinced that his actions were crucial to setting the country on a path to prosperity. Washington's immense popularity provided something of a cover for his treasury secretary, who worked assiduously among elected leaders and financial elites, making political allies with both in Northern and even in Southern states like Virginia, where opposition to the Bank was strong. He solicited ambitious Southern financiers through his treasury agents and through his own correspondence, building a network of financially powerful people to buttress support for his plan. Support for the administration was not strong everywhere in the South (in North Carolina, for example, it was particularly weak), but Hamilton's popularity, and with it, that of the Bank, grew among both political leaders and financial elites in South Carolina and in parts of Virginia, as well as cities in the North.[62]

So influential was Hamilton that he was even able to allay Washington's own misgivings about the national bank, convincing the president that it was constitutional. By contrast, Washington's secretary of state, Thomas Jefferson, considered the Bank a grossly unconstitutional violation of the rights of the states and even claimed that Washington's hesitation to veto the national bank would in effect make members of Congress "the sole judges of . . . good or evil," which, besides granting them power to do good, also granted them "power to do whatever evil they pleased." Jefferson's argument reflected his belief, shared by his fellow Republicans and Federalist opponents alike, that the president's actions would uniquely shape not only the contours of constitutional interpretation but also the moral character of the nation for years to come.[63]

In Jefferson's estimation the man doing the misleading did not come from Congress but from the executive branch. Jefferson saw "Hamilton's schemes" as the root cause of political developments that disturbed him. Jefferson and James Madison would become the leaders of the opposition Republican Party, which would come to oppose Washington's administration and his supporters and eventually take the presidency in a decisive

1800 victory that would signal the beginning of the end for the Federalists. At the time, though, as Jefferson noted later in his "Anas," the secretary of state saw Hamilton, not Washington, as the corrupting influence within the executive branch. The "real ground of the opposition which was made to the course of administration," Jefferson explained, "was to preserve the legislature pure and independant [*sic*] of the Executive, to restrain the administration to republican forms and principles, and not permit the constitution to be construed into a monarchy, and to be warped in practice into all the principles and pollutions of their favorite English model." But this was not "an opposition to Genl. Washington," who, by Jefferson's assessment, "was true to the republican charge confided to him." Rather, it was an opposition to Hamilton, who "was not only a monarchist, but for a monarchy bottomed on corruption."[64] Hamilton had a willing cadre of legislators "who, having swallowed his bait were laying themselves out to profit by his plans," Jefferson confided to Washington. Indeed, the avarice of Hamilton and his ilk appeared limitless. "No longer the . . . representatives of the people," Jefferson argued to Washington, construing these members of Congress as "deserters from the rights & interests of the people," a haughty "corps under the command of the Secretary of the Treasury for the purpose of subverting step by step the principles of the constitution."[65]

So too did Hamilton draw venom from James Madison, who seethed at Hamilton's tactics alongside his fellow Virginian. In their correspondence, Jefferson and Madison began using what Stanley Elkins and Eric McKitrick have called "tag-words": derogatory terms that described the worst features of Hamiltonian political principles. Terms like "tories," "monocrats," and "anglomen" appeared frequently in their missives to describe this "anti-republican" affinity for British politics. Other terms, like "stock-jobbers," and "speculators" were specific jabs at the elite financial interests that Hamilton targeted to the exclusion of the majority of the American citizenry.[66]

The pair hired Philip Freneau, a French writer and Madison's old college classmate, to publish the *National Gazette*, a new newspaper intended to publicly criticize the abuses of executive power emanating from the Washington administration. The *National Gazette* never achieved the circulation of the *Gazette of the United States* (in fact, it folded in 1793), and even within its limited existence, it embraced its role as a critic of the administration's policies only gingerly. Still, historian Jeffrey L. Pasley has credited the paper with attempting, for the first time, "to fashion and project the image of a coherent opposition party."[67]

Madison wrote a series of anonymous essays in the *National Gazette* between October 1791 and December 1792. In these pieces he joined Jefferson in voicing alarm at the aggrandizement of executive power and in identifying Hamilton as its source, although he never mentioned the treasury secretary by name.[68] In one essay, "Spirit of Governments," Madison distinguished among three types of government, one of which derived power from "a permanent military force," and one of which "operat[ed] by corrupt influence; substituting the motive of private interests in place of public duty," an oblique reference to Hamilton's financial schemes, though Madison asserted that this type of government did not exist west of the Atlantic. A less subtle reference came in "A Candid State of Parties." There Madison described "antirepublicans" as those who believe "that mankind are incapable of governing themselves," "that government can be carried on only by the pageantry of rank, the influence of money and emoluments, and the terror of military force." Madison also channeled his hostility toward Hamilton's financial plan into indictments of such governmental schemes and into praise for the people he believed were exemplary of the true, majority American citizenry: the yeoman farmer: "The class of citizens who provide at once their own food and their own raiment, may be viewed as the most truly independent and happy. They are . . . the best basis of public liberty, and the strongest bulwark of public safety." Madison is not renowned for populist political arguments, but here he claimed that Hamilton manipulated the power of the executive branch to serve the interests of the wealthy at the expense of humble farmers, who were the truest American citizens. Through Hamilton's underhanded schemes, the government that Washington had been elected to lead was betraying its fundamental purpose.[69]

The publication of such critical pieces is a testament to how seriously Republicans took the role that political dissent played in ensuring that the government's power served the populace it represented. The Virginia state general assembly made the importance more explicit in their criticism of Hamilton's plan for the assumption of state debts. It was "[a] system which has . . . insinuated into the hands of the Executive an unbounded influence," the assembly and senate asserted, "which pervading every branch of the government bears down all opposition, and daily threatens the destruction of every thing that appertains to English liberty.—The same causes produce the same effects!" The assembly described its members "[a]s the guardians of the rights and interests of their constituents, as centinels placed by them over the ministers of the federal government." As such, the assembly claimed a sacred duty to appeal to Congress (the states' representative body) to oppose the measure, thus holding the executive branch within its proper bounds and maintaining the delicate balance between national and federal authority that the expansion of executive power threatened. By defending Virginians from "encroachments" on their liberties, by refusing "silently to acquiesce in a measure which violates that hallowed maxim" that the states' duty was to sanction general government power in accordance with their citizens' rights, the assembly was in effect protecting the republican nature of the general government. It was actively participating in defining a boundary for the government's power and insisting that no executive measure could stray beyond it.[70]

Madison's references to "military force" spoke to Republicans' belief that the Federalists were obsessed with military strength and sought to make the United States into an empire in the mold of Britain. Washington himself appeared to agree that the military needed to be increased when, in his first Annual Message, he expressed concern whether the existing military force would be equal to the task of repelling the threats from "hostile tribes of Indians" on the nation's "Southern and Western frontiers." Washington recommended to Congress provisions for building up the nation's military forces "to afford protection to those parts of the Union; and if necessary to punish aggressors." The nation's military force totaled no more than five thousand men at the time, a paltry sum by anyone's standard.[71]

Washington's call to build up arms was not incompatible with his commitment to peace. But his argument for building up the size of the military rested in part on a view that Indians on the frontier were not only not Americans but potential enemies who could pose an existential threat to the United States. Washington interacted with Indians constantly through his long career as a soldier and statesman. He smoked ceremonial pipes with Indian leaders and negotiated with them on a regular basis prior to becoming president. Throughout his career he had expressed the view that Indians could become a civilized people if they took up farming instead of hunting and adopted white cultural practices. He condemned frontier whites who encroached on Indian lands, often with harsher language than what he used to criticize Indians themselves. Yet he never relinquished his fundamental belief that Indians were not as civilized as white Americans and never really could be. As president, Washington approached Indians as separate nations, not present or even potential citizens. He sought treaties with the powerful Creek Indians in the southeast, and with the Cherokee, hoping to avoid a costly and likely prolonged war. His call for arms prompted Congress to debate how to prepare for war, a debate that forced

Congress to contemplate what provisions would be needed; how Congress should raise the funds to pay for them; whether state militias or a more robust standing army would be best suited to repel a potential Indian attack; the role of the states, especially states like Georgia and Kentucky; and how that all comported with America's status as a peaceful nation. His call to build up arms had allies, in part because his prejudice against Indians was widely shared.[72]

In December 1792, Washington's secretary of war, Henry Knox, delivered a message to Congress from the governor of Georgia, Edward Telfair, providing an account of "certain citizens of this state, who have murdered some friendly Indians, and committed other depredations." Telfair began by condemning the attack as an "outrage" but ended his message by saying, "From what I can learn, this violence on the part of the offenders has proceeded from the circumstance of four whites having been killed, horses stolen, and other depredations committed by the Cherokees." Though he concluded by saying that did not give whites an excuse not to follow the laws, his characterization framed the incident as an act of violence that Indians had provoked.[73]

Georgia Congressman John Milledge, and a "Correspondent" in a Virginia newspaper, echoed the view that Indians were violent threats to the nation, especially "the several frontier states," which "would be more or less exposed to the cruel ravages of a savage warfare." Milledge told his colleagues. "If the customs of savage tribes did not direct them towards us, they were incessantly excited by the British and Spaniards to amuse us with false pretences of peace while they were engrossing the advantages of their trade; the aged Indians kept to hunting, and the young men gratified in the military exploits with the blood of our fellow citizens." The Virginia "correspondent" thought "it would seem bad policy to reduce the present army establishment, before the conclusion of something like a firm and general peace with the Indians. Disarming any part of our war establishment, before that period, will leave us at the mercy of the savages, to settle matters upon their own terms.—It has always been a European maxim, *to make peace with the sword in our hand.*" The western edge of the United States was becoming so populated by whites, the correspondent went on, "that the Indians now find it easier to get a living by plunder than by hunting; and they will not fail to prefer the first of these modes, if they are not restrained by a certainty of punishment from a superior force."[74]

Such a call to build up the military lent credence to Madison's charge that the Federalists led in part by "the terror of military force." Yet in time this charge would take on another irony, for as president during the War of 1812, Madison and the Republicans would invoke the terror of Indian attacks to marshal whites to serve in the war. Even within white Americans' debate over how building up the military would affect the president's power, whites broadly agreed that Indians were not included in the nation they envisioned. Indians were, at best, a separate people with whom the nation might conduct treaties, and at worst, a malevolent threat whom the whites, political leaders, and commentators contemplated were building up for war.[75]

In addition to violent clashes between whites and Indians on the American frontier, Washington had to contend with the outbreak of war between Britain, France, and their respective allies in 1793. The British and French sought to cripple one another's oceanic trade, and ships from the United States sometimes got caught in the middle. After commandeering a vessel, British seamen sometimes arrested American sailors as fugitive subjects of the crown, a practice known as impressment. Hostility on the high seas imperiled American trade. The United States was economically fragile, and trade with Europe, unencumbered by an official alliance with either party that might pull it into a war, was essential to its financial well-being.

Washington and his Federalist allies agreed with Republicans that peace was in the best interest of the American nation and that all true Americans desired peace over war. As the chief executive, Washington took it upon himself to take dynamic measures to keep the nation out of war. The French Revolution began to devolve into a bloodbath just as Genet arrived in April, but that did little to dampen public enthusiasm for his arrival. Genet arrived in the United States to great fanfare after beginning his journey across the Atlantic on the same night that France executed King Louis XVI. Republicans in South Carolina (where he landed in April) all the way northward to Philadelphia greeted him with lavish parties, so much so that he marveled that "I live here in the midst of perpetual fetes." Unbeknownst to Genet, however, Washington had already issued a proclamation that same month declaring the United States neutral in France's war with Britain, and he was unwilling to go further than agreeing to the most boilerplate well wishes for France. The neutrality proclamation strategically avoided the word "neutral"; instead, it declared the government would "conduct" itself in a "friendly and impartial" manner toward both sides. Genet vowed to take his case to the American people directly, a move that revealed Genet's profound underestimation of Washington's constitutional authority and popularity. It also perturbed Thomas Jefferson, who confided in a letter to James Madison that Genet's actions, especially his rumored plan to foment popular upheaval in Spanish Louisiana, confirmed him as the most "calamitous appointment" the United States had ever seen, an opinion that put him decidedly at odds with the Democratic-Republican Societies, who saluted "Citizen Genet" with gusto.[76]

Jefferson's position as secretary of state, which placed him in the unenviable position of trying to ease tensions not only between the French and US governments, but between Genet and the Washington administration, surely played a role in Jefferson's negative assessment of Genet. Jefferson noted in the same letter, "He renders my position immensely difficult." Feeling himself pinned between his sympathy for France and the administration's official line, Jefferson would resign his position, while his rival in Washington's cabinet, Alexander Hamilton, defended Washington's action as a constitutionally sound action that would keep the nation out of war.[77]

Hamilton, writing under the pseudonym Pacificus, defended Washington's actions vigorously in a series of essays that are best known for advancing Hamilton's expansive theory of executive power. "[T]he EXECUTIVE POWER of the Nation," Hamilton argued, "is vested in the President; subject only to the *exceptions* and *qu(a)lifications* which are expressed in the instrument." In other words, the president was permitted to exercise any power that the Constitution did not expressly forbid. Even though Congress, not the president, had the power to declare war, the Constitution did not expressly forbid the president from declaring the nation at peace.[78]

Invoking Washington's service in the American Revolution, Hamilton sought to depict the president's critics as dangerous factions intent on poisoning citizens' minds against the president, and in so doing, pushing the country toward "a state of continual revolution and change." When "the presses begin to groan with invective against the Chief Magistrate of the Union, for that prudent and necessary measure," Hamilton explained, they undermined "a measure calculated to manifest to the World the pacific position of the Government and to caution the citizens of the U[nited] States against practices, which would tend to involve us in a War the most unequal and calamitous, in which it is possible for a Country to be engaged." They sought "to disparage in the opinion and affections of his fellow citizens that man who at the head of our armies fought so successfully for the Liberty and Independence, which are now our pride and our boast" and who now as president sought "to aid in the glorious work of ingrafting that liberty, which his sword had contributed to win, upon a stock of which it stood in need and without which it could not

flourish—endure—a firm adequate national Government."[79] Hamilton
argued that Washington had led the American people in a glorious act
of dissent against British tyranny and now exercised his constitutional
powers to keep the nation out of war. True Americans recognized this and
supported him. Those who criticized him posed a threat to the nation.

On this point, the secretary of the treasury was adamant. Those who
criticized Washington betrayed the spirit of the Revolution for which
Washington and all American patriots had fought and on behalf of which
Washington, as president, now acted. This "most dangerous combination" was a kind of tyranny that threatened everything Washington, acting with the support of the American people, was attempting to preserve.
"Those who for some time past have been busy in undermining the constitution and government of the [United States] by indirect attacks, by
labouring to render its measures odious, by striving to destroy the confidence of the people in its administration—are now meditating a more
direct and destructive war against it," Hamilton warned. Proof that the
Constitution's enemies were "embodying and arranging their forces and
systematizing their efforts" lay in the efforts of "Secret clubs," and "dis-
organising corps," who concocted a whole "language" on a foundation of
lies.[80] To many of Washington's supporters, Hamilton was a sure-footed
statesman, a man of supreme confidence, possessed of a mind of almost
unparalleled brilliance. But his remarks read like those of a suspicious,
shifty-eyed sentry, scanning the political horizon for any sign of an immi-
nent threat.

Hamilton's rhetoric was certainly alarming, but he was right that polit-
ical dissenters were growing louder and more organized and that they directed their words and actions increasingly toward President Washington.
These voices directly contradicted Hamilton's claim that dissent against
President Washington was patently un-American and dangerous to the
peace and prosperity that Americans expected the president to promote.
In fact, they argued that the presidency carried with it obligations to the
American people that Washington was not living up to—and that by criticizing him, they were not betraying the nation's dissenting tradition, but
rather acting in accordance with it, bringing the executive office back in
line with its obligation to act always subject to their collective voice. It
was the natural corollary to the message communicated by celebrations
of Washington's "unanimous" election to the presidency in 1789: if "the
people" had elevated Washington to the office, vesting him with authority,
as the countless poems, songs, open letters to Washington, and professions
of support for the first president asserted, then the president was bound to

listen to the people and heed their voice, just as they were bound to obey the just laws he carried out in their name. Washington's neutrality proclamation and Genet's mission exposed and exacerbated a growing partisan divide over the relative obligations of the president and the people of the United States. Federalists like Hamilton—and Washington himself—stressed the public's duty to obey the constituted authorities, from the president on down. Republicans—especially members of the Democratic-Republican societies—emphasized the president's and the entire national government's obligation to listen to the American people.[81]

In early June 1793, a series of essays appeared in the *National Gazette*, written by a critic of Washington's neutrality proclamation who used the pseudonym Veritas. The identity of Veritas was a matter of dispute at the time, and it remains a mystery to this day. French Ambassador Edmond Genet thought Jefferson was Veritas, while Jefferson suspected it was one of Hamilton's underlings assuming the guise of a Washington critic in order to discredit the president's political opposition.[82] Whoever Veritas may have been, this critic of Washington contended that a basic distinction existed between the presidency and the man who occupied it. Veritas placed a great deal of importance on "character," speaking about both "the character of [the] first magistrate" and what Veritas called "American character" in Letter 1. Veritas made it clear that the two were interdependent. The true "character" of the presidency exemplified what distinguished the representative system of the United States from monarchies like Great Britain, but that character depended upon a robust back-and-forth between the president and the people. In monarchies such as Great Britain, Veritas pointed out in Letter 2, "*the people* have little or no share in the government," and in such governments "it is not uncommon for the executive to act in direct opposition to the *will of the nation*." But not so with the president of the United States. "Consider that a first magistrate in every country is no other than a public servant, whose conduct is to be governed by the will of the people, as expressed in their constitution and laws," Veritas urged Washington in Letter 3. The president's representative character depended upon the willingness of citizens to voice not only their approbation, but even more crucially, their objections when they feared the president's actions might prove harmful to the country. "At this momentous crisis of our public affairs, when solemn treaties and the sacred rights of American citizens seem to be openly violated," Veritas began Letter 3, "it were treason against the dearest interests of America not to warn her first magistrate to shut his ears against the whispers of servile adulation, and to listen to the solemn admonitions of patriotic truth."[83]

As Veritas's comment suggests, the president had an obligation to listen to the people just as much as the people had an obligation to speak. Deploying the same pejoratives that Jefferson and Madison used to describe the Federalists, Veritas worried that the neutrality proclamation was evidence that Washington erroneously took the opinions of an "aristocratic few, and their contemptible minions, of speculators, tories, and British emissaries," to be "the exalted and general voice of the American people." For years, Veritas claimed, Washington had clearly favored the voice of a few aristocratic toadies over the voice of the majority of the populace. In short, he was failing to fulfill his duty as president, and the nation was suffering thereby.[84]

The result, Veritas concluded, was "conduct" by the government "with respect to that of Great-Britain," extending back "some years," which could only be described as "shamefully pusillanimous." The craven actions on the part of the government in no way equaled the "character" of the American people, which for Veritas was rooted in a fierce, fearless, and uncompromising love of liberty and a boundless willingness to defend it. This spirit of independence, born in the American Revolution, owed a great debt to the French, whose "generous exertions . . . in the cause of American liberty" were critical for America's "national existence." Besides betraying the country's established diplomatic and commercial relationship with its old Revolutionary ally, Veritas argued, Washington's neutrality declaration betrayed the very essence of who the American people were—the very "character" that defined them as free people and allies to the French in their war against British tyranny.[85]

For too long President Washington had acted in a manner too far removed from the people, too unreceptive to any assessment of his conduct other than unequivocal approval. The fate of the country hinged on a more intimate connection between the president and the people. Washington's distance from the people, in Veritas's estimation, was nothing short of a betrayal of the very cause of liberty that the young country stood for and for which Washington himself had fought. If Washington refused to recognize and act in accord with "the real state of the nation," the people of the nation would amplify their voice more; a new concerted act of dissent would be needed to reclaim dominion over an office that was rightfully theirs. "The spirit of 1776 is again roused," Veritas trumpeted at the conclusion of Letter 2, "and soon shall be mushroom-lordlings of the day, the enemies of American as well as French liberty, be taught that American whigs of 1776, will not suffer French patriots of 1792, to be vilified with impunity, by the common enemies of both."[86]

Veritas was not alone. Beginning in 1793, inspired by the French Revolution and provoked by the administration's actions, the Democratic-Republican Societies (although they usually referred to themselves simply as Republican Societies, or more commonly, Democratic Societies), began to be founded across the country. Society members came from a variety of professions, among them doctors, grocers, merchants, and printers, constituting just a portion of a public citizenry that manifested its objections to the administration through collective political expression beyond just voting—the only form of political disapproval that Washington and the Federalists recognized as legitimate.[87]

In the spring of 1793, the first of the Democratic-Republican Societies convened in Philadelphia. By the end of 1793, eleven known chapters had been established in New York City, Charleston, South Carolina, and Norfolk, Virginia and as far west as Kentucky. By the end of 1794, the number of known chapters stood at thirty-five, including new chapters in Vermont, Maryland, and North Carolina. Unlike Jefferson and Madison, society members were more willing to blame Washington, rather than Hamilton, for the disturbing expanse of executive power they saw before them. The societies received help from an emerging opposition press, led by the Philadelphia *General Advertiser* and its editor, Benjamin Franklin Bache (grandson of the famed American inventor, scientist, and sage). In November 1794 Bache renamed his paper the *Aurora General Advertiser* and turned it into the premier anti-administration newspaper in the country. The *Aurora* specialized in aggressive political polemic. Criticism of the president—such as the *Aurora*'s gleeful statement that Washington's retirement should be a time for "rejoicing," because "the name of WASHINGTON from this day ceases to give a currency to political iniquity; and to legalize corruption"—could be fashioned like razors to snag and slice Washington's thin political skin, exposing the vulnerabilities in its target's uniquely formidable public stature. Bache's paper also published minutes and resolutions from Democratic-Republican Societies, helping to disseminate their message publicly, especially within the capital city of Philadelphia.[88]

Sympathetic to France and the French Revolution and repelled by almost anything British, members of numerous Democratic-Republican Societies referred to one another as "citizen" and spoke frequently about "the rights of man," while condemning anything that even hinted at the presence of "aristocracy," "luxury," or "ambition" within the US government. The link between France's beleaguered position against the belligerent forces of Britain and the United States' own perilous position with regard to both Britain and the administration—the Democratic Society of Pennsylvania argued—could not be overemphasized. The war by Britain against France was not a "war against that Nation solely, but against liberty itself." Therefore "all attempts to alienate our affections from france and detach us from her alliance, and to connect us more intimately with great britain" were worthy of the fiercest resistance, for they represented an "unnatural succession" by persons who "ought to be considered by every free american as enemies to republicanism and their country." The French cause, like the American cause, was the cause of liberty. As such, maintaining "our national engagements" with France was a test of "our national dignity." It would determine whether the American people truly possessed the capacity for "firm and manly conduct" ("the best calculated to secure to us the blessings of peace"), or whether "timid and wavering measures will expose us to numberless insults and outrages, and after a painful career of humiliation, finally draw us ingloriously into a war, which firmness and decision might have prevented."[89]

Crucially, the societies identified Washington's presidential actions as uniquely indicative of the strength of the republic. They accused him of an affinity for British monarchy and aristocracy and argued that his actions captured the disturbing gap between the general government and the American people.[90] Like Veritas, the Democratic Societies argued that they were performing a necessary civic duty by dissenting from Washington's actions. As one New York society put it, "[A]lthough we entertain a high sense of the integrity of the President, it is our duty, as republicans, to presume every man fallible."[91] The German Republican Society of Philadelphia agreed. "In a republican government it is a duty incumbent on every citizen to afford his assistance, either by taking a part in its immediate administration, or by his advice and watchfulness, that its principles may remain incorrupt." "[F]or the spirit of liberty, like every virtue of the mind, is to be kept alive only by constant action," it declared in April, 1793.[92] It was nothing personal, simply a matter of reasserting the supremacy of "the people of the United States" over "their President," and in so doing, claiming authority over an office that, though occupied by Washington, belonged to them.[93]

The mounting criticism of Washington appalled both the president and his Federalist supporters and convinced them that the dissenting voices aligning against him posed a uniquely potent threat to the country. Like Hamilton, Washington saw them as a toxic, partisan attack on the very legitimacy of the government. To be sure, Washington argued, the people had the right "to meet occasionally" and "to petition for, or remonstrate against, any Act of the Legislature." But they had no right to form "self-created bodies" that acted as *"permanent* Censors." Such bodies undermined "order & good government" by poisoning citizens' minds against their elected representatives. They questioned not only discrete laws but governmental authority itself.[94]

For Washington, the societies had provoked "the Incendiaries of public peace & order," in particular the critics of taxes that the government had levied on whiskey in 1794. The brief uprising of some rural western Pennsylvanians has earned historical renown as "the whiskey rebellion." For Washington, "the Insurrection in the Western counties" of Pennsylvania provided "striking evidence" of these subversives' "attempts to spread their nefarious doctrines, with a view to poison & discontent in the minds of the people against the government; particularly by endeavouring to have it believed that their liberties were assailed, and that all the wicked and abominable measures . . . that can be devised under specious guises . . . are practiced to sap the Constitution, and lay the foundation of future Slavery." Convinced that these rebellions "may be considered as the first *ripe fruit* of the Democratic Societies,"[95] Washington condemned the societies as "self-created societies," a remark credited with blunting their political impact.[96]

It is a testament to Washington's lasting popularity, even in the face of public criticism, that his words could have such a devastating impact on the societies' political influence. On one level the influence of Veritas and the Democratic-Republican Societies was limited. Fears that organized groups and clubs, and even private individuals, that challenged the authority of constituted authorities posed a fundamental threat to the government, and thus to political order and stability and ultimately the Constitution itself, were widespread. The idea that political parties could be a "loyal opposition"—critical of those in power but supportive of the system of government itself—was in its infancy.[97]

Yet, as Hamilton suspected, the president's public critics were not going away. Washington had yet to name Supreme Court Chief Justice John Jay as a special envoy to negotiate a treaty with Great Britain. That action would provoke renewed protests against Washington, and with them, the most cohesive vision of the presidency's place within the national political arena that dissenters had yet to produce.

3

Claiming the Presidency for the People in the Jay Treaty Controversy

WASHINGTON'S EARLY CRITICS demonstrated a political vision fundamentally at odds with the president and his allies. They disagreed that Washington's exploits in the Revolution made him above political reproach. They insisted that their expressions of disapproval were essential to sustaining the people's authority over their government, thus preserving the republican character of the country. They questioned his actions and asserted not just a right but an obligation to do so. Washington's early critics attempted to pry the man apart from the office, insisting that Washington, for all his accolades, was falling short of its uniquely demanding standards.

When news broke that Washington had appointed Supreme Court Chief Justice John Jay to negotiate a treaty with Great Britain in 1794—and then news of the treaty leaked to the press shortly after its arrival in the United States in 1795—public criticism intensified. Demonstrations of dissent ran the gamut from earnest letters pleading with Washington not to endorse the treaty to acts of vandalism and violence in the streets. Prompted by an issue of pivotal diplomatic and domestic significance for the young nation, critics of the treaty articulated more fully than ever before the presidency's unique importance to the health and vitality of the nation and the value of political dissent to holding the president publicly accountable at all times.

Opposing what they characterized as Washington's aloof comportment, his curt response to their concerns, and his and the Federalists' dismissal of their criticism as illegitimate and even dangerous to order, these critics advocated more than just a rejection of the treaty. They urged an embrace of a presidency that embodied the political culture they envisioned. Arguing that the president was subject to public scrutiny at all times, not just during elections, critics made the presidency the cultural touchstone of a more democratic and even contentious political culture: one in which

78

non-elite citizens across class lines, in cities and in small towns, enjoyed wide access to their elected leaders and exercised their right to question and even oppose actions with which they disagreed. This perpetual public accountability, they insisted, was foundational to a healthy, lasting American nation.

"THE FIRST SERVANT OF THE PEOPLE"

News that American sailors were being impressed—that they were essentially being kidnapped and forced to enlist in the British navy—provoked anger and alarm among Americans in the government and outside it, and the solutions favored by Washington's cabinet members further intensified the partisan divide between Federalists and Republicans. Britain did not recognize American sailors' claims to citizenship, holding that no one could renounce one's status as a subject to the crown. Federalists like Alexander Hamilton held that commercial and diplomatic ties with Britain were essential to the future of the United States, while Republicans like Thomas Jefferson and James Madison believed that the cozy relationship Hamilton advocated for would relegate the United States to abject dependence upon Great Britain. Reflecting their belief that Britain depended on American imports and that that dependence could act as leverage against British impressment, Madison and Jefferson had come to favor measures that would raise tariff rates on the British. Since the Constitution did not specify any role for the House of Representatives in negotiating treaties, Hamilton saw a treaty as a way to preempt House Republicans' push for a tariff and maintain peace with Britain. George Washington, too, was convinced that a treaty could avoid war, and on April 16, 1794, he selected John Jay, chief justice of the Supreme Court, as envoy extraordinary to Britain, to negotiate a treaty. The controversy that would erupt over the treaty Jay negotiated would prove especially pivotal, not only because it pertained to a foreign policy issue at a time when foreign policy dominated national politics and not just because it would exacerbate and harden the divide between the Federalists and Republicans. It would also prove to be a litmus test for a critical question that citizens beyond the halls of government would play a pivotal role in answering: How much direct say would the American public have over actions that their government undertook in both domestic and foreign affairs?[1]

The actual treaty that Jay negotiated took almost an entire calendar year to reach the United States. By the estimation of recent scholars, it was about the best that the United States could have reasonably expected. The most severely restrictive article—imposing a seventy-ton limit on American cargo ships carrying goods to the British West Indies—ultimately did not pass the Senate. The treaty called for the relinquishment of military posts on the western frontier held by the British since the end of the Revolutionary War and established a five-person commission to determine the debts owed to British creditors by American debtors. It said nothing directly on the matter of impressment. Alexander Hamilton, who corresponded with both Jay and Washington and wrote recommendations that heavily influenced Edmund Randolph's written instructions to Jay, had his own misgivings about the treaty, but he penned a series of essays under the pseudonym Camillus in its defense. Hamilton argued that a commercial and diplomatic relationship with Britain was essential to the nation's future: the treaty, whatever shortcomings it might have, would keep the United States out of war. Hamilton's actions did nothing to move Jefferson and Madison from a belief, developed over the previous several years, that Hamilton served the interests of a "speculators," "tories," and other monied elites at the expense of ordinary citizens. For their part, Jefferson and Madison, along with other Republican leaders, were convinced that the decision to negotiate a treaty—where the executive and the Senate had the authority, and the influence of the House (where Republicans were strongest) was minimized—was purely a partisan ploy.[2]

Washington, too, had reservations about the treaty, but he ultimately agreed with Hamilton that the treaty would promote peace. He praised Hamilton's Camillus essays as a valuable counter to the public criticism he considered a threat to peace and national stability. Washington drew a distinction "between the friends, and foes of order, & good government," confiding to Hamilton that, "the latter are always working like bees, to distil their poison; whilst the former, depending, ofte[n] times *too much,* and *too long* upon the sense, and good dispositions of the people to work conviction, neglect the means of effecting it." After the Senate ratified the treaty, Washington refused to submit pertinent documents to the House of Representatives, claiming both the need for secrecy and that only the executive and the Senate possessed the constitutional authority to negotiate treaties. To John Adams, Washington reiterated his frustration with the treaty's critics. "As the ratification thereof, agreeably to the advice of the Senate, has passed from me," Washington grumbled in August 1795, "these meetings in opposition to the constituted authority, are as useless, as they are *at all times* improper and dangerous."[3]

The treaty's defenders were so concerned about opposition to it, in part, because that opposition was so undeniably strong and widespread. In early March 1795 news began to circulate that Jay had brokered a treaty with Great Britain and that Federalists in the administration and in the Senate were trying to keep its contents out of the public eye. Two Republican senators, Pierce Butler of South Carolina and Stevens Thompson Mason of Virginia, leaked the treaty to the press. The treaty "produced immediate public discussion" throughout the United States, a back-and-forth between the treaty's Federalist backers and a robust Republican opposition. "Town-meetings were quickly convened in Boston, Charlestown, New-York, this City, Baltimore, Wilmington, Charleston in South Carolina, and various other places," one Philadelphia commentator wrote. These town meetings varied in size from dozens to hundreds of participants, ranging from wealthy merchants to plebeian farmers and mechanics. Reports of the meetings often noted that attendees were "unanimous" or "almost unanimous" in their condemnation of the treaty, though some meetings also featured debates with treaty supporters, and newspapers also published statements of support that explicitly called such assurances of unanimous opposition overblown and misleading.[4]

Critics also published essays and open letters under a variety of pseudonyms. Pieces circulated in the country's two most widely circulated partisan newspapers, both located in Philadelphia, the country's seat of government: for the Federalist supporters of Washington's administration, it was the *Gazette of the United States*, edited by John Fenno; for the emerging Republican opposition, it was Benjamin Franklin Bache's *Aurora General Advertiser*. From there, these essays and letters were reprinted in other newspapers, especially in New York and Philadelphia. Their influence extended beyond those two cities, however. Newspapers all over the country printed commentary mentioning these pseudonymous critics by name, and in some cases printing essay-length rebuttals to their arguments. The back-and-forth between Federalists and Republicans in the press provides an excellent illustration of the importance of early newspapers as a forum for public political discourse and as a reflection of the political arguments that citizens outside the elite echelons of government encountered and expressed.[5]

To critics, the treaty was rife with glaring deficiencies. Not only did it fail to address the issue of impressment at all, it also appeared to place the United States in a position of economic dependence on Britain. Critics charged that the whole treaty appeared to cater disproportionately to Britain's needs while downplaying or entirely ignoring those of the United

States. "[T]his Compact professes to have no reference to the merits of the complaints, & pretensions of the contracting parties," a "Committee of Bostonians" decreed, "but in reality the complaints & pretensions of Great-Britain are fully provided for, while a part only of those of the United States have been brought into consideration." The treaty's favoritism to Britain was so blatant, critics charged, that it amounted to a betrayal of the country's commercial and diplomatic relationship with its old revolutionary ally, France ("that Gallant people," a group of Virginians from Fredericksburg called them, who shared with the American people "congenial sentiments of Liberty & Equality"), and perhaps a return to a state of colonial dependence on Britain.[6]

Given this, critics were shocked and dismayed when rumors circulated that Washington actually endorsed the treaty. For citizens, the president was supposed to pursue policies that reflected the interests of the nation; no other duty was more fundamental to his job. Some essays sought to ease readers' trepidation by assuring them that the president had not—and, some went so far to say, *would* not—sign the treaty, even after Washington had actually signed the treaty in mid-August. Discussion of the president's "signing" the treaty was so widespread that a New York essayist who was more sympathetic to the treaty complained that the whole "absurd" matter was concocted "merely to excite popular meetings to interfere with the constituted authorities."[7]

As such professions suggest, even in the midst of the treaty debate, public esteem for the president remained high. Thus, a strident critic of the treaty in late July 1795 remained stubbornly convinced that "our good old commander will never offer his name to any treaty, with any nation, that will in the least clip the wings of freedom," considering it simply unthinkable that Washington would pursue an action so blatantly antithetical to the nation's interests. And yet the debate over the treaty also revealed how different the was the political vision of the president and his Federalist allies from the treaty's critics; how readily critics imagined the presidency distinct from its illustrious first occupant; and how emphatically they rebutted the Federalists' condemnation of political dissent. Indeed, one of the sharpest arguments that treaty critics made was that Washington's brilliant luster actually blinded citizens to the dangers the treaty posed and cultivated a dangerous sense of deference to his actions that was antithetical to a healthy republican polity. "In vain has the constitution pointed out the duties and the powers of the servants of the people, if the citizens are debarred from investigating the omissions of absolute duties, and the abuse or usurpation of power," Portius wrote in September, one month after Washington had in fact endorsed the treaty. "If there be a country in which the influence of one man prevents or deters this investigation, that country is already enslaved. The name of Washington has too long had this effect, and those who call themselves free, have deserted the standard of principles and enlisted under the banners of a man."[8]

This argument, repeated over and over again during the treaty debate, owed important intellectual debts to both the dozens of Democratic-Republican societies that emerged beginning in 1793 and to Veritas. The controversy over the treaty provided fuel for this argument, and through it opponents articulated more than just a position on a matter of foreign policy. They advanced a thoroughly democratic vision of the relationship between elected leaders and citizens, placing the presidency at its center. Projecting onto the presidency an expansive and egalitarian definition of citizenship that differed markedly from the one advanced by Washington, his administration, and its Federalist supporters, treaty critics asserted that no one, not even a man as celebrated as Washington, should be above public criticism and that the health of the republic depended upon presidential accountability to constant, unrelenting scrutiny. The president had an obligation to act in the best interests of the nation, and the people had an obligation to voice their disapproval if he did not. This constant and potentially contentious back-and-forth between the people and the president was not a threat to national stability or government legitimacy, as Washington and the Federalists maintained. Rather, critics argued, it exemplified the dynamic public dialogue between the people and their elected leaders that was the lifeblood of a healthy republican body politic.

Crucially, this dialogue as treaty opponents envisioned it encompassed more than just elite citizens and political insiders. Many published essays addressed middling and even plebeian audiences, articulating concerns about the treaty that affected plebeian laborers and yeomen. The citizens of America were not just "merchants and traders," Hancock insisted. Indeed, the same "interests" that concerned these well-to-do members of society also "affect[ed] the farmer[,] the manufacturer, or the mechanic." What separated these free citizens from unfree subjects was the former's capacity to disagree with those in political power. In a despotism, disagreement was simply not an option.[9]

For these critics the treaty decision was a defining moment in the nation's early history. On this they stood in complete agreement with their Federalist adversaries, who initially strove to keep the treaty out of the public eye. Washington himself sought to keep the treaty a secret immediately after he received it during the first week of March and then refused to provide the House of Representatives with any documents its members requested when debating whether to fund it in the spring of 1796. Like other treaty allies, Washington had hoped to reduce public criticism of the treaty. No doubt many treaty opponents revered Washington the way Federalists wanted, but that veneration made Washington's actions appear all the more egregious when he signed the treaty in August 1795. Federalists continued to condemn criticism of the administration as inherently dangerous. Washington's actions on behalf of the treaty, and the Federalists' efforts to defend it, provided fuel for the charge that public veneration for the president had gone too far. Critics attacked Washington's actions as a betrayal of their confidence, arguing that his refusal to explain himself fully to the American people undermined the relationship between elected leaders and citizens upon which a republican government depended.[10]

The critics' reactions demonstrated that for them the debate was not just about the treaty. It was the most blatant example of a president who considered himself beyond public reproach, who expected the public to approve his actions without question—in short, a president who profoundly misunderstood his office's most fundamental role. In their criticism of the treaty negotiated by Jay, the dissenters advocated a remarkably cohesive, president-centered vision of republican nationhood, one that was more democratic than the Federalists', championing the constant critical voice of an informed and vigilant national citizenry, and identifying the president's accountability to that citizenry as the truest measure of the people's sovereign rule. The ubiquity and intensity of their criticism conveyed that this understanding of the presidency was the will of a growing portion of the country's population—that it was an undeniably national vision rooted in a widely held understanding of the relationship between presidential leadership, government authority, and the inalienable rights and civic obligations of citizens.

Public criticism ranged from peaceful meetings to public acts of vandalism and even assault. One critic's observation that the opposition to the treaty contained a "spirit" as well as an "order" "as great as ever appeared on any former interesting subject" captures both the reactionary violence and commitment to respectability that made up the different dimensions of that opposition. At the height of the public backlash against the treaty, in the summer of 1795, critics gathered to protest in cities from New England to South Carolina. Several cities, including New York and Philadelphia, modeled their meetings after Boston's, which included a voting process for "selectmen" to draft open letters to Washington explaining their reservations about the treaty—a testament to their commitment to order and representative government.[11]

The resolutions drafted at opposition meetings often presented objections in scathing but respectful language and frequently reiterated the critics' love of country and their confidence in the constituted authorities, especially the president. Critical appraisals of the treaty sometimes mentioned Hamilton's influence—what Atticus called "the *cat's paw* of Hamilton"—behind the scenes. Hamilton had resigned as treasury secretary in January 1793, but he remained integral to the administration. For all intents and purposes, Hamilton had written Jay's negotiation instructions and had crafted an article-by-article analysis of the treaty for Washington that would become the basis for his "Defence" essays. Essayists pointed to Hamilton to underscore what they considered to be dangerous executive influence over the legislative branch. But the focus of their attention was Washington, both because he headed the executive branch and because he commanded the "superstitious veneration" that critics considered so toxic to both the Jay Treaty debate and to the office of the presidency (and thus to the overall political well-being of the nation). It was through Washington that treaty supporters made the claim that those who dissented against the treaty were subversive partisans whose criticism could only weaken the government and the nation as a whole.[12]

Repeatedly, the essays directly challenged Federalist claims that a good American citizen was an obedient citizen. On the contrary, they argued, the opposite was true. "*Passive obedience and non resistance* are now the order of the day," Atticus declared, "and he who will not subscribe to the divine attributes of the President is excommunicated, and the dire interdict of anarchist, antifederalist and traitor is fulminated against him with all the fury which characterized the vatican of Hildebrand." On the contrary, treaty critics argued, the opposite was true. Unequivocal deference, Pittachus opined, was appropriate only for "slaves." A third writer, Belisarius, took that idea further in an open letter to Washington himself. "Believe me, sir, your fellow citizens are not moulds of wax, calculated to receive any impression which the *dicta* of a magistrate may attempt to make upon them; neither are they too timid to resist."[13]

Critics of the treaty held that a true citizen in a free society held leaders to account at all times and was even prepared to defy them if they abused the authority with which the people had entrusted them. That, they relentlessly insisted, was precisely what separated free and independent citizens from the mindless toadies that the Federalists insisted they become. "While the real friends of America have been branded with all the opprobrious epithets which malice could invent, the impenetrable shield of Presidential inviolability has been held up to cover their opponents from attack," Portius explained. "The name of Washington . . . was a protection to all who were happy enough to be leagued against the people." But "[t]imes are now changed, the people begin to see that you are not infallible, to perceive that you have erred, and to distrust the high sounding encomiums so often re-echoed by the pretended Federalists." The administration's expectation that the people not think, not speak, and not inquire about the actions of their government was so preposterous to critics that it was the subject of parody. "I say the treaty is a good one, Messrs. Printers, and all those are fools and Jacobins that do not say so," an essayist writing under the pseudonym Passive Obedience and Non-Resistance declared, pantomiming a Federalist sycophant. "I say so, not because I think so, for I do not think about it, and there is none but your Jacobins who think any thing respecting it. I say they are all Jacobins that presume to think any thing about this sublime instrument. For what did we choose the senate for, and send them to Philadelphia, but to think for us[?]"[14]

But the issue was no laughing matter. Condemning critical thinking and dissenting expression as unpatriotic and dangerous stripped the people of their rightful position "as the arbiters of their own fate," as yet another essayist, Valerius, put it. It made elected leaders the masters and the people their servants—precisely the opposite of the relationship that the Constitution was designed to promote. "Passive obedience and non-resistance, base-born souls, who would thus dare to prostitute the dignity of freemen! What!! because the President, *the first servant of the PEOPLE*, has done an act which concerns every man, woman, and child in the country, must all discussion cease—must every *pen* and every *press* be stopped? Forbid it heaven!" Hancock cried. "Must we submit and tamely surrender our *country*, our rights, liberties and our children without opposition; I trust not, the idea is too *insulting*, too *humiliating* for freemen." Instead, Valerius declared, "[l]et them [the people] consider that the President and the Senate are their servants." Relegating the people's agency merely to voting them in or out of office separated the people from the men they vested with authority, rendering the government less reflective of their shared interests. It was true that, "for the present," elected leaders "exercise certain de[1]egated powers," "yet these powers may be reclaimed by the people. Let them [the people] proclaim, to the dismay of ambition, the eternal truth, that, *salus populi suprema lex*, the safety of a people is the supreme law." The people's "birth-right to freedom" was under assault, and "we cannot be silent when our rights are invaded: Revering our constitutional fabric, we cannot slumber while it is falling in ruins around us: Glorying in our national honour as the best pledge of safety, we cannot think ourselves secure while it is tarnished by abject submissions." Dissenters insisted that their public assault on the Jay Treaty was a testament to the American people's commitment to liberty. It was not the threat to freedom that Federalists believed; on the contrary, it was freedom's only true guarantor.[15]

"ARE WE A REPUBLIC, AND IS THE PRESIDENT AN OFFICER DEPENDANT UPON THE PEOPLE?"

Critics focused their opposition on George Washington, discussing his role in the treaty controversy at length, and often addressing their remonstrances to him personally. Calling into question the constitutionality of the treaty, specific provisions contained within it, and Washington's judgment in sending Jay to negotiate it, opponents also took aim at Washington's presidential behavior. They focused on his justification for the treaty, condemning it as an insulting encapsulation of how out of step he was with the people's expectations. When the Boston selectmen published a statement to Washington respectfully describing their reservations about the treaty in mid-July 1795, Washington issued a response that became his stock answer to statements from groups around the country complaining about the treaty. "My system for the attainment of this object"—by which he meant "the happiness of my fellow-citizens"—"has uniformly been, to overlook all personal, local, and partial considerations; to contemplate the *United States* as one great whole." He assured the selectmen that he took every argument for or against the treaty into consideration. Nonetheless, he continued, "the Constitution is the guide which I never can abandon. It has assigned to the President the power of making treaties, with the advice and consent of the Senate." The president and the Senate alone "ought not to substitute for their own conviction the opinions of others, or to seek truth through any channel but that of a temperate and well informed investigation." "While I feel the most lively gratitude for the many instances of approbation from my country," Washington concluded, "I can no otherwise deserve it than by obeying the dictates of my conscience." Signing his response "with due respect," Washington no doubt genuinely believed that his message was an appropriately cordial but firm explanation of his actions. The *Columbian Centinel* obviously agreed. The staunchly Federalist Boston paper published Washington's reply to the Selectmen under the headline "Worthy to Be Written in Letters of Gold."[16]

To the treaty's opponents, however, Washington's words belittled the intelligence of ordinary Americans. It was indicative of a disturbingly regal aloofness that they argued had come to characterize Washington's presidential conduct. In his "answer to the Town-meeting at Boston," Belisarius scoffed in an open letter to Washington, the president "insinuat[ed], that under the impulse of sudden and erroneous impressions *they* had not consulted the substantial and permanent interests of their country, which, without regard to personal, local and partial considerations, had uniformly directed *your* system of administration." "Then declaring that *the constitution is the guide which you can never abandon*, you . . . conclude this paragraph of your answer, with another insinuation, that yourself and the Senate have sought the truth, through the channel only of a *temperate* and well-informed investigation." The president's statement that "[t]o the high responsibility, attached to it, I freely submit," Pittachus believed, amounted to "an evident *sneer* at the remedy which the people are said to have by the Constitution." "[T]o hold a language of such superlative pre-eminence neither indicated wisdom, prudence nor republicanism," Pittachus declared. "It was in fact saying I am your superior, your President, and I will do as I *will*, in defiance of you and your opinions!" Valerius went so far as to dub Washington "the royal brat, whose first articulations have been *Noli me tangere*" and who sought "to impose a specious scheme of reciprocity on the minds of the people" whose "concomitant language has been, while you treat me with majestic respect, I will treat you with distant politeness. The less we see of each other the better—While I command your awe and submission & am surrounded with a wall of impervious gold, you may riot in all the grovelling pleasures of the swinish multitude, undisturbed by my awe-inspiring presence."[17]

Such snobbishness, wholly inappropriate conduct for the president of the United States, critics found especially troubling because of Washington's centrality to the Jay treaty issue. The president was the treaty's "real father," Pittachus explained, even though Jay had negotiated it and the Senate advised and consented on the treaty. The senators were merely "his machines," approving of the measure out of an inability to resist the sheer weight of Washington's reputation. Washington's actions gave form and shape to the treaty, and Washington's decision in the future would determine its ultimate success or failure.[18]

The critics' commentary makes clear that they believed Washington's actions set powerful precedents for the presidency beyond the treaty's ultimate fate, which in turn would indelibly shape the lived reality of representative government in the young United States. The promotion of the

Jay treaty by Washington and the Federalists reflected values that above all were designed to elevate the presidency to a position beyond the people's direct reach. Opposing this vision, and establishing a precedent that promoted the democratic republic that the treaty's opponents championed—one that valued the political participation of citizens beyond voting and prized dissent from the views of government as both a civic right and a cornerstone of liberty—required a redefinition of the presidential office.

The critics held the president's essential duty to be intimately attuned to the majority of the citizenry, to recognize public criticism as a legitimate voice, and to work assiduously to facilitate their will into government action. They believed the president's representative role extended well beyond elections and well beyond belittling and insulting explanations for his action. The president was first and foremost an exemplar of their direct and constant control over the national government. Nothing less than the very legitimacy of the nation's claim to be a republic hinged on the president's fulfilling that role. "The revolution was certainly never designed to benefit the President alone," Pittachus declared, "and if he can exercise unconstitutional and unlawful powers, because he was the commander in chief of the American army, then the revolution was designed alone for his aggrandizement." Pittachus's comment echoed those of other critics: The people "never intended to establish a species or royalty in fact, tho' not in name, and put it in the power of *one man* to legislate for them by means of treaties," Atticus wrote. Such an arrangement contravened the basic principle of representative government, that "public men are public property," as Valerius stated. "They never cease to be responsible to the constituent authority. The hour in which they neglect the voice of the people, is the date of their infamy. The hour in which they declare a contempt of that voice, makes them as impotent as base." The point could not be overemphasized. "Are we a republic, and is the President an officer dependant upon the people?" Hancock asked. For the treaty's Republican opponents, the answer to the former question depended entirely upon the answer to the latter.[19]

The critics agreed with Washington and the administration that the president of the United States should act in accordance with the shared interests of the citizens. Indeed, citizens from Charlestown, Massachusetts, offering their objections to the treaty, echoed the sentiments of many other petitioners when they assured Washington that they were "fully persuaded, that every sentiment of your heart, with every action of your life, is directed toward the public good." But they disagreed that that obligation elevated the president above the voice of the people. In point of fact, the

president should be the "man of the people," the channel through which
the values expressed by disparate individuals coalesced into a singular national interest, the agent of voting and nonvoting citizens alike, responsible
for translating that interest into government action. "The People being
the legitimate Sovereign in our Government, they have the same right to a
knowledge of the affairs of state as a Monarch, and every restraint upon
this knowledge is an abridgement of their rights. . . . [T]heir Magistrates,
therefore, can only be their *Ministers*," a pseudonymous Philadelphia
democrat argued under the pen name Franklin. "[H]ow absurd then for
the Ministers to arrogate to themselves a privilege which the Sovereign
does not possess, or cannot be entrusted with. This is making the creature greater than the creator, and is an inversion of the natural order of
things." In reality, Valerius explained, the president's interests and the
people's interests "are the same, and there is not an honest member of
the Republic who does not pray to heaven that they may forever exist in
indissoluble union."[20]

Lest Washington or his allies interpret this as a call for unequivocal
presidential assent to the masses, Pittachus and Belisarius were more than
happy to clarify further. "If the people were in an error respecting the
Treaty it would have been but decorous in him to have endeavoured to
undeceive them," Pittachus explained. "It would have been no dishonor
to him to have attempted to convert them to his opinions." The people
were not insulted by Washington's attempt to explain his justification for
the treaty, Belisarius wrote. They objected to Washington's attempt, in
league with senate Federalists, to keep the treaty a secret, "positively ex-
clud[ing] every light of information, preclud[ing] every argument, which
could have been brought into view." Keeping the treaty from the people
made it impossible for Washington to live up to his assurance that his
decision was based upon "the best means of information" obtained by "a
well-informed investigation." The people wanted the president to be open
with the people, but they did not expect him to be a passive receptacle for
their opinions. They wanted him to engage openly with them and to lay
his evidence before them. If the people found it compelling, they would
support him. If they did not, their perspective would help him make a better decision on behalf of the nation. In order for a president to act in accordance with "the manifest sense of the great body of [his] constituents,"
the relationship between the incumbent and his citizens could not be one-
sided. It had to be a dynamic and transparent back-and-forth. In short, it
had to exemplify the ideal intimacy between citizens and elected leaders
at every level of government. As critics saw it, the presidency ought to set

the standard for democratic liberty to which all local, state, and national leaders and their constituents should aspire.[21]

Critics also had a very particular notion of who counted among "the people" whom the president served. The "people" critics envisioned as the true sovereigns were not merely elected officials or economic elites. They were "the Freemen of the United States," including also laborers in the cities and in the countryside who comprised the majority of the national populace. Some published accounts of meetings by treaty opponents stressed the "respectable" nature of the meetings. Highlighting the participation of "merchants, tradesmen, and other citizens," their goal was to counteract Federalist characterizations of treaty opposition as dangerous and mob-like by connecting it to the upper classes. But speeches, statements by pseudonymous essayists, and accounts of public action by everyday citizens make clear that opposition to the treaty extended well beyond those limits. Statements critical of the treaty often underscored how every citizen would feel the effect of the treaty's acceptance or rejection, from sailors on the high seas to frontier farmers and their families. The president's actions regarding the treaty, Hancock noted, were "well deserving the notice of the great bulk of the citizens of this country." Washington's "answer to the merchant and traders of this city is in a stile so different from that addressed to the people, that we should be tempted to believe the merchants and traders were the only people who had any claim of respect, who possessed any information and who had any rights among us." This, for Hancock, was a grave mistake. The president should never "measure men's information by their wealth," nor "estimate the respect due to them by the length of their purse," nor "determine on their rights by the quantum of bank stock, or six per cents they possess, that he thus introduces casts among citizens." For "[w]hat interests have merchants and traders in our government that are exclusive, and that do not affect the farmer[,] the manufacturer, or the mechanic?" It is important to notice that Hancock not only stressed the stakes of non-elites in the outcome of the treaty but also claimed that middling artisans and plebeian farmers had an equal right and obligation to take an active part in the public political conversation.[22]

Other critics shared Hancock's perspective and did not shy away from openly saying so. "The late Treaty agreed to by Mr. Jay, between the British nation and the United States, having the appellation of a Commercial treaty, may not be considered by the Agricultural interest, as a matter that immediately concerns them," a critic publishing under the pseudonym of A Republican conceded. But that view, the writer explained, was clearly mistaken. A profound "connection" existed "between the commercial and agricultural interest of this country; for if commerce is injured, it must inevitably operate on the agriculture; as the principal support of the produce of our lands, ultimately depends on the extension of navigation." For A Republican, article 6 of the treaty was especially troubling for "the Yeomanry of the United States," to whom the essay was addressed. Article 6 addressed debts owed to British creditors by Americans, dating back to the American Revolution. Citing legal "impediments" to collection, the treaty stipulated that the United States government would *"make* full and compleat compensation" to the British creditors, which A Republican predicted would only be possible through the imposition of a land tax that would fall disproportionately on farmers. "This is the clause, fellow citizens, to which at present I wish you to attend. In this article your interest is particularly concerned; for by it your Farms are mortgaged to discharge the debts due to British creditors, for *what ever reason* they have been prevented from '*receiving full and adequate compensation.*'" Farmers had to voice their objections to the president, who undoubtedly "wishes to know the minds of the citizens in general at so important a crisis." A Republican urged farmers to act swiftly, "as it may soon be too late, to remedy this evil."[23]

A New York essayist agreed. Farmers "throughout . . . this country" were known for their "enmity against the British government" due to Britain's "savage and active cruelties, during the last war, the hatred displayed to us during the peace, and their unparalleled depredations on our trade, since the commencement of their war with France." Indeed, "that part of the yeomanry who wish not to see the constitution infringed on, or the power of their respective States fritter'd down to that of small corporations, will universally oppose it." Washington, this writer was convinced, "never will give his sanction to an irrevocable act, which he has the most convincing proofs of the great body of his fellow citizens viewing with hatred, horror, and contempt." Another writer claimed that "[a]ll men" across "all ranks" in society found the treaty "universally unfavourable" and stood "united in condemning it." "Had a petition immediately been prepared to be presented to the President, against its ratification," the writer conjectured, 90 percent of merchants would have endorsed it, "and not a mechanic would have refused." "When the people with one voice condemned a measure, of which they are competent judges, it furnishes a violent presumption against the expediency of it."[24]

Highlighting the stakes of the middling and plebeian majority of the country in the treaty's outcome and claiming that non-elites were both entitled and obligated to voice their opinion were effective ways for critics to advance a far more thoroughly democratic vision of republican union and to contrast that vision with the Federalists' stratified, deferential model. Associating supporters of the treaty with elite "speculators," financiers, and British tories—echoing Veritas's indictment of Washington and the administration—the critics rejected Federalist expectations of public deference to the administration and instead stressed the necessity of mass engagement in national political discourse through public objection to the president's actions. An open letter "[t]o the enlightened Freemen of America" urged the author's "Fellow Citizens" to "Read, and Judge for yourselves.—Evil is intended you.—The revenue officers, stock holders, and office hunters of the union are combining to subjugate you to regal domination, and British despotism." Pittachus asked his readers, "Are the men of respectability the *speculators* of our country, who, like drones live upon the industry of others, but like hawks are constantly watching for prey[?]" Were "they *the knights of the funding system* who have grown fat upon the blood and sweat of the poor soldier, and are now thirsting for distinction which alone can not give?" Were "they *the broke*[rs] *and usurers* who have started u[p] like mushrooms under the hor[ri]d influence of a funding system, and like the devil are constantly running about seeking whom they can devour?" Perhaps they were "the *Royalists* of our country, who sicken at the sound of equality and republicanism, and sigh for the crown and sceptre." In any case, "[i]f such are the men of respectability, who are to weigh against the yeomanry, the mechanicks, the manufacturers, and the independent merchants[,] I would exclaim in the language of the litany, from men of respectability, good Lord deliver us!"[25]

Ordinary citizens answered the call. They participated in the town meetings that produced the published remonstrances against the treaty. They debated the treaty on street corners and in public houses. They accosted political and economic elites. They even engaged in violence, shattering windows, assaulting treaty supporters, and burning so many effigies of Jay that he reportedly remarked that they could light his path from one end of the country to the other. Rumors of mob violence circulated. Not all of them were always entirely accurate, but they reflected a capacity for violence that was very true for groups critical of the treaty—so much so that Federalists fretted about it in private correspondence and public statements. "I am sorry to perceive that Boston is in a very inflammatory state," Federalist congressman Fisher Ames wrote on July 9, 1795, from his home in Dedham, Massachusetts. "I was there two days ago, and I learnt that the Jacobins have been successful in prejudicing the multitude

against the treaty. . . . A town-meeting is expected, and if it should be convened, I expect its proceedings will be marked with folly and violence."
Bringing up popular acts of violence by treaty critics was a way for Federalists to attack opponents as irrational and violent—and thus illegitimate.
But it was also a reflection of Federalist frustration with an opposition that
remained strong, and even appeared to be gaining ground in some places,
despite the best efforts of Federalist to argue on the treaty's behalf.[26]

For their part, critics often professed that meetings exemplified peaceful civility—a reaction to the Federalists' widespread condemnation of
the opposition as unruly and anarchic. "[T]he People . . . have shewn
themselves worthy of freedom by the calm dignity of their opposition,"
Valerius asserted. It might be tempting to view the incongruity between
prominent and well-connected Republicans, who authored many of
the most influential and well-circulated essays condemning the treaty,
and who stressed critics' commitment to "order" and decorum, with
everyday citizens' capacity for violence, as evidence of a disconnect between opposition writers and people in the streets. Yet ordered and violent approaches could blend together. One midsummer account of "the
proceedings of the town-meeting" in Philadelphia demonstrates treaty
opponents' capacity for both ordered political debate and out-and-out
mayhem. "[T]he committee appointed to bring forward resolutions
were, perhaps, as respectable as ever appeared on any public occasion,"
the account began. "The business was settled with the greatest harmony,
and without a dissenting voice in both meetings." Upon concluding their
meeting, the account continued, this "respectable" group of dissenters
marched to the front doors of two British officials, George Hammond
and Phineas Bond, and a well-to-do American merchant, William Bingham, and "proceeded to acts of violence" against each man's home, "by
breaking Hammond's windows, burning the treaty before Bingham's
door, and stoning him, as he rode in his carriage, with P. Bond." Such
incidents offer a reminder that though the authors of antitreaty essays
appealed to the masses, they could not entirely control how the masses
expressed their objections to the treaty. Criticism of the treaty included
violent protest as well as peaceful petitions—and critics could profess
peaceful, "harmonious" intent even as they committed acts of vandalism
and assault—whether the Federalists liked it, or Republicans like Valerius cared to admit it.[27]

But though their approaches varied, the critics' message was remarkably
consistent, whether made by the well-educated and politically connected
or by middling and plebeian citizens, with ink and paper or with bricks,

fists, and fire: The president's essential job was to exemplify a political system in which the government engaged with the people, all of them, all of the time. Statements from yeomen and farmers repeated arguments about wealthy elites manipulating the government according to their whim at the expense of the people's will. "We, yeomen, do not feast our imaginations with golden prospects arising from importations of British pedlars, or their trumpery," a piece published in the *Aurora* declared. "No—We would prefer the home spun garb of simple independence, made and worn under the virtuous patronage of civil liberty and genuine republicanism to the most pompous parade of wealth, gained by commercial treaties and influence, that tend to wound the cause of freedom, either at home or abroad." Replicating the antifinance language of Valerius, Pittachus, and others, the yeomen demonstrated their understanding of Republican partisanship and their agreement with its basic tenets, while adding their voices to the chorus of criticism. Plebeian Americans were among the "very numerous" gatherings of citizens around the country, participating in assemblies and rallies alongside merchants, lawyers, political leaders, and other members of the upper crust who argued that the treaty was bad for the nation and that nothing less than the future of popular sovereignty itself hinged on the president's obligation to listen to the voice of the people. These public gatherings also stressed how critical it was for citizens to voice their assessment of the treaty to the president. Frequently these gatherings included a diversity of opinions, resulting in shouting matches, underhanded tactics, and scuffles. In one such encounter, Federalist elites, led by Alexander Hamilton, tried to engage with treaty critics at a meeting that, according to one account, was "every moment more tumultuous and noisy." Some critics threw stones, one of which struck Hamilton in the forehead, while another hit one of Hamilton's comrades standing beside him. Despite the blending of peaceful and violent tactics, a common message united the treaty's elite, middling, and plebeian critics.[28]

Contrary to what Washington and the Federalists insisted, the critics maintained that they were motivated by a desire to preserve the government, not destroy it, and they believed that informing the president about their objections was the way to correct what they viewed as an essential perversion of government power stemming from a dangerously expansive exercise of executive authority. They would maintain order, if orderly petitions alone sufficed to get Washington to follow their lead and reject the treaty according to their expressly stated wishes. But if the president demonstrated that he had turned a deaf ear to the public voice, a little disorder might be necessary for the people to reassert their dominion.

"[N]o man more fervently wishes than I do, to see the citizens of the United States unanimous in their obedience to the laws of the land," a New York essayist concluded, adding the all-important qualifier "as long as those laws are founded on the immutable principles of justice, good faith, and national honor." If raising a little hell was necessary for the people to be heard, then so be it. Shattered windows, bruised foreheads, and burning effigies were well worth it if they compelled Washington to fulfill his duty to act in accordance with the people's clearly expressed wishes.[29]

When that did not happen—when Washington's responses to the critics conveyed a clear intent to endorse the treaty over their objections—the critics howled at the dire consequences of the president's decision. For all its disturbing particulars, the treaty's fundamental problem was that it aligned "the President and Senate supported by Great Britain, on one side, against the Representatives of the people, their constituents, & the constitution of the U[nited] States, on the other side."[30] Crafting the treaty on constitutionally questionable grounds and ignoring—or outright condemning—the mass of citizens who objected only further confirmed the critics' suspicion that Washington sought to use his immense national influence to replace the country's representative system with a regal government, controlled by a king-like president and a courtly Senate. Jay's appointment and the treaty that followed from it was "bottomed upon *deception*, obscured by a dereliction of the cause of an honorable ally, and at war with the wishes and the sentiments of the Freemen of the United States," Franklin lamented, and thus "could beget no confidence."[31]

Critics promised that the president's action with regard to the treaty would send a clear and unmistakable message about the true power of the people's voice in the new republic. Given that so many were against the treaty and so many were exercising their right and obligation to speak out against it, for the president to ignore this voice and endorse the treaty would mean nothing less than that "the term, *Majesty of the People*, was, like the children's rattle, used merely to keep them from murmuring and complaining," explained the same New York critic, who assured readers that Washington would never sign his name to the treaty when so many viewed it "with hatred, horror, and contempt." By contrast, if the president heeded their voice, it would be a clear testament that "in this land of Liberty," the majesty of the people "had an absolute and real existence, calculated for much more important purposes."[32]

The treaty controversy was a microcosm of this larger point. Because the president's actions reflected the national citizenry's direct influence over the general government, it was imperative that the president be accountable at all times to public sanction and censure. Like other critics, Franklin believed that public confidence in the president was the key to the people's confidence in the system of government as a whole. But that confidence could not come from an expectation of abject obedience. In Britain, Franklin explained, "the King is considered infallible, and here, the President is deemed incapable of error, and to question the purity of the administration of either, is productive of the same calumnies." The point in both cases was "[t]o stifle free enquiry." Yet only by resisting such invectives and insisting upon public accountability could the country regain "the unbounded confidence which was *once* reposed in the present Chief Magistrate of the Union." To regain public control over the presidency and thus restore confidence in the system of government, the president had to be a responsible citizen who embraced such scrutiny as an essential part of the job, not as a bothersome impediment to his ability to govern. "But . . . we can never under our *present* constitution have a President, who has not been, or who is not, a citizen," Valerius wrote in his sixth essay, good citizens being "the best sureties for democratic virtue." This was why it was imperative that "our President, as a citizen, be upright and enlightened. For though many good citizens would make bad Presidents, yet no good President can be a bad citizen."[33]

The president's accountability to the populace was the hallmark of political importance. Contrary to what the Federalists believed, the critics maintained that this public accountability actually increased the prestige of the office—and by extension the government. The power of the people's presidency can be seen in Pittachus's call for Washington's impeachment. It was not because any real chance of impeaching the president existed, Pittachus acknowledged, because the senators were "his machines," and their actions were as "criminal" as his. Nonetheless, "there are important purposes to be gained by even a vote of impeachment." Pittachus's elaboration on those purposes is worth quoting at length:

> It would convince the world that we are free and that we are determined to remain so. It would be a solemn and awful lesson to future Presidents: it would exact a scrupulous administration in future of the Constitution; it would give confidence to the people in the government; it would exact a respect for the laws, and it would impress the strongest conviction of the virtue of our representatives and the justice of our country .—Lessons like these would not be useless; for when even a *Washington* would not be permitted to sport with our

rights, and trifle with things sacred, we might calculate upon trans-
mitting our inheritance to posterity, and insure a secure asylum to
the persecuted patriots of the other hemisphere, who would not look
here in vain for liberty.[34]

It is worth stressing that this criticism of Washington—like other statements of dissent against Washington and the treaty—was grounded on a
set of expectations of presidential conduct that represented an affirmative
vision of the presidential office. It is also worth emphasizing how cohesive
was the dissenters' vision for the presidency and how radically it diverged
from the major elements of the administration's approach to presidential leadership. The critics agreed that the presidency set the tone for the
people's relationship to the government, but there the agreement ended.
The obedient, compliant citizenry; the aloof executive; the insistence that
direct public civic engagement began and ended with voting in elections—
all of this the treaty's critics summarily rejected. They also defied the Federalist belief—articulated even before the treaty was published—that too
much democratic influence would dilute the significance of the presidency
and thus corrode the strength of the union. Critics countered that the
American people were not the complaisant, deferential servants that Federalists insisted they should be. Instead, they were a dynamic, engaged
people, united by a jealousy of their liberties and an uncompromising belief that they ruled over the government, not the other way around. Their
engagement with, and even criticism of, the president did not diminish
the power of the presidency or compromise the young country's political health. On the contrary, public criticism of the president *strengthened*
the republic by establishing a level of constant public accountability and
demonstrating that this accountability applied to all elected officials. By
insisting that such robust criticism of the president was a necessary prerequisite to a truly strong and lasting union, the critics simultaneously
separated Washington from the office he currently occupied and drew a
direct link between the presidential office and the republican character of
American society.

John Beckley, clerk of the House of Representatives and Thomas Jefferson's political ally, illustrated both elements in a series of essays under the
pseudonym A Calm Observer. Beckley's pieces were primarily focused on
Washington's finances as president. Washington had declared he would
not take a salary, yet Beckley argued that Washington, with the aid of his
former and current treasury secretaries, Alexander Hamilton and Oliver
Wolcott, had accepted government loans for expenses beyond what his

salary would have been, in effect stealing government money with the help of his own advisors. Beckley hammered home the egregiousness of the action by highlighting the "precedent" it potentially set for "other public officers"—the same basic theme that treaty critics emphasized. "[H]ow many hundred thousand dollars per annum would thus be lawlessly taken from the public treasury and saddled upon the people?" Beckley's Calm Observer wondered. Yes, Wolcott and Hamilton were certainly complicit, as it was their duty "to have checked and restrained the abuse of power." But "[i]s there any other man in the government of the United States" besides Washington " . . . to whom [Wolcott and Hamilton] would have presumed to grant the like favour?" Washington's actions, Beckley claimed, would reverberate well beyond his time in office and could potentially shake the public's "respect for the constituted authorities of their country"—in effect, turning the Federalists' most familiar talking point against them. After wondering "[w]hat will posterity say to the man who has acted in the manner I have stated," Beckley quoted from Washington's own vow not to accept a salary, and then seemed to answer his own question: "Will not the world be led to conclude that the mark of political hypocrisy has been alike worn by a CESAR, *a* CROMWELL *and a* WASHINGTON?" Like public pieces focusing on the Jay Treaty, Beckley's Calm Observer pieces argued that Washington's own actions as president had made him unworthy to hold an office of uniquely vital public trust.[35]

If anything, critics argued, it was the Federalists and Washington who failed to understand the full extent of the presidency's political significance. The American people deserved a president who embraced above all "the voice and the interest of his country," Atticus insisted, a president who exemplified their sovereignty over the government, and the informed and even potentially critical political engagement that ensured it would always remain theirs. The people deserved a president "who," in Valerius's flowing phrase, "should in all things think and feel with the people, whose mind should be the focus of the wills of converging millions."[36]

The best testament to critics' lasting impact on presidential politics lay in the Federalists' reaction to it. Fisher Ames, in a speech before his House colleagues urging Congress to fund the treaty, suggested that Republicans were pandering to the emotions of the masses in order to sabotage a treaty whose imperfections paled in comparison to the benefits it afforded. "If we listen to the clamor of party intemperance, the evils are of a number not to be counted, and of a nature not to be borne, even in idea. The language of passion and exaggeration may silence that of sober reason in other places, it has not done it here," Ames assured his audience. "The Treaty must appear to be bad. . . . And . . . this ought to be ascertained by the decided and general concurrence of the enlightened public."[37]

Ironically, Ames himself played upon the emotions of his audience, making the most of an illness that left him visibly pale as "a mere ghost" to maximize the emotional drama of his speech, and invoking the violence on the frontier by "savage" Indians—the result of the British abandoning the western military posts if the treaty were rejected, leaving white American settlers defenseless from the inevitable slaughter. "Will the tendency to Indian hostilities be contested by any one? Experience gives the answer. The frontiers were scourged with war till the negotiation with Britain was far advanced, and then the state of hostility ceased." Ames continued.

> If any . . . should maintain that the peace with the Indians will be stable without the posts, to them . . . I will appeal directly to the hearts of those who hear me . . . I resort especially to the convictions of the Western gentlemen, whether, supposing no posts and no treaty, the settlers will remain in security? Can they take it upon them to say that an Indian peace, under these circumstances, will prove firm? No, sir, it will not be peace, but a sword; it will be no better than a lure to draw victims within the reach of the tomahawk.[38]

The image of hostile Indians charging innocent white settlers, tomahawks raised to the sky, conveyed a powerful and unmistakable message about who posed a threat to the country. Ames knew it, and he pressed the image further.

> On this theme, my emotions are unutterable. If I could find words for them . . . I would swell my voice to such a note of remonstrance it should reach every log-house beyond the mountains. I would say to the inhabitants, Wake from your false security! Your cruel dangers—your more cruel apprehensions—are soon to be renewed; the wounds, yet unhealed, are to be torn open again. In the day time, your path through the woods will be ambushed; the darkness of midnight will glitter with the blaze of your dwellings. You are a father: the blood of your sons shall fatten your corn-field! You are a mother: the war-whoop shall wake the sleep of the cradle![39]

Ames effectively linked support for the president's agenda to a racially grounded national identity. Republican protests against the Jay treaty were not just belligerent and uncouth; they portended a potentially irreversible decline into savagery. Ames's speech was widely disseminated and discussed practically from the moment Ames stopped talking, drawing effusive praise from Federalists, and even grudging admission from Republicans that his speech, especially his dramatic depiction of white women and children butchered on the frontier, had made opposition to the treaty no longer possible. The House would vote narrowly in favor of the treaty, and though Ames's speech was not solely responsible for treaty support, observers admitted that his dramatic flourishes had changed the minds of key congressmen. Ames's approach anticipated a tactic that Federalists, pushed back on their heels by Republican dissenters' insistence on a publicly accountable president, would wield even more forcefully after Washington announced his retirement in the fall of 1796, commencing the first contested presidential election in United States history. As Thomas Jefferson emerged as the leading Republican contender to succeed Washington, Federalists would make the white supremacist and nativist foundation of their vision of American nationhood more explicit than ever before. Ridiculing Jefferson as an effeminate coward, Federalists argued that a firm nation depended on a firm president: a man who understood the "character" of the American people and who possessed the courage and moral commitment to resist infiltration by foreign enemies, nonwhites, and radical partisans. Neither the presidency, nor national politics, would ever be the same.[40]

4

Jefferson's "Want of Firmness"

BY 1796, GEORGE WASHINGTON's limited patience with his critics had run out. Referring to Benjamin Franklin Bache's radical Republican newspaper, the *Aurora*, Washington confided to David Humphreys in June that "the Gazettes . . . will give you a pretty good idea of the state of Politics, and Parties in this country;—and will shew you, at the same time (if Bache's Aurora is among them) in what manner I am attacked for persevering, steadily, in measures which, to me, appear necessary to preserve us (during the conflicts of the Belligerent powers) in a state of tranquility." Washington vowed that "these attacks, unjust, and as unpleasant as they are, will occasion no change in my conduct,—nor will they produce any other effect in my mind than to increase the solicitude which, long since, has taken fast hold of my breast, to enjoy." For Washington, the point could not be overemphasized. "Malignity, therefore, may dart its shaft, but no earthly power can deprive me of the consolation of *knowing* that I have not, in the whole course of my Administration (however numerous they may have been) committed an *intentional* error." For the first president, as for his Federalist supporters, all that public criticism of his leadership could ever be was a baseless attack by self-interested partisans on his honest and consistent attempts to do his presidential duty.[1]

Yet despite this resolve, Washington did decide to retire from the presidency that year, commencing the first truly contested presidential election in American history.[2] The standard story, told then and often now as well, is that Washington's decision to retire was further proof that he was immune to corruption from power. But Washington had also grown sick of the partisanship that surrounded him, and he never let go of his conviction that public criticism undermined public faith in the government, and thus threatened the peace, prosperity, and unity of the nation. Washington would continue to act as a reference for Americans as they chose their next president, but his departure meant that the Federalists had to communicate the significance of presidential leadership to the populace in the absence of Washington's illustrious example.

Republican dissent had not dissipated, despite Federalist attempts to discredit the dissenters as an inherent danger to the country, and in fact Thomas Jefferson emerged as a leading contender to succeed Washington. The Republicans' insistence that the president stand accountable to the populace struck directly at Federalist insistence on public deference for elected leaders, from the president on down. To Federalist commentators during the election, Jefferson's own political career, views, and even private conduct made him the face of a dangerous democratic faction that belied everything America stood for. To them, a Jefferson presidency portended a cataclysmic and potentially irreversible national slide into anarchy, as dangerous "foreign" (particularly French) ideas and people infiltrated the nation, and nonwhites clamored for the rights and liberties reserved for whites. During the presidential contest of 1796, Federalists made more explicit than ever their own national vision, rooted in a fundamental relationship between the presidential office that Washington would no longer occupy and an American populace who shared a common "character" that distinguished them as one people.

Federalists accused Jefferson of a "want of firmness," claiming that he lacked a key characteristic of presidential leadership that they asserted was vital to maintaining a strong national union. By focusing on "firmness"—a gendered and racialized trait that could be applied to individuals as well as groups, to elite leaders as well as ordinary citizens alike—Federalists not only launched an attack against Jefferson's personal courage and capacity for paternal leadership in the mold of Washington, they also made a claim about the presidential office, apart from any single candidate. A man worthy of the presidency had to understand the collective "character" of the American people—the unwavering resolve, the "firmness" to defend themselves and their liberties from any internal and external threat that sought to impose itself upon them—and he himself had to possess the fortitude, the resolve, the "firmness" to ensure the perpetuation of that character. By denying that Jefferson possessed the "firmness" for the presidency—and thus the "firmness" to maintain the nation against its enemies—Federalists, pushed by Republican dissenters, took Republicans' insistence on a direct link between the president and the people one step further. Not only must the president engage with the populace as their representative. He had to understand the essential liberty-loving courage and resolve that made them Americans, and exhibit that quality himself.[3]

FIRMNESS

For all their differences, most Americans in the late eighteenth century considered civilization to be about motion, across time and across terrain. To the extent that a concept of "American" held any tangible meaning, this movement, from one continent to another and then over a vast, untamed land, to settle it, subdue it, cultivate and thus improve it, was essential. It was a vision that excluded far more types of people than it embraced. Women had a role to play, but not as political or social equals. Native Americans were a separate people, vested with potential for civilization, but distinct from white Americans, dependent upon whites to learn to be truly civilized. Poor whites moved aimlessly, rather than with purpose, consuming far more than they cultivated. They were separated from blacks—considered the ultimate dependents—only by the color of their skin, which gave even poor whites a vested interest in maintaining a system that designated blacks as inherently inferior. Black people could never be Americans because in America freedom was reserved for whites—a freedom whose very definition depended upon the enslavement of black people. Benjamin Franklin preached this vision, Thomas Paine popularized it, and Thomas Jefferson and George Washington believed it.[4]

Yet this narrative of civilization-as-principled-movement relied on a crucial corollary of principled stasis. What distinguished intrepid, masculine, white Americans from Indian "savages," black slaves, and poor white dependents was not that they moved from place to place, but that they eventually stopped moving. They built homes, improved the land, and staked a permanent claim. They put down roots and resisted any encroachments upon land they had made their own. Being a man, being white, being civilized—being an American—meant to be courageous, decisive, and strong. In practice, that meant demonstrating one's mastery by imposing one's will onto land and people and one's independence by resisting encroachment from outside forces. In a word, it meant being firm.

In the eighteenth-century firmness referred to the ability of an object, an individual person, or a group to resist being acted upon by an outside, foreign force. It was a common term that suggested individual characteristics like hardness, bravery, fidelity, and devotion, as well as national qualities like unity and order. It could be invoked to refer to health (its opposite in this context was "infirmity," or sickness), constancy ("firm continuance"), resolve ("firm belief"), and cohesion ("the Unity of the Whole, and the firm Coherence of the Parts").[5]

So ubiquitous was its use, in fact, that it was used to define a wide array of other terms. Thomas Sheridan's dictionary in 1789 defined "firm" as "not easily pierced or shaken; constant, steady, resolute." A children's dictionary published in 1797, which gave no entry for "firmness," used the term to define other entries, providing clues to the broadness of its application. The dictionary defined "flabby" as "not firm," "indissoluble" as "binding forever; firm," and "indissolubleness" as "firmness, stableness."[6] The term's range of meaning made it useful for describing a variety of character traits held by one person, a group of people, or an entire society.

This range of meaning also associated firmness strongly with masculinity and with whiteness. More specifically, firmness was closely associated with a sense of independence that only American men—not foreigners, not cowards, and not nonwhites—were thought capable of achieving. This was what the Declaration of Independence implied when it lauded "the manly firmness" displayed by the state legislative assemblies in the United States in opposing the British king's "invasions on the rights of the people." Women were occasionally praised for their "firmness," but such approbation did not function as a challenge to gender norms. On the contrary, it reinforced them. Sometimes, such praise for feminine "firmness" was meant as a not-so-subtle dig at men who failed to exhibit such a manly trait—the point being the men's lack of firmness by comparison. Firmness could also function as a synonym for faithfulness or loyalty, thus underscoring women's roles as domestic helpers for men. Hence, a group of Southern men at a Fourth of July celebration in 1793 honored the "firmness," "resolution," and "patriotism" of the women in their midst, declaring that these traits "made an embellishment to their charms."[7]

So too did the occasional mention of a slave's "firmness" reinforce, rather than challenge, racialized assumptions of freedom and independence. As the slave Gabriel, the leader of a failed Virginia slave revolt in 1800, was being led to the gallows, a popular (and possibly apocryphal) account of his execution goes, he "lost all firmness," openly displaying "nothing but abject fear." Pointing out that Gabriel "lost all firmness" suggested that he had it to begin with, but it also revealed the tenuousness of his possession. The purpose of the story was to depict him as an "abject" slave, not a wrongly bound man deserving of freedom. Losing his firmness revealed Gabriel's inherent incapacity for freedom, thus proving the illegitimacy of his failed Virginia insurrection. Despite the occasional attributions of firmness to women and blacks, then, firmness was unequivocally—one might even say firmly—a white, masculine trait, reflecting the late eighteenth-century belief that true liberty was reserved for white men alone.[8] But, as these examples show, this did not mean that the firmness of a white man—or that of a group—could never be called into question. Quite the contrary. Any action a man took that might be deemed craven or weak, dishonest or merely inconsistent, could be held up as proof of that man's want of firmness.

WASHINGTON'S FAREWELL

Washington had been contemplating retirement since before he even became president. In fact, Washington's repeatedly stated longing for private life was integral to his image as a man who could be trusted with power precisely because he did not want it to begin with. Not that such professions were disingenuous posturing. Washington's words leave no doubt that he sincerely longed for retirement, and that he agreed to stay on as president as long as he did because he genuinely believed it was in the best interests of the country to do so. In 1792 he wrote a letter to James Madison, describing his intent to retire and even providing a sketch of the retirement address he wanted Madison to write. He wanted his retirement address written "in plain & modest terms," he told Madison, and it should emphasize how "honored" Washington was to hold the presidency, and how important it was for the entire system of government, and the unity of the nation, that he step down. He stressed to Madison that his address should emphasize a common American identity, fostered and maintained by citizens' shared commitment to peace and independence, borne out of the Revolution and their common support for the government. "[W]e are *all* the Children of the same country," Washington wrote to Madison, describing the points he wanted included in the address, in substance if not in precise wording. "That our interest, however diversified in local & smaller matters, is the same in all the great & essential concerns of the Nation . . . That the established government being the work of our own hands . . . may . . . bring it as near to perfection as any human institution ever approximated . . . That however necessary it may be to keep a watchful eye over public servants, & public measures, yet there ought to be limits to it; for suspicions unfounded, and jealousies too lively, are irritating to honest feelings; and oftentimes are productive of more evil than good."[9]

Washington would decide to stay on for another term, but when he did decide to retire in 1796, Madison saw to it that his address did, in fact, emphasize these points. The address, published in September 1796, stressed to readers throughout the country that they were all members of a single, cohesive nation, defined by their shared commitment to liberty, peace, and prosperity, unique among the people of the world—what the address referred to as a "Union & brotherly affection"—and that the strength of that union rested upon their willingness to trust and even obey the leaders they vested with power. The address only used the word "firmness" once—in reference to Washington's neutrality declaration in 1793—but the concept was all over the address. The address assured readers that the national bond was strong but threatened by both partisan dissenters at home and foreign forces abroad. The durability, the strength, the firmness of their "indissoluble community of Interest as *one Nation*" hinged upon their willingness to choose capable leaders to govern—and then to fall in line behind them.[10]

The American people's shared national "interest" had been forged in the "common cause" of the American Revolution, Washington's address explained; Americans had "fought & triumphed together" for it, and "the independence & liberty you possess" was the result of this collaboration. Now, the general government, "a Government for the whole," sustained that national bond, and its further perpetuation hinged upon choosing capable leaders to vest with authority, lending them support, and recognizing those who dissented from the government's authority as "designing men," whose arguments "tend to render Alien to each other those who ought to be bound together by fraternal affection." The people had to stand resolute against such forces, and that meant placing their unfailing confidence—meaning their obedience—in the people they vested with power. "The very idea of the power and the right of the People to establish Government presupposes the duty of every Individual to obey the established Government," Washington's address stated. "All obstructions to the execution of the Laws, all combinations and Associations, under whatever plausible character, with the real design to direct, controul, counteract, or awe the regular deliberation and action of the Constituted authorities are distructive [*sic*] of this fundamental principle and of fatal tendency.—They serve . . . to put in the place of the delegated will of the Nation, the will of a party." Obedience to the government was not weakness, but strength. In the face of dangerous dissensions that sought to inject a "spirit of innovation," and altering the government constantly in order to undermine it, a pledge to obey the government vested the government with the "vigor" it needed to act as the "surest Guardian" of common liberty. "It is indeed little else than a name, where the Government is too feeble to withstand the enterprise of faction, to confine each member of the Society within the limits prescribed by the laws & to maintain all in the secure & tranquil enjoyment of the rights of person & property."[11]

Though not written by Washington, the address captured how the outgoing president's nationalism related directly to his discomfort with political dissent. Published in newspapers across the country in September of 1796, it touched off the electoral contest of 1796. Not surprisingly, praise for Washington often highlighted the first president's "firmness" as a way of advancing the Federalists' favorite talking point: that Washington was the ideal "paternal" national leader, a father figure who stood as the protector of the citizenry beneath him.[12] "Had it not been for the firmness and prudence of this wonderful man," a Boston preacher told his congregation in a 1795 sermon, "long ere this by the artful machinations of foreign agents joined by domestic foes should we have been involved in European broils, and been obliged to lavish our blood and treasure, without any probable prospect of advantage to a single class of the community." The *Gazette* proudly reported "that sentiments similar to the above, adorned the prayers and sermons of almost all persuasions of Ministers on Thanksgiving day."[13] Washington's farewell address, which bestowed "good advice" on the public, had been "expressed in the language of firmness and paternal affection," another piece proclaimed.[14] Any successor could only hope to emulate "that wisdom and firmness which have hitherto adorned and supported [Washington's] official conduct," a group of Federalists from Winchester, Frederick County, Virginia, described the first president's virtues.[15] The New Jersey legislature voiced its "hope and expectation, that his successor in office, will be emulous to imitate his virtues, and pursue the wisdom and wholesome system of politics, which has . . . so effectually secured to us the inestimable blessings of Peace, and present unparalleled prosperity of our country."[16]

Crucially, though, praise for Washington's "firmness" also suggested that the contest of 1796 provided a chance for Americans to prove their collective firmness by choosing a worthy successor to Washington. As an article in the *Maryland Journal*, reprinted in the *Gazette of the United States*, explained, whoever followed Washington had to "pursue the thread of his views, give continuity to his system, and carry into practice those inestimable political precepts which he has sanctioned at his parting advice to his grateful country." The election of such a successor would not only do honor to Washington's legacy. It would also reflect the people's firmness in their commitment to an ordered, stable society. "In this country and under the constitution of the United States, it will be by no means a difficult thing to avoid this evil, if the people have discernment to comprehend the true principles of the government, and virtue enough to endure them in practice," the Maryland piece explained. "They will shew in their elections, whether they possess this penetration and firmness."[17] That claim was important, for it highlighted the significance of the contest and the importance of the presidential office in a way that simultaneously echoed and departed significantly from the standard Federalist Party line. Praise for Washington characterized his "firmness" as an essential personal character trait qualifying him to command the loyalty of the American people, but that was because it was a trait that he held in common with the American people. In supporting his leadership, they not only recognized his firmness but demonstrated their own. It was an early iteration of a formula that dominates national politics to this day: the president is not a patriot king, standing over the people, but the leading figure of American democracy. In personal and public word and deed, the president is expected to be the standard-bearer and living example of the values, beliefs, and traits—the "character"—that all Americans supposedly hold in common. That this is an impossible standard, predicated on a fiction of a uniform American "character," does not make it any less significant or powerful. In perhaps the greatest of all political ironies, the praise for Washington—and, during the contest of 1796, the condemnation of Jefferson—by Federalists, the party that favored elite governance and a deferential public, would begin to mold the presidency into the nation's most powerful symbol of democracy.[18]

Before the month was out, newspapers carried predictions that the choice would come down to Thomas Jefferson, Washington's former secretary of state, and Vice President John Adams.[19] Neither man participated directly in the campaign. The dictates of republican virtue forbade it. The prevailing eighteenth-century wisdom about political leadership, as demonstrated by public acclaim for Washington, was that only those who did not openly pursue power for selfish gain (who were "disinterested") were worthy to hold power. Modern-day political campaigns involving stump speeches, public debates between candidates, and open solicitation of voters for support fly directly in the face of this republican ideal of disinterested virtue. Of course, that did not stop candidates from attempting to influence voters. Dating back before the Revolution, candidates for office (including Washington himself) frequently held parties to woo voters with food and alcohol. Politicians also took advantage of their connections with printers and state and local political leaders, who could write and circulate essays lauding their qualities and lambasting those of their opponents while they themselves maintained their distance from such dirty political business. In the election of 1796, however, Jefferson and Adams remained about as legitimately removed from the campaign as they could be. Adams traveled to Quincy, Jefferson to Monticello, and there is little evidence to suggest that either maintained some sort of campaign command that controlled the public message their respective supporters produced.[20]

The campaigning was not limited merely to elites. Public interest in the contest is evident not only in the published electioneering materials but also in voter turnout in places where presidential electors were directly elected and in the political participation of citizens beyond the electorate. An estimated 40 percent of eligible voters participated in the vote for electors in the nation's capital city of Philadelphia. As far away as Georgia, over 18,000 Republicans cast votes for the state's four victorious electors. The Republican campaign also mobilized Philadelphia women and children, who could not vote. Public crowds on election day featured Jefferson supporters chanting "Jefferson, and no king." Newspapers around the country featured essays addressed to electors, attempting to sway their vote. Because neither Jefferson nor Adams participated directly, they could not dictate the tenor of electoral discourse. Elites who might prefer a deferential public nonetheless had to acknowledge the public's central role in the electoral debate and frame their particular arguments to convince this active, engaged American public. The election, then, was not reflective of merely the competing political philosophies of two presidential candidates, or even just their closest political allies. Rather, it was the invention of a larger American public made up of elite, middling, and plebeian sorts, women and men, young and old, all with a vested interest in selecting a firm president to succeed Washington.[21]

Commentary at the time did not fail to note the significance of the moment. The presidency was "the greatest office that can be conferred by a free people," as one essayist put it, and the results of the election would have far-reaching ramifications for every American.[22] "Little need be said to prove to you the importance of having that high office properly filled," but another commentator, Sidney, said it anyway in the New York *Argus*, a Republican newspaper. The president of the United States "has been the great pivot upon which our affairs have turned and no doubt whoever is placed in the presidential chair . . . will retain that pre-eminent importance which we have found attached to the Presidency under George Washington."[23] A Federalist writing in the *Gazette of the United States* under the pseudonym National Pride agreed completely with the election's momentous importance. "The approaching election for your Chief Magistrate, is the FIRST which has been a *contested* one under your present constitution—indeed, since your existence as an independent nation," National Pride pointed out, referring to the lack of competition for the presidency to that point due to the widespread knowledge in 1788 and 1792 that Washington would be the president. "How careful ought you to be to preserve its PURITY." The key to winning the election, Federalists concluded, would be to play off the significance of the office that even Republicans acknowledged and convince the public that the Republicans' standard-bearer, Thomas Jefferson, was unfit to be president.[24]

"SO HIGH AND IMPORTANT A STATION AS THAT OF CHIEF MAGISTRATE"

Federalists' attacks on Jefferson during the presidential contest condemned Jefferson as a cowardly, immoral, excessively intellectual, and dangerously egalitarian leader whose "want of firmness" would undermine the firmness of the American union should he win the presidency. Through attacking Jefferson's firmness, Federalists linked his presidency to national decline on every conceivable level. It was not just that Jefferson was unequal to the task of governing, although Federalists argued that too. It was not just that his leadership would practically serve as an open invitation to foreign belligerents and black slaves to take over the country, although Federalists were convinced that it would. It was also that Jefferson's cowardice and weakness would have a deleterious effect on the entire country, infecting the American citizenry with an infirmity from which it might never recover. It was through their attacks on Jefferson's want of firmness, even more than their praises of Adams, that Federalists made the point that the presidency set the tone for the nation's morality and values. Federalists insisted that the president, by his words and actions, exercised a unique and singular influence over not only what America did, but who Americans were.[25]

The Federalist assault focused on two specific moments in Jefferson's career as a government official. As governor of Virginia during the Revolution, Jefferson had retreated twice from the approach of British troops, once in Richmond in late 1780, and again six months later in his hometown of Charlottesville. This, and his decision to step down as secretary of state in 1793, demonstrated Jefferson's unfitness for the presidency. "I think it my duty to declare, that Mr. Jefferson's conduct, when governor of Virginia, in the year 1781, in abandoning the trust with which he was charged, at the moment of an invasion of the enemy," Virginia Federalist Charles Simms argued in a speech that would be reprinted, quoted, and cited throughout the contest, "and his retirement from the office of the secretary of state, at a time when the peace and tranquility of the United States appeared in extraordinary peril, are, in my opinion, strong objections against his appointment to the office of President of the United States." "These instances," Simms concluded, "shew him to want firmness."[26]

Federalists repeated Simms's accusation of Jefferson's cowardice throughout the campaign and for years to come. Indeed, the episode dogged Jefferson for the rest of his political life, providing fodder for political opponents looking to make him out as a weak leader whose inept ability predated even the nation's system of government. Federalists used the accusation to associate Jefferson with radical democracy, with partisan self-interest, even with blacks urging an abolition to slavery. Jefferson was not merely unfit for the presidency because he was a coward, Federalists insisted. He was unfit for the presidency because he and his party posed a threat to everything that made Americans a free and independent people. A Jefferson presidency would lead to a rapid and likely irreversible decline from Washington's firm, paternalistic example. Federalists were convinced that this decline would encompass more than just the nation's system of government; it would include the personal values, beliefs, customs, and "character" that united the nation and defined its people as Americans.[27]

Simms was the earliest author of the "want of firmness" charge, but he was not its most influential proponent in the contest. That distinction fell to William Loughton Smith, a British-educated South Carolina congressman and one of Alexander Hamilton's closest Southern political allies. A staunch Federalist, Smith maintained that radical democracy could never promote liberty; all it could do was undermine the authority of the learned gentry who alone possessed the wisdom to govern. By the time Washington's retirement announcement was public, Smith shared his colleagues' alarm that corrosive political criticism was everywhere and the Republican Party's influence in spreading it was growing seemingly by the moment. During the contest of 1796, Smith published a two-volume pamphlet, entitled *The Pretensions of Thomas Jefferson to the Presidency Examined; and the Charges Against John Adams Refuted. Addressed to the Citizens of America in General; and Particularly to the Electors of the President.* The pamphlet appeared in serial installments in the *Gazette of the United States*, under the pseudonym Phocion, after the Greek general and politician. Newspapers around the country, from the Portsmouth *New Hampshire Gazette* to the Charleston, South Carolina, *Columbian Herald*, reprinted the Phocion essays, and they became the foundational texts for the Federalists' public assault on Jefferson's presidential candidacy. In these essays Smith used Jefferson's inadequacies as a private citizen and political leader to describe the essential character of the American people and to connect a Jefferson victory to irrevocable national catastrophe. Attacking Jefferson's leadership abilities, Smith offered the most explicit definition of American national identity to date and projected that identity directly onto the presidential office.[28]

Smith's pamphlet was itself a response to a pro-Jefferson essayist, "Hampden," whose praise for Jefferson went beyond the realm of Jefferson's actions as an elected leader. Jefferson was a keen "philosopher"; a stalwart republican; "a friend to the civil and religious rights of mankind"; a supporter of the Constitution and the general government; a supporter of the French Revolution and, at the same time, of "the independency and self-government of America," a leader who would have addressed "the perfidious conduct of Britain toward us" in a way superior to the approach of the administration; a superior diplomat; and a keen scientific mind. These qualifications Smith took to be Jefferson's merits, not only according to Hampden, but according to those of his supporters more generally. From the outset, then, Smith's *Pretensions* envisioned Jefferson on political as well as moral and intellectual grounds. His was an attempt to grasp every component of Jefferson's "character" that was relevant to his supporters' claim that he was worthy to occupy the presidential office.[29]

Smith's analysis was not just an attack on Jefferson but an assault on the people who comprised the dissenting Republican Party and the principles they promoted. Like his fellow Federalists, Smith believed that social order could only be maintained through specific inequalities: men over women, white masters over enslaved and free blacks, wealthy statesmen over common citizens. Smith was convinced that the weak-willed Jefferson had become the leading apostle for radical equality, the standard-bearer for a democratic movement that threatened the essential inequalities of an ordered, stable, firm society.

Firmness was everywhere in Smith's pamphlet. To buttress his point, Smith approvingly quoted from Simms's accusation that Jefferson "wanted firmness" and reiterated Jefferson's retreat from British invasion in 1781 and his retirement from Washington's cabinet in 1794 as evidence of his cowardice, his inconsistency, in short, his inadequacy for presidential leadership.[30] He cited another Virginia Federalist, Leven Powell, who had argued that "when *Tarleton*, with a few light horse, pursued the assembly to Charlottesville"—referring to the attack in June 1781—"Mr. Jefferson discovered such a *want of firmness* as shewed he was *not fit to fill the first executive office*." He contrasted Jefferson's cowardice with Adams's "*firm and steady*" political leadership. Attacking Jefferson's personal religious views, Smith quoted Washington's characterization of religion and morality as "these great *pillars* of *human happiness,* these *firmest props* of the *duties of men and citizens*." He praised Washington's neutrality proclamation as "supported by *his* [Washington's] energy and *firmness,* and by the good sense of an enlightened nation," and explained why Jefferson's resignation in 1793 demonstrated a lack of "a firm and *virtuous independence* of character." The point was clear: any successful presidential successor to Washington had to possess at least some modicum of the firmness Washington demonstrated. Jefferson, for Smith, clearly did not measure up.[31]

For Smith firmness was an essential, personal presidential trait as much as it defined the fundamental character of American citizens. Smith considered a Jefferson presidency to be a threat to every element of this character, and his pamphlet's primary objective was to explain why. Jefferson had written a letter to the black scientist and writer Benjamin Banneker in 1791, striking what Smith considered to be a disturbingly cordial tone. Jefferson questioned the necessity of religious homogeneity to a stable society. He kept up correspondence with Thomas Paine and was influenced by Paine's and Revolutionary France's dangerous democratic radicals. These facts, Smith concluded, made Jefferson wholly unqualified for the job of president. Insinuating the catastrophic national collapse should Jefferson be elected, Smith attacked both Jefferson's private quirks and personality, as well as his public actions.

Addressing "the CITIZENS of AMERICA in general; and Particularly to the ELECTORS of the PRESIDENT," Smith's attack on Jefferson was designed to tap into a variety of ordinary Americans' fears and concerns, including their suspicion of men of lofty intellect—"philosophers," as Smith called them. Smith meant his attack on Jefferson to appeal to a deep suspicion of intellectuals shared by Americans across class and political lines around the country. Jefferson's intellectual personality was especially manifest in his personal conduct as a private citizen. Bookish, soft-spoken, and possessing a staggering range of intellectual curiosity about nearly every subject, Jefferson conducted scientific experiments and published academic papers; corresponded with intellectuals around the globe in multiple languages; and devised strange contraptions that filled his house (along with an eclectic range of items from around the world). Beginning in the early 1770s, Jefferson acquired mockingbirds for his home and grew so fond of them that he kept one, named Dick, during his presidency, letting it fly around the room, land on his shoulder, and eat food from his lips. Not all of these specific incidents had occurred or were well known in 1796, but they all spoke to Jefferson's quirky, contemplative personality. It was Jefferson's intellectual personality that Smith targeted in order to attack intellectuals in general, with Jefferson playing the role of the flaky, professorial foil for the common sense of regular Americans. Unlike the "Old-World" aversion to intellectuals voiced by the likes of Edmund Burke, who criticized attempts by artists and intellectuals to "break free of" the control of the nobility and aristocracy who funded their pursuits "and seek power and influence on their own," Smith, as historian Jeffrey L. Pasley argues, "simply sneer[ed] at the professors and eggheads" through his ridicule of Jefferson. "When William Loughton Smith attacked Jefferson as a 'professor' and a 'theorist,' he was tarring learning and intellect in general, in an effort to flatter the relative ignorance of the common people in just the way Burke had warned against, as one of the dangers of democracy." In so doing, "Smith had pioneered one of the most dangerous and damaging weapons in the arsenal of know-nothing demagoguery."[32]

For Smith, Jefferson's "philosophical" personality hamstrung his ability to act as a competent public official. The evidence, Smith suggested, was plain in Jefferson's endorsement of the French Revolution and of its most radical supporters, Thomas Paine. "If it can be shewn that he [Jefferson] has disapproved of the *cruelties* which have stained the French revolution, that he has reprobated, instead of countenancing, the *impious doctrines* of Thomas Paine, that he has been an advocate for *peace, order,* and submission to the laws, that he has never recommended in a public character, a profligate violation of public faith," Smith wrote, "in that case, his qualities as a good *moral* philosopher, would be valuable ingredients in the character of President of the United States." The problem from Smith's perspective, of course, was that Jefferson had done none of these things. In fact, he had done just the opposite: he endorsed the French Revolution, was one of Paine's most trusted confidants, and stood at the forefront of public criticism of the Washington administration. The people were better off without "philosophers" in power, Smith suggested, because philosophers made terrible executives. Men like Jefferson dawdled in theoretical pursuits while the job of the executive was to act with strength and conviction in the real world. Adrift in intellectual flights of fancy, philosophers lacked the fortitude, the firmness, to act in the people's interests when pressure mounted. For Smith, Jefferson's actions while governor of Virginia and secretary of state established a clear pattern of action that undermined public trust in the government. Without that public trust in the people's legitimate leaders, "stability" and "order" in society were impossible. In this way Smith linked Jefferson's personal cowardice to profound national decline at the hands of a dangerous, democratic "disorganizing spirit"—a spirit Jefferson himself had helped cultivate—that ran contrary to the nation's values.[33]

Smith saw evidence of this democratic "disorganizing spirit" everywhere he looked, including in Jefferson's private correspondence with a black intellectual. In Smith's view Jefferson's treatment of Benjamin Banneker suggested an ambivalence about racial hierarchy, and perhaps even an affirmative endorsement of racial equality, that threatened the racial stratification Smith considered an essential element of American nationhood. Smith took all of two pages before diving into his analysis of Jefferson's "confusion of ideas" about race. Jefferson's *Notes on the State of Virginia* had revealed him to be an ardent white supremacist, even if he was conflicted about the moral implications of slavery. Jefferson's "confusion," Smith posited, lay in a labored meditation on whether blacks were "a peculiar race of animals below *man* and above the *oran outang*," or fellow humans alongside whites. Interracial sex and racial "mixing" lay at the heart of Jefferson's analysis. Blacks possessed physically inferior traits that instantly distinguished them from whites, an arrangement that distinguished American slavery from the slavery practiced in ancient Rome. Black people's black skin rendered them less physically attractive, Jefferson had written in his *Notes*. They lacked the "flowing hair" and "more elegant symmetry" that whites possessed. They also possessed a more pungent bodily odor, because "they *secrete less by the kidnies* [sic] *and more by the glands of the skin*." Males "are *more ardent after their female*; their griefs are transient; in general their existence appears to participate more of *sensation* than reflection." Thus, emancipation of enslaved blacks could not simply consist of an end to slavery, as it had in Rome. "Among the Romans, emancipation required but one effort: the slave when made free might mix *without staining the blood of his master*," but the natural inferiority of black people in America required an additional, unprecedented step: they had to be "*removed beyond the reach of mixture*" with whites to prevent the degeneracy of the white race.[34]

Yet Smith thought Jefferson's letter to Banneker completely undermined Jefferson's own stated commitment to white supremacy. In his letter to Banneker, Jefferson noted his desire "to see such proofs as you exhibit, that nature has given to our black brethren, talents equal to those of the other colours of men, and that the appearance of a want of them is owing merely to the degraded condition of their existence both in Africa and America." Declaring Banneker's almanac, which Banneker had included in his correspondence to Jefferson, "a document to which your whole colour had a right for their justification against the doubts which have been entertained of them," Jefferson signed the letter "Your most obedt. humble servt." Smith declared the letter "a fraternizing epistle," disturbingly collegial in its tone toward its intended recipient. To drive the point home further, Smith referred to Banneker as Jefferson's "brother author" and "Brother Benjamin," appellations that conveyed the equality between Jefferson and Banneker that Jefferson's letter suggested to Smith. "What shall we think of a *secretary of state* thus *fraternizing* with negroes, writing them complimentary epistles, stiling them *his black brethren*, congratulating them on the evidences of their *genius*, and assuring them of his good wishes for their speedy emancipation[?]" Smith asked. The answer was obvious. Observers should think that a white man who sought, or even valued, the approval of blacks posed a threat to the racial hierarchy that reserved full membership in the American nation for whites alone.[35]

Jefferson's letter no doubt contained a performative aspect to it. Jefferson notoriously hated conflict, and Banneker's missive to Jefferson demanded that he explain the obvious contradiction between the words of equality and liberty contained in the Declaration of Independence and his own practice of slavery. Jefferson was caught in the contradiction that has made him such a fitting embodiment of America's essential hypocrisy. Recognizing that he was writing to a black man whose accomplishments so thoroughly disproved his own racist dismissal of black intelligence, Jefferson knew he could not possibly double down on what he wrote in his *Notes*, and so he chose a more amenable tone.

Nonetheless, Jefferson's letter to Banneker was a private matter, revealing Jefferson's personal struggles to reconcile his own white supremacist views with his awareness of its evil. "For if a slave can have a country in this world, it must be any other in preference to that in which he is born to live and labour for another: in which he must lock up the faculties of his nature, contribute as far as depends on his individual endeavours to the evanishment of the human race, or entail his own miserable condition on the endless generations proceeding from him," Jefferson wrote in his *Notes*. "And can the liberties of a nation be thought secure when we have removed their only firm basis, a conviction in the minds of the people that these liberties are of the gift of God? That they are not to be violated but with his wrath? Indeed I tremble for my country when I reflect that God is just: that his justice cannot sleep for ever."[36] Jefferson's letter to Banneker went well beyond annoying public theorizing on race. Instead, it was a private expression of hope for a more racially just world with an actual black man. It revealed a conflict in Jefferson's private mind on the morality of white supremacy which, for Smith, posed potentially irrevocable public harm if he were to win the presidency.

Through his characterization of Jefferson's letter to Banneker, Smith asserted that the stability and strength of the American nation rested on the ability of the president to reinforce the country's white identity. A Jefferson presidency, Smith warned, threatened the very fabric of social order by granting a sense of government sanction, and thus legitimacy, to equality in what Smith considered its most radical form. Most fundamentally, it portended a "fraternizing" between the races that could result in a mixed-race national political arena. In such a political future, slaveholders' claims to their human "property" would be crushed by a wave of active, public political engagement by nonwhites that possessed the sanction and the support of the general government. Jefferson had already said, "The rising race (in the United States) are *all* republicans." Jefferson was referring to a rising generation of *white* Americans, and his intention was to voice a confidence that this younger generation had no love of the "royalism" of the nation's colonial past. But Smith saw in Jefferson's language an ominous suggestion about what republicanism might become if he were to ascend to the presidential position. The idea of republicanism *itself* might become synonymous with racial equality, with the emancipation of slaves, and with the "mixing" of black civic engagement with government authority. "For my part, were I a southern planter, owning negroes," wrote Smith, himself the scion of Southern slave-traders, "I should be ten thousand times more alarmed at Mr. Jefferson's ardent wish for *emancipation*, than at any *fanciful* dangers from monarchy. *Emancipation* is a *possible* thing; but *apostasy* to *royalism*, according to Mr. Jefferson, is *impossible*."[37] By linking a Jefferson presidency with the possibility of racial equality, Smith made presidential firmness synonymous with the nation's racial identity. Insisting that the president of the United States had to reflect and preserve the young nation's status as a white nation, Smith claimed that white supremacy was a foundational element of American culture and that presidential leadership was essential to preserving it.

So, too, did Smith consider Jefferson's religious views a threat to the sanctity of religious authority in American society. The American nation, Smith believed without equivocation, was a Christian nation, and

Washington's presidential leadership was the essential tie that bound it together. Washington's "sublime" and "admirable" evocation of the essential role of religious morality in cultivating patriotic unity stood in marked contrast to Jefferson's act for establishing religious freedom in Virginia. This, too, was a public action, but it stemmed from Jefferson's own personal conviction that religious doctrine should not be the basis for a just society's laws. Moreover, Smith believed that decoupling morality from the Christian religion would have a deleterious effect on the private morality of all citizens. Society would degenerate into licentiousness and violence without stern moral guidance from religious leaders. The only tangible result of Jefferson's act was "an immediate *tendency* to produce a total disregard to *public worship*, an absolute indifference to *all religion whatever*."[38] Smith was incensed by Jefferson's belief, again stated in his *Notes*, that having a neighbor who was a pantheist, an atheist, or anything in between, did not harm him in the least. "What? do I receive no injury, as a member of society, if I am surrounded with atheists, with whom I can have no social intercourse[?]" Smith wondered. "[I]s this the man the *patriots* have cast their eyes on as a successor to the *virtuous Washington*, who, in his farewell address, so warmly and affectionately recommends to his fellow-citizens, the *cultivation of religion*[?]"[39]

In truth, Washington was not quite the devout Christian that Smith pictured. The first president attended church periodically (although not regularly) and himself had spoken of religious freedom for non-Christians. Historian Gary Scott Smith has characterized Washington as a "theistic rationalist," one whose theology blended "natural religion, Christianity, and rationalism," with rationalism trumping the other two. Theistic rationalists believed that God intervened in human life and that religion existed above all to cultivate morality. Notably, Gary Scott Smith considered Jefferson a theistic rationalist as well.[40] But to William Loughton Smith, Washington's leadership had been essential in cultivating "those religious and sacred ties, which restrain mankind from the perpetration of crimes." If Jefferson's acceptance of atheism and non-Christian religion were to supplant Washington's support for Christian morality—or, put another way, if Jefferson's want of firm moral leadership were to replace Washington's devout reverence for Christian obedience—those sacred "ties" would simply disintegrate and "civil society would soon degenerate into a wretched state of barbarism, and be stained with scenes of turpitude, and with every kind of atrocity."[41] As he had with racial inequality, Smith linked the moral foundation of the country—which he equated with Christianity—directly to Jefferson's personal conduct and argued that, if elected president, Jefferson's immorality would begin the slippery slope toward the breakdown of American society.

The leveling tendencies that Smith perceived in the nation's future under Jefferson's presidency, he viewed as a clear indication of "foreign" influence from France. Smith called the Republicans "Jacobins," a favorite Federalist invective for Republicans, linking them to the French Revolution's most radical, violent, and oppressive turn under Robespierre. Smith drew a direct link between Citizen Genet and Republican newspapers like the *Aurora* and the *National Gazette*, holding them collectively responsible for "the disorganizing spirit" that had "then prevailed" during the controversy over neutrality. In language brimming with national exceptionalism, Smith furthered his case against a Jefferson presidency by identifying the president of the United States as the primary agent responsible for ensuring the nation's autonomy from France. "The President of the United States ought to be an *enthusiastic* admirer of no cause, but that of *his own country, enthusiasm*, in a politician, is closely allied to *error* and *passion*, both of which are the *bane* of good government," Smith wrote. "[B]ut enthusiasm for a *foreign country* leads *directly* to subservience and devotion to *foreign interests*; a chief magistrate, *enthusiastically* attached to France, will therefore soon become a *devoted tool of France.*"[42]

By elaborating on the possible damage that a Jefferson presidency could do to American society as a whole, Smith suggested in vivid and ominous language the presidency's central role in defining national political culture in the present and in the future. For Smith, the presidency's impact radiated far beyond the government itself, amplifying its occupant's personal and political character—for better or for worse—and in turn shaping every facet of American cultural identity. This was why a Jefferson presidency would be potentially disastrous for the nation. A firm nation required firm presidential leadership, and Smith maintained that meant a president who embodied the essential "principles" and "character" that defined the American nation and its citizens. As Smith put it, "so high and important a station as that of Chief Magistrate" required "sound and correct principles of government, great purity and firmness of character, rectitude of views, and strong *national* attachments." The firmness of the president had to be worthy of the firmness of real Americans. Without it, the nation's independence from foreign influence and immorality would be compromised, perhaps irrevocably. An infirm president, "capricious and wavering, often warped by the most frivolous circumstances," "timid, inconsistent, and unsteady," with "political principles" that were "whimsical and visionary" or "subversive of all regular and *stable* government"—a president like Jefferson—would undermine the firmness of the nation and destroy the very fabric of republican national union. "[I]n short . . . his elevation to the Presidency" would result "in the *debasement* of the American name, by a whimsical, inconsistent, and feeble administration," and perhaps even "in the *prostration* of the United States," before radical anarchic influences, "the *subversion* of our excellent *Constitution*, and the consequent *destruction* of our present *prosperity*."[43]

Smith's accusation that Jefferson "wanted firmness" provided the basis for other Federalist commentaries on Jefferson, informing both their depiction of the nation's political moment and their critiques of Jefferson's fitness for the presidential office. In addition to the *Gazette*, individual Phocion essays were published in the Hartford, Connecticut, *American Mercury*; the Charleston, South Carolina, *Columbian Herald*; the New York *Minerva, & Mercantile Evening Advertiser*; and the country edition of the New York *Herald*. Essays responding to Phocion appeared in the *Gazette of the United States*; the Charleston, South Carolina, *City Gazette*; the New York *Argus; Greenleaf's New York Journal and Patriotic Register*; and the Portsmouth *New Hampshire Gazette*.[44] Like Smith, a Federalist writing under the pseudonym A Friend to the Union argued that Jefferson was unreliable and cowardly, a "Sun-shine patriot," willing to pay lip service to national devotion in peaceful times but lacking the fortitude to "stand at the Helm in a *Storm*, as Washington has always done," refusing to leave "his Post in the most Perilous Times."[45] The phrase "sunshine patriot" was a clear reference to Thomas Paine's first "Crisis" essay, published in 1776 ("These are the times that try men's souls. The summer soldier and the sun-shine patriot will, in this crisis, shrink from the service of his country: but he that stands it *now*, deserves the thanks of man and woman").[46] Quoting Paine, who by 1796 was a known sympathizer of the French Revolution as well as a known friend to Jefferson, hinted at Jefferson's status as a "Jacobin," while at the same time labeling Jefferson with the same disparaging term that Paine used to describe unpatriotic cowards. The point was to link effeminacy and cowardice to French influence and to present all three as threats to government-provided national strength and stability both from within and from without.[47]

Federalists echoed Smith's contention that the choice of Washington's successor would be the nation's ultimate litmus test, reflecting their current values and "character," and that the future president's character would determine who the American people became, as individuals and as a collective.[48] All true Americans were firm, but the nation could only be as firm as the president they chose. The result would either be a lasting nation of upright, moral, courageous citizens, or a sickly, fissiparous society of moral, racial, and national degenerates participating in a dangerously democratic free-for-all. For that reason, other Federalist commentaries, following Smith's lead, fixated more on attacking Jefferson than they did on promoting Adams. Their attacks insinuated that Jefferson, like other non-Americans, moved around too much, intellectually and politically, if not also physically. He meandered aimlessly from one ludicrous, half-baked idea to another. He changed political positions at the slightest hint of pressure. He questioned the moral basis of religion. He tucked tail and fled when threats loomed. In stark contrast to real Americans, who were so firmly committed to Christian morality, republican order, and white supremacy that they were prepared to take up arms in their defense, Jefferson flitted about, untethered and ungrounded.

Attacking Jefferson's deficiencies allowed writers to describe the nation they envisioned in vivid detail, heightening the drama with predictions of disastrous decline should Jefferson win the presidency. The Federalists' approach illustrated what has become a classic political smear tactic, and an articulation of nationalism, that thrives to this day. Jefferson could not lead the American people because he was everything real Americans were not: too intellectual, too cowardly, too amenable to black people, too indifferent to timeless Christian morality, too willing to bend whichever way the political wind blew—in short, too weak to stand firm against everything that threatened Americans.

That was why the next president could not be Jefferson. If Jefferson could not be trusted to stand his ground against an invading British force literally penetrating deeper into the Virginia countryside—"to act the man," as one pamphleteer writing under the pseudonym Aurelius colorfully put it—and if he had failed to stand firm "when *Genet* the French Minister, invaded the United States and made a furious Attack upon our Government with all the Artillery of disorganizing and anarchical Opinions, and endeavoured by Artifices and Threats to drag us into the European War," as A Friend to the Union stated, why should anyone believe he was the right man to preserve republican order in the midst of the "violent measures" exerted against the government by an unruly, partisan public? The nation was under attack from dangerous democratic impulses, just as it had faced assault from British soldiers during the American Revolution. Jefferson appeared not only ill-equipped to oppose these dangerous forces, Federalists argued, he actually appeared to side with them.[49]

For Federalists the relationship between the candidates' personal character and the future of what Aurelius called "American character" was all-important.[50] True national strength had to start with decisive, resolute presidential leadership. The president provided an example of moral, uncompromising character for other elected leaders to emulate and ordinary citizens to follow with pride and confidence. On this point some commentators did shift the focus to Adams. An Adams presidency, Americanus trumpeted, "will prove that a community may be perfectly free, and at the same time discreet, preferring certain good to every uncertainty whatever, averse from change however artfully recommended, superior to the vile calumnies of a daring faction, and paramount [to] the digested machinations of a foreign power."[51] The "principles" of a sound government "must be established and confirmed as the political creed of every friend of freedom," a piece in the *Gazette of the United States* explained. A vote for Adams was a vote for the firm commitment to those principles. It was a vote in favor of government itself and a promise that "those monsters, the jacobins . . . are not to erect a murderous revolutionary empire on the ruins of our laws and liberty."[52]

"AN EXAMPLE TO THE WHOLE WORLD OF AN EXTENSIVE NATION ACTING COLLECTIVELY"

Federalists' attacks on Jefferson's want of firmness were so pervasive that they actually forced Republicans to respond. John Beckley took up his pen, assuming the name A Subscriber, and went after Phocion directly, publishing a rebuttal to what he called the "shamefull mis-statements of the writer . . . under the signature of *Phocion*" and "his friend Charles Simms" in an essay published in the *Gazette of the United States*. Beckley provided an account of Jefferson's conduct while governor of Virginia, and "a full enquiry into" Jefferson's actions by the Virginia legislature, retorting that the legislature's conclusion had found in favor of Jefferson—a testament to "Mr. Jefferson's ability and integrity," that was, Beckley emphasized, *"altogether silent on the want of firmness."*[53]

Beckley thought Alexander Hamilton was Phocion and wrote to James Madison in mid-October that he did "not think" the first essay appearing in the *Gazette of the United States* "will produce any great public impression in this State [Pennsylvania], for which it is intended; whilst at the same time I consider it as an Evidence of fear on their [the Federalists'] part."[54] As time went on, Beckley's confidence waned. While the Republicans were "all busily engaged in the Election and are sanguine in our hopes of success for Jefferson," "[t]he other side are equally active and equally sanguine," he reported in early November to William Irvine. By mid-December, he confessed to Irvine: "After all our Exertions I fear Jefferson will fail altogether, and that Adams & [Charles Cotesworth] Pinckney will be, one of them president, the other Vice president."[55]

Though Beckley did not identify Simms's and Smith's attacks on Jefferson as the reason for his soured outlook on the election, it is clear that their accusation that Jefferson lacked firmness struck a nerve. Following Beckley's lead, Republican defenses of Jefferson—and their criticisms of Adams—remained focused on each man's public conduct while in office. Republicans were less willing to engage with Federalist insistence that the president's private character would have profound public consequences and instead sought to turn the Federalists' accusations of Jefferson to their advantage.

Federalist attacks had made the election of 1796 a referendum on Jefferson's Revolutionary credentials, an approach that Republicans countered by repeatedly bringing up the obvious point that Jefferson was the primary author of the Declaration of Independence. In 1776 Jefferson's authorship of the Declaration was not widely known, but twenty years later, knowledge that Jefferson had written it was far more widespread.[56] Republicans took advantage of this by invoking the document to defend Jefferson against the Federalists' accusations that he wanted firmness. "Did he display no firmness when he stood forth the ablest advocate of independence, of that bold measure which broke your chains, which rent asunder a vast empire, & which proclaimed in thunder to the whole world liberty and justice?" an essayist asked readers of the *New Jersey Journal*.[57] Another pro-Jefferson publication agreed. "While praise is due and freely given to Mr. Adams, for having seconded the motion for declaring the Independence of America; is it recollected, that this much admired composition almost entirely flowed from the pen of Mr. Jefferson!" The writer went on. "Is it recollected . . . that the instrument which declares the Independence of Virginia, and which preceded the declaration of Congress and of the other States, owes its existence to the same author!—It is surely the most unaccountable persuasion of reason to attribute firmness to Mr. Adams, because he seconded and voted for the Declaration of Independence; and to deny to Mr. Jefferson the possession of this manly quality, when Mr. Jefferson fabricated the instrument itself, and afterwards voted for it."[58]

Republicans were more than happy to make the election a contest over which man had done more on behalf of the Revolutionary cause. The Declaration of Independence stands without peer as a statement of America's

Revolutionary spirit, of course. But it also allowed Republicans to counter
Federalist attacks on Jefferson's personal courage by steering readers' focus back to Jefferson's public actions. They pointed to Jefferson's authorship of the Declaration of Independence as proof that he understood the
American people and the obligation of elected leaders to listen to and
follow the public voice and that he had devoted his public career in its
service. Everyone who signed the Declaration of Independence (Adams included) had risked everything—"our Lives, our Fortunes, and our Sacred
Honor," as the Declaration stated—by endorsing the American campaign.
But Jefferson had *written* it. What could be a greater testament to a man's
firm commitment to the people, Jefferson's supporters asked, than the act
of capturing and immortalizing the expression of an entire people's collective will to be free?

From here, another essayist expounded on the Republicans' favorite
hobbyhorse: the concept of popular sovereignty and elected leaders' accountability to the people. It was the people's collective "ability," "spirit,"
and "firmness to govern themselves without the interference of British
merchants, agents, and spies," this essayist argued in *Greenleaf's New-
York Journal*, not the power of would-be kings or aristocrats, that defined
the American nation. "What says our Federal Constitution?" another
commentator writing under the pen name Sidney queried. "It is founded
on the equal rights of the citizens; all are politically equal; all power ema-
nates from the people."[59]

Republican campaign strategy stayed the course that Washington's
critics had charted during his presidency, stressing each man's capacity
and willingness to listen to and act in accord with the will of the people.
Rather than engage with the Federalists' obsession with personal "character," much of the Republican rhetoric adhered to the more traditional
view that only an elected leader's public conduct was fair game for public
criticism. Most Republican campaign literature did not question Adams's
personal religious convictions, his private intellectual pursuits, or his particular commitment to white supremacy. Instead, they attacked Adams's
highly publicized words, especially his *Defence of the Constitutions*. Adams himself insisted his intention was to distinguish the unchecked furor
that had given birth to the French Revolution with a more stable—one
might say more firm—governing structure that balanced elements of aristocracy and monarchy against the anarchic inevitability of excess democracy. Republicans characterized the sprawling multivolume comparative
commentary on "democratical," "monarchical," and "aristocratical"
governments as essentially a monarchist manifesto. The *Defence* provided

an obvious contrast with the Declaration of Independence that cast Jefferson in an even more favorable light.[60]

Numerous pieces invoked the *Defence* by name, or quoted it at length, to condemn Adams. Sometimes a whole published newspaper essay consisted of quotes or paraphrases from the *Defence*, with a brief introductory paragraph urging readers to read Adams's words and judge for themselves.[61] "*Kingly* government best; Tyranny worst," Americanus, paraphrasing Adams, wrote in a piece appearing in the New York *Minerva*. "No city is more wretched than that under tyranny, nor any more happy than that under *regal* power." Americanus included a dozen such paraphrases from the *Defence*, complete with page numbers, highlighting Adams's candid statements about the inevitability of hierarchy in society and his endorsement of a powerful, independent, "regal" executive to balance the competing forces of the many and the few.[62]

A Republican writing under the name Juno expanded the criticism beyond Adams, suggesting that Adams's affinity for kingly government was indicative of an entire "Royalist" Federal Party whose members sought to stifle the rising tide of political dissent outside government. "[T]o direct the deliberations in the choice of an Executive Officer . . . is of no trifling nature, and of no less consequence than the salvation of your country, and the preservation of national liberty," Juno informed all "Patriots of America and Friends of True Constitutional Principles."

> To exalt a man to Executive eminence, who is so religiously devoted to the cause of monarchy, would be to confess a contrition for having permitted this great empire to be formed into a Republic. You cannot, as patriots attached to your country's cause, remain silent spectators and behold, without emotion, a groupe of *brazon* [sic] *fronted Royalists* fomenting sedition, and endeavoring, by artful means, to subvert the Republic, and totally annihilate the elective system, which is the immaculate basis of your Political Independence, and all your rights, liberties, and free suffrages. . . . If a love of your country will prove stimulous to your actions on the important day of election, we trust that your decision in the choice of President, will be the faithful criterion of your patriotism.[63]

Republican attacks on Adams continued the theme established during Washington's presidency and amplified during the Jay treaty controversy: a man worthy of the presidency did not stand apart from the people, commanding their unquestioned assent from above, but rather acted as a conduit for their collective sovereign will, especially against tyrannical forces demanding their silent assent.

For Republicans, Adams's political philosophy illustrated the difference between a leader's desire for power and his fitness to be trusted with it. Adams's preferred system of government was undoubtedly powerful—a stratified system that reflected the inevitable division between gentry and commoners, with a strong, independent executive above them both, balancing their interests. But it was designed to keep ordinary people at arm's length. Such a scheme, sold by Adams as more reliable, was actually a reflection of his discomfort with the idea that anyone but a select few should possess any authority to govern. This was not a formula for national strength or popular sovereignty. As Tench Coxe put it, Adams considered "the *hereditary union and descent of* landed estates, legislative and executive power and rank in the families of emperors, kings, and nobles" to be the sole source of mankind's "energy" and "dignity."[64]

Such arguments could lend themselves to more personal attacks, and for all their resolve to keep the focus on each man's public conduct, Republicans did sometimes stray into more personal territory. At times their comments echoed their Federalist counterparts' insistence that their target's elevation to the presidential office would amplify his personal deficiencies, leading to profound and possibly irrevocable national decline. Sidney argued in the *Argus*, a Republican newspaper in New York, that the "*Kings, Lords, and commons*" favored by Adams were "living monuments of pride, ambition, effeminacy and hypocrisy."[65] Affinity for monarchy and aristocracy, Republicans insisted, weakened everyone involved. Commoners were rendered "miserable and oppressed," A Plebeian pointed out, prostrated "in abject submission before the shrine of arbitrary power, and where millions of victims are slaughtered to gratify the capricious and foolish ambitions of an idiot and a sot."[66] The author of a pro-Jefferson pamphlet echoed that theme, describing Adams as not only "advanced [in] years," but plagued by "infirmities, which are evident to every discerning eye" and an "energy of mind" that was "much impaired." The consequences of choosing a man so philosophically, intellectually, and physically ill-equipped for the office's responsibilities would be dire: "The choice of one not possessing general confidence, of suspected honesty, or mental imbecility, will necessarily endanger the glorious fabric of Independence, in the rearing of which the blood of heroes has been drained!"[67]

This same pamphleteer agreed with Federalists that whom the people chose as their next president revealed as much about them as the man they chose. The selection of the president of the United States set "an example to the whole world of an extensive nation acting collectively, more from prudence than from passion or prejudice," the pamphleteer concluded. The president would be the focal point of an attentive and watchful citizenry that distinguished the American republic as an "immense globe of fire and light, which enlightens, warms and vivifies immensities of worlds" from monarchy and aristocracy's puny "opaque and dwindled star." As such, "the chief magistrate of this extensive republic, should possess courage, fortitude, equanimity and impartiality." But he was "the President of a free people"; his "fortitude" originated with them. In the presidency's capacity to reflect the public will lay the essence of the nation's "character."[68]

It was here, Republicans argued, that Jefferson revealed his greatest qualification for the presidency by his commitment to protecting his liberty and the liberty of others from the encroachments of tyrannical forces. Cosmopolitan and insatiably curious, Jefferson's "masterly correspondence with the French, British, and Spanish ministers are universally admired wherever they are read."[69] "No man can boast of a more profound knowledge of politics," the author of *President II* argued of Jefferson, "no man is better versed in governmental systems, or has a more complete knowledge of the causes which have transpired in aggrandizing or extinguishing states and empires."[70] As president, Jefferson could "conciliate the mass of the people of America more effectually to the general government," one Pittsburgh Jeffersonian wrote in a letter reprinted in the *Argus, Greenleaf's New Daily Advertiser*, "as they have an idea that he has a leaning towards Republican equality, and is opposed to aristocratic pride and destinction [sic]."[71] Jefferson "combines in himself every requisite qualification for the Presidency," the author of *President II* declared: "a consistent uniformity of conduct, firmness and intrepidity, with an unconquerable love of liberty." By electing Jefferson, the people "will give dignity and stability to the government, and effectually cement and fraternize every description of persons throughout this extensive country, and thus transmit our equal rights inviolate to the latest posterity."[72]

In early October 1796, Beckley reported to William Irvine that "many of [the Federalists] prefer [Charles Cotesworth] Pinckney to Adams, and there will be great Schism amongst them."[73] Two weeks later Beckley told James Monroe to "rest assured that Adams, if [Alexander] Hamilton can prevent it, without danger, is not designed as Ws [Washington's successor]," even though "Jefferson & Adams are the only candidates publicly held up for president," and "[Aaron] Burr & Pinckney for V.P." Beckley predicted that "it will be a very close election & that this State [Pennsylvania] must decide it."[74] The election was indeed close. Adams won, but only by three electoral votes, 71 to Thomas Jefferson's 68.

The election of 1796 had been bitter and divisive, but its significance lay in more than the insults each party had lobbed at their opponent's candidate. Far more significant was the direct line the Federalists drew between the personal "character" of whomever occupied the presidency and the "character" of the entire nation. In the election of 1796, Federalists argued that all true Americans were firm—moral, courageous, and committed to resisting racial equality and encroachments by dangerous foreign influences—and that the fate of the nation hinged on the election of a president who held that firmness in common with his fellow Americans. Racial parity and "foreign" infiltration were noxious threats to the nation, and a president who was excessively intellectual, cowardly, and insufficiently guided by Christian morality would all but ensure the penetration of these threats deeper into American society. Just as the Republicans' relentless criticism of Washington had forced the Federalists' hand, so too did the Federalists' arguments during the election of 1796 push Republicans to defend Jefferson on these terms. For all their resolve to focus on Adams's public record, they nonetheless had to defend Jefferson against the Federalists' "want of firmness" charge. A few even discussed the importance of the president's "character," mirroring the Federalist approach.

Adams won the election, but the Federalists failed to quash Republican dissent. Indeed, Beckley's mention of a "schism" among Federalists would prove prophetic. Adams found himself surrounded by strident criticism throughout his single presidential term. Some of that criticism would come from within his own party, much of it from Republicans. All of it Adams took as a personal attack and as the sign of a nation in decline from its bedrock national values. This attitude, so often described as a character flaw that made Adams uniquely ill-suited to presidential leadership, made him reflective of a perception that was gaining across the country. Seeking to silence the voices of Republican dissenters, the Federalists argued that the presidency was not only deeply personal but fundamental to the American people's collective sense of themselves. The people's choice of president expressed what they valued, who they were at the moment, and what they must be in the future. The office, in turn, amplified the character of whomever they chose, which would undoubtedly determine the character of the country far into the future. To dissent against the president was to dissent against the people themselves. That was why the Federalists during Adams's single presidential term would take unprecedented measures designed to silence political dissent once and for all.

5

John Adams's Presidency and the Moral Fate of the Nation

JOHN ADAMS ENTERED the presidency determined to be his own man. In early November 1797, the president wrote to his son, John Quincy Adams, that he admired "Mr Washingtons Character and Conduct in all Things: but" the new president was determined to "imitate him *servilely* in nothing."[1] Given who had preceded him, this was no easy task. Imitating Washington was the obvious temptation, for despite all the controversy that surrounded Washington in his second term, he was still beloved, and would remain so for the remainder of his life and beyond. But Adams recognized that copying Washington's approach to the presidency would spell inevitable doom. For one thing, nobody could truly imitate Washington; any attempt to do so would be transparent and unconvincing. For another, Washington remained the target of substantial criticism from Republicans, even those who expressed hope that Adams and Jefferson could work together across party lines. Any politician would love to avoid such insults, but many skilled leaders develop a thick skin to weather them; Adams, by contrast, took everything personally.

That, for many historians, has been his essential political flaw. Adams's inability to separate the personal from the political; his constant fretting about his own character and his sensitivity to any slight, real or perceived; his belief, bordering on obsession, that his own personal failings would have real, potentially irredeemable consequences for the country—in short, his own insecurities, coupled with his understanding that he performed on a public stage, at a time that would be studied painstakingly by the world for centuries to come—harmed his legacy when compared with men like Washington, Jefferson, and Madison (men to whom Adams also compulsively compared himself). Often overshadowed by both his predecessor and his successor, Adams is almost always depicted as a man whose political genius was constantly undermined by his sensitivity to slights and his unwillingness to keep his mouth shut.[2]

Yet it is those precise qualities that make Adams such a valuable historic figure. Principled to a political fault, Adams said explicitly what his more prudent contemporaries would have never dreamed to utter aloud. His willingness to state bluntly what he believed to be true, consequences be damned, has made him "such a remarkably instructive and cooperative historical source precisely because he was so difficult for most of his contemporaries to work with," the historian Alan Taylor has rightly observed.[3] Moreover, Adams's insecurities give him a human dimension his contemporaries often lack. In works of history, to say nothing of textbooks, documentaries, and films, Adams's political contemporaries often seem to be chiseled in marble. Washington, Jefferson, and Madison—and Benjamin Franklin, though he never became president—frequently come across as unapproachable, flawless "Founding Fathers," rather than flesh-and-blood human beings. By contrast, Adams has gone down in history as an all-too-human figure. That makes him very relatable to anyone who has ever had to follow a really tough act, anyone who has had to weather comparisons between themselves and immensely gifted peers, or anyone who has ever felt that they have not been fully appreciated for their efforts or intellect (in other words, just about everyone). Yet it can also lead Adams's political contributions, especially his presidency, to be undervalued. Insecure men who gripe about not getting their due as leaders and who fret constantly about their own legacies make for uninspiring copy. They just don't fit the mold of what most Americans expect of their leaders, especially their presidents. Yet Adams's inability to conform to the standard model of presidential leadership—his penchant to take everything personally—is precisely what makes his presidency so significant.

Despite his own pledge, Adams *did* look to Washington as the obvious (and only) model of presidential behavior for himself. An elitist and unapologetic admirer of the British system of government, Adams favored an executive that would be powerful enough to invite comparisons with European monarchies, a position that drew derision from Senate colleagues like William Maclay and public critics during the 1796 election. He hated being told what to do, yet he expected public support and obedience, and like his predecessor, he saw political dissent as an existential threat. Adams believed that civic conduct was indelibly linked to personal virtue, meaning that presidential leadership was more than simply a matter of Constitutional interpretation. It was deeply personal and deeply moral.

John Adams's letter to his son, John Quincy, offers a window into the second president's views of the intimate connection between the president and the citizenry who elect him. The elder Adams was writing in response to his son's stated misgivings about being appointed minister to Berlin. His son's "aversion," the second president assured him, was not merely unfounded; it was grounded in "a false Principle," and "an unjust Principle." Simply put, Adams told his son, "[t]he sons of Presidents have the Same Claim to Liberty, Equality, and the benefit of the Laws with all other Citizens." Why should a government disqualify an otherwise capable man from serving the country, simply because he happens to be a family member of the president? Neither the framers of the Constitution nor Congress thought it necessary to include such a disqualification, he reminded John Quincy. And if they had, the elder Adams vowed, he would have refused to serve in the government.[4]

The second president of the United States continued with the point. In the span of two sentences, John Adams invoked the example of his peerless predecessor, claiming that though Washington had a personal policy not to name his own relatives to high-ranking positions, Washington *would* have nominated his own sons, if he had had any sons of his own "and those Sons had been qualified." The elder Adams also said he would have refused to serve in office if he had felt he had to follow such a rule as a matter of law. Then, in the next sentence, he parted ways with Washington, noting that he would "imitate" Washington "*servilely* in nothing." If we look beyond Adams's trademark insecurity and his propensity to never leave well enough alone, we see the second president making a point about the young nation's political culture that Americans during his presidency, Federalist and Republican, would widely share. All citizens were equally members of the American family, and it was "false" and "downright Injustice" to draw distinctions among them that suggested otherwise.[5]

As president Adams saw it as his job to cultivate and maintain a common national character, one that guided the most private and intimate actions of private citizens and linked them to one another and to their government. The controversies that dominated his presidency revealed that both his critics and his allies agreed. Adams viewed political diversity and partisan division as toxic to the domestic tranquility he had been elected to ensure. During his single presidential term, his Federalist allies would justify their response to France in the "Quasi-War," and a series of laws granting the president broad-ranging power to arrest and prosecute "seditious" political dissenters and even to deport "alien enemies" whom the president deemed dangerous to the nation, as moral imperatives, necessary for preserving the character that bound the American people to their leaders as members of one unified national family.

These policies would provoke unprecedented backlash from Republicans, culminating in Adams's defeat in 1800 at the hands of his rival and vice president, Thomas Jefferson. For all that dissenters disagreed with Adams and the Federalists, they concurred on one key point: Americans were part of a single national family, held together by a profound moral bond that linked them to one another and to their government. But Republicans argued that intense public scrutiny—in other words, the capacity of the people to dissent—was what made this intimate bond possible. They argued that the measures undertaken by Adams, and the powers vested in the presidency by the Alien and Sedition Acts, threatened the nation's moral fabric by placing the president above that intense public scrutiny.

Adams's tendency to take politics personally put him on the vanguard of a transforming political landscape, one deeply divided along partisan lines yet in agreement that the powers exercised by the president in office profoundly shaped the moral fabric that bound the people to their elected leaders and to one another. It would be this shared belief that convinced Adams's critics and supporters alike that the political divide over the "Quasi-War" and the Alien and Sedition Acts would have profound and lasting effects on the moral character of the nation.

"COME FORWARD AS ONE MAN"

John Adams's best-known and controversial political commentaries, the *Defence of the Constitutions* and *Discourses on Davila*, reveal him to be equal parts wary of the power of the masses and admiring of the potential of executive power to "balance" the competing interests of the many and the few. Adams certainly held these views—and paid dearly for them—but focus on Adams as a political theorist risks obscuring his view that government's essential role was to cultivate a set of values and morals that would unite the people of a society together.[6]

It was not easy to define an American. The word "Americans," Adams thought, was "very comprehensive . . . & has a tendency to conciliate all the inhabitants of the continent & the islands." That was a good thing, as "[w]e are such an Hotch potch of people," he observed to William Tudor, Sr., "such an omnium gatherum of English, Irish, German Dutch Sweedes, French &c"—that it was tough to pin down what being an American even meant.[7] Yet Adams was convinced that morality made America great, and he knew that not everyone within America's borders shared the same moral values as true Americans.

Adams was deeply interested in the legacy of the American Revolution on the international stage, and he found himself pulled, as many of his generation were, in two directions at once. On the one hand, Adams believed that the American Revolution proved the United States to be, at least potentially, unique in all the world, poised to succeed in crafting a successful representative government where all other societies dating back to antiquity had failed. On the other hand, Adams recognized the practical reality that United States, if it were to succeed, needed a strong, independent executive who could forge diplomatic and economic relationships with powers around the world.

Adams's dilemma did not just encompass issues of political theory—of governmental structures and abstract balances between the interests of the few, the many, and the one. Crucially, it encompassed both the public virtues of elected leaders and reached into the private depths of individual citizens: their personal values and morality, indeed their very manhood itself. Adams understood that the American nation had to exist in a global context if it were to survive. But he remained convinced that Americans were a distinct people whose brief history had already demonstrated exceptional qualities that emanated from deep within each individual. These qualities united the American people together in a bond of virtue and sentiment. In this union, Adams was convinced that he had a uniquely vital duty to play as president: to stoke this sense of common values in defense against threats to the nation.[8]

Adams reached back to antiquity to further explain where such a deeply ingrained moral character came from and what it produced. For Adams, "virtue" was the natural byproduct of morality; it was the basis for the "sentiment" that connected every citizen and strengthened their collective bond against forces seeking to undermine it. So long as "[t]he Republicks of Antiquity," remained true to "the Virtues on which alone they were founded," Adams explained to a gathering of Richmond citizens, they could overcome the internal "divided . . . opinion[s] . . . and dissentions" and external "foreign Intrigues" that threatened them; "a foreign War, or a prospect of it, never failed to unite them as one Man at home."[9]

Adams's reference to true republicans uniting "as men" was not limited to long-dead ancients. Over and over again, in statement after statement, Adams framed Americans' commitment to liberty, in defiance of such forces, as a masculine trait. And invariably he contrasted the image of Americans uniting, like the ancient republics, peacefully and deliberately "as men," or "as one Man," with condemnation of French and Republican opposition as comparatively effeminate, irrational, and prone to violence.

Adams's affinity for comparing the American and French nations by their respective revolutions was such that he even borrowed from the language of his political rival and vice president, Thomas Jefferson, in his public appeals to supporters. "Whenever our Country shall be driven to the last dread Appeal, I have no suspicion that you will be found wanting, as Men, Citizens or soldiers ready to hazard your Lives and fortunes in the support of our national Independence against every Attack," Adams assured the militia of Prince George County in early June, 1798.[10] Taking advantage of the significance of his location nineteen days later, Adams appealed to a gathering in Concord, Massachusetts, by quoting from the close of the Declaration of Independence and invoking the 1775 battle that marked the official outbreak of the war. "[O]ur ancient Maxim was 'Ennemies in War, in Peace Friends,'" the president told them. Referring to the words of a twenty-two-year-old document as "ancient" allowed Adams to connect the Declaration—and by extension, the American Revolution—to the virtuous republics of antiquity, while emphasizing the Declaration's hope for a strong alliance with Britain. "If Concord drank the first Blood of Martyred freemen," Adams continued, "Concord should be the first to forget the Injury when it is no longer usefull to remember it."[11]

By invoking the Declaration, Adams sought to cast support for himself—and, by extension, the entire national government—as the culmination of a uniquely American commitment to liberty that had been forged in the American War of Independence. This was not mere public grandstanding: Adams's private correspondence bears out his belief that the relationship between the government and the people had to consist of a strength and consistency on the part of the government and boundless trust and unshakable "attachment" among the citizenry. Anything that interfered with that relationship was subversive to a functioning republican society. Even for a political theorist like Adams, this relationship between the people and their government was not an abstract academic concept; it was a moral matter. This was why he predicted that France's experiment in republican government was doomed to failure. The French, he wrote to Henry Knox, were vain and conceited; they "Consider nobody but themselves," and "have no other rule but to give reputation to their Tools & to destroy the reputation of all who will not be their Tools." Adams believed the lack of moral selflessness on the part of French leaders had a direct impact on the spirit of immorality that infected the entire country. That same spirit of selfishness existed in the United States, as the election of 1796 had demonstrated. Adams had won the election, but only by three electoral votes over "such a Character as Jefferson," he griped, and by twelve votes over "such an unknown being as Pinckney," rather than the "hundreds of other men infinitely his Superiors in Talents, Services, and Reputation." (Here, Adams probably meant Thomas Pinckney, who received fifty-nine electoral votes, and not Charles Pinckney, who received only one, although Adams did not specify in his letter).[12]

Adams would not be the last president to complain about the outcome of an election that he had won. But Adams was doing more than being a sore winner. He was discussing what the election for president revealed about the American people. The revelation that such unqualified "characters" could come so close to being elected "filled me with apprehensions for the Safety of us all," he confided to Knox. The reason was strikingly straightforward: the people's choice of their president revealed the people's "Sense of Honor Equity and Character" or their lack thereof. An alarming number of people in America must be "a Sordid people indeed, a people destitute of a Sense of Honor Equity and Character, that could submit to be governed, and see hundreds of its most meritorious Public Men governed by a Pinckney under an Elective government."[13]

The people seemed infected with a "Universal Ambition and Avarice" that repelled "all the best Men" from public service, making them "sick & weary of the perpetual Anxiety, which electioneering Projects and Exertions occasion." This made American society especially vulnerable to manipulative appeals by dissenting forces bent on undermining public confidence in the government. Adams maintained his hope that "our Republican system" could endure well into the future, he told Elbridge Gerry. "But it will not, if French Influence as well as English is not resisted."[14]

Such sharp criticism of the American people did not make its way into his public statements, but Adams certainly did publicly distinguish between what he referred to before the people of Concord as one "foreign Power [France] . . . whose ill Will we experience every day, and who will very probably in a few Weeks be acknowledged to be an Ennemy in the sense of the Law of Nations," and "a Power [Britain] that has never had the Insolence to reject your Ambassadors," and who "at present Conveys your Trade and their own at the same time."[15] For Adams, the British were a trusted international trading partner; the French, by contrast, were a dangerous "foreign" influence that threatened the nation.

In short, Adams was the country's first presidential culture warrior: the first sitting president to view American greatness as an ongoing crusade by patriotic Americans against foreign influences and homegrown subversives promoting moral relativism, selfishness, disdain for traditional values, and disregard for the rule of law. Where Washington sought to be an example of nonpartisan virtue who stood above the political fray, Adams sought to enlist everyday Americans in a moral campaign whose outcome he believed would determine the country's fate. To the Citizens Committee of Boston and Vicinity in early August, 1797, Adams warned that there would be some "worthy Citizens" who might be lulled into the false belief "that Calumnies and Contempts against the Constituted Authorities will not make a dangerous Impression upon a public opinion," because the public was adept at separating misleading falsehood from tried-and-true fact. Yet he was "of the opinion, that the profligate Spirit of falshood [*sic*] and malignity, which has appeared in Some, and the unguarded disposition in others to encourage it, are Serious Evils and bear a threatening aspect upon the Union of the States, their Constitutions of Government and the moral Character of the Nation."[16]

Adams did not have to look far to see evidence of such assaults on public confidence in "the Constituted Authorities." Less than two weeks after he took office, the *Aurora* published a piece that blamed Washington for a decline in national "character." The piece concluded with "the hope, that a change of administration will produce a change of system, and that our country, through the wise and judicious policy of the present Chief Magistrate, will be restored to those enjoyments of which it has been deprived."[17] Ostensibly an expression of optimism for Adams's new presidency, the piece was actually a cleverly framed attack on one of Adams's most sensitive political nerves. The only way for Adams to live up to the expectations before him, the *Aurora* piece suggested, would be to imitate Washington in nothing. Despite Adams's privately expressed resolve to do just that, his invocation of Washington in his reply to John Quincy about the latter's appointment to Berlin revealed the truth: Adams, like nearly all Americans, looked up to Washington and sought to follow his example. Adams would almost certainly try to imitate Washington, at least in some respects—and he was all but doomed to fail. But even in the unlikely event that he succeeded, the *Aurora* was assuring him that he would be met with the same vigorous resistance that Washington had faced.

Adams did continue Washington's example in one important respect, right from the start: he retained several of Washington's cabinet members, Charles Pinckney as secretary of state, James McHenry as secretary of war, and Oliver Wolcott as secretary of treasury. He also inherited the foreign policy fallout from the Jay treaty. Since the Senate had approved, Washington had signed, and the House had voted to fund the treaty, the French Directory had cut off talks with the US Minister to France, James Monroe. It not only refused to see his successor (Pinckney), but went so far as to expel Pinckney from Paris.[18] The French claimed that the Jay treaty violated the existing treaty between the United States and France and in effect made US ships fair game for confiscation by French vessels. Before the debates over the Jay treaty had even concluded in the Senate and the House, French privateers began freely attacking American ships in the Atlantic and the Caribbean. Timothy Pickering, Washington's secretary of state, estimated that in 1795 alone French privateers were responsible for the capture of over three hundred American vessels. Sometimes they confiscated the ship and its goods; other times they stripped it of its sails or damaged it severely enough to make it unseaworthy.[19]

The "misunderstanding with France," as Adams described the diplomatic tensions that arose in the wake of the Jay treaty, consumed Adams's presidential term as few single issues have in presidential history.[20] Adams sent a three-man envoy, consisting of Elbridge Gerry, John Marshall, and the exiled Pinckney, to France to negotiate with the French Directory. When the trio arrived in Paris to meet with French officials, they were met by three agents of the French Foreign Minister Charles Maurice de Talleyrand-Périgord—agents identified only as X, Y, and Z—who demanded a tribute (essentially a bribe) before negotiations could commence. Gerry, Marshall, and Pinckney refused, and negotiations ground to a halt.[21]

The United States and France had commenced the "quasi-war." The two countries were locked in a tense diplomatic stalemate that in some key respects anticipated America's Cold War with the Soviet Union in the twentieth century. As during the Cold War, America teetered on the edge of an all-out war with a world power, its political leaders and everyday citizens fearful of what would happen if the political posturing and diplomatic tit-for-tat ever escalated to all-out war. As during the Cold War, political leaders from the president on down often viewed dissidents in the United States as dangerous "foreigners" or at least as subversives whose criticism of America's leaders undermined public confidence in its political institutions, thus aiding America's adversary. And as during the Cold War, political leaders acted on that belief.

Nervous that the United States faced possible violent conflict on multiple fronts, and partisan intrigue from Republicans, the Federalist-controlled

Congress passed, and Adams signed, a series of laws known collectively as the Alien and Sedition Acts. Taken together, the acts were meant to empower the president to stymie political dissent through a variety of powers. The Alien Enemies Act of July 6 granted the president authority to determine whether a resident alien from a hostile nation (such as France, if hostilities continued as many Federalists thought they would) was an alien enemy, and to recommend that individual's arrest, detention, or deportation as he saw fit. The Alien Act, passed eleven days earlier, vested in the president power to declare any resident alien, no matter from where, "dangerous to the peace and safety of the United States" and to incarcerate the person without trial if they refused to leave the country. The Sedition Act, passed on July 14 (ironically Bastille Day), granted the president authority to prosecute any criticism of the president, the administration, or Congress (but not the vice president, a clear indication of the partisan nature of the acts) as seditious libel and to impose a fine or imprisonment as a penalty for criticizing the government.[22]

Obvious partisan infringements upon constitutionally guaranteed civil liberties, the acts nonetheless reflected the Federalists' desire to distinguish between true Americans and loyal alien "friends," on the one hand, and subversive "foreign" forces that posed a threat to the nation, on the other. Adams believed that the Alien and Sedition Acts helped promote what he called "a Union of sentiment," a shared moral mission to root out radical, democratic, foreign forces where ever they might lurk. Adams was convinced that it was moral "sentiment" that was under assault from radical, Frenchified democrats from within and from without.[23] While dissidents like Matthew Lyon and Benjamin Franklin Bache faced criminal prosecution for opposing the administration, the president basked in public professions of loyalty from individuals and groups around the country.[24]

Printed in newspapers, often alongside Adams's reply, these statements ranged from open letters to the president, professing support for his power to root out foreigners, to descriptions of military drills by civilians to show their readiness to take up arms against the French—and anyone else the president deemed a threat—at Adams's command. Seven state legislatures expressed their support for the laws as not only a constitutional grant of power to the president, but "in the present critical situation of our country, highly expedient," as the state legislature of New Hampshire put it.[25] But public professions of support for President Adams more accurately reflect the intensity of nationalistic zeal that captured much of the American public in 1798—an intensity that blended the Federalists' paternal and populist messages and revealed how the Federalists' longstanding profession that real Americans were a peaceful people could be used to justify calls to violence and the denial of civil rights. Affirming the longstanding Federalist vision of the president as the paternal protector to an obedient nation, these professions of loyal support were also meant to demonstrate Adams's considerable rapport with the American people. The president needed the support of the American people in order to successfully defeat the un-American forces threatening their country, and Americans were willing to give it, these professions collectively claimed, because he clearly understood and valued what separated them from their enemies. Militaristic in tone and message, these professions nonetheless suggested that the president's supporters desired peace but had been pushed to prepare for war by French radicals and Republican partisans, whose aggression gave them no other choice.

The publication of a letter by Jefferson to an Italian confidant, Philip Mazzei, in May 1797, appeared to lend credibility to the Federalists' contention that Republicans were traitors to the country, who had pushed the administration to take drastic measures. The letter, published initially in France, then in the New York *Minerva,* and then in Federalist newspapers throughout the country, suggested that Federalists, "an Anglican monarchical, & aristocratical party," had taken over most of the government, and Jefferson appeared to imply, Washington was among the infiltrators. "It would give you a fever were I to name to you the apostates who have gone over to those heresies," Jefferson wrote to Mazzei, "men who were Samsons in the field & Solomons in the council, but who have had their heads shorn by the harlot of England."[26]

The language of firmness, echoing the Federalist rhetoric of the campaign of 1796, remained a powerful tool with which Adams's backers cast their support as exemplary of an American nation demonstrating its resilience against French threats and Republican apostasy. While "the Mayor, Aldermen, and Citizens of the City of Philadelphia" marveled at "the prudence and moderation with which our Government has received the unprovok'd aggressions of France, and the sincerity and equity of your endeavors to conciliate her friendship," and "feel the independent pride of AMERICANS in your dignity and firmness," they also pledged to the president "our utmost assistance in the time of difficulty and need."[27] "The Subscribers, inhabitants and citizens of *Boston,* in the state of Massachusetts," told Adams they were "deeply impressed with the critical and alarming situation of the United States; and convinced of the necessity of UNANIMITY and FIRMNESS at this interesting moment"; they promised the president and Congress "their fullest approbation of the measures adopted by THE PRESIDENT, relative to our Foreign Relations," another address, published in a Boston newspaper, announced.[28]

Like Adams, the Federalists often drew upon the language of the Declaration of Independence—often pledging their "lives and fortunes" to support the president and Congress in the execution of national law. Appropriating the document that Jefferson had principally authored, Adams's supporters drove home the connection between the American people's capacity to dissent against tyranny (which they had demonstrated in the American Revolution) and the power conferred on Adams to eradicate dangerous, French influence.[29] While they often pledged to support the president and Congress together, public demonstrators also noted the president's primary role in foreign and military affairs and framed their "affection" and support for the president as the ultimate act of patriotism. "Our confidence in the wisdom and integrity of the Executive of the United States, has always been unshaken and entire, and we find it daily augmented by the development of events," declared "the Inhabitants of the Townships of Windsor and Montgomery, and the Towns of Princeton and Kingston," in New Jersey. Reiterating the group's "warm and unequivocal approbation of the wise and temperate system which has hitherto been pursued with regard to our foreign relations, and our undiminished confidence in those who preside over the affairs of the nation with so much wisdom and prudence," the address announced, that "[w]e are prepared for every event. If you should deem it necessary to impose a restraint upon foreign commerce, we will cheerfully forego the conveniences of living, which commerce yields. If, on the other hand, you resolve to claim your rights and bravely to defend them, we make not indeed any boastful professions of chaining victory to our arms, but we fear not to meet either in the field or on the ocean, those who have been accustomed to boast."[30]

"We are fully satisfied with the measures taken by the Supreme Executive, for accommodating the differences subsisting between the *United States* and the French Republic," another group announced in an addressed published in the *Massachusetts Mercury*:

> We are determined, at every hazard, to support the Government of our choice: and to those, with whom the Powers of Government are entrusted, we will afford our hearty concurrence and aid, for carrying into effect such measures as they may see fit to adopt; holding in the highest estimation our Rights and Interests as a free and independent People—those Rights and Interests for which we have once contended, and which it is our settled purpose never to resign.

Without a shred of irony, Adams's supporters made it clear that a pledge to resist dissenters by supporting the president—even taking up arms if the president commanded—was an expression of patriotism in keeping with the dissenting tradition of the American Revolution. As the *Mercury* piece demonstrated, supporters framed their pledge to Adams as a pledge of support for a republican government—a "government of our choice"— which had been won through valiant resistance to oppression, the ultimate act of independence. It proved that one remained uncorrupted by and thoroughly resistant to dangerous (meaning French) ideas or influence.[31]

Conflating one's commitment to the president, to the principles of the American Revolution, and to the American nation, supporters mirrored Adams's tendency to link together national and presidential "character," describing the two as inextricably linked. Professions of public support for Adams described the political stakes in strikingly personal terms, construing public and private acts as expressions of one's patriotism (or lack thereof), and infusing nearly every public action, and even the most intimate of acts, with political meaning. Supporters showed their approval by serenading the president with lavish approbation when he appeared in public, and even in the midst of his frequent trips back and forth between the national capital (Philadelphia and, near the end of his term, Washington City) and his Quincy, Massachusetts, home (he was away from the capital 385 days of his four-year term, far more than Washington's 181 days of absence in eight years' time). Even when not greeting the president personally, Federalists found occasions to demonstrate their support for the administration and to vilify anyone who even hinted at support for France. They wore black-cockaded hats, eschewing the red, white, and blue–colored variety that signified sympathy to France. Concert attendees demanded that bands play the "President's March" over and over again; hisses and boos awaited anyone who dared request the French Revolutionary tune "Ça Ira."[32]

The depth of public devotion to Adams extended even to times when the president snubbed his own adoring public. A Philadelphia paper published an account of one group of "federal" citizens who had prepared a reception for the president's arrival. But the Federalists' cheers upon seeing the president's carriage approaching turned to perplexed silence when his carriage actually sped up, passing them by with hardly a gesture of acknowledgement from its occupant. Bewildered, the group, "like true patriots, . . . soon recovered the disaster, gave the fleeting president three cheers, and closed the *honours* of the day with the noble song of *Hail Columbia*." Assuring readers "that the president, in treating the *respectable*

young men with so much neglect the other day, could not possibly mean
'*to blast the buds of their patriotism*,'" the author of the account ultimately concluded that the president's actions "does him honour, and such
as becomes the first magistrate of a free people. He studiously avoided
empty parade and idle pageantry."[33]

Like the president, Adams's adoring public cast American resilience in
masculine terms. Even descriptions of children and elderly men made the
connection between love of country and one's own claim to masculinity,
as young boys and their elders demonstrated their patriotism by pledging their service and even their willingness to engage in combat against
enemies at the president's command, even when social norms imposed
on them no obligation to do so. In June militia officers in New Jersey,
a group of "Boston youth," and a gathering of Federalists in Carlisle,
Pennsylvania, each published statements of loyalty to the president, drawing explicitly upon language from the Revolution. The "Boston youth"
emphasized their birth during the Revolution and promised their lives
in service to President Adams. Meanwhile, The Rev. John Chalmers of
Baltimore, Maryland, "exempted from military duty, both from his age
and his profession, offered himself to head a company," gushed a brief
account in the Richmond *Observatory, or, A View of the Times* entitled
"Eminent Patriotism." "His aged colleagues . . . endeavoured to prevail
on him to relinquish this purpose; but being joined by a large majority in
the opinion, that the urgency of the present crisis out-weighed every other
consideration, he was finally elected to the command, and has therefore
exchanged the pulpit for the field."[34]

Adams clearly relished this public adulation. "The confidence of the
people" of the states in his leadership, Adams remarked, demonstrated a
confidence in the government more generally, a confidence that "evinces
a tendency to a restoration of that harmony and union" that the people
demonstrated during the War for Independence, "but which has been ap-
parently interrupted since the commencement of the federal government."
As Adams told the residents of Accomac County, Virginia: "Your promise
to cooperate in whatever measures government may deem conducive to
the interests, and consistent with the honor of the nation, and your pledge
of your lives and fortunes, and all you hold dear, upon the success of the
issue, are in the true spirit of men, of freemen, of Americans, and genuine
republicans."[35] At times, he was even more blunt. In reply to the words
of praise and support from "the inhabitants of Chester county" in Pennsylvania, he remarked: "While the solemn declaration of your confidence
in Government, is a great encouragement; your engagement to support

administration, and submit cheerfully to obey pecuniary burthen that may be thought necessary, for the safety and independence of your country, becomes the character of excellent citizens, and is a laudable example to all."[36] Adams sometimes became so caught up in the political moment he barked commands to his audience to gear up then and there and prepare for combat. "To arms, then, my young friends,—to arms," he exhorted to "the Young Men of Boston, Massachusetts," "especially by sea, to be used as the laws shall direct, let us resort."[37]

So committed to maximizing public support for his administration was Adams that, in the summer of 1798, he selected Washington to be commander of the national army. Washington would not be literally leading the army into battle; instead, he would be offering "advice and assistance," Adams explained to his predecessor. Adams needed "your Conduct and Direction of the War," should it ever come. The "reasons for this measure, will be too well known to need any explanation to the Public," Adams went on to say. "Every Friend and every Enemy of America, will comprehend them, at first blush."[38]

By coaxing Washington out of retirement and into a position that was mostly advisory and symbolic in nature, Adams hoped to enlist Washington's still-unparalleled reputation in the campaign to drum up public support for his administration, oppose Republican dissent, and intensify preparation for possible war. In yet another layer of irony, the move invited comparisons between Adams and the man from whom he had vowed to distinguish himself. Washington's acceptance of the appointment "should be read in churches," one essayist breathlessly remarked, underscoring the choice as part of the president's efforts to strengthen the moral character of the citizenry. "His presence will blow every latent spark of patriotism into a flame; brace every nerve; turn every pruning hook into a sword; and call thousands to arms, who before never handled a musket." "Nothing," another letter remarked, "could have preserved the American character from disgrace, but the firmness of John Adams, in demanding protection for a defenceless country." "Your countrymen know not how much they owe to the man who has placed himself in a situation big with danger. If they are inheritors of the spirit of their fathers, they will make a rampart of their bodies around the ark of their country's independence, and placing ADAMS and WASHINGTON at their head, swear to be a tributary to no nation on the globe." Administration supporters celebrated Washington's appointment as evidence that Washingtonian bravery, so essential to securing national independence during the Revolution and guaranteeing national order earlier in the decade,

Figure 5.1: "A New Display of the United States," Amos Doolittle, (1799).
Courtesy of the Library of Congress Prints and Photographs Division.

continued unabated with the current administration. Adams had enlisted
the services of Washington against foreign elements threatening the union
of the republic.[39] It was an unprecedented blending of former and current
executive power that further galvanized public loyalty around presidential authority.

Expressions of that loyalty extended beyond public commitments by men to take up arms, encompassing the public actions of children and even the most intimate of acts between men and women. Construing themselves as defenders of their nation, Federalist men described women and children as especially vulnerable to the French—underscoring the immorality that separated them from patriotic, liberty-loving Americans. Federalist speeches often insinuated that women, the mothers of the nation's untold millions of unborn, were being targeted by the French, who sought to duplicitously win the "hand" or the "smiles" of the "American Fair" for themselves. One poem, reprinted in the Republican *Herald of Liberty*, claimed the French simply sought to "r****h [ravish] all our women."[40]

Resistance to such a scheme required that patriotic women demonstrate their steadfast devotion and fidelity to the nation by publicly supporting the men who themselves had pledged their service to the president and by reserving sexual intimacy only for truly patriotic, Federalist men. In Pennsylvania, the "Ladies of Potts-Town" praised the Volunteer Light Infantry Company for their bravery, presenting them with a standard to carry with them into battle and urging them: "Go then, Volunteers, obedient to your country's call." The officers replied with gratitude at having "receive[d] from the fair hands of virtue and innocence, the emblem of your approbation of our military exertions." The officers conveyed to the ladies, "With you we hope, that under the wisdom of an ADAMS at the helm of our councils, the valour and prudence of a WASHINGTON in the field of battle, our efforts will be crowned with success, while acting in the defence of our Rights, Independence and Religion, purchased with the blood of our fathers." In Massachusetts, "the ladies of *Deerfield*" gathered on Independence Day to drink tea and promise to "*perceive* and *pursue* the *infallible system* of *extinguishing* Jacobinism," starting in their own beds. "While we open our arms to the lovers of our hearts, may we never be deceived to Jacobinic embraces."[41] Mutual esteem between patriotic women and men, and even romantic and sexual affection between lovers, ensured the survival of pure American ideals, unsullied by degenerate French democracy. It was a crucial expression of the affection that bound all Americans together and united them with their president.

The statements by Adams and by the Federalists reverberated off one another, creating a political feedback loop that conflated support for the president with affection for and commitment to defend the nation's fundamental political principles. The shared portrait that emerged was that of a nation of moral Americans—women and men, young and old—united in their belief that at stake in their support for "the patriotic, manly, and decisive measures of [the President's] administration," as a piece in the New York *Commercial Advertiser* put it, was nothing less than "American character" itself.[42] As Adams himself told a gathering in Plymouth County, Massachusetts, he took every "Pledge" from supporters as proof that "in any arduous Issue to which the Arts or Arms of successful Violence may compell Us, you will, as becomes faithfull Citizens of this happy Country, come forward as one Man, in defence of all that is dear to Us."[43]

Yet not even all who called themselves Federalists were convinced. Outpourings of support contained such fanatical devotion, one former Federalist wrote in an open letter to Bache, the editor of the *Aurora*, that they collectively began to take on the look of a new religion that replaced God with the president. For this writer, such a development had the potential to undermine not only freedom of thought and expression but also the very religious morality that Federalists (including Adams) claimed to champion. "I believed, that each man was free to think for himself, and that he was free to act according to his own convictions, if within the bounds of the constitution and the laws: when I discovered, however that there was to be but one standard of opinion, and that all men's minds were to be governed by that standard, I began to doubt the uprightness of the creed," the apostate wrote in a letter renouncing his partisan affiliation, "and to believe that persecution for political opinions might terminate in persecution for religious ones, and that political faith might beget a religious one that would lead to oblige all men to worship God after the presidential manner."[44]

Critics of Adams, the Federalists, and the Alien and Sedition Acts were no less convinced that an intimate, even familial love for one another and for their liberty bound all Americans to one another and that the president should act as the exemplar of that intimate national bond. But a fine line existed between familial love and blind fanaticism. As the groundswell of dissenting voices provoked by the Alien and Sedition Acts would argue, one signified the people's strength and citizenship, while the other made them slaves.

"AND NOT EVEN A PRESIDENT OF THE UNITED STATES SHOULD BE AN EXCEPTION"

Three months after passage of the Sedition Act, Timothy Pickering complained to George Washington that he was flabbergasted "to hear what audacious lies are propagated by the partisans of France." He told

Washington the story of "an honest merchant" named William Bell, who encountered "some of the country people (Germans)" who were angry about the Alien and Sedition Acts, which they misunderstood as "the *alliance* and *seditious* bills." As Pickering told the story, these "country people" thought that "a son of the President," presumably John Quincy Adams, "was to marry a daughter of the King of Great Britain; and General Washington was to hold the United States in trust for that King!" The commoners who accosted Mr. Bell, Pickering concluded, thought that was the reason "that an army is to be raised, and *window* taxes levied!" Pickering saw the story as a baseless conspiracy theory, peddled to the public to whip up a frenzied public anger. He deemed it the most "foolish and absurd" story he had heard about the Alien and Sedition Acts, the most outrageous of the widespread rumors "of an *Alliance* between the U[nited] States & Great Britain," which circulated widely, "held up as a scarecrow before the eyes of the people."[45]

The "country people" misunderstood a lot about the Alien and Sedition Acts, but they knew well enough that the acts were about control; they were about a king-like imposition of conformity upon the populace, from the president on down. These people may have simply misunderstood a single word—"alliance" instead of "alien"—but they, like the Federalists and President Adams, believed that the bond between the president and the American people was both public and personal, encompassing both formal governmental actions as well as informal intimate conduct. Adams and the Federalists believed that the acts equipped the president to relentlessly enforce American values against all dissenters. Republicans saw them as evidence of a personal, familial bond in the works between the president and the king of Great Britain: clear evidence of the president's misplaced affection for monarchy and thus a betrayal of who Americans were as a people. This love for British monarchy over the liberty of the president's fellow-citizens would reverberate throughout American society. It threatened the peace, prosperity, and unity of the American nation. To take their country back, Americans had to resist with both public statements of dissent and intimate acts of defiance. They had to reclaim the presidency.

The message of dissent, carried across the country by a Republican press, stridently criticized Adams and his supporters, while echoing the Federalists' essential themes about the American people and their relationship to the president. Slamming the Federalists as unabashed Anglophiles and Adams as a wannabe king, Republicans nonetheless expressed a willingness to give their affectionate assent to a president who truly governed in the name of the people. Through their criticism of Adams, dissenters advanced their own vision of who the American people were that encompassed both public actions as well as private choices. Convinced that the Alien and Sedition Acts granted the president dangerous power, dissenters also argued that the president's power both reflected and ultimately determined what Americans stood for as a people.

Though Federalists had always enjoyed a distinct advantage in the press, the Alien and Sedition Acts touched off a surge in Republican newspapers. On the eve of the passage of the acts, the ratio of Federalist to Republican newspapers stood at better than two-and-a-half to one. And the Republican press that had been established, historian Jeffrey L. Pasley has argued, "was relatively inconsequential: unstable, widely scattered, vastly outnumbered, and in many cases, unsure of its mission." All that changed when the acts became law. Outrage at the administration's belligerent attempt to silence political criticism and violate the basic rights of the press and of individual citizens made the Republican press more prolific, more widespread, and more radically anti-Federalist. In the year 1800 alone, eighty-five new Republican newspapers appeared around the country. By the time Thomas Jefferson delivered his first inaugural address, pro-Republican newspapers outnumbered their Federalist counterparts, dominating political print for the first time in the young nation's history.[46]

The unprecedented numerical superiority of Republican newspapers was critical to the mobilization of what was in reality a well-established opposition message: Federalist practices were violating the public will, thus undermining the Constitution, the government it described, and the nation that government was designed to represent. Never was the evidence of the Republicans' assertion more clear than in 1798. Never was executive power so clearly the core of the Federalists' plan to quash dissenting opinion. And most importantly for the Republicans, never was the people's firm resistance to executive tyranny and active promotion of a stronger link between the public and the presidency more essential to rescuing the republic from the clutches of what Albert Gallatin called the "Executive Party" and the force of regulars and volunteer militia—over forty thousand strong, according to one newspaper report—that formed what Thomas Jefferson ominously termed "the Presidential army, or Presidential militia."[47]

As during Washington's presidency, opponents cast themselves as proud defenders of a beleaguered Constitution under attack from executive-obsessed "royalists." One piece in a Virginia newspaper provided the classic expression of this depiction, describing in dramatic, uncompromising terms the "*external alarms*," raised "for the purposes of *internal impression*," and the "dangers [from] abroad" enlisted "to further the work of injustice at home." Refusing "to blow the trumpet of alarm with a feeble or equivocal sound," the essay stated in no uncertain terms that the nation was no longer only being ignored by a president who preferred to broker deals with Britain and ignore the plight of France. Now, the government had launched an all-out attack on its own people, initiating what the essayist called an unprecedented "system of *legalized* terror" that "menaced" anyone who would not voluntarily muffle his own criticism and cheerfully, enthusiastically promise to support the government's every action.[48]

Dissenters accosted officials in the streets. They mobilized at every level of government, keeping a close eye on political developments at the local, state, and national levels. They shared news, speculation, and updates in correspondence. These actions were all components of a fervent campaign to resist the Federalist politics of limitless executive power and the stifling of political dissent. "Our domestic concerns afford little matter except on the subject of Elections," John Beckley wrote to Tench Coxe in late October 1798. Beckley tabulated the gains that Republicans were making in state-level seats, as candidates challenged Federalist incumbents in legislative assemblies from New England to Maryland, and even predicted that Matthew Lyon's "persecution and sentence" under the sedition law earlier in the month "will certainly do good in Virginia." In early November he announced that "the Aurora has arisen with *poison* (to Aristocracy) under its wings," alongside the New York–based *Argus*, which Beckley predicted would "extend its enlightened vigil thro' this & other Eastern States."[49]

The acts provided even more impetus for opponents' identification of the executive as the root cause of government despotism. In Congress, New York Representative Edward Livingston declared:

[B]y [the Alien Act] the president alone, is empowered to make the law, to fix in his mind, what acts, what words, what thoughts or looks, shall constitute the crime contemplated by the bill, that is the crime of being *suspected* to be dangerous to the peace and safety of the U[nited] States. . . . [T]he president then, having made the law, the president having construed and applied it, the same president is by the bill authorised to execute his sentence, in case of disobedience, by imprisonment, *during his pleasure*. This then comes completely within the definition of despotism, an union of legislative, executive, and judicial powers.[50]

The Kentucky Resolutions and the Virginia Resolutions, drafted by Thomas Jefferson and James Madison, respectively, are today the most famous statements of opposition to the Alien and Sedition Acts. Like other early expressions of dissent against the acts, the resolutions emphasized the threat that the acts posed by vesting the president with powers that violated the limits imposed on the government by the Constitution. Jefferson's Kentucky Resolutions repeatedly invoked the Tenth Amendment, arguing that the acts amounted to an assertion of authority on the part of the national government that the Constitution did not grant and that was reserved to the states and to the people. Thus, Jefferson argued, the acts were "unauthoritative, void and of no force."[51]

The Kentucky Resolutions would prove especially influential over the decades, for reasons Jefferson could not have predicted at the time. The Resolutions' most recurrent argument was that the states, not the federal government, possessed a legitimate "right of judging how far the licentiousness of speech and of the press may be abridged without lessening their useful freedom, and how far those abuses which cannot be separated from their use, should be tolerated rather than the use be destroyed." It was the states' collective assent that formed the "compact" from which the national government drew its power and legitimacy. It is an argument that twenty-first-century readers might find unusual, because it expresses a discomfort with the specific governing body tasked with limiting political speech, rather than with the limitation itself.[52]

Jefferson showed a draft of his resolutions to Madison, who used them as the model for the Virginia Resolutions, though Madison's document was briefer and employed less strident language. Nonetheless, Madison retained Jefferson's insistence that the Alien and Sedition Acts were unconstitutional and a violation of an affective bond that not only connected the people of each state but also transcended state boundaries and linked all Americans with one another. The people of Virginia "felt, and continu[e] to feel, the most sincere affection for their brethren of the other states," Madison's resolutions declared. That was really what the Constitution was: "the pledge of mutual friendship, and the instrument of mutual happiness." It was a pledge to which all people, in all states, and even "friendly strangers" were a party, Jefferson's Kentucky Resolutions argued. The Kentucky and Virginia Resolutions claimed that the Alien and Sedition Acts were an affront to the intimate bond that defined the people both as members of autonomous states and ultimately of one American nation.[53]

Embedded within each document's criticism of the power that the acts conferred on the president was an affirmation of the essential role the president should play in cultivating and strengthening the affective bond that all Americans, and all those aspiring to be Americans, shared. The resolutions affirmed the expectation, which Federalists enthusiastically shared, that the president should act as the voice of the nation, facilitating "the mild spirit of our Country" and acting on behalf of "the sacred force of truth," "law," and "justice." But the president could not act as his own source of authority. This was where the Alien and Sedition Acts went astray; they made "the bare suspicions of the President," rather than the sentiments of the people, the basis for the law. Such a government, the Kentucky Resolutions concluded, could only be "a tyranny" where the authority vested in "the President of our choice" violated, rather than strengthened, the bond of friendship that all liberty-loving people held in common.[54]

The Virginia and Kentucky Resolutions argued that the Alien and Sedition Acts drove a wedge between the people and the government by vesting in the executive expansive authority to prosecute political dissent that the people of the several states did not grant. The result was a strengthened government but a weakened nation—"an absolute, or at best a mixed monarchy," as the Virginia Resolutions concluded—a government that acted apart from the people, rather than drawing its strength from them. By declaring the acts unconstitutional, the legislative assemblies of Virginia and Kentucky contended, they were actually affirming their "warm attachment to the Union of the States" and their "duty to watch over and oppose every infraction of those principles, which constitute the only basis of that union." Though affirming the right of states to declare national laws null and void, the Kentucky Resolutions—and, to a lesser extent, the Virginia Resolutions—argued that the Alien and Sedition Acts threatened the nation because it dangerously expanded presidential power, thereby undermining the public confidence in and affection for the government that connected Americans across state lines.[55]

Republican critics throughout the country echoed this point. The basis for liberty itself was the equality of not only citizens' political views, but also their emotions.[56] Their affection for one another and for their government was paramount in any nation that was truly free. That meant that no one's "feelings"—*especially* those of the president—should be immune from harsh, uncompromising criticism. As a Richmond Republican questioned, "Is it sacrilege to call 'your beloved President' a despot? Is it an offence punishable by every junto, whose servile and courtly feelings it may wound?" The writer, using the pseudonym A Friend to the Sovereignty of the People, asked readers of the Richmond *Examiner* in July, 1799, "Is it sacrilege to ascribe to any of your public servants impure motives? Or are you bound to attach infallibility to those, who derive all their power from you, and whose acts are binding no longer than they are declaratory of your will? If so, farewell to your boasted liberty!"[57]

Notably, some pieces even went so far as to suggest that the criticism need not even be reasonable or civil to be protected. When a disgruntled Adams critic, Luther Baldwin, was jailed by the marshal "for dropping an expression, in an unguarded moment, amounting, as it is said, to a *wish*, that the President of the United States was dead," the ardently Republican Boston newspaper *Independent Chronicle* howled at the injustice. "That it is highly improper and unbecoming for any person to wish the death of another, all will allow—but that it ought to be made the subject of a prosecution, all will *disallow*; and neither ought it to be if made respecting one of the officers of government, for that would be placing them, who are the servants or agents of the people, above the people themselves. Here's *Liberty* for you!"[58]

There was the crux of the argument. For all the legalistic arguments marshaled to defend or condemn the acts, Republicans argued that the fundamental problem with them was that they privileged the president above everyone else—and in the process undermined the mutuality of affection for one another and for their government that only the constant promise of unrelenting criticism could provide. Republicans agreed that the people loved their government because it was subject to their will and that whoever occupied the presidency should be the focus of that affection. Insisting on blind loyalty to the president, ironically, undermined the more substantive affective bond between the president and the people that only the capacity to dissent made possible.

This argument is remarkable in that it followed the Federalists' insistence on a fundamental connection between the president's "character" and that of the people at large. While never abandoning their insistence that the president listen to and engage with the American people, Republican resistance to the Alien and Sedition Acts echoed the Federalists' point that what was at stake was not simply a line of public communication linking the president to the populace. Rather, the power granted the president by the Alien and Sedition Acts made a statement about the American people themselves. For Federalists, the acts provided a rallying point where patriotic Americans could affirm their love of country through pledging their support to the president. For Republicans, the acts undermined the very love that bound American citizens to one another and to their government—the very love that the president was trusted to cultivate by listening to, engaging with, and acting to serve the interests of, the people. That love would always be contingent. It could not be commanded, and it could not be coerced.

One of the most explicit indictments of Federalist enthusiasm for the power that the Alien and Sedition Acts conferred on the president, manifested by their breathless pledges to take up arms at Adams's pleasure, was written by a Virginia Republican under the pen name Civis. By professing unwavering and unequivocal support for the president, Civis argued, Federalists revealed their preference for a nation of mindless "slaves." Using a term that carried not only governmental but racial implications that no reader in Virginia—or elsewhere—would have missed, Civis claimed that to pledge publicly one's devotion to the president was to embrace such enslavement and abandon citizenship itself, to shackle one's own mind and become a part of the president's army of sycophantic soldiers. Supporters of the administration "who have offered their services to the president," were *"regulars"* in his army, Civis explained. "A soldier is a slave; a citizen is a freeman. A soldier is bound under the severest penalties of martial law, to obey without deliberating—a citizen is subservient to the civil laws, and to them only; and if they are obnoxious to him, he has the power and the right to change them. But not so with a soldier—he has no will but that of his commanding officer." Quoting from "a very ingenious, eloquent, and patriotic English writer," Civis further expounded upon the voluntary enslavement that was the essential role of the regular soldier, who forfeited all of his civic powers with his pledge of unequivocal support for the president:

The strict discipline which is found necessary to render an army a machine in the hands of its directors, requiring under the severest penalties, the most implicit submission to absolute command, has a direct tendency to familiarize the mind to civil despotism. Men, rational, thinking animals, equal to their commanders by nature, and often superior, are bound to obey the impulse of a constituted authority, and to perform their functions as mechanically as the trigger which they pull to discharge their muskets. They cannot indeed help having a will of their own; but they must suppress it or die. They must consider their official superiors as superior in wisdom and virtue, even though they know them to be weak and vicious. They must see, if they see at all, with the eyes of others; their duty is, not to have an opinion of their own, but to follow blindly the behest of him who has had interest enough to obtain the appointment of a leader. They become living automatons, and self acting tools of despotism.[59]

Civis certainly intended to invoke a comparison with, and capitulation to, the violent, militaristic European empires, like Britain, that boasted a powerful standing army that included mercenaries. In this, Civis joined other Republicans in declaring that the resemblance was not a cause for celebration.[60] But Civis also used a term—"slaves"—that carried with it an obvious racialized meaning. In 1800 James Callender—the same James Callender who would turn against Jefferson and the Republicans and publish the accusation that Jefferson kept an enslaved woman, Sally Hemings, as a mistress—published a series of attacks on the Federalists and Adams that made that connection even more explicit. Callender did not limit himself to the Alien and Sedition Acts. Instead, Callender meticulously described the Federalists' attempts to fund Adams's lavish home furnishings with government money. This, to Callender, was another "scene of swindling, by which the people of America must be robbed of twenty, thirty, or fifty thousand additional dollars." Why should the "Men of Virginia," to say nothing of Americans around the country, "submit in silence to work like this . . . to kiss the hoofs of despotism?"[61]

Callender rattled off a series of grievances against Adams, from imprisoning men who drank to the health of Thomas Jefferson; to his foreign-policy decisions; to defaming the widows of his opponents, including Benjamin Franklin Bache, the editor of the *Aurora*, who was jailed under the Sedition Act, went essentially bankrupt paying the $4,000 bail set by the court, and died in September 1798. Adams's immorality betrayed the trust of the American people on every conceivable level. The president was stealing money from people's pockets. He was sending critics to jail. He was denigrating families.[62]

And, Callender added, Adams was obstructing the immigration of "gallant but unfortunate patriots" from worthy nations like Ireland, while "embrac[ing] an official compact with an African rebel, and plac[ing] the signature of the United States alongside" the name of Toussaint L'Ouverture, the former slave who led the revolution in the French colony of Saint Domingue. The revolution, begun in 1791, would culminate in 1804 with the establishment of the independent, black republic of Haiti. But even at the turn of the century, the rebellion had already forced France to end slavery in the colony and then to abolish slavery throughout its empire. Adams had supported establishing a commercial relationship with Saint Domingue, thinking that doing so might prove useful in the diplomatic struggle between the United States and France. Jefferson would reverse the decision once he became president, and the United States would not recognize Haiti officially until the 1860s.[63]

But in 1800 Callender suggested that such a gesture, no matter the reason, granted legitimacy to a violent rebellion of free and enslaved blacks. Like Civis—and like William Loughton Smith in the contest of 1796—Callender's attack highlighted the racial politics to the young nation's partisan divide. While Civis claimed that sycophantic Federalists who pledged their service in a potential war to Adams lowered themselves to the level of "slaves," Callender claimed that the president himself was lifting violent black rebels closer to the level of whites. To regain control of their country, the people had to wrest the presidency from the Federalists' grasp.

The political mobilization to do so would require more than just those who could formally vote. Republicans met Federalist insistence on sexual intimacy as a gesture of loyalty to the nation by inverting the equation, making women's choice of a Republican lover—who would oppose the president's power rather than become his abject "slave"—a powerful political act that would stir men to action. As a Virginia newspaper's account of a gathering of New Jersey Republicans put it: "The fair Daughters of America" should "never disgrace themselves by giving their hands in marriage to any but real republicans." The New York Tammany Society toasted "the American Fair—May none enjoy their smiles but true Republicans." The Carlisle (Pennsylvania) *Gazette* published another Republican toast to "the fair Daughters of Columbia. May their smiles be the reward of Republicans only."[64] Some Republican praise for the "fair" hinted at a level of gender equality: to "entrust the rights of women, to those who slight the rights of man," a Boston paper argued, would be a grave injustice to both the woman herself and her country.[65]

By 1798 both Federalists and Republicans considered the presidency to be the crucial gauge of a powerful and deeply personal bond between citizens and their elected leaders, one rooted in a shared civic morality at the heart of Americans' commitment to maintaining liberty. Republican dissenters considered an intimate, affective bond between the president and the people to be the bedrock of a lasting American nation no less than did the president's supporters, or the president himself. But that love could not exist if the president was held in higher regard than the people he represented. Here, during Adams's presidency, was where Republican dissenters echoed the argument first put forward by Federalists in the election of 1796: to cultivate a truly lasting love of country among the American people, the president had to be one of them. Ensuring that, Republicans maintained, required the very exposure to public criticism that the Federalists sought to quash.

Resistance to the president's power was not a violent betrayal of national character. On the contrary, Republicans argued it was an act of patriotic bravery, an attempt by the American people to save the nation by resisting attempts by the president and the Federalist Party to strip ordinary citizens of their liberties and render them cowed subordinates. "No, sir, we are not cowards," a Republican response read. "We would as soon crush a domestic tyrant, or any man who would propose an hereditary president, as we would repel the French, or any other foreign foe." What Federalists mistook for cowardly "leveling principles," as the Federalist impersonating a Republican put it ("democratical—that is, faction-*atical*, or mob-*atical*, stir[r]ing up opposition to the constituted authorities, and vociferating on every occasion—Liberty! Liberty! the People! the sovereign of the People! &c."), was actually essential to preserving what the Federalist agenda threatened. "Nor need you fear, as it seem[s] you do, 'that we will place any man *above* the constitution and laws of his country.' Be assured, sir, that we will not place him there; and if he places himself there we will hurl him down headlong, with as little ceremony as we would run an invading enemy through the body with a bayonet." Republicans chorused that real Americans recognized that every man—from the president on down—had to be subject to the laws.[66]

Republicans made this pledge—to bring the president down to the level of the people—the hallmark of their message. In case the connection between the present moment and the country's revolutionary origins was not explicit enough, this same Republican commentator spelled it out: the Federalist position "that there is too much liberty of the press, and of speech" would be unrecognizable to the nation's Revolutionary "forefathers," who "were not *monarchy ridden*, as some of our federalists are; they were then republicans in name and reality."[67] Republicans agreed that the honor of the nation was inextricably bound to the "honour" of the president ("for HONOUR is personified in her CHIEF MAGISTRATE," a Federalist commenter declared). But they countered that by holding the president above all criticism and empowering him to prosecute dissenters, Federalists were perverting the honor of the office and the nation. It was the Republicans who adhered to the nation's noble dissenting tradition by insisting that public scrutiny apply foremost to the president. As one Republican, responding to a Federalist critic, put it: "I agree with you, 'that the language and deportment of men in exalted stations are never to be regarded with indifference, and that it becomes the duty of the press to expose and censure when they forget the demeanor of good citizens.'" But the two parted ways on "the application of this maxim." The Republican "should extend it from the lowest to the highest man in office, and not even a President of the United States should be an exception." The Federalist, on the other hand, "will be disposed to go no higher than a Vice President." Republicans argued that political dissent showed them to be everything that supine, monarchy-obsessed Federalists, who willingly "enslaved" themselves, were not: strong, independent, free, and bound together in solidarity by a love of liberty that not even the threat of arrest or prosecution by a wannabe-king and his toadies could extinguish. In their dissenting message, in their insistence that their president share the people's love of liberty, and not demand the people's unquestioned loyalty to his authority—Republicans proved themselves real Americans.[68]

ADAMS "HAS SUNK THE TONE OF THE PUBLIC MIND"

John Adams began his presidency by resolving to stand apart from his predecessor, yet his own words to John Quincy reveal that he did look to Washington as an example, leaning on what he was certain Washington *would* have done, had he any sons who were qualified for appointment to posts by the president. Adams's well-documented independent personality thus blended with an desire to invite favorable comparisons between himself and Washington whenever the opportunity presented itself. Both would, in their own way, contribute to Adams's own political downfall.

Adams named Washington commander of the army in mid-summer of 1798, just as he signed the Alien and Sedition Acts into law. Washington agreed, and "formed a List out of Names" of men to appoint to positions of command beneath him, subject to Adams's approval. On the list were two men that Adams patently disliked: Henry Knox, Washington's secretary of war, and Alexander Hamilton, his former treasury secretary. Yet Adams placed trust in Washington that he would never appoint men who would damage *"the Honor, personal Influence, or Character* of the Chief of our Nation." Anyway, he told Oliver Wolcott, Washington knew that Adams was now the president and had made it clear to Adams that he had no "Wish to interfere with any of the Powers constitutionally vested in the President," and recognized, as Adams did, that "the whole must depend upon the President."[69]

Yet Adams despised Hamilton, and though he maintained that he disliked Knox just as much ("I have no kind of Attachment to him or Affection for him more than for Hamilton"), the first treasury secretary evoked a special kind of suspicion from the second president. For one thing, the Caribbean-born Hamilton did not meet Adams's nativist criteria for a full-fledged American. "Hamilton is not a native of The United States but a Foreigner," Adams stated bluntly to Oliver Wolcott, Jr, "and I believe has not resided longer, at least not much longer in North America than Albert Gallatin," the Swiss-born Republican congressman who would go on to serve as Thomas Jefferson's treasury secretary.[70]

For another, Adams was convinced that Hamilton continued to exercise immense influence over Pinckney, McHenry, and Wolcott, the cabinet members that Adams had retained from Washington's presidency. Such meddling in the executive branch by a "foreigner" was bad enough, but compounding it was Hamilton's hawkish view of the potential war with France, which contrasted sharply with Adams's commitment to maintain peace at all costs. Hamilton especially had his eye on Florida and Louisiana, two colonies he believed the United States must possess to counteract French or Spanish aggression. "I have been long in the habit of considering the acquisition of those countries as essential to the permanency of the Union, which I consider as very important to the welfare of the whole," Hamilton had remarked to James Gray Otis in late January 1799. "If universal empire is still to be the pursuit of France, what can tend to defeat the purpose better than to detach South America from Spain which is on the Channel, th[r]ough which the riches of *Mexico* and *Peru* are conveyed to France? The Executive ought to be put in a situation to embrace favorable conjunctures for effecting that separation."[71]

Adams's desire to follow Washington's example, then, had led him to retain several members of Washington's cabinet and to accept men to positions of command that he did not trust. The rift between Adams and these men widened to a chasm, eventually leading Adams to fire McHenry and Pickering in 1800. The divide between Adams and Hamiltonian Federalists yawned still wider as Adams deviated from his own tough talk in his Annual Message (what today is called the State of the Union) the year before. In addition to calling on American citizens to prepare for war, Adams and the Federalists had also insisted that the French had done nothing to meet the United States halfway at the negotiating table. French actions toward American ships and American diplomats sent a clear message that the French had no interest in peace, which made it necessary for American citizens to show their commitment to independence by gearing up for war. In order to convince the United States that this was not the case, the onus was on the French to change course, and the draft Annual Message that Adams had in front of him in 1799 specified that France would have to signal its seriousness about peace talks by sending a minister to America.[72]

Peace with France threatened to derail Hamilton's imperial designs, but Adams's commitment to peace was genuine: so genuine, in fact, that he went off-script, unbeknownst to his bewildered cabinet members. Adams's address as given altered the wording, requesting from France "more determinate assurances" that an American minister "would be received," suggesting that he was indeed open to the possibility of sending another minister to France, an action that the draft of his speech had called "an act of humiliation to which the United States ought not to submit without extreme necessity." As if that were not enough, Adams also announced his plans to send another mission to France, as a gesture of the sincere desire of the United States for peace. He noted that he had been given assurance by France that the Americans would be received, "and I have directed them to proceed on their mission to Paris. They have full power to conclude a treaty, subject to the constitutional advice and consent of the Senate."[73]

Such a change amounted to a pivot that undercut the fundamental message that Adams and the Federalists had promoted, and which their public supporters had willingly echoed back, for more than a year and a half. The crux of the Federalist message was that France's actions had pushed the two nations toward war, and that it was every patriot's duty to profess support for the president in quashing dissent at home and taking up arms in preparation for war abroad. The president, they insisted to one another, had to be the focus of the public's unyielding faith in the government and of a martial spirit that resisted foreign forces that threatened the nation. Here was the president himself committing an act that he and his supporters agreed was patently un-American.

Adams's impromptu change to his Annual Message demonstrated his desire to avoid war with France. This desire is very much to his credit, especially given that it flew in the face of the fundamental political position that he and his party had taken to demonize and silence their political opponents. But it only added Federalist voices to the crescendo of Republican criticism of his presidential leadership. In the Federalists' view, war and patriotism were intimately linked. Peace with the nation's enemies was nothing less than cowardly capitulation—a betrayal of the American family and an abdication of one's duties as an American. In modern political parlance, Adams had alienated his base.

Hamilton led the charge. The former treasury secretary wrote a scathing private letter to his Federalist confidantes, indicting Adams's presidential leadership. The letter was intercepted by Republicans and appeared in the Republican press. His disapproval of Adams publicly exposed, Hamilton doubled down, publishing his letter in 1800 in the form of a pamphlet entitled *Letter from Alexander Hamilton, Concerning the Public Conduct and Character of John Adams, Esq., President of the United States.* In the pamphlet Hamilton attacked Adams with a line that had become the lingua franca of national politics: that the "character" of the president and the nation were indelibly linked.[74]

As president, Hamilton argued, Adams had initially proven himself capable of acting decisively and boldly in response to French maritime belligerence and its attempts at diplomatic extortion—precisely the president's proper job. "Without imitating the flatterers of Mr. Adams, who . . . ascribe to him the whole merits of producing the spirit which appeared in the community, it shall with cheerfulness be acknowledged, that he took upon the occasion a manly and courageous lead," Hamilton conceded. Adams "did all in his power to rouse the pride of the nation—to inspire it with a just sense of the injuries and outrages which it had experienced, and to dispose it to a firm and magnanimous resistance; and that his efforts contributed materially to the end."[75]

But then it all changed. "It was suggested to him," Hamilton explained, concealing the agency of Adams's cabinet members—loyal Hamiltonians all—behind the passive voice, "that it might be expedient" to require France to send an envoy to the United States if it desired reconciliation with the United States. Adams at first dismissed the suggestion, declaring *"that if France should send a Minister to-morrow, he would order him back the day after."* But not two days later, the president "underwent a total revolution—he resolved not only to insert in his speech the sentiment which had been proposed to him, but to go farther, and to declare, that if France would give explicit assurances of receiving a Minister from this country, with due respect, he would send one." This action, so in contrast with his initially bold presidential action, "has sunk the tone of the public mind," Hamilton lamented. "It has impaired the confidence of the friends of the Government in the Executive Chief—it has distracted public opinion—it has unnerved the public councils—it has sown the seeds of discord at home, and lowered the reputation of the Government abroad." Adams's own weakness and indecisiveness (one might say a want of firmness) had compromised the people's confidence that he could act on their behalf, that he could exemplify their "spirit." By demonstrating a lack of presidential "character," Adams had compromised the "spirit" and "dignity of the nation" itself.[76]

THE DEATH OF WASHINGTON
AND THE ELECTION OF 1800

On December 14, 1799, George Washington drew his final mortal breath, dying in his bed at Mount Vernon. His death inspired public and private acts of mourning across the country. Americans wrote poems and songs, painted portraits, and recounted Washington's life in ways that reveal as much, if not more, about the creators as they do about their common subject. In some respects the public rituals of mourning could be quite inclusive, drawing together people who seldom convened and cutting across vocational, gender, class, regional, and even political lines. In New York businesses closed, streets were cleared, and a lengthy procession consisting of various groups of citizens—military personnel, "Incorporations, Societies," and "girls in white robes" snaked its way through the town, down Bleekman and Pearl Street to Wall Street, past City Hall and the Bowling Green, and ending at St. Paul's Church. Yet the most common themes in Americans' mourning rituals emphasized the traits that distinguished Washington above his fellow Americans. Some portraits—such as a fantastic image of Washington being welcomed to heaven by Benjamin Franklin, who had died in 1790—have become classic testaments to Washington's legacy as the nation's "Kind and venerated Patron and Father."[77]

Such reverence for the first president stands in stark contrast to contemporary Americans' understanding of the office that Washington was the first to hold. The office is prestigious precisely because Americans expect the occupant to exemplify what they consider best among themselves: to occupy a position of unique power and authority given by the people as recognition that he (at least thus far) exhibits the "character" that they believe all Americans possess: values and characteristics that unite American citizens with their elected leaders. That view of the presidency, so pervasive among twenty-first-century Americans that it is easy to take it for granted, had come to dominate American politics across partisan lines for the first time in the twilight of the 1790s. Like the man himself, Washington's presidential ideal—that of an executive who stands beyond the partisan fray, a father figure commanding the people's respect and support from above—had gone the way of all flesh.[78]

In the election of 1800, Federalist and Republican partisans repeated many of the arguments they had made four years earlier, their arguments infused with the urgency of the political moment. Once again, Jefferson emerged as the top Republican contender and thus the target of Federalist attacks that, as in the election of 1796, predicted Jefferson's victory would lead to the downfall of American society. Federalist pieces predicted a dangerous, democratic leveling of society, the persecution of religious leaders, and even the sexual assault of innocent daughters, should Jefferson win the presidency. "Is it that we may see the Bible cast into a bonfire, the vessels of the sacramental supper borne by an ass in public procession, and our children . . . chanting mockeries against God, and hailing the sounds of Ça ira the ruin of their religion, and the loss of their souls?" Timothy Dwight asked his Connecticut parishioners. As hyperbolic as his sermon, entitled "The Duty of Americans at the Present Crisis," may sound, it resonated with his audience so much that Federalists widely reprinted it during the presidential campaign of 1800. The nation's very republican "soul" was at stake in the selection of the president. Other preachers emulated its message, haranguing their congregants about the dire consequences of looming French and Republican threats and the subversion of religious, moral, familial, and governmental order that would result if Jefferson were elected.[79]

Numerous Republican publications countered that Jefferson was "the man of the people," a man whose "patriotic talents and virtues" warranted "elevat[ion]" to the presidential chair by "the voice of his countrymen."[80] While the rift continued between Adams and the Hamiltonian Federalists, both the president and his party found their insistence on public assent to the government drowned out by the loud acclaim for "the People, the Sovereign of the United States," and "*the sovereign people's* man," Jefferson, their "friend and favorite," and the "faithful Guardian of our rights," as the True Republican Society of Philadelphia trumpeted.[81] Jefferson was the author of the Declaration of Independence, the brilliant philosopher of freedom "whose name will be revered as long as patriotism shall be esteemed a virtue, or philosophy and science ornaments to the character of man," a group of "Citizens of Richmond" declared.[82] He above all others had proven his capacity to convey "the Republican cause throughout the world"; he above all could claim "honest and patriotic exertions in the cause of universal Liberty," as the Tammany Society of New York exclaimed.[83] Throughout his entire political life, Republicans throughout the country argued, Jefferson's cause had been the people's. That meant that his actions as president, as "the pilot of the federal ship," would not be the independent actions of an aloof executive but the energetic actions of an independent people. As much as the presidential actions of Washington and Adams (and those of their supporters within the government and without) had perverted the republican experiment and rendered far too many of its citizens willing "slaves of monarchy," so Jefferson's presidential actions would embody the will of "the PEOPLE, the only sovereign of the United States."[84]

The election came down to a tie in the Electoral College between Jefferson and fellow Republican Aaron Burr, which required thirty-six separate ballots in the House of Representatives to resolve. Despite the indirect electoral methods imposed by the legislative selection of electors (which was still the method in most states), as well as attempts by Burr's allies to sway the vote in the House, Jefferson eventually emerged victorious.[85] By electing Jefferson to the presidency, Republicans claimed that the voices of dissent—the people themselves—had become the voices in power. Commentators across the political spectrum were convinced that Jefferson's presidency would confirm one prediction or the other: the American people were either poised to fully realize their long-sought status as an independent people, or they were standing on the precipice of a decline into degeneracy, savagery, and despotism.

6

President Jefferson's Nation of Dissenters

"FRIENDS AND FELLOW CITIZENS," Thomas Jefferson began his inaugural address on March 4, 1801, standing in the Senate chamber in Washington City. That salutation, like Jefferson's choice of attire, was meant to send a message. He wore no elaborate "badge of office," one newspaper reported. No ceremonial saber adorned his hip, as it had for Washington and Adams during their first inaugural addresses. Instead, the third president dressed as "a plain citizen." Rather than ride to the Capitol in an ornate carriage, as his predecessors had done, he walked. Newly sworn in and standing before both members of Congress and private citizens (many straining to hear his soft-spoken delivery), Jefferson began his first speech by addressing his words to the citizenry and not, as Washington and Adams had done, to Congress itself. Right down to the particulars of his inaugural ceremony, Jefferson sought to convey that the presidency—and with it, the government—now belonged to the people.[1]

Jefferson's First Inaugural Address, one of the most celebrated and studied of presidential addresses, did offer some important conciliations to Federalists—a point often emphasized in analyses of his speech. "[E]very difference of opinion is not a difference of principle," Jefferson said, in probably the most frequently quoted passage of his address. "We have called by different names brethren of the same principle. We are all republicans: we are all federalists."[2]

Jefferson devoted nearly a third of the speech to describing the "principles" that united all Americans. They were "federal and republican principles," the principles that Republican dissenters had advocated throughout the previous decade: religious pluralism; support for individual rights such as the right to vote, assemble, and express one's political beliefs; freedom of the press; a commitment to strong but peaceful foreign and domestic policies; and the right of minorities to criticize, free from persecution by those in power. Protection for minority rights was a "sacred principle,"

Jefferson stressed, the connective tissue between the other principles, without which the country's other federal and republican principles had no meaning. "[T]hough the will of the majority is in all cases to prevail," Jefferson stated, "that will, to be rightful, must be reasonable; that the minority possess their equal rights, which equal laws must protect."[3]

This respect for the rights of dissenters was ultimately what distinguished American freedom from "oppression," Jefferson went on to say, "as despotic, as wicked, and capable of as bitter and bloody persecutions" as the religious intolerance which the American people had "banished from our land." For Jefferson, the rights of political and religious minorities could not be overemphasized. "If there be any among us who would wish to dissolve this Union, or to change its republican form, let them stand undisturbed as monuments of the safety with which error of opinion might be tolerated, where reason is left free to combat it."[4]

Jefferson appeared to be embracing the Federalists as a loyal opposition, though doing so by offering some assurance to them that he would not target them for their criticism of his actions the same way they had targeted the Republicans. His assurance to Federalists—who had lost the presidency and would soon be the minority in Congress as well—that minority rights would be respected under his administration was at least as much a promotion of Republican superiority as it was an olive branch to Federalists. It was a back-handed promise, meant to send the clear message that Republicans would govern more equitably and responsibly than the Federalists had, but it was a promise nonetheless.

Yet even as Jefferson appeared to promise that Federalists' right to dissent would be respected, his First Inaugural Address also described his election as "the voice of the nation" and made clear his expectation that the partisanship that had defined the campaign would cease and that citizens would "unite with one heart and one mind" to build a stronger, more harmonious nation. That unity would occur only when the majority agreed to protect the rights of the minority, *and*, the president stipulated, when the minority agreed to "absolute acquiescence in the decisions of the majority." The first of these requirements highlighted the Federalists' great failure to live up to the lofty standards of republican governance that citizens expected. The second underscored the Federalists' current obligations now that they were no longer in power. Now that the people had spoken, Jefferson noted, "all will of course arrange themselves under the will of the law, and unite in common efforts for the common good."[5]

Jefferson intended his inauguration on March 4 to stand as the culmination of a profound political change. Years of relentless dissent against

British tyranny had birthed the United States. Years of dissent by Republicans during the 1790s had toppled Adams and the Federalist majority. The result, Jefferson assumed, would be unprecedented unanimity by all Americans around the government he now led. "Reasonable" political debate would continue, but intractable, bitter partisanship would cease now that the very ideals that had animated political dissent of the national government served the government itself.

During Jefferson's two terms as president, political division would crystallize over a shared belief that Jefferson's presidency signaled an unprecedented democratization of the American political landscape, with both Republicans and Federalists invoking the nation's dissenting tradition to make their respective claims about the nation's future under Jefferson's presidential leadership. Jefferson's supporters were convinced that with Jefferson's election to the presidency, the promise of a truly democratic nation would finally come to fruition. To be sure, Republicans conceded, if Jefferson failed to fulfill his duty to promote the people's liberty and oppose any threats to it, the people had a solemn duty to dissent, with the knowledge that they would be free from official persecution from the government. But if a president *did* fulfill that singular, stratospheric duty—and Republicans argued that Jefferson was doing so—all true Americans had an obligation to show the president their unequivocal, enthusiastic support. Federalists, meanwhile, drew precisely the opposite conclusion about Jefferson's election and subsequent presidency. Jefferson's policy decisions and his private life proved the folly of democracy carried to its logical conclusion; the president, the head of a party dominated by slave-owning Virginia aristocrats, was leading the nation to precipitous and possibly irreversible national decline. Ironically, Federalists insisted that they had the patriotic duty to dissent, to save the nation from the clutches of an administration professing to serve "the people" but one that sought the subordination of all to the interests of a slaveholding Southern gentry—to make "slaves" out of liberty-loving Americans. Proceeding from the same basic assumption about presidential power, national character, and public accountability, partisan commentators drew dramatically different conclusions about the nation's democratic character during Jefferson's presidency.

THE REIGN OF "MASSA JEFFERSON"

Early in January 1801, a poem titled "The Triumph of Democracy" appeared in the *Connecticut Courant* describing the disastrous consequences of a Jefferson presidency. The Electoral College would not deadlock on the "Sage of Monticello" and his future vice president, Aaron Burr, until February, and the tie between the two men would not be resolved by the House of Representatives until February 17. Nonetheless, unmistakable change was in the air, and more than a month before Jefferson would emerge victorious over Burr on the House's thirty-sixth ballot, the *Courant* poem marveled: "Lord! How the Federalists will stare/At JEFFERSON in ADAMS' chair!" The poem offers an early example of a contention that Federalists would make relentlessly throughout Jefferson's two presidential terms: that Jefferson's presidency marked the beginning of the end of the nation that Washington, Adams, and all their citizen-supporters had sought to build. "The Triumph of Democracy" located the source of this decline in both Jeffersonian democratic ideas—which Federalists predicted would commence an inevitable slide toward lawlessness, chaos, and eventually tyranny as those meant to be ruled stood shoulder-to-shoulder with those meant to rule—and Jefferson's position as a Southern slaveholder, who would inevitably use the power of the presidency to cater to the interests of fellow plantation aristocrats at the expense of Northerners.[6]

The dangers posed by Jeffersonian democracy, Federalists were convinced, began in Jefferson's home state of Virginia, and in the South more generally, which Federalists described as a haven for foreigners and their radical, un-American ways. "Thieves, traitors, Irish renegadoes,/ Scape-gallowses, and desperadoes,/ All sorts of rogues stripp'd off the masque,/ And enter'd on the glorious task,/ Prepar'd to flounce with highest glee,/ In JEFFERSON's 'tempestuous sea.'" Jefferson and his ilk won the favor of such reprobates by making fantastic promises and pantomiming religious piety—by "telling lies" and "aping prayer." Without vigilance by states that had not become deaf to the "Jacobinic Tocsin," the Republicans' democratic poison would spread throughout the entire country. "In such a virtuous congregation," the poet ominously predicted, "some fruits must ripen for the nation."[7] The poem's prediction that democratic excess would flow from Virginia's disproportionate political influence laid the foundation for the second, somewhat contradictory, prediction: that Jefferson's presidency could commence an unprecedented sectional battle between Northern states, especially those in New England, and an oligarchy of Southern slaveholding aristocrats who now wielded control of the national government—and, perhaps worst of all, violence at the hands of black slaves themselves.

Historians are hesitant to posit counterfactuals, but it is difficult to imagine any action Jefferson could have taken that would have met with unequivocal Federalist approval. This is not meant to exonerate Jefferson from criticism. Rather it is to say that years of dire predictions of national decline at the hands of Jeffersonian democracy had primed Federalists to view almost anything Jefferson did as confirmation of their suspicions. Nonetheless, the specific actions Jefferson did take in his first term added tangible examples to fuel Federalist fears.

The first of these was Jefferson's decision, beginning immediately after taking office, to replace Adams's so-called "midnight appointments" with loyal Republicans. Prior to leaving office, Adams had used his presidential authority to appoint Federalists to last-minute posts as a way of shoring up the party's strength throughout the government. Less than three weeks after taking office, Jefferson declared these appointments "nullities" and replaced them with his own appointees.[8] Of the "412 officers at the disposal of the President," a piece in the *Newburyport Herald* reported in July 1802, "nearly 200 . . . [have been] filled since he came into office." By the time his first term was half over, Jefferson's own count was even higher, attesting to Republican control of better than 50 percent of the offices subject to presidential removal.[9]

Jefferson's removal of Adams's so-called "midnight appointments" was a widely publicized and debated political event. One Adams appointee, ousted by Jefferson, came to be the public face of Jefferson's executive action. Elizur Goodrich, a New England Federalist, had served two years as a congressman from the still heavily Federalist state of Connecticut. Recently reelected to that position, Goodrich had vacated his seat in order to accept Adams's appointment as collector of the port of New Haven. But his appointment was among those Jefferson deemed "nullities," and the new president promptly replaced Goodrich with Samuel Bishop, thirty-seven years Goodrich's senior and father to Republican printer Abraham Bishop.[10]

News of Goodrich's ouster was followed closely by news of a peculiar gift given to the president by loyal Republicans in the traditional Federalist stronghold of New England. On New Year's Eve, 1801, a group of Baptists from Cheshire, Massachusetts, greeted Jefferson at the president's mansion with a giant block of cheese weighing over half a ton, a gift to Jefferson meant to demonstrate the entire town's support for his administration. Attracting dumbfounded stares during its journey of more than four hundred miles, the cheese was known to many Americans before it arrived in Washington, and the further publicity it received from the Federalist press only added to its novelty. Odd though it was, the "Mammoth Cheese," as the Federalists dubbed it, was irrefutable evidence that support for the Republican president was making headway even in places where the Federalist Party remained strong. News of Jefferson's removal of Goodrich demonstrated Jefferson's willingness to wield the power that such public support gave him. A piece in the *American Citizen* remarked that stories about the "Mammoth Cheese" and Goodrich likely provoked "more *federal* objections against the *New* Administration, than any other two measures." Republicans defended Jefferson's actions as essential to ensuring that only true servants of the public will carried out national law.[11]

Federalists responded by arguing that Jefferson's use of the appointment power was an exercise in partisan "persecution," a dismissal of proven experienced public servants for party interests that was not in keeping with the president's job of acting in the best interest of all Americans. "A President in the exercise of his power, should not discard every reflection on the people's happiness. He should so act, as to come as near the will of those who delegated him as possible," remarked A Citizen in the *Philadelphia Gazette*.[12] Federalists insisted that Jefferson's removal of Goodrich demonstrated his partisan disregard for the people whose authority he was obligated to serve: a detriment that they argued would drag the entire country down into the muck of partisan one-upmanship. Goodrich was a Federalist, from a Federalist state (Connecticut), in the most heavily Federalist region of the country (New England). The people he would be tasked with serving were overwhelmingly Federalist, and besides, Federalists argued, Goodrich had already served the government well for years. Removal of such qualified public servants was a gross usurpation of the people's power by the president. "That conduct which would discover the friend and father of his people, the impartial administrator, the true patriot; that conduct, which, were a Democrat ever to be trusted, we had a right to expect from solemn protestations needlessly and unexpectedly made, evidently appears to be abandoned for a systematic course of persecution and revenge," a Federalist argued in the *New York Gazette*, "a course consistent with a barbarous station, but incompatible with the dignity, the virtue, the integrity, the amiable feelings, the heroic sentiments, that ought to distinguish the first magistrate of a great, of a civilized nation." For Federalists, that was the real point. The action simultaneously portended a dangerous broadening of presidential power and an alarming decline toward the kind of backward absolutism that Americans had rejected in favor of republicanism. Jefferson's actions did not just betray the formal mechanisms of government but the very character of a "civilized" society.[13]

One of the most colorful criticisms of Jefferson's appointment decisions, written by a pseudonymous Federalist under the pen name Fidelis,
managed to convey this point by depicting Jefferson as both effeminate
and domineering, disparaging the third president by comparing him to
an obstinate and unpredictable housewife. "If the hereditary despots of
the old world exercise it [the appointment power] in gratifying their own
partialities, in providing for their minions, friends and flatterers—the
American people never suspected that in the hands of a President of their
choice, it would be thus abused," Fidelis argued in the *Columbian Centinel.* "When they made *you* mistress of the family, they had no idea that
you would act the virago, clear the house, and without giving them an
hearing instantly drive out all the old servants, as though they were a par-
cel of rogues or scoundrels." Quite the opposite, Fidelis contended: "the
generality of federalists believed that the new bride would have entered
with an air of complacency, and previous to any symptoms of ill humour,
would have tried, at least, to manage the family-affairs with the help already accustomed to them and acquainted with the ways of the house."[14]

Remarkable about the essay is the way it feminizes both Jefferson and
Washington to completely opposite ends. "That a WASHINGTON under
similar circumstances, would have conducted thus, his life from beginning
to end, is a proof," Fidelis went on. "Though he should have known that
all those public servants had been opposed to his election, yet, believing
them to have acted conscientiously, they would not have been, on that
account, less in his esteem, nor considered by him as less qualified to co
operate with him in the public service." The result? A country bitterly
divided by partisanship and oppressed from the top by a domineering
shrew of an executive. "Instead of the melting down of parties and their
extinguishment, what an irritation to their passions, and sharpening of
their spirits against each other! What an accumulation of fuel upon the
fire! What an effusion of oil upon the flames of discord."[15]

Scholars of gender would rightly have a field day with a political piece
that disparages Jefferson by likening him to a stubborn housewife and
then essentially calls him a bitch. For our purposes, the piece is more
significant for what it reveals about the presidency. Using the position of
housewife as a metaphor for the presidency, the piece underscores how the
president's exercise of the appointment power set the tone for the entire
household: the metaphor that Fidelis chose for the nation as a whole. An
institutional power like the president's appointment authority had palpa-
ble cultural significance, encouraging either the amiable cooperation that
Americans extolled as a unique virtue of their republican system or the

partisan division that was the curse of inferior, "old-world" societies. Jefferson's exercise—Federalists would say abuse—of his appointment power would lead to a national decline into primitive political persecution.

Such a decline carried an obvious racial subtext, made all the more glaring by Jefferson's own status as a Southern slave-owner. Jefferson's dismissal of Adams's appointments confirmed Federalist predictions that under Jefferson's presidential leadership any person and any state that did not completely adhere to the president's agenda would be stripped of any voice or influence whatsoever, dividing the country into a Federalist Party and a New England region rendered "slaves," and a Jefferson-led Virginia aristocratic "faction" that wielded absolute power.[16] The complaint was so common in Federalist writing that by the end of Jefferson's presidency and the beginning of Madison's first term, the Republican press characterized it as a tired political cliché. It was not "worth the while to notice the pitiful slanders that have been circulated in the federal papers to effect an hatred between the northern and southern states," an exasperated Republican writer sighed in 1807. "Geographical distinctions have been countenanced by the most expert praters of the day; and the freemen of Massachusetts have been told that their liberties were in danger from the slaves of Virginia."[17]

But Federalists were deadly serious. Federalists railed against the leveling effects of Jeffersonian democracy, arguing that Jefferson's actions proved his intent to establish a rigid and permanent political hierarchy where Southern slaveholding elites stood permanently over everyone else. "Our Constitution's strength is gone,/ Its pride, its Justice overthrown," lamented another poem, "Sketches of the Times." Published in the *Courant* and Alexander Hamilton's *New-York Evening Post*, the poem articulated the Federalists' belief that they were all that stood in the way of Jefferson's ultimate goal of making abject slaves out of free citizens.

> Lo, now, the servile Band engage,
> With party fire, and maddening rage,
> To force our freeborn souls to obey,
> And bow beneath a despot's saw,
> To fix their Man, tho' noise and strife,
> A KING OR PRESIDENT FOR LIFE!
> In one vast vortex sink the fates,
> And freedom, of the Northern States,
> Place in Virginia's hands the reins,
> But bind our Sovereignty in chains.[18]

Fears that Jeffersonian democracy threatened the freedom of white, American citizens were not new in the early years of Jefferson's presidency. But Jefferson's exercise of the appointment power seemed to offer tangible proof that the Republicans, led by Jefferson, sought to subordinate Northern, white Federalists to their will, essentially pushing them down to a status that looked to Northern whites alarmingly similar to that of black slaves.

The Federalists' attack functioned as both a personal attack and a statement about the office Jefferson now held. The president's appointment power was intimately connected to the nation's status as a nonpartisan republic, a political distinction inseparable from whites' understanding of their own superior status over free and enslaved black people. Anything that smacked of arbitrary, unaccountable authority reminded whites of the very authority they exercised over people with dark skin. Thus, anything that appeared to exercise such authority over white people brought their social and political status, if not their physical bodies, into closer proximity with those of black people. By claiming that Jefferson's actions expanded the power of the presidency in service of the slaveholding South, seeking to "bind" Northern states and citizens in "chains" to Southern interests, Federalists implied that the president's duty to exercise the appointment power in a nonpartisan manner was part of a more fundamental duty to safeguard a republican citizenship rooted in white supremacy.

Federalist views about the connection between Jefferson's presidential actions and the racial integrity of the nation could explain why James Callender—who, after languishing in jail for violating the Sedition Act and seething after Jefferson had denied him an appointment to a postmaster position in Richmond—decided to seek revenge by publishing a salacious, but at the time baseless, accusation that Jefferson was having sex with Sally Hemings, one of the women he enslaved. Callender's attack on Jefferson is usually characterized as a political blunder stemming from Callender's profound misunderstanding of the rules of American political culture regarding what was, and what was not, fair game to be discussed publicly. Sex between white masters and black slaves was an open secret in the South. Evidence of it was everywhere, from the light-skinned enslaved children birthed by black women on their master's plantation to the whispers of indignation (and often outright fury) by white plantation mistresses to their closest confidantes. Yet slaves were considered property, and therefore, the thinking went, what a master did with his property should be nobody else's concern. For this reason, sex between a white man and his female slave was not openly discussed in polite society, despite widespread knowledge that it occurred frequently. By publishing his accusation that Jefferson was keeping a black mistress, the historical account usually goes, Callender committed a colossal political miscalculation: he attacked Jefferson the plantation owner for having sex with one of his slaves, in the hopes of ruining Jefferson's reputation. Callender's plan boomeranged on him, costing him his reputation and leaving Jefferson relatively unscathed. Even if true, Jefferson's sexual involvement with one of his slaves was accepted in American society. Discussing it openly, by contrast, was not. Jefferson refused to respond to the accusation directly, thus preserving the expectation of silence that surrounded the subject. Callender's reputation, meanwhile, was irreparably ruined.[19]

But emphasizing Callender's failed attack on Jefferson the Southern plantation owner glosses, or completely ignores, Callender's attack on Jefferson the president. This latter attack was not a violation of social norms. In fact, it was consistent with the message that Federalists and Republicans had been conveying for years. The presidency was more than just a political office; it was the exemplar of those social norms, and as such even the most intimate of personal conduct was fair game for public criticism because it revealed much about American society as a whole. Callender's willingness to bring up Jefferson's sexual activity fit as part of Federalist commentary (echoed by Republicans) that suggested that the president's job was to reflect and uphold the essential character of American society. For Callender, at the core of that character was white supremacy, and because Jefferson was the president, Callender argued, his action portended a rapid and potentially irreversible leveling of society, a dangerous dissolving of the natural hierarchies that maintained social order.

Callender certainly accused the third president of making a personally damaging choice by fornicating with a black woman. At one point, Callender lamented that Jefferson, who "wrote so smartly concerning negroes, when he endeavored so much to belittle the African race," was now "the chief magistrate of the United States" and "the ringleader in shewing that his opinion was erroneous," electing "an African stock whereupon he was to engraft his own descendants." And there is no doubt that Callender had an ax to grind. Callender's initial essay challenged Jefferson and Republicans to respond to his explosive accusation, claiming that silence would amount to a tacit admission of Jefferson's guilt. The final sentence makes reference to "so many unprovoked attacks upon J.T. CALLENDER," a reference to the extent to which Callender had been all but purged from Republican circles.[20]

Yet Callender's personal attack was rooted in a statement about the presidency and the obligations of the president to maintain a social and cultural status quo. Callender's initial essay accusing Jefferson began by referring to Jefferson as "the man, *whom it delighteth the people to honour*," and throughout, it highlighted Jefferson's occupation of the office alongside his debauchery with his black "concubine." "By the wench Sally, our president has had several children," Callender went on to say. "Behold the favorite, the first born of republicanism! the pinnacle of all that is good and great! in the open consummation of an act which tends to subvert the policy, the happiness, and even the existence of this country!" In a subsequent essay the paper referred to a son Jefferson supposedly had with Hemings as "our little mulatto president, the fellow TOM."[21] Both references highlight the people's possession of Jefferson, referencing his station as president, and not-so-subtly underscoring the widespread repercussions of Jefferson's actions on "the people" as a whole. Viewed as simply an attack on Jefferson as an individual, these statements make little sense. But viewed within the context of many years of Federalist commentary on Jefferson's impact on the presidency, Callender's meaning becomes clear: Jefferson's intimacy with a black slave was simply one more way that, as president, Jefferson was compromising the nation's racial integrity.

In this sense Callender was not really introducing a radically new criticism but rather claiming that an old Federalist fear of the corrosive impact that Jefferson's presidency would have on American society was materializing on Jefferson's plantation and radiating out through the entire country. Much Federalist criticism of Jefferson, dating back to the 1790s, stemmed from a belief that too much intimacy between members of groups that were meant to remain separate and unequal would inevitably lead to a breakdown of society. The ultimate expression of that dangerous breakdown of order was racial mixing—a belief that Jefferson himself expressed in his *Notes on the State of Virginia*. Yet Federalists remained convinced that Jefferson's egalitarian ideals would poison the country's system of governance—and society more generally. With the apostle of equality as the nation's president, those who were never meant to rule would get dangerous ideas that perhaps the dream of equality should include them, too.

A piece signed by a "correspondent" to the *Recorder* writing under the pseudonym "A Poor Dutchman" bore out the point that the president's sexual intimacy with a black slave portended a national decline into degeneracy. Praising the paper for providing "information . . . respecting the president, so far as it concerns negro Sally," the piece condemned Jefferson's behavior as a permanent "stigma upon his character, by all religious and genteel citizens." "He has broken the laws of God and man," A Poor Dutchman went on to say. "It is therefore to be hoped that the people of the United States will never continue in the honorable post of presidency, a man who has been guilty of such an irreligious and dishonorable act. And indeed should they do so, we shall have sufficient reason to think the time is not far distant when all will become fornicators and mongrels; for it is well known how apt most people are to imitate, as near as they are capable, the actions of those we call great men."[22]

The writer's chosen pseudonym, the editors' insistence that the letter was "the genuine production of a person beyond the Blue Ridge," and their praise for the author's "plain intelligent mind" suggests that the paper is going out of its way to confirm its veracity as a condemnation of Jefferson by a poor, rural Virginian. Callender was certainly capable of fabricating the piece himself, but whether it was actually written by a far-flung westerner or not, the piece provides another testament that presidential "character" was now subject to scrutiny by non-elites. Jefferson himself is often credited with romanticizing rural farmers as the archetypal Americans. The *Recorder* piece proceeds from that same assumption in order to maximize Jefferson's humiliation. For Callender, no less than for Jefferson, rural farmers were the real America that the president was tasked with representing. Callender clearly operated under the widely shared assumption that democracy in America was only for whites and that holding the president accountable for maintaining an acceptably hierarchical relationship with black people in his public as well as private interactions was essential for ordinary, white Americans to ensure that the racial basis of their democracy remained intact.[23]

Callender's caustic attack on Jefferson was far from alone. Months before the *Recorder* published Callender's first essay about Jefferson and Hemings, the Philadelphia-based Federalist newspaper *Port Folio*, edited by former Adams administration official Joseph Dennie, published a poem (reprinted in the *New-York Evening Post*) that used interracial sex and slave violence to illustrate the inevitable cost of democracy, now that democracy's champion held the highest office in the land.[24] The poem's protagonist, a fictitious slave named Quashee, who shares Jefferson's ideals of equality and liberty, takes those ideals to their logical conclusion, which includes his right to express himself sexually to white women and violently toward white authorities, in open defiance of established white supremacist norms.

Den tell me, why should Quashee stay,
To tend de cow and hoe de corn!
Huzza for massa Jefferson;
And if all mans alike be free,
Why should de one, more dan his broder,
Hab house and corn! for poor Quashee
No hab the one, no hab de oder.
Huzza, &c.
[. . .]
For make all like, let blackee nab
De white womans—dat be de track!
Den Quashee de white wife will hab,
And massa Jef. shall hab de black
Huzza, &c.

Why should a judge (him always white)
'Pon pickaninny put him paw,
Caus he steal little! dat no rite!
No! Quashee say he'll hab no law.
Huzza, &c.
[. . .]
Huzza for us den! we de boys
To rob and steal, and burn and kill;
Huzza! me say, and make de noise!
Huzza for Quashee! Quashee will
Huzza for massa Jefferson![25]

The poem—from its crude pantomime of slave dialect, to Quashee's resentment at racial injustice at the hands of judges, to his ultimate resolution to reject white laws, take a "white wife" and make violent "noise"—uses the threat of unbridled black violence and sexuality to illustrate in visceral terms the consequences of the equality that the president and his party promoted. Jefferson's election was clear evidence that his ideas were gaining traction throughout the country. While Southern aristocrats used the language of democracy to strip Northerners of political power and influence, what was to stop enslaved blacks from invoking democracy's ideal of equality to justify violent resistance to their enslavement and sexual congress across the color line? Jefferson's democratic ideology provided slaves like Quashee the intellectual justification to target white women for sexual conquest and in the process "make all like"—breaking down the racial hierarchy that kept whites in power and blacks enslaved.[26]

The Quashee poem is more than just a particularly vile example of racism deployed to further political ends. More specifically, it is also a reflection of Federalists' insistence that Jefferson's ascent to the presidency amplified the power and influence of his dangerous democratic political philosophy and the Southern-based Republican Party he led in persecution of Northern Federalists. The result, they were convinced, would be a once-noble republican nation reduced to a Southern slave-ocracy. While plantation masters ran roughshod over the rights of Northern free men, relegating white Northerners to a level that approximated that of their black chattel, the slaves themselves would eye equality with a lustful, unbroken gaze—and then act, to the horror of formerly free white Americans.

The Louisiana Purchase in 1803, Jefferson's most celebrated presidential accomplishment and one of the most momentous feats in all of American statecraft, nonetheless became, to Federalists, further evidence that the president orchestrated a massive takeover of American society, with the ultimate result being the subjugation of white Northerners to the rule of Southern aristocrats. To this, Federalists added fears of racial, cultural, and linguistic decline, predicting that the acquisition of Louisiana, with its population of Indian "savages," foreign French and Spaniards, and their slaves, would irreparably degrade the American nation.[27]

Jefferson inherited from his predecessors an uncertain political climate shaped by the violence of foreign nations, especially the on-again, off-again war between France and Great Britain. In 1802 the Treaty of Amiens between Britain and France led to a détente that lasted only a year. In the interim Napoleon Bonaparte, who rose to power in France in 1799 and crowned himself emperor in 1804, obtained from Spain the vast expanse of land west of the Mississippi known as Louisiana, leading Jefferson and his administration to worry that France would use the acquisition, particularly its control of the port at New Orleans, to strangle American trade. Jefferson sent James Monroe to France to negotiate a deal. To both men's surprise and delight, the French government agreed to sell the United States not only New Orleans, but all of Louisiana.[28]

The purchase of Louisiana had far-reaching implications. Diplomatically it certainly eased the stress felt by the Jefferson administration that French aggression would lead the United States to a war that would further increase its alliance with Britain. Financially it was a steal: fifteen million dollars for more than 820,000 square miles of land. Politically, it allowed Jefferson to further bring the nation and the government more in line with his political ideology and his party by naming Republicans to leadership positions within the territory. It also opened up the Great Plains for American westward expansion. For decades, the political and economic fate of the United States would be tied to the western frontier. The states carved from the Louisiana Territory would facilitate the expansion of slavery westward. To Jefferson, who never believed that black and white people were capable of living together as equals, the opening of slavery to westward expansion would act as a kind of safety valve, relieving the pressure that inevitably mounted when the slave population increased over the generations in a limited geographic area. John Quincy Adams, the son of Jefferson's predecessor, would assess the situation more accurately during the Missouri Crisis more than a decade and a half later, presciently observing that the West was not relieving the pressures of slavery but exacerbating them as supporters and opponents of slavery scrambled to expand or limit the terms by which western lands could be admitted as slave or free states. Indeed, the lands purchased by Jefferson in 1803 would serve as both figurative and literal battlegrounds over the spread of slavery that would eventually erupt in the bloody and cataclysmic Civil War.[29]

Federalists, meanwhile, saw in the purchase a far-flung wilderness, filled with "savage" Indians, dangerous French and Spanish foreigners, and their slaves. The acquisition of Louisiana confirmed their fear that Jefferson was dangerously abusing the powers of his office in ways that would lead to inevitable and irreversible decline, as these populations— uncouth and unschooled in representative government, many of them unfree and unfamiliar with English—would now become incorporated into the country. Railing against the introduction of barbaric Indians, Spanish- and French-speaking foreigners, and their slaves, Federalists made it clear that they expected the president to uphold the very moral, racial, and political purity that Jefferson's actions threatened.

Federalist accusations that the purchase of Louisiana was a clear example of Jefferson's own ambitions to make himself a king went hand in hand with the contempt and suspicion they harbored for the people who inhabited the country's newly acquired territory. Jefferson, they argued, surely intended to populate the country with so many detestable people in order to make them his minions, solidifying his political grip at the expense of the nation's moral, racial, and political character. "Mr. JEF-FERSON, the man who dreads executive patronage and the influence of office so much, Mr. JEFFERSON, has bought Louisiana, a vast half savage region which will ever require myriads of placemen and dependents, civil and military, on the President as long as we keep it in possession," the *Hampshire Federalist* exclaimed. "Here Mr. JEFFERSON has derived from an act of Congress giving the whole power of a monarch into his hands, more *patronage* than Mr. ADAMS ever enjoyed."[30] "Hitherto it has been our wise endeavour, at least it was certainly a part of the system of the *late administration*, to create among the people of the several states, a strong attachment to each other; to unite their interests where possible; to assimilate their views where practicable; and to form in as great a degree as was feasible, a firm, consistent *national character*," A Merchant recalled, referencing Adams's administration. This "national character" could only degenerate once Louisiana was incorporated. "[W]hen a population of Frenchmen and Spaniards, which with their slaves, will it is supposed amount to 250,000 souls, shall be introduced into our government, shall participate in its functions, and shall hold (as by the treaty they are entitled to do) the highest offices in our nation, what sort of national character shall we possess?"[31]

For A Merchant the fears of national degeneracy were of a piece with "the greatest evil resulting from this incorporation into our Union," namely "the great preponderance it will give" to some states over others. Could foreigners, "bred up in the arms of despotism . . . suddenly be fitted for self-government, and republicanism?" The answer was clearly no. Frenchmen, Spaniards, and their slaves, "with their ignorance of our constitution, language, manners, and habits," could not "be intrusted with the weight and authority, which a state in its sovereign capacity, must and ought always to hold in the union." The very notion that "two Spaniards from New-Orleans," would "have the same influence in the Senate, with the two Senators from Virginia, Pennsylvania or Massachusetts" was not only "absurd" but "highly dangerous to our peace." Not only was Louisiana crawling with foreigners, it was prime real estate for westward expansion by slaveholding Southerners bent on dominating the entire country. The "assistance and support" that citizens, especially those in such a vast, remote place, needed could only be provided "by a *strong and vigorous administration*," which would upset the balance of power between the states and grant unprecedented supremacy to the South and its champion, Jefferson. "No member of the Conservative Senate" of France, "base and servile as it is, would venture to propose [to] vest such powers in Bonaparte, as Mr. Breckenridge in *the Senate of the United States* has dared to attempt to grant to Mr. Jefferson. Such indeed are the measures which are to be expected from an extension of terr[it]ory. It is as adverse to our republicanism as it is to the increase of our population a[n]d power."[32]

A Merchant echoed the sentiments of critics throughout the country who saw Louisiana as both a far-flung backwater filled with foreigners and a site for the dangerous and potentially irreparable national domination of the Jefferson-led slaveholding South.[33] The nation is "now ruled by a President elected by means of *Southern Slaves*," an essay in the *New-York Evening Post* cried out in 1804, "so we must ever continue under the controul of a Virginia faction, unless we unite in the choice of men who will administer the government for the benefit of the UNION, and not of an INDIVIDUAL STATE."[34] An 1803 piece in the *Newburyport* (Massachusetts) *Herald*, quoting from Jefferson's *Notes on the State of Virginia*, asserted that in the Old Dominion "the right of electing *members of the legislature, who* in turn, elect the *governor and council*, and generally '*all the chief officers, executive and judiciary*' is confined to a '*roll of freeholders;*' which 'freeholders,' let it be remembered, consist of a landed ARISTOCRACY, who are the owners and possessors of—*three hundred and forty-five thousand slaves*." That "inequality," the author assured readers, "has continually been increasing" since Jefferson penned his *Notes* twenty years earlier. "When Mr. Jefferson writes more 'Notes on Virginia,' he will be compelled to acknowledge that 'below the falls of the rivers,' the *blacks* increase in a ratio of *two to one*, compared with the *whites*," the author concluded, "and this indisputable fact may, if he pleases, be cited as a pertinent illustration of the position assumed by PUBLIUS, 'that the principle of investing wealth with immediate political power, has covered the earth with slaves.'"[35]

It all added up to an assault on the white population by Jeffersonian democracy from above and below—from both the Virginia "aristocracy" that now ran the country, as well as the "foreigners" they embraced and the slaves they owned. In the purchase of Louisiana, Federalists saw further evidence of the party's long-predicted political apocalypse. They declared that the influx of dangerous foreigners, uncivilized Indians, and slaves into the rest of the country, and the all-but-certain domination of Republican appointees within the newly acquired territory, would signal a decline from which the country would never recover.

Adding still more fuel to Federalist opposition were Jefferson's religious views, especially his longstanding belief in religious toleration, his opposition to government support for religious establishments, and his friendship with avowed critics of Christianity. In an 1802 address to a Baptist congregation in Danbury, Massachusetts, Jefferson spoke of his belief "that religion is a matter which lies solely between Man & his God," and that the First Amendment to the Constitution establishes "a wall of separation between Church & State." One year earlier, the same month as his inauguration, Jefferson had written a letter to Thomas Paine, the literary firebrand of both the American and French revolutions, whose work *The Age of Reason* many devout deemed blasphemous. The letter, widely reprinted in the press, reportedly offered Paine transport on a "public vessel" to the United States. Federalists decried the use of government money to support the travels of the once-celebrated revolutionary writer.[36] Paine's *Age of Reason* was "a blasphemous, though weak, attack on the divinity of our Saviour, and the whole Christian system," one piece declared. "[I]t may be of *no importance* whether a man believes in "NO GOD OR TWENTY," the author continued, referencing Jefferson's own observation that his neighbor's religious beliefs did not affect him personally and thus were not his concern. "[Y]et, the serious Christian sees, alike in *both*, a deadly enmity to the church of Christ, an habitual hatred to the principles of true religion, and a *mutual co-operation* to root out and destroy the ONLY SOLID FOUNDATION OF PUBLIC PROSPERITY AND PRIVATE FELICITY."[37]

For William Emerson, Boston minister and father of Ralph Waldo Emerson, France was clearly the source of such moral decline, and the presidency that Jefferson now occupied was the conduit through which it worked to undermine what Emerson called the "principle of cohesion," established by the Constitution for the entire country after the American Revolution. Moral decline threatened Americans' status as a free people. If "the rulers of our country" decided to "deviate from the course prescribed by their wise predecessors," Emerson warned, "deplorable will be the consequences."[38]

More than simply an attack on Paine, France, or even on Jefferson's personal failings, Emerson's sermon was a statement about how Jefferson's actions as president threatened the downfall of the nation's essential institutions—and with them, the "feelings," "manners," *principles*," and ultimately the "character" of the American people themselves. "From an head so sick, and an heart so faint, disease will extend to the utmost extremities of the political body," Emerson warned. Citizens "owe it to the ashes of him, who, whether considered as a man among men, an hero among heroes, or a statesman among statesmen, will command and love the admiration of every future age." Emerson meant, of course, the "immortal Washington," but he also implored his audience to remember the example of Washington's "great successor, who has now carried into retirement the sublime and delightful consciousness of having been an everlasting benefactor to his country." Highlighting the service of Washington and Adams, Emerson identified these men as the steadfast leaders who had governed according to the principles of the Revolution, and the "character" of its participants. In so doing, he implied that the office they held was the "head" whose health determined the well-being of the entire "political body." To ensure the body's continued health, the people must, "[w]ith daily and obstinate perseverance," work to "[p]reserve unchanged the same correct feelings of liberty, the same purity of manners, the same principles of wisdom and piety, of experience and prescriptions, the same seminaries of learning, temples of worship, and castles of defence, which immortalize the memory of your ancestors." This persistent resistance to the corrosive effects of Jacobinism and libertinism—never more danger-ous now that the champion of these vices stood at the "head" of the "po-litical body"—was the key to "prolong to your enraptured eyes *the age of Washington and of Adams.*"[39]

It is tempting to view such commentary as little more than disingenu-ous political hyperbole, concocted by Federalists as a strategy to stir up panic and fear in an unscrupulous attempt to regain power. Certainly it is true that Federalists recognized the volatility of their arguments and de-ployed them to play upon the apprehensions of any white American who feared where the ideals of Jeffersonian democracy could lead if carried to their logical conclusion. But the fact that many Americans had those fears reminds us that such racist arguments cannot be dismissed as purely political mudslinging. Obviously calculated to rile up political opposition, this criticism nonetheless reflected a sincere belief that the office Jefferson now occupied was inseparable from white Americans' collective sense of themselves. The balance of power between the states and the national government, the moral, linguistic, cultural, and racial purity of its people, the accountability of elected leaders *to* that people, all hinged on the pres-ident's actions. For Federalists, that was what made everything Jefferson did so terrifying.

Yet for all their protests Federalists appeared to be losing ground. In 1804 the Twelfth Amendment to the Constitution was ratified, stipulating that electors would specify votes for president and vice president, mak-ing it all but impossible for a Federalist runner-up for the presidency to become the vice president, thus eliminating the possibility that the results of the 1796 presidential election could happen again in reverse. That same year Jefferson larruped Federalist Charles Cotesworth Pinckney by 148 electoral votes (162 to 14), a more lopsided margin than even Washington had mustered with a vote from every single elector. In his Second Inaugural Address, Jefferson pointed to the victory as a triumph of "truth" over "falsehood and defamation." But his argument was not merely majoritarian. His overwhelming reelection was evidence that most Americans recognized "right" and "truth" when they saw it, but what Jefferson and Republicans sought was not right simply because the majority believed it. His reelection was further proof that "the union of sentiment" flourished, "manifest[ing]" itself "so generally, as auguring harmony and happiness to our future course." The result was a kind of political tautology. Republican principles were "right" and "true" because most citizens supported them (as evidenced by Jefferson's election and now his reelection). But their support was evidence that those principles were "true" and "right" no matter how many or how few people subscribed to them. As evidence of this, Jefferson pointed to his signal Constitutional triumph: the Louisiana Purchase. Once alone in "a country which left them no desire but to be undisturbed," indigenous peoples were now finding their lands increasingly occupied by whites. The purchase of Louisiana was not the catastrophe critics believed it to be. On the contrary, it was an opportunity for Americans to settle among "strangers of another family" and bring them into the fold by teaching them civilization they had never known. "[N]ow reduced within limits too narrow for the hunter's state, humanity enjoins us to teach them agriculture and the domestic arts; to encourage them to that industry which alone can enable them to maintain their place in existence, and to prepare them in time for that state of society, which to bodily comforts adds the improvement of the mind and morals," Jefferson explained. "We have therefore liberally furnished them with the implements of husbandry and household use; we have placed among them instructors in the arts of first necessity; and they are covered with the aegis of the law against aggressors from among ourselves." Right was right, truth was truth, and civilization was civilization, whether adhered to by a small minority or an overwhelming majority. The capacity of indigenous Americans to become civilized attested to their ability to learn how to become Americans as they found themselves becoming minorities in a land they once solely occupied. That statement worked as an analogy for the Federalists. "With those, too, not yet rallied to the same point," Jefferson continued, clearly referencing his political opponents, "the disposition to do so is gaining strength." It was not just that "a mass of their fellow citizens" held views contrary to their own. It was that those views were objectively, unavoidably superior.[40]

More than three years later, Jefferson's reelection continued to stand for the triumph of an objective national "truth" over repugnant Federalist dissenters peddling a dangerous "falsehood." "Every one is convinced," crowed a Jefferson supporter in 1807, writing under the pseudonym

Livingston, "that were we to a man united and firm in support of our government, no incendiaries would attempt to disturb us—no other nation could hope to wrest from us any essential right or deprive us of any valuable privilege." Why had that national unity in support of the government failed to materialize? The answer, to Livingston, was obvious: intransigent Federalists, stubbornly convinced of the superiority of their political ideology, were "continually opposing our own government, slandering and ridiculing the men who have been elected to administer it, and condemning and thwarting the measures they adopt for our security and welfare." But how could they be right if Jefferson's margin of victory in the Electoral College had been so lopsided? "But, you will ask, how can we support our government when we know it is wrong?" Livingston queried, then answered the question with a barrage of questions of his own. "Are you *sure* it is wrong?—*May* you not be wrong yourselves? Have you divested yourselves of party feelings and prejudices, and sought for truth *impartially* and *diligently*[?] Or have you closed your eyes, as it were against the evidence of facts, shut your ears to the voice of truth, and relied only upon party news-papers, and party pamphlets for information?"[41]

Knowing that the Federalists would never regain the presidency, historians have often marked Jefferson's reelection as a precursor to the Federalists' steady downward plunge into political obscurity. New and better methods of collecting data on voting in the first decades of the nation's history, however, has led to a reevaluation of the Federalists' political vitality. New studies demonstrate that Federalists remained a formidable political force at the state and local levels through the War of 1812. Taking advantage of the public controversies surrounding Jefferson's and Madison's actions, Federalists competed for state legislative seats and congressional seats from Massachusetts to Georgia, and even in western states like Kentucky and Ohio. They founded new partisan newspapers in Vermont, New York, Maryland, and as far south as Charleston, South Carolina.[42]

Yet Federalists' efforts to maintain and grow their political power at the state and local level—and Republicans' responses—were never wholly removed from the presidency. Both Federalist gains and Republican actions to counter them reflected the designs of the former to recapture the presidency and the latter's commitment to stopping them. Federalist efforts led Republican-controlled legislatures in states like North Carolina, Vermont, and most notoriously Massachusetts, to alter their electoral methods specifically to keep Federalists from regaining power. Recognizing the political advantage to be had through such schemes, Federalist-controlled assemblies in New Jersey did the same, changing how the state chose its presidential electors in order to maintain its authority. Many of the elections that took place during the presidencies of Jefferson and Madison witnessed record voter participation: a testament that, despite their renowned suspicion of democracy, the Federalists proved themselves remarkably adept at mobilizing popular discontent.[43]

Federalists also circulated petitions at the state level that objected to Jefferson's actions and even called for changes to the presidential election process. "[S]carcely had the auspicious inauguration of 1801, been celebrated . . . when symptoms of ambition and intrigue; of jealousy and discontent; of disunion and disorder; awakened the patriotic mind, to a sense of new troubles, and new sorrows," a piece in a Pennsylvania paper explained. Apostate "malcontents resolved to coerce, whom they could not persuade; and to ruin, what they could not enjoy" and were seeking to undermine the very freedoms that Republicans had long championed and for which Jefferson's presidential leadership now stood. Most ominously, the piece reported, these malcontents were collecting signatures for a petition that called for a new state constitutional convention: an act that Pennsylvania Republicans saw as an attempt to strike at the legitimacy of Jefferson's authority and undermine the authority of the national government as a whole. No one denied "[t]he inalienable right of the People, to assemble for the alteration, or abolition, of their form of Government; and the absolute authority of the Citizens, to select whom they please, for their Chief Magistrate," the piece conceded, but this was not the sentiment of the people of the state. Rather, it was a blatant attempt, "through the example and influence of *Pennsylvania*, to subvert the Federal Constitution at the hazard of civil war, and a dissolution of the Union." It was the petulant "cry" of a "faction," and therefore could not be given the same "obedience . . . which is due alone to the legitimate voice of the People." Republicans responded by circulating a remonstrance against the petition; they gathered 5,590 signatures, exceeding the petition's total by 646 names. "Our Fellow-Citizens, of every political description, feeling, at length, the necessity of a prompt interposition, hastened to rally round the Constitution, as the ark of their common safety," the piece trumpeted, "[a]nd now the Malcontents beheld, with terror and dismay, the People, whose name they had craftily assumed, and whose indignation they had justly excited; rising, in the native majesty of their power, and their virtue, to vindicate the dominion of the laws."[44] Political maneuvering at the local and state levels thus reflected how important the presidency was to Americans, regardless of their party ideology. Federalists remained a force to be reckoned with at the state level, but they had not removed their

sights from the presidency. Jefferson's second presidential term would provide Federalists with more fodder to attack Jefferson—and Republicans
with more alarm at the dangers those attacks posed.

Beginning shortly after he killed Alexander Hamilton in a duel in 1804,
Aaron Burr, Jefferson's vice president, set his sights on the west to reclaim
his political reputation. Enlisting the help of some sixty men, Burr solicited financial backing from Britain and led his band down the Mississippi
River. His precise goal was unclear, but it set off rumors that his actions
threatened "the peace and safety of the Union," as Jefferson himself put
it in 1807 in a special message to Congress. Jefferson feared the worst
and justified his actions in response to the alleged conspiracy as a fulfillment of his presidential duty to enact "measures . . . for suppressing" such
threats. Though the "fidelity" of the western country was "known to be
firm," Jefferson argued that the nation could not afford to take chances.
Jefferson notified the governors of the Orleans and Mississippi territories,
sent orders "to every intersecting point on the Ohio and Mississippi, from
Pittsburgh to New Orleans, for the employment of such force either of the
regulars or the militia" as would be enough "to arrest the persons concerned, and to suppress effectually" their progress. After Burr was arrested
and paroled in Kentucky, and arrested again in Virginia and tried for treason in 1807, Jefferson insisted that Burr's guilt was "beyond question."[45]

The whole bizarre ordeal struck Federalists alternately as evidence of a
more insidious tyrannical plot (of which, some suggested, Jefferson himself was a part) and a spurious excuse cooked up by one of Jefferson's
informants to prosecute Burr. On the one hand, some Federalists believed
that Jefferson knew about the Burr plot for upwards of a year before
acting. "Mr. Jefferson was warned of the designs of this Cataline twelve
months ago; and it is said he hooted at the information!" exclaimed "A
Sentinel" in the *Washington Federalist*. This was as clear a sign of executive weakness in light of a potentially serious threat as any, and the public
needed to hold Jefferson accountable. On the other hand, Jefferson's haste
to prosecute Burr struck others as evidence that Jefferson was exercising
too much political power, rather than too little. "I am an unbeliever in the
truth of the principle charges against the said BURR," one skeptical Federalist wrote in a letter published in the *Hampshire Federalist*. "The evidence
of his guilt comes the wrong way." But whether they held the president accountable for doing too much or not enough, Federalists invariably interpreted Jefferson's handling of the Burr conspiracy as evidence that he had
fallen away from his presidential duty to act dynamically for the safety
and security of the nation. "Good people of the United States," A Sentinel

implored readers, "how long will you submit to be the dupes of weak and wicked measures?"[46]

Federalist cries of "weak and wicked measures" only swelled after the imposition of Jefferson's embargo in 1807, widely considered to be the great foreign policy blunder of Jefferson's presidency.[47] Britain and France's on-again, off-again decades-long war resumed again in 1803, and each side sought to stymie the other's trade with other countries in an effort to wound the opponent economically. Britain—which enjoyed a naval superiority over France, while France's army dominated the battlefield in Europe—continued to impress American seamen on the high seas. To protect American ships and their crew members, prepare the nation for a possible war, and hurt Britain and France economically by denying them goods from the United States, Jefferson imposed an embargo, forbidding American trade to either belligerent nation.[48]

The embargo came after two widely publicized attacks on American vessels by two different British ships, the *Leander* and the *Leopard*, caused waves of public outrage at both British aggression and Jefferson's presidential leadership. Both attacks—the *Leander*'s in 1806, on a vessel just outside New York, the *Leopard*'s on a ship off the Virginia coast in 1807—cost American lives, and both were public spectacles. Federalists channeled this public anger into a demand that the president sufficiently enable the nation's capacity to defend itself and a condemnation of Jefferson's inability to do so. "*Resolved*, That the citizens of the United States are of right, and according to the constitution and laws of the land, entitled to the enjoyment of life, liberty, and property; and that it is the primary and most important duty of government to defend, preserve, and protect the same," a coalition of New York "Federal Republicans" declared just days after the *Leander*'s attack. Asserting that the responsibility for national safety fell to the administration, the Federal Republicans argued that Jefferson's administration had done nothing to prevent the British vessel from entering American waters without cause, and through its clear inability or indifference to its responsibility, had facilitated the death of John Pierce, a sailor who had perished in the *Leander* attack. Calling Pierce's murder "an act that excites our detestation and abhorence [*sic*]," deserving of "the adoption of prompt and vigorous measures" on the administration's part "to prevent a repetition of such wanton and inhuman conduct, and so flagrant a violation of our national sovereignty," the Federal Republicans declared that they would attend Pierce's funeral, "and that it will be recommended to the ships in the harbor to display the customary signs of mourning."[49]

The Federalists intended to make a show of the overwhelming public demand for satisfaction, directed squarely at the president. Making good on their promise to honor Pierce, Federalists held public observances of his life, as the Federalist Republicans requested, "not only for the purpose of manifesting the public sorrow, for the violent & untimely end of a fellow citizen, but as a solemn and impressive testimony against that system of administration, which . . . withholds all adequate protection from our city, and sea-fairing brethren, and thereby leaves us and them defenceless and exposed to the violence of depredations of the free-booters of the ocean."[50] Jefferson's leadership was rendering the nation more susceptible to attack, while his actions—a condemnation of the attack, in which Jefferson called for the arrest of the ship's commander, Henry Whitby, while also ordering the ship to depart and forbidding any American trade with the vessel—all but blatantly advertised the nation's inability to find and prosecute those responsible. "The President of the United States, has, by Proclamation enjoined our citizens to apprehend Henry Whitby, commander of the British ship Leander, *wherever he may be found*," one paper commentator explained, "and, in the last paragraph, we find Mr. Jefferson, with the correctness and consistency, which mark all his measures, prohibiting our citizens from going to the only place, where it is probable the same Henry Whitby *could be found*."[51]

Federalists accused Jefferson of a failure to act with the swiftness and decisiveness the American public demanded. In effect, they were calling upon strong presidential resistance to British tyranny, claiming that the people were prepared to follow such leadership when it arose, and stating in no uncertain terms that the current incumbent fell woefully short of the mark. Funeral processions and public acts of mourning accompanied printed accusations of Jefferson's executive inadequacies, of his failure to act when the public demanded it.

Taken together, Federalists deemed the attacks by the *Leander* and the *Leopard* and the embargo a fitting summation of the nation's decline since Jefferson took office. "Eight years ago these United States saw no nation or people so great and so blessed," an open letter to New Jersey electors asserted in the New York *Evening Post* in September 1808. "Our federal constitution was unchanged—our law, wisely framed and ably executed;— The fruits of industry and rights of property were sacredly respected." The economy flourished, the nation "at *peace*" at home and abroad, not by "surrender of rights—but by our own justice and valor. We had not been bowed to French influence, but maintained our independence, when threatened, by adequate means to defend it." All of this, the writer stressed, was "the fruit of twelve years of precious government under our WASHINGTON and ADAMS!" Since Jefferson's inauguration, however, every one of these trends had reversed. Loyal public servants had been "suddenly *dismissed*" simply for being Federalists. A Republican Party that had long charged the Washington and Adams administrations with capitulating to foreign (British) interests counted among its ranks men like William Duane—a pugilistic partisan journalist who would inherit editorship of the *Aurora* after Benjamin Franklin Bache. Though American-born, Duane was the son of Irish immigrants and thus a prime example of "foreign" influence within the Republican ranks—as was Albert Gallatin, Jefferson's treasury secretary, "a *Swiss emigrant*, who scarcely pronounces our language." The Louisiana Purchase was a fifteen-million-dollar boondoggle that netted the United States nothing but a "disputed country" that was "already . . . the scene of treachery, contention and war." And now the embargo, the act of a president and a party that had long accused Federalists of being British sycophants and warmongers, showed the capacity of the president to submit to British aggression, while directing the power of his office to harm his own people. "Commerce, ships, seamen, all are wiped from the face of our country—not by England, or France—but by our *own rulers.*"[52]

For this writer, the embargo was the culmination of a downward national decline that began with Jefferson's election. "Never in so short a time," the writer concluded, "has any country suffered so much in its character and interests, from a change of public men in all the executive, legislative, and judicial departments." A nation once prosperous, united, strong, and independent now saw its "constitutions," its "independence," its "rights of commerce and property," and its "personal liberty, union, and security" in tatters. The culprit was an administration that was too hostile to the moral, upright "principles and views of the friends and supporters of the WASHINGTON SYSTEM" that persisted around the country, especially in Northern states, and too weak-willed to meet foreign aggression with anything but "blustering and impotence."[53]

For Federalists, the embargo perfectly captured the cowardice, partisan self-interest, and immorality that belied the ideals of Republican democracy and the lofty promises of its apostle in chief. It was the latest example of a president who had long proven himself incapable of standing up to the aggression of foreign armies, dating all the way back to his term as Virginia governor. The accusation that Jefferson had fled in the face of approaching British forces during the Revolution appeared again, but this time a Hudson, New York, paper linked Jefferson's cowardice

to his penchant for a black mistress. Not only had "the peril of the times
. . . frightened" Jefferson "to a 'dignified retreat,'" the then-governor
had sought safety "in the *bosom* of Carter's mountain—or, to that of his
faithful slave."[54] The embargo was but the latest example of Jefferson's
cowardly retreat from foreign pressure—and another opportunity to link
that cowardice to sexual immorality and racial impurity. But it was also
evidence of his bald-faced willingness to subjugate and enslave Northern states, making him what one piece called the "arbitrary and absolute" ruler of American commerce, less than two months before James
Madison took the oath of office. The president's "mere *instructions*, one
thing to day and another to-morrow, one thing in this part of the union,
another in that, issued without notice and never made public, are rendered paramount over the laws of the land, over the municipal policy
of the states, and the constitution itself."[55] In the embargo Federalists
saw evidence of Jefferson the dangerous race-mixing democrat, Jefferson
the cowardly leader, and Jefferson the partisan Southern aristocrat. Into
their criticism of the embargo, they poured their long-held insistence that
Jefferson betrayed everything the American nation stood for—and thus
failed the essence of what the president of the United States should be. By
any reasonable measure, Federalists chorused, Jefferson did not live up to
this standard—and the entire nation suffered as a result.

From objections to the embargo emerged calls on citizens to dissent
from Jefferson's presidential leadership, praising citizens and public officials who opposed it as the nation's saviors.

By Jefferson's second term, dissent came even from some Republicans,
most notoriously John Randolph of Virginia, who believed Jefferson was
abandoning the principles of the Republican Party, and DeWitt Clinton
of New York, who gained Northern supporters apprehensive about the
pervasiveness of Southern influence. In June 1803, the *Aurora* disparag-
ingly referred to these critics as a "*tertium quid*" (Latin for "third thing"),
accusing these Republican separatists of blending "true" Republican principles with "false" Federalist ones. The name *Quid* became something of
a favorite term of disparagement among Jeffersonian Republicans, hissed
at Republican turncoats that Jeffersonians considered traitors.[56]

For Jefferson's critics the partisan nastiness that defined politics in the
age of Jefferson made it all the more imperative that citizens keep a suspicious eye over those they entrusted with power. As John Randolph, writing
as Philo-Laos one year after Jefferson's retirement put it, the one "lesson"
that the present political situation taught the public was "that, *here*, as
well as in the unhappy country from which we are descended; with all the

clamour and inveteracy of hate between whig and tory—whigs, *in power*, become *tories*, and tories *out of power, whigs*." For that very reason, it was imperative "to watch them accordingly."[57]

Calls to keep a stern eye on the president and oppose Jefferson's measures, a staple of Federalist political commentary, reached peak intensity with Jefferson's embargo. The Massachusetts assembly called the embargo "grievous to the good people of this State" and praised the governor for refusing "to designate persons to carry into effect, by the aid of *military power*, . . . the Embargo."[58] A series of resolutions passed by the town of Springfield, Massachusetts, declared that the administration's policies were indicative of a dangerous overreaching of executive power, "which in our opinion vests in the President powers wholly unknown to the constitution, violates the first principles of civil liberty, prostrates the sovereignty of the states at the foot of the Federal Executive, and tends directly to the establishment of the worst of all possible Governments,—A MILITARY DESPOTISM." Resistance to such laws by the states and by the citizenry, uncompromising demands that the president hear and respond to their grievances—"expressing our opinions of the measures of our rulers," as the town's resolutions put it—was "one of the dearest privileges of Freemen, . . . a duty peculiarly incumbent upon the citizens of our country," because it was the only way "to restore the United States to that commanding situation of happiness and prosperity to which they were exalted by the *Patriots* of former times, the illustrious founders of our *Republic*."[59]

An address to the electors of New Jersey, published in the Federalist New York *Evening Post* (with a heading praising the piece as having been composed "with ability"), made clear the importance of mass public dissent against the president. "It is for the PEOPLE to speak out, and no longer conceal their sentiments of those *public agents*, whose *ignorance* or *mal-conduct*, have produced these calamities." the unnamed author of the address declared, "[O]ur dispositions are those of countrymen and brothers—We speak to the *great body of voters*, whatever may have been their former opinions, in the spirit of affection, but in the language of freedom."[60]

Linking Jefferson's embargo to such profound decline, opponents of the embargo asserted their right to criticize the president in order to restore the nation's former glory. Federalists insisted that the nation needed a president who possessed an uncompromising commitment to everything that made Americans civilized, sovereign, and free. On this, Republicans wholeheartedly agreed.

THE OTHER FOURTH

"THE FOURTH OF MARCH Has become a glorious *aera*, in the annals of our country!" an account of a Republican celebration of the second anniversary of Jefferson's inauguration announced. "If it did not, like the FOURTH OF JULY, give existence to a *nation*, it yet renovated the declining spirit of *Freedom*, and rescued a *nation* from impending destruction." Jefferson's election to the presidency "appalled the enemies of our constitution: it paralized [*sic*] their efforts, to sap the foundation of our liberties;—it demolished their air-built fabric of hereditary glory: it arrested the wild career of profligacy and corruption—it checked the shameful aggressions of executive power, and proclaimed to the daring spirit of usurpation, '*Thus far shall thou go, and no farther!!*'"[61] Pieces like this appeared year after year on March 4, the anniversary of Jefferson's inauguration, both during Jefferson's presidency and even into the presidency of his successor, James Madison. Fourth-of-March celebrants cast the date as the anniversary of the day that patriotic Americans had finally triumphed over the nation's enemies, in a "bloodless revolution of 1801," the peaceful culmination of their bid for sovereignty and independence that had begun in the American Revolution. During Fourth-of-March anniversary celebrations, Jefferson's supporters refuted the Federalists' essential argument. Jefferson's election marked the culmination, not the betrayal, of American freedom.[62]

March 4 had been designated the date for presidential inauguration since the beginning of Washington's second term in 1793 (Washington's first inauguration took place on April 30). Indeed, public celebration of March 4 was a Federalist invention, or perhaps more accurately, an adaptation. Attendees of a Fourth-of-March celebration encountered much the same fare as at a reception for Washington during his national tours, or during a celebration of Washington's birthday or the Fourth of July. Songs, toasts, and oaths were common, as were the firing of weapons, and attendance by the community's respectable sorts. This replication of established patriotic traditions was essential to its significance. Fourth-of-March celebrations applied these nascent holiday rituals explicitly to the rhythm of presidential politics.[63]

Federalists had hailed the Fourth of March as "the first day of the federal year," the day when the advocates for liberty and the champions of order came together to salute the ascent of the leader who was tasked with protecting the former and maintaining the latter. Though never as popular as Fourth-of-July celebrations or observances of Washington's birthday during the 1790s, Fourth-of-March observances provided Federalists an occasion to articulate their vision of presidential leadership and link that vision explicitly to loyal Americans' civic duty. For Federalists, this meant demonstrating civilian support for military strength, which demonstrated the nation's cohesiveness, its citizens' obedience to leaders, and its preparedness against foreign threats. "Discharges of cannon" and fireworks were staples of these celebrations. Drills by militia (preexisting, or, in some cases, formed by "youths" who yearned to emulate the great man) were also ubiquitous.[64]

Appropriating many Federalist traditions—public gatherings, toasts, speeches, even appearances by military personnel and discharges of cannon—Republicans nonetheless refashioned the Fourth of March to reflect their own vision of American independence, predicated upon democratic principles. In their celebrations of Jefferson's election, Republicans feted principles such as religious pluralism, civilian control of government, individual liberty, federalism, and peace with other nations. Their songs, toasts, and open letters to Jefferson heaped praise upon the man himself, but by making his election to the presidency the culmination of these national principles, Republican celebrants emphasized the indelible link between the office Jefferson now held and the fundamentals of American identity they all shared.

The exact number of Republican Fourth-of-March celebrations is difficult to ascertain, but we know that Republicans in the North and in the South celebrated the holiday during Jefferson's presidency, and that Republicans publicized these celebrations as a way to fete Jefferson's leadership and to demonstrate the ubiquity of his support. Even in New England, where Federalism was still the strongest, Republicans drank toasts and gave public orations declaring their support for Jefferson, praising him as the exemplar of principles for which they had been advocating throughout the previous decade. To drive home the point that Republicanism was making inroads even in New England, the Richmond *Argus* published an account of an 1803 celebration in New Haven, Connecticut, that drew over 1,000 people.[65]

Celebrants of the Fourth of March cast Jefferson's inauguration as the culmination of a lengthy battle between patriotic champions of American freedom and would-be oppressors from England and from within America's own borders, stretching from the outbreak of the Revolution through the 1790s and climaxing with Jefferson's election. It was, in other words, the triumph of years of steadfast dissent by liberty-loving patriots. The Fourth of March marked "the complete and triumphant success which has crowned [republicans'] exertions," an account of a celebration in Westfield, New Jersey, declared on March 24, 1801. "It was indeed a proud day to the friends of liberty. Since the 4th of July '76, none more auspicious has opened upon the United States."[66] One week earlier, another gathering of New Jersey Republicans made the point that the Fourth of March was nothing less than "[a] day which forms a new aera in the annals of freedom: and evinces to the world that the raised expectations of the venerable Franklin, Price, and others, on the pleasing prospects of the American revolution, have survived the thunders of aristocracy."[67] Both were crucial and interconnected points, repeated by Republican gatherings over the years. Jefferson's election to the presidency was a testament to the power of popular dissent against Federalists who sought to impose British-style monarchy and aristocracy. The peaceful "revolution of 1800" proved the commitment of true Americans never to relinquish their liberty.

Over the course of Jefferson's two presidential terms, and beyond, supporters of Jefferson gathered year after year to commemorate the anniversary of his historic election and to reiterate this fundamental point. Year after year they referenced Jefferson's own words and actions as president to further attest to the transformative impact of his ascent to the presidency. The *National Intelligencer*, which functioned as the administration's de facto newspaper, set the tone. Just two days after Jefferson gave his inaugural address, the *Intelligencer* published a breathless assessment of the speech, praising Jefferson's delivery as "plain, dignified, and unostentatious," and stressing the "principles" that Jefferson enumerated as "pure, explicit, and comprehensive." In short, the *Intelligencer* concluded, the address showed that the "principles" of the new president and the people he served were one and the same. Jefferson's First Inaugural Address was "the Address of the Chief Magistrate of a People, who have shewn themselves amidst the storm of war and the calm of peace equally competent to protect their rights and establish their common happiness; and who in the enjoyment of sovereign unlimited power, have betrayed neither the intoxications of prosperity, or the depressions of fear."[68]

Throughout his presidency Jefferson's supporters referenced, quoted, and reprinted his First Inaugural Address more than any other address. Part of Fourth-of-March festivities often included celebrants reading it aloud. They incorporated lines from the address in their toasts. The point was to reinforce the link between Jefferson's words and the "principles" held by the liberty-loving citizens he represented and to contrast that with the Federalists, who fetishized monarchical pomp and aristocratic privilege. A play dramatizing Jefferson's ascent to the presidency, *Jefferson and Liberty*, included selections from the address describing "the essential principles of government" that will guide "the duties which comprehend every thing dear to you" (but notably omitted Jefferson's assurance that "we are all federalists, we are all republicans").[69] A Maryland printer, John Winter, invoked the address to take a playful potshot at his Federalist subscribers. Reporting that he dined by himself rather than attend "the respectable company of young gentlemen" who gathered at a local tavern on March 4, 1801, Winter sat alone in his office, drinking toasts to John Adams ("May he carry with him in retirement, *a self approving conscience*, the sweet reward of every honest man"), Jefferson, and six more subjects. Then, perhaps feeling the effects of the alcohol, Winter drank his ninth toast to "[m]y *Ninety-five* subscribers, who withdrew their subscription, because *I dared* to think, not exactly as *they* tho't: May they remember that '*a difference of opinion is not a difference in principle.*'"[70]

Winter's toast might read as a Jeffersonian kind of olive branch to his subscribers, a statement that though divided by political perspective, they remained united in the "principles" that made them all Americans. But the message being communicated to Federalists, and to Republican Quids who criticized Jefferson's leadership, was that Jefferson upheld the principles of independence and democracy that all true Americans shared. Opposing the president was tantamount to a betrayal of the very principles that distinguished true American citizens from the would-be despots in their midst.

Fourth-of-March celebrants praised Jefferson as the champion of Americans' collective independence, fleshing out what American "principles" specifically were in practice. They ticked off a litany of Federalist abuses, from burdensome and odious taxes to violations of free speech to an insistence on moral and religious conformity. Federalists, Republicans chorused, were enemies of every iteration of American freedom, every facet of true American citizenship. Jefferson championed precisely what the Federalists condemned. That not only made him uniquely qualified to lead all Americans, it disqualified Federalists from full membership as Americans.

"My countrymen have we reason to doubt the patriotism of our administration?" asked a New Hampshire pamphleteer writing under the pseudonym One of the People. During Jefferson's tenure, "we have been relieved from internal taxes, among which were an odious *stamp* tax, and land tax," not to mention "a *host* of tax gatherers, whose wages amounted to about *two hundred thousand dollars* per annum" as well as "sixteen *useless* judges, whose salaries amounted to 33,000 dollars, annually, and who

were created, not for the people, but for the *Government.*" In addition,
the people "have been relieved from a sedition law:—behind the *palings*
of which Mr. Jefferson never entrenched himself."[71] An 1806 gathering
of Sag Harbor, New York, Republicans likewise recounted "those times
when federalism and terror were the order of the day . . . War abroad and
probably at home—our debt increasing by millions—our jails crouded
[*sic*] with the victims of sedition laws, and our houses with tax-gatherers."
Fast forward to 1806, and "[m]ark the contrast":

> Our public debt diminishing in the ration of eight millions annu-
> ally—stamp acts, and a long chapter of other vexatious taxes abol-
> ished—an over-flowing treasury—peace at home and abroad—our
> citizens happy, and free to "manage their own affairs in their own
> way"—our friendship courted, and our country respected by the na-
> tions of Europe. The effects of an honest, wise, and economical ad-
> ministration, warmed by the patriotism, and guided by the counsels
> of a JEFFERSON.[72]

Supporters praised Jefferson as a worthy exemplar of the American
people's commitment to their liberty, invoking the example of George
Washington in explicit and implicit ways, a move that offended and incensed Federalists. Invoking the same passage from the Book of Micah
that Washington had paraphrased in his address to the Hebrew Congregation of Rhode Island in 1790 (in which Washington had assured the congregation that they would be safe from persecution in the United States),
a group of celebrants of Jefferson's 1801 victory toasted "the President of
the United States, Thomas Jefferson; may we live happy under his administration, and eat our bread in peace with thankfulness and a merry heart,
under our own vine, and under our own fig-tree, and have none to make
us afraid."[73]

Presenting Washington as a champion of religious liberty, Republicans
cast Jefferson as Washington's worthy successor. Religious liberty, to Jefferson and the Republicans, was first and foremost about *liberty*, about
the right to worship as one saw fit. In Republicans' telling, both Jefferson
and Washington shared the American people's support for a clean separation between church and state. Those who did not share that view were
decidedly out of the national fold. Some Republican gatherings included
messages directed toward Federalist religious leaders, imploring them to
stop combining religious and political messages and fall in line.[74] But others employed more defiantly combative language, urging Republicans to

use their newfound power to demonstrate how wrong Federalists' beliefs about using the coercive power of government to enforce religious morality had truly been. Now that Jefferson was president, Republican minister Stanley Griswold told his New England audience, the people had a remarkable opportunity to follow the example of the founders of New England, who exemplified "the leading, most distinguishing traits" of "*liberty* and *religion*" that could now combine "into one character," demonstrating that the people were capable of morality and goodness without the coercive force of government compelling them. Cleaving religious morality from government coercion ensured that the people's republican morality could be the driving force behind the government, not the other way around. "Amaze once more the tyrants of the earth when they look toward this land: let them see that men can be free without licentiousness, orderly without needing the shackles of despotism, religious without the impositions of bigotry. By assuming this character, be invulnerable to your foes; baulk the hopes of the envious."[75]

"BY THE CESSION OF LOUISIANA, WE SHALL PRESERVE PEACE"

Jefferson's crowning achievement, the Louisiana Purchase, provided evidence that he shared Americans' commitment to peace with all nations through diplomacy that forged strong ties while still maintaining America's autonomy. As the *National Intelligencer* boasted: "By the cession of Louisiana, we shall preserve peace, and acquire a territory of great extent, fertility, and local importance. However great the latter object may be, the former is of inestimable value, and it is principally in relation to it that the importance of the cession is to be estimated. A nation, whose population is doubled in twenty-four years, whose resources increase with still greater rapidity, and which enjoys a free government, only requires peace to elevate her in a few years above the storms which[,] with so little intermission, agitate the European world."[76]

Republicans turned the Federalists' pessimism about the far-flung, "savage" wilderness of Louisiana on its head. Rather than pollute a pristine nation with degenerate Indians, suspicious foreigners, and their slaves, Republicans insisted that Louisiana would attest to the American nation's ability to uplift and assimilate brutish, uncivilized peoples and teach them how to be free. As another gathering proclaimed, "*Louisiana*" was the "[y]ounger sister of American independence, proceeding from the same common parentage." Its non-American inhabitants would soon be a part of the nation, not through coercion but through their affirmative desire to do so. Native Americans, foreign-born European migrants, creoles, and slaves: they were all "new-born children of our National Family," who could "speedily learn to write and speak with propriety, the language of Liberty," a gathering of celebrants declared in 1805. "Figure to yourselves what would have been the situation of our frontier settlement on the western waters in case of a war with France, while her emissaries had their numerous tribes of Indians in Louisiana, firmly attached to her interest, and ready, when called upon, to make war upon our dispersed and defenceless inhabitants," David Ramsay told his listeners in an oration given in South Carolina in May 1804 and widely reprinted in the months leading up to the election, emphasizing the acquisition's promise of peace that made it so popular with Republicans around the country. "These Indians are now all our own. . . . The cession of Louisiana has wrested the scalping knife and tomahawk from their hands, and laid the foundation of perpetual peace." Through the Louisiana Purchase, Republicans insisted, Jefferson had brought the freedom that all true Americans shared to a people who surely desired it but had never experienced it. The acquisition of these new people would be a testament to the capacity of Americans to bring up even savage, backward people in American freedom.[77]

The timing of the Louisiana Purchase aided Republicans in their attempt to connect the two Fourths—the Fourth of July and the Fourth of March—in a narrative that depicted Jefferson's ascent to the presidency as the fulfillment of a democratic republican national character that had drawn its first breath with Jefferson's pen twenty-four years earlier. As a gathering of Newburyport, Massachusetts, Republicans succinctly put it, "The *three* great events in our national history" were "[t]he declaration of *independence*, the conquest of the British armies by GEORGE WASHINGTON & the restoration of our government by THOMAS JEFFERSON."[78]

Of course, Jefferson stood at the center of that story. As in the election of 1796, Republicans touted Jefferson's primary authorship of the Declaration of Independence as the ultimate patriotic act, repudiating Federalist accusations of cowardice and duplicity, and positioning Jefferson as the scribe of American liberty. Republicans pointed to Jefferson's authorship of this document to reinforce their characterization of his commitment to peace, while simultaneously enlisting George Washington as an ally of Jefferson against warmongering Federalists. Republicans insisted that Jefferson's pen had proven no less crucial to the war effort than had Washington's sword. In fact, it had been Jefferson's words that had articulated the reasons for seeking independence. In this way, Jefferson's words were what separated the nation's glorious military campaign from the other countless run-of-the-mill bloodbaths that stained the pages of history and that now consumed Europe. Washington's sword served the nation's collective aspiration to independence, but Jefferson's pen had given that aspiration form, shape, and ultimately, immortality. The "principles" of liberty "handed down" by New England's "forefathers" "to their sons" have "in every period of the country's progress . . . been conspicuous," Griswold sermonized to his listeners. "They broke out in full splendor in 1775 and '76, of which the *Declaration of Independence* is an illustrious proof."[79] That made Jefferson and Washington more than simply broth-ers-in-arms. To Griswold and other Republicans, it made them true Amer-icans, like the people they served—distinct in every way from Federalists who seemed to lust for war simply for war's sake.

Yet for all their adoring praise, Jefferson's admirers also made it clear that Jefferson would only command their affection so long as he faithfully served the principles of democracy and independence that all Americans shared. Changing men was meant to signify a radical change in the princi-ples by which the government operated: it was loyalty to those principles, not loyalty to men, that true Republicans possessed.[80] As such, Jefferson's supporters lent him their sincere hope for his success. But they would watch Jefferson as carefully as they had watched Adams and Washington before him, maintaining their vigilance in order to ensure that the man who occupied the presidential office was performing the task the office required. Celebrating Jefferson's 1801 triumph, a group of Republicans toasted, "[t]he invulnerable Thomas Jefferson, President of the Union; May he indeed be a safe depositary of the people's rights, a terror to evil doers, and a praise to republicans. 3 cheers. 1 gun."[81] The "may" in that sentence was crucial. His supporters hoped that he would fulfill the office's lofty task, but if he failed to exemplify the people's principles, they would find someone who could. One 1805 gathering made such a warning ex-plicit, drinking this toast: "THOMAS JEFFERSON—May he continue to sub-mit to the Constitution, and the equal rights to man; when he forsakes the principles on which they are founded, may the People forsake him."[82]

Republicans, thus, maintained that it was not really Jefferson they were celebrating, at least not unequivocally. They were really celebrating an *office* onto which they had projected their vision of their nation, and through which they demonstrated their membership in it. On this, they echoed their Federalist opponents. But their pledge to watch the president carefully and hold him to account also justified characterizing any critic of the president as a traitor to the nation. Since the capacity of Americans to dissent maintained their control of the presidency, all Americans were obliged to support the president so long as he acted in accordance with their national vision. Republicans maintained that Jefferson was doing just that, which meant that dissent against Jefferson was patently un-American.

What defined the partisan divide, then, was a shared belief that the president's actions, and the people's response to those actions, determined the nation's fate. Where one stood on the political spectrum depended upon the extent to which Jefferson was living up to the immense duties that years of partisan debate had projected onto the office he now occupied. The Federalists considered themselves patriots for dissenting against Jefferson's presidential actions. Republicans, by contrast, considered opposition to Jefferson a betrayal of the very spirit of dissent that had placed him in office.

THOMAS JEFFERSON'S SCRAPBOOK

Jefferson's assertion that the right of the people to disagree with one another—and with their government—was the foundation for self-government and represented more than Inauguration Day ornamentation. He repeated this belief again and again in his correspondence to political allies. Looking back over his presidency more than a decade after he retired from public office, Jefferson called his election in 1800 a "revolution," one that "was as real a revolution in the principles of our government as that of 76 was in it's [sic] form," with one key difference. The "revolution of 1800" had not been "effected . . . by the sword . . . but by the rational and peaceable instrument of reform, the suffrage of the people."[83] To a far greater extent than either of his predecessors, Jefferson openly embraced the role of the presidency as the symbol of the people's possession of a government that rightfully belonged to them. It was the people's shared trust in the president that Jefferson believed the people had won in the "revolution" of 1800. That trust brought the American people together and kept them together, so long as the sitting president actively worked to cultivate and maintain it. Thus, "in a government like ours," Jefferson explained, "it is the duty of the Chief-magistrate, in order to enable himself to do all the good which his station requires, to endeavor, by all honorable means, to unite in himself the confidence of the whole people." Only this crucial act of the president, Jefferson explained, "can produce an union of the powers of the whole, and point them in a single direction, as if all constituted but one body & one mind," only this "can render a weaker nation unconquerable by a stronger one."[84] As president, Jefferson fully intended to govern according to the belief that the people possessed both the ability and the right to govern themselves. "[M]y countrymen are so much in the habits of order, and feel it so much their interest, that they will never be wanting in the support of the existing government, tho' they may disapprove & mean to change it at the first return of their right of election," he boasted.[85]

Nonetheless, as certain as Jefferson was that the people's essential claim as a free people rested on their capacity to dissent, he was equally sure that all true Americans would unite in support of this basic philosophy. "I hope to see shortly a perfect consolidation, to effect which nothing shall be spared on my part, short of the abandonment of the principles of our revolution," he wrote to John Dickinson just two days after taking the oath of office. The government of the United States would be a shining example to the world "that a free government is of all others the most energetic, that the enquiry which has been excited among the mass of mankind by our revolution & it's consequences will ameliorate the condition of man over a great portion of the globe."[86] This led Jefferson to prize dissent as his supporters did: as the essential tactic that had given rise to an independent American nation and then to a Republican ascent that had culminated in his 1801 election to the presidency. It also led him, along with his followers, to condemn those who criticized him as something other than fully American and possibly a dangerous threat to the nation.

Not long into his first term, Jefferson surveyed the state of the Federalist Party, and predicted that the party would die a rapid death. The evidence of this Jefferson saw not only in state-level and national elections (both of which he monitored through his perusal of the dozens of newspapers to which he subscribed throughout his presidency) but also in the attacks that Federalists leveled against him. "[T]heir bitterness increases with their desperation," he wrote to Levi Lincoln in 1802. In the throes of their own demise, the Federalist Party thrashed about in a last-ditch, desperate attempt to bring down the party of the people's choice, "trying slander now which nothing could prompt but a gall which blinds their judgments as well as their consciences." Now that he was president, Jefferson vowed to do what the Federalists had not: "I shall take no other revenge than by a steady pursuit of the economy, and peace, and by the establishment of republican principles in substance and in form, to sink federalism into an abyss from which there shall be no resurrection for it."[87] Jefferson was as good as his word. He let the odious Alien and Sedition Acts expire and never replaced them with a law that targeted Federalists for their political beliefs.

Yet the third president still resented the slanders he received from Federalists. Even in retirement he complained of the "putrid state into which our newspapers have passed, and the malignity, the vulgarity, & mendacious spirit of those who write for them." "[A]s vehicles of information, and a curb on our functionaries they have rendered themselves useless by forfieting [*sic*] all title to belief," Jefferson wrote of the press in 1814.[88]

Jefferson knew well how partisan the press coverage was. He read dozens of newspapers throughout his presidency and kept a scrapbook of materials he read (see figure 6.1). The contents of this scrapbook, which swelled to multiple volumes before Jefferson was done, were eclectic, much like Jefferson's interests. Not only do the entries come from dozens of different publications (mostly US publications but some reprints from Europe as well), they cover a wide range of topics. There are essays on lofty intellectual subjects, like honor, religion, and piety, and more practical subjects, like gardening. The scrapbooks also contain numerous published accounts of holiday celebrations, essays, poems, and songs, mostly from Republican sources but some from Federalists as well, commenting on Jefferson's presidential leadership. The contents are by no means a comprehensive, objective reflection of public opinion surrounding his presidency. Instead, they offer us a glimpse into public perception of the office and Jefferson himself—as Jefferson chose to see it.[89]

Jefferson was well versed in the use of scissors, paste, and paper to create his desired intellectual landscape. A religious skeptic who nonetheless expressed an admiration for Jesus of Nazareth, Jefferson cut out biblical passages that he approved of and pasted them into a booklet he called "The Life and Morals of Jesus of Nazareth." This volume, often called the "Jefferson Bible," was completed by Jefferson after his retirement from the presidency. The "Jefferson Bible" can be read as his attempt to cull the impossible stories of nature-defying miracles that, to Jefferson's mind, were fantastical stories distracting from Jesus' teachings on matters such as fellowship, forgiveness, and love.[90]

So, too, Jefferson's four-volume scrapbook is an attempt to fashion a particular environment over which he had limited control—in this case, the partisan climate surrounding his presidency—according to his particular specifications.[91] Jefferson includes Federalist pieces in his scrapbook, but the contents of the scrapbook are overwhelmingly Republican. On

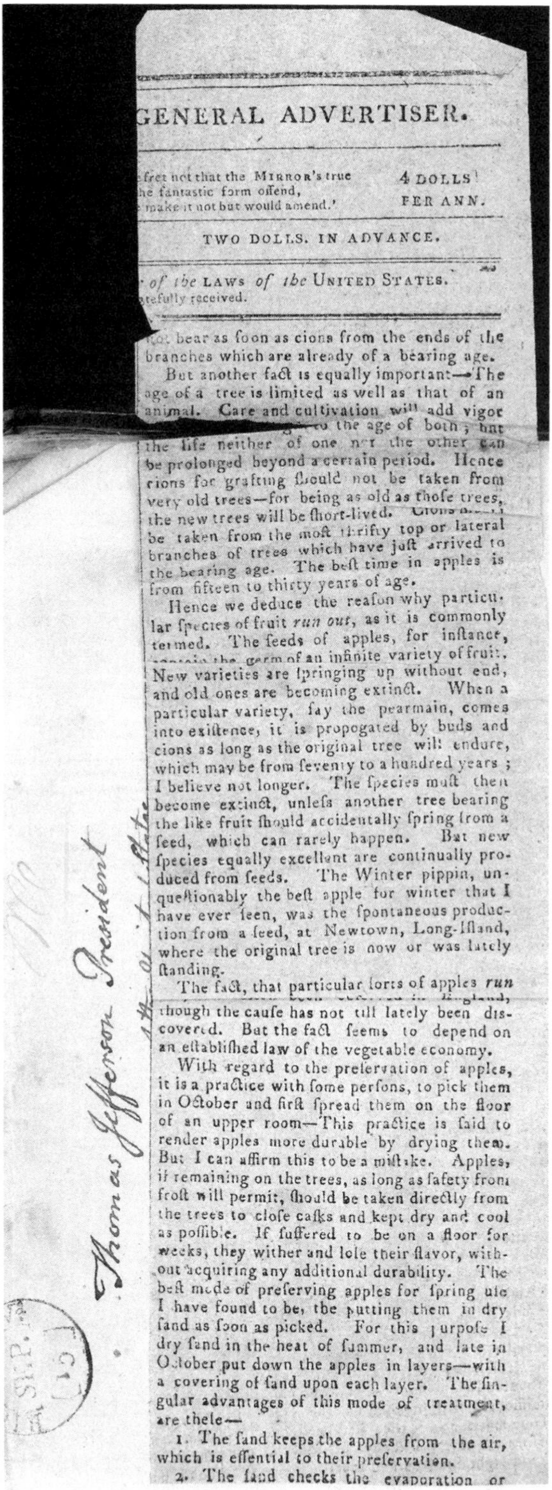

GENERAL ADVERTISER.

'fret not that the Mirror's true   4 DOLLS
he fantastic form offend,
make it not but would amend.'   PER ANN.

TWO DOLLS. IN ADVANCE.

of the LAWS of the UNITED STATES.
tefully received.

bear as foon as cions from the ends of the
branches which are already of a bearing age.
But another fact is equally important—The
age of a tree is limited as well as that of an
animal. Care and cultivation will add vigor
                    to the age of both; but
the life neither of one nor the other can
be prolonged beyond a certain period. Hence
cions for grafting fhould not be taken from
very old trees—for being as old as thofe trees,
the new trees will be fhort-lived. Cions a.
be taken from the moft thrifty top or lateral
branches of trees which have juft arrived to
the bearing age. The beft time in apples is
from fifteen to thirty years of age.

Hence we deduce the reafon why particular fpecies of fruit run out, as it is commonly
termed. The feeds of apples, for inftance,
contain the germ of an infinite variety of fruit.
New varieties are fpringing up without end,
and old ones are becoming extinct. When a
particular variety, fay the pearmain, comes
into exiftence, it is propagated by buds and
cions as long as the original tree will endure,
which may be from feventy to a hundred years;
I believe not longer. The fpecies muft then
become extinct, unlefs another tree bearing
the like fruit fhould accidentally fpring from a
feed, which can rarely happen. But new
fpecies equally excellent are continually produced from feeds. The Winter pippin, un-
queftionably the beft apple for winter that I
have ever feen, was the fpontaneous production from a feed, at Newtown, Long-Ifland,
where the original tree is now or was lately
ftanding.

The fact, that particular forts of apples run
though the caufe has not till lately been discovered. But the fact feems to depend on
an eftablifhed law of the vegetable economy.

With regard to the preferration of apples,
it is a practice with fome perfons, to pick them
in October and firft fpread them on the floor
of an upper room—This practice is faid to
render apples more durable by drying them.
But I can affirm this to be a miftake. Apples,
if remaining on the trees, as long as fafety from
froft will permit, fhould be taken directly from
the trees to clofe cafks and kept dry and cool
as poffible. If fuffered to be on a floor for
weeks, they wither and lofe their flavor, without acquiring any additional durability. The
beft mode of preferving apples for fpring ufe
I have found to be, the putting them in dry
fand as foon as picked. For this purpofe I
dry fand in the heat of fummer, and late in
October put down the apples in layers—with
a covering of fand upon each layer. The fin-
gular advantages of this mode of treatment,
are thefe—

1. The fand keeps the apples from the air,
which is effential to their prefervation.

2. The fand checks the evaporation or

[handwritten: Thomas Jefferson President]

Figure 6.1: A clipping from Volume 1 of Thomas Jefferson's Scrapbook. Courtesy of the Albert and Shirley Small Special Collections Library, University of Virginia.

some pages, a single Federalist piece appears on the page literally surrounded by Republican rebuttals.[92] The scrapbook is evidence that Jefferson understood that, as president, he stood at the center of the vitriolic political exchanges taking place during his presidency, yet he possessed limited ability to control the debate. He could not change the minds of all Federalists, just as he could not change the global contours of Christianity. But he could control the pages of his scrapbook. Within the confines of those covers, Jefferson could present a picture of an overwhelming groundswell of American voices drowning out a comparatively minimal Federalist opposition.

Jefferson proved himself adept at identifying pieces that reflected the major themes emphasized in Federalist pieces denouncing him and the Republicans. The *Courant* poem, "Sketches of the Times," is in there, with its praise for New England states like Massachusetts ("free and bold,/ Too proud, too STRONG to be controul'd"), and its condemnation of Virginia's dominance of the government to the detriment of Northern whites. That poem, along with some other pieces in the scrapbook, specifically discuss the political advantages that slavery gave to the South and even make reference to Sally Hemings.[93]

Jefferson's scrapbook also includes Federalist criticism of Jefferson's embargo—specifically the charge that the embargo demonstrated Jefferson's inability to protect the nation from an obvious attack on its people. One of the most remarkable texts in the scrapbook is a fictitious dialogue between Peter Pallet, the pseudonymous author of a piece in the Hudson, New York, *Balance*, published in the last year of Jefferson's presidency and included in volume 1 of Jefferson's scrapbook, and a Miss Pertly. Pallet was dumbfounded by the sheer array of women's fashion trends he saw all about him, each "distinguished by some popular name.—We have had Truxons hats—Suwarrow boots, Nelson hats—Jefferson boot and shoes—Trafalgar ribbands—Nelson's wave and Nelson's bell callicoes—and more other sort of boots[,] hats, shoes and ribbons, &c. than I can remember." One fashion statement in particular, sported by Miss Pertly, caught his eye: an "enormous new fangled bonnet . . . called a *gun-boat*," "thus named," Miss Pertly explained, "in honour of Mr. Jefferson." But how was a bonnet like a gunboat? Under Jefferson's watch, Pallet explained, gunboats, like bonnets, "are calculated to make a *mere show of defence* . . . while in fact they *invite aggression*." As Miss Pertly blushed at the suggestive double entendre, Pallet elaborated. "I beg your pardon madam—but let me see a young lady with a gun boat bonnet—a proclamation tucker—and a spider net embargo—while all her prominent points (I mean her elbows, &c.) are naked and defenceless—and I'll bet you my ears against a pair of picnic gloves that she can be conquered."[94]

One way to read this exchange is the way the author intended: through Federalists' eyes, as a fitting metaphor for Jefferson's embargo. Deluded and deceived by Jefferson's promises, the American people had been rendered effeminate, weak, "naked and defenceless" against the lustful stares of hostile foreign forces—as unfirm and unmanly as the president himself. But another way to read it is a testament to the Federalists' preference for war and their predilection to view any political solution that did not involve the threat of violence as evidence of feminine weakness. Pallet leers at Miss Pertly, declaring that government policies are like women's clothes: the ones that do not actually provide "defence" instead "invite aggression," and wagering that both are ripe to "be conquered."[95]

Republicans chose the latter reading of the embargo, defending Jefferson's action as a testament to the American people's commitment to peace and the Federalists' irrational lust for war—a quality, Republicans charged, that Federalists shared with the British. Jefferson's embargo was not a sign of weakness but a sign of restraint. That made public support for him all the more necessary and expected of all true Americans. "Let us not be misunderstood. We are not the friends of a blind confidence in any executive, " the *National Intelligencer* explained, reiterating the Republican refrain that they were loyal to the national principles the president was expected to uphold, rather than Jefferson himself, "but we do say that at a period like this, when the whole world is convulsed, when justice is unknown by those nations with whom we have intercourse . . . [and] when this executive too has uniformly manifested a love of peace; under all these circumstances we hesitate not to aver that confidence is the best of virtues, and that it is such a virtue as a true republican will not blush to own."[96]

Federalists and Republicans agreed that "[t]he President of the United States ought to be in reality the chief magistrate of *the nation*," as pseudonymous writer, A Freeman, succinctly wrote in the *Salem* (Massachusetts) *Gazette* just months after Jefferson's retirement.[97] But this shared understanding of the president's duty to promote everything that separated free Americans from foreign subjects, Indian "savages," and free and enslaved blacks, only fueled the political divide that defined Jefferson's presidency. Federalists, horrified at what the nation was becoming under this president, claimed that dissent against him was necessary to save the nation from certain ruin. Republicans argued that support for the president was essential to protect the nation from the dangers posed by the president's opponents, in league with dangerous foreign (especially British) forces. By commemorating the Fourth of March, a group of Massachusetts Republicans explained in 1806, "We tell the world we love our country and *will* support its defenders."[98]

Jefferson stepped down after two terms and remarked that he felt great relief in his retirement, happy that his successor, James Madison, now shouldered the considerable "burden" of the office.[99] Yet even in retirement, Jefferson remained convinced that "republicans are the *nation*," and "their opponents are but a faction, weak in numbers, but powerful & profuse in the command of money, & backed by a nation, powerful also & profuse, in the use of the same means." That other nation, of course, was Britain. As far as Jefferson and the Republicans were concerned, opponents were not only outside the nation simply by virtue of their dissent, they were specifically "backed" by the very British monarchy from whom the nation had won its independence and by whom it had suffered violations of its maritime rights, even attacks on its citizens and vessels. Such opposition to the president could only be opposition to the self-evident truths of American nationhood that Jefferson and his party championed. Silencing this faction was everything, for, Jefferson noted, "the last hope of human liberty in this world rests on us." The nation should "sacrifice every attachment & every enmity" in favor of political unity, and "leave the President free to chuse his co-adjutors, to pursue his own measures, & support him & them, even if we think we are wiser than they are, honester than they are, or possessing more enlarged information of the state of things. If we move in mass, be it ever so circuitously, we shall attain our object: but if we break into squads, every one pursuing the path he thinks most direct, we become an easy conquest to those who can now barely hold us in check."[100]

As Jefferson transitioned to retirement and Madison began his first presidential term, tension between the United States and Britain grew over continued British aggression against American ships and citizens. Republicans in Congress railed at British threats to America's sovereignty on the seas. Some looked in almost every cardinal direction—Canada to the north, Florida to the south, and further west—for opportunities to take over more territory. Their desire to stand up to Britain, assert their young nation's independence, and perhaps annex new territory in the process, plunged the United States into its first declared war. More than ever before, Republicans, and eventually Federalists, would assert that demonstrating the character that bound the American people to their president would involve engaging in armed combat against the nation's foreign and domestic "enemies."

7

To Bear Arms at the President's Call

"YE TRUE HONEST demo's and friends to the nation,/ Whom nothing can sway from these United States,/ Lend your hearts and your hands to the administration,/ So likely to render us happy and great. . . . / The chief of this nation once more shall behold us/ The truest republicans the world does contain;/ In spite of the tories who fain would have sold us,/ Our rights and our liberties still to maintain." So went a tune, titled "Unanimity," meant to inspire Americans to patriotic action. The bodies of those killed during the War of 1812 were barely cold, and the ashes left in Washington after the British had invaded the city had barely stopped smoldering, when the song appeared in the *American Patriotic Song-Book* in 1816. In the same songbook, another song specified what such a show of patriotism should look like:

> The blood-hounds of Britain again we now spy,
> Unkennel'd, uncoupled, and all in full cry
> [. . .]
> There's all the old Tories and old Refugees,
> And merciless Indians united with these,
> At the sound of the bugle they follow the track,
> And join in the chase with the old British pack.
> [. . .]
> For lashing the puppies half train'd to the chase,
> We'll send them to Scotia again in disgrace.
> Though spies, and though traitors should practice their wiles,
> Fair Freedom shall ne'er be entrapped in their toils,
> Like true-blooded Yankees, we'll smoke their stale tricks,
> And play them the game of old seventy-six.
> John Bull may bellow, his lion may growl,
> His bullies may bluster, his war dogs may howl,

Like our fathers our freedom we'll ever maintain,
They beat the whole pack and we'll beat them again.[1]

Though the War of 1812 is one of the least well known among Americans today, its impact on early United States presidential politics was profound. Beginning late in Jefferson's presidency, and continuing through James Madison's two terms and the nation's first declared war, white Americans across partisan lines deployed racialized language to distinguish themselves from their political opponents—and more generally white liberty-loving Americans from foreign and nonwhite "enemies"—more explicitly than ever before. As many Native Americans allied with the British against the United States, enslaved black people sought freedom, and some free black critics of the war openly added their voices of dissent to "Mr. Madison's War," Republican pro-war propaganda stressed that the nation the president embodied was a nation of native-born whites and that demonstrating one's patriotic devotion meant answering the president's call to "bear arms" in the nation's defense against "enemies" who threatened the nation from within and from without. These professions, made by Republican supporters of the administration during the War of 1812, echoed those made by Federalist during the "quasi-war." But in the War of 1812, professions turned to action.[2]

At the beginning of 1812, Congress called for 35,000 troops for a formally declared war against the United States' former mother country. However, political and military incompetence, partisan criticism, and the formidable alliance of British troops, Indian allies, and free and enslaved blacks dampened the ardor for war and hampered the administration's recruiting goals. To inspire patriotic white men to service, pro-war propaganda conjured horrific images of British soldiers facilitating the scalping of innocent whites by "savage" Indians, the rape of white women by black men, and the murder of innocent white families on the frontier. A relentlessly aggressive British government, in concert with Indians and black "internal enemies," had pushed native-born white Americans to the brink. Violence was necessary to counter the uncivilized, barbaric assaults by the nation's threats. Federalist resistance to such propaganda rested on insistence that Madison was incompetent and being pushed into war by Napoleonic France and that the war served only Southern interests at the expense of the Northern states, who disproportionately felt the brunt of battle. Setbacks and blunders by American officers, and even by the president's cabinet members, culminating in the British invasion and burning of Washington, provided devastating evidence to justify Federalist reticence.

Yet news of the Treaty of Ghent, formally ending the war, and subsequent news of Andrew Jackson's spectacular victory at New Orleans forced Federalists to alter their political message, echoing Republicans' insistence that all true Americans demonstrated their love of country by responding when the president issued a call to arms. By the end of the war, white Americans across party lines asserted that they expected their president to channel their zeal for their liberty into decisive martial action, and in return, all true Americans were expected to take up their weapons and go to war when the president called. Doing so was the true measure of one's claim as an American and one's commitment to promote and protect America, civilization, liberty, and sovereignty against all foreign and domestic threats.[3]

BEARING ARMS

James Madison's election was not inevitable. Indeed, division existed among Republicans, and Madison's first two years as president would witness division between mainstream Republicans, "Old Republicans"—the "tertium quids" led by John Randolph—and "malcontents" like Wilson Carey Nicholas, William Branch Giles, and Robert Smith. The latter, who served for a time as Madison's secretary of state, disagreed with Madison's decision to accept a letter from Napoleon, via the Duc de Cadore, in 1810. The letter proffered what historian J.C.A. Stagg has characterized as a "hypothetical," worded to sound like a promise: in the event that the United States could compel Britain to stop violating its maritime rights, or Britain voluntarily rescinded the Orders in Council, Napoleon would lift his own restrictions on neutral ships. The letter was not, in fact, a promise to lift the Berlin and Milan decrees, but Madison took it as such. Smith objected to Madison's decision, and Madison fired him, replacing him with James Monroe as secretary of state. The decision opened Madison up to a criticism that would be repeated (especially by Federalists) throughout the war—that Madison was little more than a pawn, or perhaps an enthusiastic ally, of Napoleon. This criticism, though unfair, underscored the predominant objection of Madison's Republican critics: that Madison's foreign policy catered too much to belligerent foreign powers. To their mind Madison's attempt to use economic restrictions to compel France and Britain to respect American maritime rights was misguided. So too did Republicans vary in their reasons for supporting war. Some professed to favor war to defend American rights on the high seas and the liberties of American citizens impressed by the British. Others looked to the war as an opportunity to acquire coveted territory in Canada and in the west. Nonetheless, when Madison announced that Congress had declared war in June 1812, most Republicans enthusiastically applauded the news.[4]

Despite the friction that existed among Republicans, once Madison won the election of 1808, his victory lent an air of inevitability to the Republicans' narrative of national fulfillment, which cast Jefferson's election to the presidency as the culmination of a peaceful resistance to Federalist abuse of executive power, a "Revolution of 1800" that echoed the democratic essence of the War for Independence. The American people, Republicans chorused, were peaceful, democratic, and independent. United by a revolutionary act of dissent against Britain, they had forged a government unlike any in the world, one that epitomized their democratic, independent character by remaining at all times accountable to them.[5]

Picking up right where it left off with Jefferson, the *National Intelligencer* chronicled the widespread celebration of the Fourth of March in 1809. Celebration took place throughout the country by Republicans whose "spirit of harmony" linked them together across vast geographic distances. "In three important respects there appears to be the most complete identity of sentiment;—in reverence for the late President; in the attachment to the new Chief Magistrate; and in the determination to maintain at every hazard our just rights." In Fourth-of-March and Fourth-of-July celebrations throughout Madison's presidency, Republicans feted Madison and Jefferson in tandem, drinking toasts to each of them, reading from the Declaration of Independence, and extolling, as the *Intelligencer* did, how fitting it was that the successor to the "patriot sage" who chiefly authored the Declaration of Independence was the man who was especially "useful and active in [the] formation" of the Constitution.[6]

Republicans continued a practice they had begun during Jefferson's presidency: comparing their Republican standard-bearer to George Washington. Washington was an unexpected choice for Republicans, given that the first president of the United States was no Republican, repeatedly acted in ways that infuriated Republicans, and trusted men like Alexander Hamilton and John Jay, who provoked Republican suspicions (at best) and contempt (at worst). But Republicans gleefully rewrote Washington's presidential history—claiming that Washington had always been one of their own—by celebrating Washington as a champion of tolerance. Jefferson, a Republican preacher announced to his congregation in 1807, was the champion of the very religious liberty that Washington himself had alluded to when he had addressed a Jewish synagogue in 1790. Washington's dream that "the Children of the Stock of Abraham, who dwell in this land, continue to merit and enjoy the good-will of the other inhabitants; while every one shall sit in safety under his own vine and fig tree, and there shall be none to make him afraid," was also Jefferson's dream, and indeed the dream of all true American patriots. And with Jefferson's election to the presidency, the preacher argued, that dream had been realized. Borrowing from Washington's own address, the preacher "thanked God, that the United States were at present blessed with *a wise and virtuous Chief Magistrate*, who, instead of *shutting up the houses of religious worship*, and persecuting the *ministers of the gospel*, as has been *falsely predicted* he would do; had left them in the *peaceable exercise of their religion*, and all, in the enjoyment of 'their own vines and fig trees with none to make them afraid.'" Characterized this way, Washington was a champion of the religious pluralism and democratic reason that Jeffersonian Republicans claimed made their party "the nation," as Jefferson himself had declared after his retirement. Like Jefferson, Republicans claimed, Washington was an exemplar of the heterogeneity that could not only exist but flourish under a democratic government that left all of its citizens free to live the life they chose, to disagree reasonably among themselves and even with their government: a democracy that respected difference and reasonable dissent.[7]

Claiming Washington was an undoubtedly effective way for Jeffersonian Republicans to troll Federalists. In the longstanding national narrative that Republicans had crafted, Federalists were the violent ones, looking to silence political dissent through threats and intimidation as well as legislative coercion. Federalists were incensed that Republicans would enlist Washington into their ranks after bitterly criticizing him a decade earlier. But adopting Washington as one of their own allowed Republicans to tell a story of the young country's entire history that emphasized the office that Washington held in common with Jefferson—and now Madison—as much as it did the men themselves. In effect, Jeffersonian Republicans invoked Washington to celebrate a nation that had finally realized the dreams of the patriots who risked their lives to rebuke British oppression and establish a free, independent, and peaceful nation of their own (see figure 7.1).

But that characterization only thinly masked grave anxiety. The Federalist Party, alongside Quid separatists, continued to criticize the president. Federalists continued to repeat their longstanding criticism that Republicans were too enamored with everything French—a charge that took on new dimensions with the rise of Napoleon. And the attacks on American

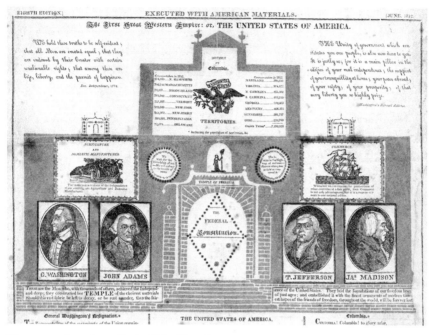

Figure 7.1: Jonathan Clark, "The First Great Western Empire" (1812). Detail. Courtesy of the Library of Congress Rare Book Division.

vessels by the *Leander* and the *Leopard* made America's continued vulnerability in the crossfire of Britain's war with France frighteningly clear. That New England states, and not Britain or France, felt the brunt of Jefferson's embargo, only added more fuel to Federalists' contention that *they* were the noble dissenters and that Republicans were the reckless tyrants who used their power to defile everything America was supposed to stand for. As one piece succinctly put it: "*democratic* policy has been our *bane*, and FEDERAL policy our SALVATION."[8]

Republicans continued to condemn such criticism as dangerous attacks on an administration that American citizens had vested with power through years of persistent struggle against Federalism. The Virginia-based *Daily Compiler* echoed the sentiments of other Republican newspapers when it vowed that its commitment to dissenting against those in power had not disappeared once a Republican president took office. "We shall not be the slaves of *any* administration; that we neither expect, nor hope, nor wish for any thing from such a quarter; and that all we have said or may hereafter say, may be considered as the pure dictate of our own minds, in the moment we say it, uninfluenced by any extraneous consideration." Such free-thinking citizens ensured that the president, and by extension, the entire government, remained the possession of the American people. But they took it as a given that such freethinking patriots would come to the conclusion that support for the administration was warranted. In case the point was not explicit enough, the newspaper titled this statement "TRUE AMERICANS."[9]

Republicans thus differentiated between dissent within their own ranks and that from the Federalists. The former was a righteous, sustained act that fueled the "Revolution of 1800" and continued to hold Republican administrations to account. The latter was a self-serving attempt by an un-American political ideology to regain power it had rightfully lost. As far as the author of a "Receipt to Make a Modern Federalist," Quids were no better than Federalists themselves. The recipe's list of ingredients included "*five* scruples of liars Tongues," "four drachms of the hatred of Truth," a gallon "of the treason of Benedict Arnold," and "eight ounces . . . of quidism."[10]

Beginning in earnest with the attacks by the *Leander* and the *Leopard*, Republicans repeatedly asserted the duty of every true American patriot to "bear arms" in defense of the country. The call to bear arms was voluntary, which distinguished militia service from the compulsory service of a standing army. In this way the call to bear arms exemplified the volitional nature of citizenship—as distinct from black slaves, who had no choice to take up arms, and British regulars, who had no choice *but* to take up arms. None other than stalwart Jeffersonian John Dickinson made the racial basis of "bearing arms" especially explicit. "Slaves are deeply, deeply injurious to the Morals of the Masters and their Families, and are internal Enemies allways [*sic*] to be watched and guarded against," Dickinson wrote to George Logan in January 1804. "As standing Armies are justly abhorred among Us, our Liberty must depend on our being an *armed* Nation; and considering the power of those with whom We may have to contend, We must be a *populous* Nation." Dickinson was more committed to abolition than virtually any of the statesmen of his era. Believing slavery to be immoral, Dickinson freed his slaves in his lifetime (first conditionally, and then unconditionally) and even tried in vain to convince George Washington to do the same. The purchase of Louisiana filled him with consternation that it would provide a place for slavery to spread, further leading to the decline in morality. But even Dickinson shared the view widespread among whites that black people, slave as well as free, threatened America from within. Calls to take up arms were calls to native-born, white male citizens to exercise their free choice to pick

up a weapon in defense of their homes, their families, and their very independence itself, from non-white "internal enemies," Indian "savages,"
and British agents. To drive the point home further, these calls frequently
invoked the American Revolution, linking the threats posed by these enemies and the response of patriotic white Americans, to the War for Independence.[11]

Several made explicit what the rest only implied: that the choice to take
up arms in defense of country was a choice to support the president in a
potential war. In mid-April 1807, the Philadelphia *Democratic Press* published an appeal from A Republican "[t]o the People of the United States":
"The right to possess and bear arms, is the most invaluable privilege of
Freemen," A Republican began. "It was that right, *exercised*, which en-
abled the President to check the machinations of *Aaron Burr*, while the
forms of law prevented the securing of his person." Invoking the word
"insurrections," which could apply to Burr's attempted scheme as well
as to armed uprisings by black people, A Republican continued: "It is
that right, by which you will enable the chief magistrate to suppress insurrections, and to arrest usurpations." That was why it was imperative
that every American citizen "support the chief magistrate of your choice
in the execution of the laws, which guard liberty, order and property" by
obtaining "for himself *a musket and bayonet, or a rifle.*" A Republican
warned readers that "[a] free man, without a musket, has but half his
constitutional strength."[12]

Later that same month, a writer using the pen name Tullius published
"Thoughts on the Nature of the Government of the United States," arguing that "[t]he people of America present themselves . . . as a body of men
associated to attain the happiness of the whole." The rights they enjoyed,
"*[t]he rights of conscience*, then, *the sovereignty of an equal people*, and
the freedom of the press, constitute the safe foundations of the free governments of the United States," connecting them, as one people, across states.
Some political leaders, "nursed in ancient prejudices," might be compelled
to erroneously believe "that there is no energy in a government, which
thus rests on the natural strength of twelve hundred thousand free men,
having the right, the power, and the duty to possess and to bear arms."
But on the contrary, it was precisely the "chief magistrate . . . powerfully
backed by the whole natural and armed strength of a people *interested*
to support him: the rich and the substantial, to prevent the subversion of
their liberty and property; the laboring and the poor, to keep themselves
from political slavery," who possessed the energy necessary to protect the
nation from both foreign and domestic national threats.[13]

"*Resolved,*" a group of Republican supporters announced in a New England newspaper in February 1809, invoking the language of "insurrection" as well, "[t]hat whereas the constitution of the United States has secured to every citizen 'the right to keep and bear arms,' we do most earnestly recommend to every good citizen, at this crisis, to provide himself with arms and ammunition, . . . for the purpose of aiding in the execution of the laws, and in suppressing insurrections against the constituted authorities." The group praised both Jefferson and Congress for "hav[ing] made an honorable stand in defence of the rights of their country" and for displaying "a patriotism which entitles them to the sincere gratitude of their country," in contrast to the opponents of the embargo, "who are endeavoring to excite rebellion and disunion among our fellow citizens." These opponents constituted a cabal of misinformed dupes and unscrupulous "leaders" looking "to erect a monarchy on the ruins of our republican government, and under the pretence of a northern confederacy to ally us again to the fortunes and the fates of Great Britain." As much as its members would "regret the occasion (if it should arise) of resorting to arms in defence of our rights," they were firmly convinced "that all the evils of such a resort are nothing compared with the evils of the anarchy, confusion and despotism which would follow a destruction of our national government." Concluding that they were committed "to support with our lives and fortunes any further measures" by the national government, "whether of peace or war," these New England Republicans echoed other statements that invoked the nation's long-professed commitment to peace to justify taking up arms to support the president, and even engaging in warfare, if it came to that.[14]

For his part Jefferson echoed these sentiments, praising citizens' willingness to support his actions through military engagement as evidence of their commitment to the country. The embargo represented Americans' commitment to maintaining its independence peacefully, yet Jefferson also considered military preparation "indispensable" and told Congress in his 1807 annual message that he had unilaterally approved additions to the nation's "existing stock" of military supplies, claiming that "to have awaited a previous and special sanction by law would have lost occasions which might not be retrieved." He went on to say that he was confident "that the Legislature, feeling the same anxiety for the safety of our country, so materially advanced by this precaution," would concur with the measure. While it remained uncertain whether formal military action would be necessary, Jefferson also "called on the States for quotas of militia, to be in readiness for present defense," and boasted to Congress "that these have offered themselves with great alacrity in every part of the Union." Jefferson thought militia service was especially emblematic of the American people's independent spirit. "For a people who are free, and who mean to remain so, a well organized and armed militia is their best security."[15]

This was precisely the argument that Republicans made after Madison took office. Federalists, too, had pushed the nation toward war, Republicans charged. (The *Aurora* even framed the presidential election of 1808 as a choice "between the policy, views, and actions of one party, and those of their opponents—one being for war, and the other being for peace").[16] But, time and again, Republicans—the *real* Americans—had demonstrated restraint, seeking diplomatic solutions that avoided war. As the tension with Britain over the *Leopard* and *Leander* attacks briefly eased, and then intensified after the British issued the Orders in Council in 1807, calls to bear arms continued. A set of resolutions published in 1811 in the *Old Colony Gazette* in New Bedford, Massachusetts (and reprinted in New York and Richmond, Virginia), declared (in almost the same language as the gathering of Republicans in 1809) that "whereas the Constitution of the United States has secured to every citizen 'the right to keep and bear arms,' it is incumbent on every honest patriot, whether exempt from Military duty or not, to arm and equip himself for the purpose of aiding, at a moment's warning in the suppression of any treasonable opposition to the laws." Whatever "civil commotions" resulted from this mobilization was a small price to pay to preserve "the liberty and independence which was so dearly bought by the Martyrs of the revolution." The authors "do not therefore hesitate to declare that we are ready again if necessary to take the field in defence of this liberty, and this independence, and to sacrifice every boon to the love of our country."[17]

Jefferson's comments, in tandem with public calls for private citizens to take up arms and for militia to be raised, revealed how central the presidency was for Republicans professing peace and readying for war and how closely related the two actually were in practice. To Republicans around the country, as for the president himself, calls to bear arms in support of the president were calls to support the government he led and the nation they all comprised. In no way did they consider these calls incompatible with their longstanding professions of peace. Even a peaceful nation had its limits. If belligerent nations, domestic partisans, and "internal enemies" pushed the American people too far, the armed response would be righteous, swift, and overwhelming. A defensive war, fought against an enemy that would not abide peaceful means, was a testament to who Americans were, not a betrayal of it. Courageous, civilized, free, and fiercely protective of their independence, Americans were committed to protect themselves at all costs.[18]

"THIS WAR OF MR. MADISON IS . . . NOT AN AMERICAN ONE"

Tension with Britain finally escalated to a formal war declaration in the summer of 1812. Like Jefferson before him, Madison argued that war was now necessary to maintain "rights which no Independent Nation can relinquish." The British government, in league with Indians on the frontier, had left the United States no choice but to go to war to defend the freedom that Americans had won in the American Revolution and which they wanted to enjoy in peace.[19]

Supporters of the president frequently invoked the American Revolution in broad, sweeping language, trumpeting the glory of the Revolution and describing in breathless language the exceptional quality of the American nation among the nations of the world, even before Madison signed Congress's declaration of war. "In all other countries, their rulers have vigilantly withheld from the body of the people the arms necessary for their defence," an essay in the Plattsburg *Republican* explained in mid-March 1812. "They have been fearful, that their atrocious acts of tyranny and oppression would be resisted, and they expelled from power, if their subjects were permitted to hold and bear arms. They have, therefore, not only not given them arms, but they have prohibited them from buying and keeping arms themselves." The piece specifically mentioned the Irish as a people denied the right to bear arms under British rule. The mention was noteworthy because Irish immigrants had been crucial in winning the states of Pennsylvania and New York for Madison in 1808. The piece went on to use the right to bear arms to contrast independent American citizenship with Ireland's abject subjection to Britain. "It is generally known that the Irish peasantry are not permitted to own or have fire arms. But in these states, we shall witness the proud example of a nation armed by their government, at the expense of the public treasury, and each individual subject to be called on to defend his rights, possessing an inalienable property in the stand of arms thus bequeathed to him by government," the piece went on to say. "We hail the auspicious prospect as promising to establish a new and bright era in the annals of civilized government, and as presenting another invincible argument in favor of the republican form." As if the message of the piece was not clear enough, the author signed it, "American."[20]

The discussion of the Irish and a reminder of the critical role they played in electoral politics four years earlier underscored the fact that 1812 was not only the year the United States declared war on Britain, it was also an election year. Political participation at the national, state, and local levels proceeded in tandem with the war, and as politics clearly informed the war, so did the war loom over the nation's politics. Madison's supporters insisted that supporting the president in the war involved one's ballot as well as one's actions on the battlefield. In 1811 a meeting of Republicans in Rensselaer County, New York, even published a resolution calling for the right to vote for all men "who have been or are liable to bear arms, and of twenty-one years of age."[21] The Republican establishment argued that supporting Madison's reelection was essential to a victory that would vindicate America's honor and independence.

Standing in the way of this message, even before the official declaration of war, were Federalists and some Republicans who criticized the war as a horrible mistake from the outset and laid the blame for it squarely at the feet of the president. The declaration of war was itself a partisan matter: while more than eight of ten Congressional Republicans supported the war declaration, not a single Federalist in either house voted for it. Opposition to the war was especially forceful in New England. Leading the charge was an attorney named John Lowell, who published a pamphlet widely printed throughout New England (going through multiple editions), which coined the term by which the war would come to be known: "Mr. Madison's War."[22]

Lowell's pamphlet emphasized three distinct but interconnected themes that his fellow Federalists would continually stress throughout the war: the first, that the war demonstrated Madison's—and the Republican Party's—clear bias toward French interests; the second, that the war would ultimately lead to irreparable national moral, political, institutional, and demographic decline; and thirdly, that to prevent such irrevocable decline, citizens were obligated not only to refuse to fight in the war but to engage openly in acts of public dissent, from voting to public statements of the war's folly, with the ultimate goal of loosening and finally ending Republicans' grip on the presidency.[23]

Elitist and deeply Francophobic, Lowell initially described Madison as an incompetent leader who had been tricked into war by the French government and later as a Napoleon fanboy who sought to help the French emperor by deliberately steering the United States into war with

France's mortal enemy. Lowell began by asserting that France had essentially played Madison for a fool, backdating the end of the Berlin and Milan decrees, which prevented American ships from engaging in commerce with Britain, a full thirteen months before it had actually stopped enforcing them. Doing so changed the message the United States meant to send when in May 1810 Congress passed a law effectively terminating its nonintercourse agreement with whichever country ended its restrictions on American commerce first. The law was grounded in the belief that both Napoleon's decrees and the British Orders in Council were in effect. France, however, "*now* declares that her decrees were not repealed until April 28, 1811," making the 1811 law look like a measure aimed at one country that violated American maritime rights (Britain) while leaving untouched the other (France), which was guilty of the same affront. "Thus it seems that in addition to the bitter pill of war, we are compelled to swallow this most nauseous and disgusting dose," Lowell concluded. "We are to admit that our retaliation upon France was *first* withdrawn, *before* she would consent to repeal her decrees, and Mr. Madison declared to the world that her decrees *were* repealed, which she *now* says were *not* repealed until after we adopted what *she* directed. . . . If this is not a triumph of France over our pride, our honour, our character, our justice, our interest, and our liberties, I confess I do not know what acts could amount to such a triumph." But just pages later, Lowell accused "our administration" of "enter[ing] into an avowed co-operation and concert with France."[24]

Whether a dupe or a French sympathizer, the point for Lowell was that "this *war of Mr. Madison* is in effect a *French* war, and not an *American* one, that is undertaken for *French* interests, and in conformity with repeated *French* orders, and at the sacrifice of our *own* best interests, and probably of our liberties."[25] Lowell also recycled the well-worn Federalist refrain that the president served not only foreign French interests but also the interests of a Southern slaveholding planter class. Jefferson had felt the brunt of this accusation through his two terms, but they applied to Madison as well. The fourth president, like his predecessor, was the son of "a slave State," in fact the same slave state as Jefferson. For Lowell, that meant that Madison was predisposed to view the issue of impressment in terms "of property seized on the high seas."[26]

Lowell's point could have supported a strident criticism of slavery itself. A staunch opponent of slavery could argue that Madison was just as wrong to think of black people as property as he was to think of impressed sailors that way. But Lowell's pamphlet was not an indictment of slavery. Rather, he meant to highlight how inappropriate it was "to intimate that the seamen ought to be carried in for *adjudication* like *other property*, instead of being subjected to the decision of military officers." Few New England merchants complained about their men being impressed by the British. From Lowell's perspective Southern states complained about this far more loudly. "Yet such is the fact, well known to every man on the sea coast—Maryland, North Carolina, South Carolina, Georgia, employ three foreign seamen to one American!" Lowell's critique of Madison was meant to disparage him as a slave-owner but not to impugn the racism upon which it was based. Lowell cared nothing that Southern aristocrats treated blacks as property. What he cared about was that a Southern, slaveholder president applied that same approach to white American sailors.[27]

Lowell's charge dripped with partisanship. Alongside Adams, he cited George Washington (another slaveholding president from Virginia) as evidence that the "evil" of impressment by the British occurred only to a "very limited extent." So limited was it, in fact, "that neither General Washington nor Mr. Adams thought this matter of sufficient importance to make it the subject of a special communication to Congress, much less did they think it reasonable to cause war."[28] His use of Washington as an example of how past presidents handled the issue of impressment responsibly reveals how little he actually cared about the evils of slavery itself. His concern was not the treatment of blacks; rather, it was the treatment of whites *in the same manner as blacks*. Lowell charged that, as a slave-owner, the Republican Madison (but not the Federalist Washington) was accustomed to viewing people as property and could only view the solution in terms of property rights. To the extent that true Americans (as opposed to foreigners) were being impressed, a solution that treated impressed sailors in any way like property relegated them to an inferior status reserved only for the likes of Madison's human chattel.

The War Hawks' wide-eyed ambition to take Canada was also misplaced, Lowell continued. "Will they [the territories of Canada] strengthen us? No—They will enfeeble us—They will increase the jarring materials of which the United States are composed, and which are already too discordant for our own peace or safety—They will open an easy entrance to French power and French intrigues." Then Lowell tied this picture of creeping French influence to Jefferson's signal diplomatic achievement. "Already Frenchmen are admitted to a seat in our national councils, and the addition of Canada would only give to France the opportunity of attacking us on both flanks; for it ought to be known that every Louisianan and Canadian is at heart as well as by habits a Frenchman."[29]

Lowell's remedy for this national calamity was straightforward: citizens had to engage actively in dissent, both by refusing to involve themselves in or giving any support for the war and by speaking out against the war and especially its leader. "[I]n a war offensive and unjust, the citizens are not only not obliged to take part, but by the laws of God, and of civil society, they are bound to abstain," he asserted to his readers. They had to assemble, publish, and speak out at every opportunity about the folly of the war. No statement was too harsh, so long as the dissenter "confine[d] himself strictly to truth in stating his facts." This concerted effort had one aim: to take back the presidency from a man and a party leading the nation to potentially irrevocable ruin. "The people," Lowell concluded, "must recollect that on the change of President depends the prospect of peace and every man, let his politics be what they may, who is attached to peace, must wish to displace the *man who alone is responsible for this war*—I mean Mr. Madison."[30]

As the war commenced, other critical commentaries echoed his point that whether Madison was a willing Francophile or not mattered less than the deleterious impact the war would have on the nation. "That administration which DRIES UP THE SOURCES OF REVENUE, WEAKENS THE POWER, DISCOURAGES THE INDUSTRY AND DEGRADES THE CHARACTER OF A COUNTRY, and especially that administration which embroils a country with foreign powers, and involves it in unnecessary wars, is a bad administration," one piece declared.[31] The result, wrote another, was a war that catered to the interests of a foreign power and which would only "preserve the Virginian dynasty, and . . . silence all, who doubt that '*the powers that be are ordained of God.*'"[32]

Ominous invocations of the "Virginia dynasty" and Virginia "junto"— already ubiquitous in critical commentary during Jefferson's presidential tenure—remained common in criticism of the war. Critics argued that foisting on Northerners a war that they clearly did not want, and claiming that their status as real Americans hinged upon their willingness to support it and the Virginia president who led it, was really a way to subordinate Northern whites to Southern aristocrats—to bring the former down to the approximate level of the latter's black slaves.[33]

A satirical 1814 story, published in London, which depicted a conniving, opportunistic cardinal and a bankruptcy commissioner selling off Napoleon's possessions, demonstrated that the criticism of Madison as a lover of Napoleonic France and the leader of a cruel Southern slave regime, were internationally known. When a set of "old blood-hounds from the St. Domingo pack" come up among Napoleon's possessions to be auctioned off, the commissioner mentions "an American merchant" interested in purchasing all of them, who "is of the opinion that his friends the planters would give any money for them, to hunt their runaway slaves with." Later, when "the crown of Lombardy" and "the sword and balances of Justice, the former rusty for want of use; the latter with only one scale" come up for sale, the cardinal claims the crown, while the commissioner awards the rusty sword and imbalanced scale to an American "friend" who "has determined to buy and forge it into thumb-screws for negroes, which he thinks will sell well." When lot 9, the "star of Napoleon" comes up, the cardinal proposes it be "*set in mud*," but the commissioner replies, "Well, for all that, I shall offer it to his adorer, Jemmy Maddison, who will set it in diamonds."[34] The humor of the story lay in the serious criticism of the cruelty of slavery and Madison's place as the leader of the American nation. The very support for the president that Republicans demanded as a prerequisite for citizenship, dissenters argued, was really meant to "completely subvert our liberties, subject us to the cruel caprice of a military despot, and eventually establish an hereditary government," and dissolve any distinction between "a President, Emperor, or King." That would make white, American citizens, at best, subjects—and at worst, something akin to the black souls that aristocrats like Madison claimed as property.[35]

In mid-August 1812, a gathering of more than 1,500 New Hampshire Federalists published a "Memorial" to James Madison, announcing that they wanted no part of the war "if the consequence of this war should be, that the American flag shall give the American character to all who sail under it, and thus invite thousands of *foreign* seamen to enter into our service, and thrust aside our own native citizens." The "Memorial" urged citizens to speak out against the president and the war and to refuse to participate. "The Chief Magistrate of a Government, which rests on public opinion, and which can only look for the support of its measures to the approbation of the People, has a right to be informed, distinctly and unequivocally, of the sentiments entertained by the community, concerning measures of great national importance," the New Hampshire gathering informed Madison. They were not unequivocally averse to war. Pointing out that many of them had fought valiantly in the Revolution, they assured Madison that "[w]e are ready to meet those scenes again, whenever it can be shewn that the vindication of our National honor, or the preservation of our essential rights, demands it." But Madison had failed to convince them that this war was worth the expenditure of "our TREASURE, and our BLOOD in its prosecution."[36] Humiliating defeats at Michilimackinac and at Detroit, at the very outset of the war in the summer of 1812—only appeared to confirm the critics' case.

The problems began immediately after the United States declared war. British forces across the border promptly arrested Americans and confiscated their goods. British Captain Charles Roberts took Fort Michilimackinac and its American commander, Porter Hanks, entirely by surprise, forcing Hanks's surrender and taking control of a fort that was crucial to the Indian trade. It was a show of force that strengthened British ties to Natives, while simultaneously playing off American fears of Native "savagery."[37]

Problems for the Americans continued when Madison, recognizing the need for an early and decisive victory, named the territorial governor of the Michigan Territory, William Hull, a brigadier general, and endorsed Hull's scheme to invade Canada. A newspaper report expressed high hopes for Hull's appointment. "Yesterday the General arrived at this place with his suite, and will immediately proceed to Dayton, where he will take command of the army destined for Detroit," the report noted on June 11. "Indeed the spirit and patriotism which now animate the people, remind us of the feelings and conduct of our ancestors in 1775." Such confidence proved woefully misplaced. More adept at issuing proclamations and speeches than at commanding a military force, Hull sought to inspire his men with vivid descriptions of Indian butchery. But these descriptions also betrayed Hull's own fear of Indians, which led Hull to hesitate, even when he had superior numbers over the British and their Indian allies. Retreating to Fort Detroit in early August, Hull surrendered the fort to British General Isaac Brock after Brock paraded a force that included more than five hundred Indians in front of the fort. Petrified, Hull almost immediately knuckled under. By losing Detroit, Americans had forfeited a place of strategic significance, along with all the weapons and resources it contained. Following Michilimackinac, the loss of Detroit dealt a body blow to national morale.[38]

Countering the claim that voluntary service was an essential patriotic duty, the governors of three states—Massachusetts, Rhode Island, and Connecticut, Federalists all—announced at the war's outset that they would not make their states' militia available to the administration for the war. Fueled by early disasters at Detroit and Michilimackinac, criticism of the war from Federalists and dissident Republicans emphasized that opposition to the war would not cease until skeptics were convinced that the war promoted, rather than threatened, America's essential national character.[39]

Critics of the war walked a fine line between asserting a sectional political identity that was distinct from those that Southern and western states pursued through the war and a single national "character" that only strident criticism of the administration could save.[40] Northern Federalists published pieces (reprinted even in Southern newspapers) that described Northerners as alternately fundamentally different from Southerners or the only hope left for a nation being destroyed by an ineptly administered war.

"In this town, . . . setting aside the officers of government, agents, contractors, expectants of office, military officers, &c., *nine tenths* are opposed to the war," wrote an exasperated Federalist in Boston, in a statement that hinted at both the reach of the federal bureaucracy and military and their dissonance from the New Englanders in their midst. "There is a plain rule by which to judge of the merits of an administration.—That administration which PRESERVES THE PEACE, CHERISHES THE INDUSTRY AND ADVANCES THE PROSPERITY OF A COUNTRY is a good administration, and deserving of public confidence," another claimed. "That administration which DRIES UP THE SOURCES OF REVENUE, WEAKENS THE POWER, DISCOURAGES THE INDUSTRY AND DEGRADES THE CHARACTER OF A COUNTRY, and especially that administration which embroils a country with foreign powers, and involves it in unnecessary wars, is a bad administration." Yet commentators on either end of this divide stressed the importance of the upcoming election. "If you regard the *union*, and the *welfare of your own state*," the Bostonian urged readers, "bestir yourselves in season to prevent the re-election of Madison." Another agreed: "The present situation of our country excites the deepest anxiety, and renders the choice of its first public officer more important and interesting than ever. This choice involves in effect a question of administration, the appointment of heads of departments, and the institution of principles of policy for conducting our public affairs, of the utmost consequence to the union."[41]

The Federalist *Pittsburgh Gazette* devoted the entire back page of its October 23, 1812, issue to the "Address of the Democratic-Republican Committee of the Borough of Pittsburgh, and Its Vicinity" to endorse New York Mayor DeWitt Clinton for president and to join Federalists in blaming Madison entirely for the war's mishaps—a clear sign of Northern states' frustration with Southern domination of national politics. Citing both Detroit and Michilimackinac, the "Address" lamented that the British "flag . . . waves in triumph over the lakes, Detroit and Mackina," evidence of victories won with the aid of Indians, whose "savage yells which proclaim murder and destruction thro' our defenceless frontier, forbid us to think of glory, and announce in impressive language, the imbecility and incompetency of the administration." The Democratic-Republicans of Pittsburgh were clear. The country needed as president a man who possessed an "energy of . . . character," capable of leading "a vigorous prosecution of the war, and an honorable and lasting peace"—a man, they thought, like DeWitt Clinton. Without such a president, a war meant to ensure the nation's independence would only compromise its character. Americans would be rendered subordinates, even "slaves," to Britain. Thus, early defeats fueled critics' contention that Madison's war was a threat to precisely the qualities that supporters argued it promoted.[42]

PATRIOTS AND THE PRESIDENT AGAINST SUBJECTS, "SAVAGES," AND SLAVES

As 1813 dawned, more news arrived of brutal slaughter. Along the Raisin River, Indians set fire to makeshift prisons housing roughly eighty wounded American soldiers who had been captured by British troops. The prisoners had been marched to their quarters in the bitter cold, and the exposure to the elements left most of them unable to escape as the flames consumed the walls around them. Those who did manage to escape were picked off by roughly two hundred Natives who waited on them, tomahawks at the ready. News of the so-called "River Raisin Massacre" circulated quickly, providing a rallying cry ("Remember the Raisin!") for soldiers and Republican politicians looking to drum up more evidence of Indian butchery to fuel their pro-war propaganda campaign. Despite such a rallying cry, public confidence in the war was hard to sustain. Even American victories, such as the victory at Sacketts Harbor in late May, came with a heavy price. Accustomed to defeat, a navy officer had set fire to a dockyard to prevent supplies from falling into British hands. Though American forces repulsed the British, they did not pursue the British in retreat. Victory thus resulted in minimal gains, fueling critics' contention that the war was a fool's errand from the start.[43]

To explain these losses while salvaging their national narrative, Republicans contrasted the violence perpetrated by the British, their Indian allies, and free and enslaved blacks with the violence they demanded of patriotic Americans. British subjects, Indian "savages," and black slaves revealed their cowardice, their bloodlust, their licentiousness, in vivid scenes of butchery, scalping, and rape that circulated among Americans by word of mouth and in print. Critics of the war, President Madison and his allies maintained, were complicit in the slaughter and abuse by undermining the war effort. Those who did agree to do their patriotic duty and answered the president's call, on the other hand, were patriots engaged in glorious combat to defend their families, their homes, and their nation all at once.

The very humiliating defeats that America incurred provided rich fuel for a gruesome and lurid story of butchery and rape by British soldiers, Indian "savages," and even freed black slaves. In his Fourth Annual Message to Congress, just months after Hull's loss of Detroit, Madison explained that "[a] distinguishing feature" of Hull's humiliating loss was "the use made by the enemy of the merciless savages under their influence," who unhesitatingly "call[ed] to his aid their ruthless ferocity, armed with the horrors of those instruments of carnage and torture which are known to spare neither age nor sex." The result of such barbarous warfare, Madison went on to say, had a silver lining: "It was followed by signal proofs that the national spirit rises according to the pressure on it." The loss at Detroit had "inspired everywhere new ardor and determination. In the States and districts least remote it was no sooner known than every citizen was ready to fly with his arms at once to protect his brethren against the bloodthirsty savages let loose by the enemy on an extensive frontier, and to convert a partial calamity into a source of invigorated efforts."[44]

Madison's explanation told a story that Republicans would emphasize in response to the defeats the United States endured throughout the war. British soldiers fought an immoral war, encouraging the basest natures of both Indians and blacks against not only valiant, armed white American men but unarmed, innocent white women and children. Such violence would inspire all true patriots to join in the war effort. By exercising their freedom to take up arms on their own—by voluntarily answering the president's call to war—these men would distinguish themselves as courageous, civilized, sovereign citizens, as *Americans*, in contrast with despotic monarchies, "savage" societies, and their traitorous Federalist sympathizers, who threatened their democracy. Contrasting "the dastardly and ferocious conduct of the British and their savage allies," against "that of our citizens who have the honour to bear arms in support of their country's rights," the *National Intelligencer* declared, "Long may a contrast, so glorious to our cause, continue to exist!"[45]

The Fourth of July, 1813, less than six months after the River Raisin massacre, and less than a month and a half after the costly victory at Sacketts Harbor, provided a forum for Republicans to praise the war effort by invoking the mystique of the American Revolution and to condemn America's enemies through stories of sexual assault and macabre slaughter. "The Declaration of Independence, which we celebrate, was hardly more important to our Country, than the Declaration of the War, in which we are engaged," one orator announced to a gathering of fellow Republicans. "The one, announced our existence as a nation: the other, announces our determination, to maintain the rights and honor of the national character." Both were acts of dissent against tyranny: the one establishing America as an independent country, and the other maintaining that independence through Americans' "just cause . . . fair object, and . . . instruments of civilized warfare." By aligning with them, the British in Canada demonstrated that they lacked "the pride of the warrior" and "the virtue of the Christian." "Allied with the savages in arms, and almost assimilated with them in nature," the orator continued, "the troops of Canada are ferocious, without courage; and treacherous, without art. Like the savages themselves, they seek not an enemy, but a victim. Excited only by a thirst of blood, they are equally gratified by the stream, whether it flows from the head of the old or of the young;—from the heart of woman, or of man!"[46]

In addition to depicting British troops and Indian allies attacking and scalping innocent white American women and children, accounts of British soldiers, often accompanied by Indian allies, liberating Southern plantations provided opportunities for pro-war propagandists to employ another vicious scene with which to contrast the civilized violence of liberty-loving, white Americans: black men raping white women. Such stories minimized women's role as independent people, instead presenting them as helpless victims of nonwhite men, existing in constant need of protection by white men. Captivity narratives, which chronicled the sexual peril of white women captured by Indians, became immensely popular during the war, as they played off two widespread perceptions at opposite cultural extremes: on one end, the view of white women as paragons of sexual and racial purity; on the other, the perception of Indians (and blacks) as brutes.[47]

A letter from an officer to the lieutenant governor of Virginia, Charles K. Mallory, published in the Philadelphia *Democratic Press* just days before the July 4 festivities, reported the violence in Hampton: "*My blood ran cold at what I saw and heard.* The few distressed inhabitants running up in every direction to congratulate us; tears were shedding in every corner—the infamous scoundrels, Monsters, *destroyed every thing* but the houses, and, (my pen is almost unwilling to describe it,) the *Women were ravished by the abandoned Ruffians . . .* and not a solitary American arm present to avenge their wrongs!"[48]

Of course, such stories failed to discuss acts of deplorable violence perpetrated by white Americans. (The very first scalping in the war, for instance, was committed by a white American, not an Indian).[49] Instead, Republicans associated stories of horrific butchery with Indians and black people, especially slaves, further associating nonwhites with acts of murder and sexual violence—an association that would remain fundamental to American racism to this very day. "The unfortunate females of Hampton who could not leave the town were suffered to be abused in the most shameful manner, not only the venal savage foe but by the unfortunate and infatuated blacks, who were encouraged in their excesses," a separate account of the violence in Hampton reported. "They pillaged, and encouraged every act of rapine and murder."[50] Such acts of violence only further marked the difference between savages and slaves on the one hand and valiant Americans on the other. Crucially, Republicans continued, such viciousness from America's enemies should only inspire truly patriotic American men to redouble their commitment to the war effort. As one Republican Fourth-of-July toast to "the daughters of Columbia" succinctly explained, "That barbarity which has inspired one sex with terror, has only inflamed the courage of the other."[51]

As the calls to bear arms suggest, ultimately it was the men who would do the fighting. It was the men who would clear the land of brutal savages, British soldiers, and their allies. It was the men would do the ploughing and the planting, both agriculturally and sexually, impregnating their fecund soil with the seed of their crops and their fertile women with the seed of the next generation of Americans. It was the men who would do the governing, the voting, and, ultimately the deciding. None of this meant that women's roles as procreators and sexual partners was any less important than men's role on the battlefield; after all, what would be the point of fighting a war for America without the promise of future generations of Americans? But it did mean that the freedom to dissent, to oppose being acted upon, was reserved in its fullest form for white men. Once they had inspired their men to victory, women were expected to submit to the dominion of their husbands, to grow and train their children, to ensure the survival of America's civilized, white democracy. For Republicans, this meant that the entire war effort, the entire future of the nation, indeed the very claim of white, patriotic, American men *as* men, *as* protectors, *as* civilized, *as* strong—in short, *as Americans*—stemmed from this free choice to bear arms in support of the president. Conversely, it also meant that anyone who *refused* to support the president in a time of war had aligned themselves with the nation's enemies and had in effect become "submissive" subjects and degenerate "slaves" themselves. Dispiriting news of American defeat circulated alongside terrifying stories of slaughter and rape by licentious blacks and barbarian Indians made it more difficult for both the war's supporters and its critics to make their respective arguments. Supporters of the war found it increasingly difficult to convince Americans that the war could be won decisively and that the cost Americans were paying would be worth it. Critics could (and did) point to these early losses as justification for their decision to refuse to fight. But they also faced the argument that their refusal to fight was the very reason for the losses.[52]

In the midst of the war's setbacks, critics doubled down on their insistence that their refusal to fight Madison's war was an assertion of their masculinity, their autonomy, their independence—their *American*-ness. Critics in the New England states who refused to hand over their militia argued that their refusal was a defense of state autonomy, as well as a necessary measure to protect the homes and families of the state's citizens.[53] Denying that voluntary service in the war was an expression of a citizen's manhood and the only certain way to protect one's family from harm, the state of Connecticut defended its decision to keep its militia within its own borders. Like Massachusetts and Rhode Island, Connecticut stipulated that its militia would not be under the service of the president but would remain in the service of the state, where militia would be used only to defend its own people from invasion. The expectation that militiamen under twenty-one fight the war was a violation of the state's rights, a piece in the *Connecticut Mirror* claimed. And since all contracts made by individuals under twenty-one were "invalid, and cannot be enforced by law," requiring state militia to serve the administration alongside the regular army struck at "the obligation which exists between children and their parents, the basis of which is laid in the nature of things, and the principle is solemnly enjoined in the fifth commandment, by GOD himself." That precedent would allow the government "with the same propriety" to "dissolve" any and all familial or social relationships, including "the obligations of the marriage contract, and authorise [sic] married women to contract." While the assertion of states' rights clearly suggested that Connecticut was separating itself from the authority of the federal government, and particularly the president's authority, the statement also grounded its claims in more universal themes of family relations and religious morality.

Connecticut's intransigence was meant to ensure that its own state militia remained within its borders to protect the state from harm. But it was also meant to send a message to the president on behalf of the entire country. The piece concluded unequivocally: "The free people of the United States, it is firmly believed, do not appreciate Mr. Madison's honor at so extravagant a rate, as to be willing to part with their liberties and independence to preserve it."[54]

Republicans countered that Federalists were un-American and unmanly, British sympathizers. Some even called them "slaves." By refusing to lend their support to the president, they argued, critics were effectively aiding the enemy and undermining everything America stood for.[55] "[W]e verily believe that our government had no other alternative, than War or an unqualified submission to the haughty mandates of the British Ministry," a group of Lancaster County, Pennsylvania, Republicans calling themselves "the Friends of Peace and Commerce" declared in early September 1812. "Can then an honorable and independent people declare, that the constituted authorities have made an improper choice of these alternatives? None but a Slave could answer in the affirmative." All Americans, the group concluded, should "not then hesitate in determining to uphold the government of our choice, and to comply, in letter and in spirit, with the patriotic recommendation of the President, by exerting ourselves.—'In preserving order, in promoting concord, in maintaining the authority and efficacy of the Laws, and in supporting and invigorating all the measures which may be adopted by the constituted authorities, for obtaining a speedy, a just and an honorable peace.'"[56]

The next month, a pseudonymous Republican, Pindar, described the decision to go to war as "an open, patriotic, and manly stand," and reiterated the Lancaster Republicans' claim that dissent against the war effort was tantamount to a betrayal of everything America stood for. "[T]here are men in America who contend that England has done us no material damage.—Such men cannot be considered as lovers of the country; on the contrary they appear to be its greatest enemies," Pindar announced. "They would sacrifice dignity and honor, at the shrine of interest. Their contact is to be avoided, and their influence obviated as much as possible, by all means consistent with the principles of honor." For Pindar, no less than for the Lancaster Republicans (or Madison's Republican and Federalist critics), the election of 1812 would determine the course of the war, and with it, the fate of the nation as well. "Let every man, who has the good of his country at heart, turnout at the present election. Democracy must triumph."[57]

The very people who opposed the war, claimed a defender of Madison writing under the pen name A Friend to His Country in 1813, contributed to the very "want of vigor" that led to the country's repeated defeats. "It was not till after the most obstinate resistance that the administration were authorised [*sic*] to raise an army, which in consequence of resistance was less than they desired. Every measure that was calculated to give energy was resisted, and delays produced by long speeches and other obstacles." Those who laid blame for the country's defeats at Madison's feet, A Friend to His Country argued, were no more justified than would be someone who claimed Congress was responsible for Benedict Arnold's treachery. "Our country is great—its resources ample and the arms of its defenders strong," A Friend of His Country concluded. "If then we are called upon—and the times seem to call on us—to declare ourselves, let us have no hesitation in proclaiming to the world that under all circumstances we have the fullest confidence in the wisdom and temperance of the administration, who equally avoid the frantic excesses of heat and passion on the one hand, and of nerveless fear on the other, but pursue that steady sober path which their great trust and important duties mark out."[58]

Celebrating the free choice of white patriotic men to bear arms by making explicit its connection with American citizenship, a piece addressed "*To the People of Massachusett's* [*sic*]," castigated the state for having fallen from its once-proud station as the leader of the American Revolution. The piece quoted from the Declaration of Independence, listing specifically the grievances that George III had "constrained our fellow citizens, taken captive on the high seas, to bear arms against their country, to become the executioners of their friends and brethren, or to fall themselves by their hands" and had "excited domestic insurrections amongst us, & has endeavoured to bring on the inhabitants of our frontiers, the merciless Indian savages; whose known rule of warfare is an undistinguished destruction of all ages, sexes, and conditions." Against such abuses, the proud patriots of Massachusetts dissented, and ignited the War for Independence. "In your might, you stood erect, you ceased to be slaves, you became men." But, the author provocatively asked readers, were the people of Massachusetts *still* free, or even still men? "Are you now what your sires were then? Do you yet love liberty? Or are you degenerated? Are you prepared again to wear the despot's yoke, again to be enslaved?" If the people of Massachusetts were still masculine, liberty-loving Americans, the author declared, it was time to prove it. Against an entrenched Federalist minority in power, which held "views" that "are uniform in an opposition to *every* measure of the general government," "the majority must rise to a man: armed by the elective franchise they must expel their present rulers from office, else a civil war may determine whether the adherents of America or those of England are the most powerful in Massachusetts."[59]

Still another piece, published late in 1813 in New York (and reprinted in Pennsylvania and Massachusetts) depicted the refusal to take up arms in support of the war effort as an abdication of one's manly duties as the protector of his family, as well as his nation. "If, then, you love your country & are determined to defend its rights—if you love your families and are determined to protect them—if you value your property, and are determined to preserve it—you will fly to your arms and hasten to meet the enemy, should they dare to set foot on our shores."[60]

Dissenters and supporters across partisan lines agreed that Americans were civilized and courageous, unlike the barbaric, "savage" Indians who prowled the frontier and cravenly preyed upon innocent women and children. Americans were free, unlike the subjects of foreign rulers who violated American rights and the abject black slaves who toiled in American plantations. Both considered the presidency inextricably connected to this national character, agreeing that ultimate credit or blame for the war rested with the president and that the core issue was whether support for the war promoted or undermined that national character. But just as the war reflected the political context out of which it was born, so too did partisans treat the political debate like part of the war.

"Alas my *friend*, Washington is hardly cold in his grave," Elizabeth Parke Custis Law lamented to the consul at Paris, David Warden, in early September 1814. "That hallow'd spot has been trampled on by Ruthless Invaders." The "hallow'd spot" she referred to was the city of Washington, which had been invaded by the British just two weeks earlier. Marching from Bladensburg, Maryland, British forces had met with little real resistance from American troops. Dolly Madison and her slaves scrambled to leave the president's mansion before the British arrived, and a story emerged—which is still told to this day—that she managed to take a Gilbert Stuart painting of George Washington with her before the British arrived and set the mansion ablaze. But no amount of paintings spared a fiery fate could diminish the humiliation of an act she considered "a prostration of national pride & Honor."[61] Madison's supporters as well as his critics shared that sentiment. For Federalists and apostate Republicans who rejected the war, as well as for the war's Republican defenders, the attack was a humiliation that spoke to the hostile forces threatening American decline.

The attack only reinforced a longstanding criticism of Madison's inadequate leadership that, by the summer of 1814, even some Republican pieces grudgingly acknowledged. "[W]hilst we acknowledge his virtues," a piece in the *Philadelphia Democratic Press* explained in late July 1814—weeks before the British invasion of Washington, "we cannot refrain from expressing our regret that indecisive measures should have proceeded from his administration during this time of war, *when firmness and energy can alone save us*." Pieces like this attest that the burning of Washington culminated a long war effort that had left even many supporters weary.[62]

For Madison's most scathing critics, the burning of Washington exemplified how a want of presidential firmness leads inevitably to national degeneration. Madison was no military leader; he lacked the fortitude to lead American forces in a successful defense of the nation's seat of government.[63] A visual depiction of the burning of Washington, "Philanthropie Moderne," shows a British statesman and officer embracing black slaves as the officer sets fire to a building labeled "Washington." The image highlighted the alliance between British soldiers and nonwhites that pro-war propagandists had used to provoke white Americans to take up arms in support of President Madison and in defense of home, family, and country. The attack on the White House and the Capitol building sent a disturbing message that, just as Federalists had long predicted, the president's weakness had compromised the nation's courage, its independence, and its capacity to resist being imposed upon by foreign forces. The very fact that a belligerent force—and the country's former mother country at that—could invade the nation and set fire to its seat of government signified how much of its sense of itself America had already lost (see figure 7.2).

Madison's stalwart supporters—including Custis Law—actually agreed with portions of this argument. "Mr. Madison is not a military man," she stated bluntly, in agreement with Madison's critics. It was an obvious and unavoidable point; for all his bona fides as a political thinker, Madison was no warrior. In fairness, neither were Jefferson or Adams. But neither of them served as president during a declared war. The fourth president was clearly in over his head. But Custis Law brought up Madison's lack of military experience for a different reason. "*I consider Armstrong the author of all*," she wrote, referring to John Armstrong, Madison's secretary of war. "He was M[adison]s enemy—he sought to injure him," she believed. "He hoped by Managing the War Office *as he has done*—to ruin the Republican cause—& make himself a king—& he hoped to gain popularity to the North & East—by causing the public buildings to be

Figure 7.2: "Philanthropie Moderne" (1813). Courtesy of the American Antiquarian Society.

destroy'd. That Congress might be obliged to remove from W[ashingto]n." For Custis Law, Madison's lack of military credentials simply meant that he depended on leaders like Armstrong all the more. Such a colossal failure could not be blamed on Madison; it had to fall on the men he had trusted. Given the significance of one's duty to serve when the president called, such a dereliction of duty called everything into question: including Armstrong's devotion to America itself. "[M]iserable wretch," she continued, "he has pull'd a mountain on himself—detestation is express'd of him by all."[64]

Custis Law was not alone in blaming Armstrong for the invasion of Washington. In fact, the president himself claimed that Armstrong was the focus of "violent prejudices" that people in Washington City and the surrounding area directed toward the government for its failure to adequately defend the nation's seat of government. In his account of his conversation with Armstrong, Madison recalled Armstrong maintaining that he had done everything he could to prepare for the invasion. Some "charges" were "destitute of foundation," Madison conceded, but not all of them. And as Washington was "the capital of the nation," the "strong feelings" that the inhabitants of the city felt would surely radiate out to "every where else also." Madison went on to say that "it would not be easy to satisfy the nation that the event was without blame somewhere." With that, Madison informed Armstrong that he did not agree that the secretary of war had done all he could to keep the city safe. Madison claimed credit for every "precaution or arrangement for [the city's] safety" and argued that Armstrong's suggestions had only "induced a reduction of my arrangements to the minimum, in order to obtrude the less on a reluctant execution." Armstrong tendered his resignation, and Madison accepted it.[65]

Shifting the blame entirely onto Armstrong for the British invasion of Washington was part of a larger pattern of blaming high-ranking officials or officers for key losses. These accusations—while not always entirely unfounded—nonetheless allowed the war's supporters to salvage the president's reputation and thus preserve the obligation to answer the president's call to fight that was foundational to the pro-war propaganda campaign.[66]

"UPON THE SKILL AND BRAVERY OF GEN. JACKSON EVERY RELIANCE IS PLACED"

The Treaty of Ghent, ending the war, returned the United States and Britain to the diplomatic relationship they had had previously (known as *status quo ante bellum*). Yet even peace did not bring an end to Republicans' celebration of violence as a fundamental national value. In fact, as the war reached its end, news of a resounding American victory in New Orleans, led by Andrew Jackson, would force Federalist critics of Madison's administration to substantially shift their criticism of the war. No longer could they insist that refusing to fight when the president called was a patriotic act. Jackson's victory was too spectacular, its publicity too widespread. Instead, Federalists joined in the acclaim for Jackson's military leadership, claiming that Jackson exemplified the obligation to take up arms when the president called. That obligation, Federalist publications insisted, was never more crucial than when a president like Madison—to their mind, incompetent and cowardly—led the nation. Attempting to register a final dig at Madison, Federalists echoed the essential message of the Republicans' pro-war propaganda campaign: that all true Americans had to be willing to take up arms—to engage in violence—when the president called, to defend their civilization, their sovereignty, their *nation*, from anything that threatened it.[67]

The prospect of peace certain filled the war's supporters with hope. One report, published even in New England, praised the treaty as a testament to James Madison's negotiating skills.[68] Another, titled "PEACE," celebrated peace with Britain by quoting from the Declaration of Independence: "*Enemies in war, in peace Friends*, was the manly and generous expression of our ancestors," the piece declared, "and we well recollect with what illuminations, transparencies, bonfires, and other demonstrations of popular rejoicing, the close of our former contest with Great Britain was celebrated."[69] Yet even amid talk of peace, there was no question that the violence of the war had transformed the nation.

"The accounts which have been received from New Orleans, since our last, are of a very vague and suspicious character," the *Boston Spectator* reported in late January of 1815. Years of military blunders and missed opportunities had conditioned the war's critics to look askance at any promising news. Reports estimated that Jackson had declared martial law in the city and that he had at his disposal a combined force of 7,000 to 8,000 men, militia from New Orleans and the surrounding areas and regulars combined. The best that the *Spectator* could surmise, that force well surpassed the estimated 1,000 to 3,000 British approaching New Orleans. Still, the *Spectator* refused to believe an initial report from New York "that the British were defeated." "[T]his we presume, is a mistake," the *Spectator* concluded. "If the fact, that the enemy had almost surprized the city, may be considered as a specimen of General Jackson's vigilance and ability, we have little room to expect any other than an unfavourable result."[70]

Reports such as this were published in newspapers across the country, though they varied in their estimation of the size of the British forces the United States faced.[71] Yet even Federalist newspapers carried letters and accounts attesting to the bravery and patriotism of the Americans, agreeing that every able-bodied man—including men of color—stood ready to fight.[72]

Subsequent stories of the battle confirmed that earlier reports of victory were not mistaken. Jackson and his men had decisively beaten the British at New Orleans, achieving a victory that would be the signal American achievement of the war and the launching pad for a national fame that Jackson would eventually ride to the presidency. Historians often point out that the victory was diplomatically meaningless; the Treaty of Ghent had already been concluded, officially ending the war before the Battle of New Orleans even began. But that does not make the battle politically insignificant.[73] Indeed, more than even the treaty itself, Jackson's victory at New Orleans forced Federalists to alter their entire characterization of the war effort.

Headlines and stories used every available superlative to describe Jackson's victory. It was "glorious," "incredible," "splendid." It prompted patriotic celebrations attended by "all classes of our citizens," as one typical account described. Republican celebrations of Jackson's victory bore some unmistakable resemblance to celebrations of Washington's arrival on his national tours twenty-five years earlier. "We this day have the heartfelt pleasure of announcing, that the Grand Expedition against New Orleans, consisting of nearly *ten thousand* of the choicest veterans of England, *has totally failed.*—. . . Thanks to the gallant JACKSON and his brave '*back woods men*' their aspiring expectations have been blasted," a Boston piece, reprinted in the *National Aegis*, announced. "The flourishing capital of Louisiana was to have been sacked and plundered, and its virgins and matrons were to become the sport of a licentious and brutal soldiery. '*Beauty and booty*' were the watch words by which the *Hunnic* leaders of the armies of the Prince Regent endeavoured to awaken the ferocity of their barbarian soldiery. . . . We cannot but repeat our thanks to the heroic '*Backwoods men*,' for having . . . preserved the city of New Orleans . . . from plunder and devastation." In addition to gatherings of citizens of all classes, the celebrations often featured military pomp and parade from local militia or volunteer corps, who would drill and parade and fire salutes to Jackson and his victory before its audience. The volunteer corps, like the militia who drilled before Washington upon his arrival to town, exemplified the voluntarism of the American fighting force, distinguishing the democratic nature of the military from the compulsory model of monarchical Britain.[74]

Republicans made Jackson's victory at New Orleans exemplary of the broader narrative they used to characterize the entire war: a triumph of citizens who freely served when their president called, saving their families and their nation from British subjects whose king compelled them to commit atrocities against innocent American citizens. A piece from the *Richmond Enquirer*, republished in New York, went so far as to say that should Britain opt for peace, "we ought to 'thank the enemy' for his attack on New Orleans. It removes the mistrust, . . . [and] binds that section to us forever. It proves that we are adequate to *their* protection, and that *they* are faithful in their allegiance. It proves that republics are not as weak as they have been represented; and that a federal government is able to stretch out its arm and cast its shield over the extremest parts of its dominion." Highlighting the potential of the victory to embrace the far-flung city of New Orleans as part of the nation, the piece also argued that Jackson's victory proved once and for all that the unwillingness of New England governors to provide their state militia was a cowardly, un-American act. "For if New-Orleans had been situated as far to the N.E." of the country "as it is to the S.W.," and if it had as its leader "such a governor as [Massachusetts Governor Caleb] Strong, . . . if the western militia had been kept back by the same *factious* spirit and *pretended* scruples for the Constitution . . . New-Orleans would, indeed, have been captured, and our country disgraced."[75]

Not surprisingly, the war's critics were not convinced. Instead, the treaty only confirmed for them that their misgivings about Madison—and their refusal to fight his war—had been correct from the beginning. Contrary to Republicans' insistence, the nation had bought peace at the expense of lives, fortune, and sacred honor, Federalists chorused. By getting none of what the nation went to war for, the *Massachusetts Spy* argued, the peace was tantamount to an acceptance of antebellum British maritime practices—in effect codifying British abuse in writing, the height of pointlessness.[76]

A number of Federalist pieces conceded the Republicans' point that the whole country was unified in support of the treaty. But they rejected the Republicans' implication that that meant the war had unified the country under Madison's leadership—as well as the claim that the war had been worth the toll it had taken. The country edition of the *Federal Republican*—edited by Baltimore Federalist Alexander Hanson, who, after being assaulted by Republicans, brazenly moved his publication to Georgetown (geographically *closer* to the administration he so abhorred)—conceded that Federalists were relieved at the news of peace. That was to be expected, the *Federal Republican* explained, since they had wanted peace all along. The treaty only proved the president's incompetence and the national humiliation that had resulted, since the nation saw cause "to rejoice here, with such men at the head of affairs, that we did not lose half the U[nited] States—that the whole country was not lost." Even Madison had agreed that "we were contending for 'national existence.'" What its supporters had promised would be a glorious war was now being celebrated as a victory because it was not the complete and total disaster it could have been. That did not vindicate the Republicans' assurances that confidence in Madison was well placed; rather, it proved that critics' fears of national decline, and perhaps even a return to a subordination to Britain, had been justified all along.[77]

The *Federal Republican for the Country*, in its piece titled "Our Truth-Telling President," could not resist getting in another dig at Madison, claiming that the negotiations at Ghent demonstrated the administration's commitment to partisan and sectional division. On Madison's orders, it alleged, "our commissioners at Ghent had formally complained of the practice of carrying off slaves and selling them." When the Senate formally requested evidence to back up the charge, the administration failed to produce any. The move, the article alleged, was a stunt "[f]or the purpose of raising a clamor in the slave holding states," revealing the fixation of the president (and, more generally, the South) with slavery—a fixation that continued to divide the country, even as it neared a peace that the president's own supporters claimed justified universal support for the war.[78]

That prediction would prove prescient, but as reports poured in of Jackson's victory, Federalists found the basis for their criticism of the war crumbling. Federalists had spent years arguing that the war was so misguided and Madison's leadership so inept that refusing to fight amounted to a statement of independence from the president's calamitous national folly. Yet Jackson and his men had fought—and won. One could argue that the United States was lucky to eke out a treaty with Britain that amounted to a draw. But how to make sense of Jackson's victory? Federalists could not suddenly join in the celebration of Jackson's triumph and pretend they had supported the war all along. Nor could they maintain their old line that refusing to fight Madison's misguided war was the truest mark of patriotism.

Jackson's victory seemed too good to be true. So skeptical were Federalists of Jackson's triumph that newspapers published reports questioning the veracity of the news from New Orleans alongside statements of approval for the Hartford Convention that December. In the same issue that reported "[t]he accounts which have been received from New Orleans, since our last, are of a very vague and suspicious character," the *Boston Spectator* noted that a Massachusetts committee had published a report, "in part, expressing the highest satisfaction in the proceedings of the New England Convention" in Hartford, "and their readiness to adopt the measures recommended by them."[79]

The gathering of Federalists in Hartford produced a document that was meant to strike at what its authors considered a flagrant and potentially irreversible expansion of Republican-controlled presidential power. Hartford Federalists called for legislation at the state level "to protect the citizens of said States from the operation and effects of all acts which have been or may be passed by the Congress of the United States, which shall contain provisions, subjecting the militia or other citizens to forcible drafts, conscriptions, or impressments, not authorized by the Constitution of the United States"—a direct rebuke of Republicans' repeated insistence that the militia must fight in Madison's ill-conceived and ineptly prosecuted war. They called for state autonomy to defend their own borders, independent of the chief executive. They wanted no naturalized foreigners in Congress, or in any office of public trust, including the presidency. They called for an end to the three-fifths clause, considered to be the source of the disproportionate power the South wielded over the government and the key to the rise of the Virginia dynasty. And if the message were not clear enough, they specified that they wanted the Constitution amended to prevent any further multiterm presidents, as well as consecutive presidents from the same state.[80] But the story of Jackson's triumph was true. And the Hartford Convention fueled more accusations that Federalists were treasonous. The same issue that carried news of the convention charged its readers to "discover in it, any thing but *the vile spirit of disunion*." The charge was not true, but that characterization by Republicans stuck. During the nullification crisis years later, South Carolinians who argued that each state could determine for itself whether a federal law was Constitutional drew condemnation from critics, who compared them to delegates to the Hartford Convention.[81]

Pushed to find a way to escape the accusation that they were traitors to the war effort, Federalists amped up their praise for Jackson and their condemnation of Madison. Reversing themselves on the subject of service in the war, Federalists joined Republicans in praise for Jackson and his men but used Jackson's victory at New Orleans to sharpen their assault on Madison's presidential incompetence. It was not Madison who had pulled victory from certain defeat but men like Jackson, who answered the call to service from a president whose entire administration fumbled every opportunity that presented itself. "All the accounts agree, that the inhabitants of Orleans, and the troops called to their aid, have acted most heroically, thinking no privation or danger suffered in defence of the city, too great," Hanson's *Federal Republican* cheered in January 1815. "Upon the skill and bravery of Gen. Jackson every reliance is placed, and our little army has already given proofs of subordination, courage and devotedness which has not been surpassed at any place or period during the war." Then the essay took aim at Madison. "What Jackson has already done, is proof of what more he would have done, if the government had turned its attention to the defence of the city only one month earlier." The *Federal Republican* conjured the very same picture of heroic, masculine, civilized Americans fighting valiantly for their freedom that Republicans had made their refrain since before the war's outbreak. But the *Federal Republican*'s primary target was not British subjects, Indian savages, or black slaves; it was the president himself. "If the American people were not the most tame, amiable good natured race of men that ever lived," the essay continued, "the President would have been hissed out of office, if not pelted with stones, the first day Congress assembled, after the flight and conflagration." Instead, Jackson and his men had saved the day.[82]

The contrast between President Madison, who was tasked with leading the American people, and the people who responded to the president's call to war, explained both Federalists' long-sung refrain that the war had been a fool's errand from the beginning and the war's unexpected conclusion at Ghent, followed by Jackson's spectacular victory at New Orleans. Against the valor demonstrated by the "tame, amiable good natured race of men" who fought on the battlefield, the *Federal Republican* compared Madison and found the president wanting. It was unclear whether Madison's deficiencies were due to "treachery, weakness, stupidity, or what it may," but what was clear was that the president simply did not live up to the character of the people he was tasked with leading, and "the effect is precisely the same upon the nation." Questioning Madison's manhood, his bravery, and his competence in one fell swoop, Hanson's *Federal Republican* compared Madison to a child: "[T]here is hardly a clerk in one of the departments, or a little boy in the Lancastrian Academy, who would not have conducted this war infinitely better than James Madison."[83]

This characterization pivoted decisively away from the line that critics had maintained throughout the war: that Americans had no obligation to serve a war that was so horribly conceived and so thoroughly mismanaged by the president and his administration. Instead, it embraced Republicans' depiction of an American people who demonstrated their masculine courage, their civilized nature, their incomparable will to be manly and independent by answering the president's call to war. The image the *Federal Republican* created was one that amplified the heroism of Jackson and his men by doubling down on Federalists' longstanding claim that the folly of the war originated with Madison's presidential incompetence. Madison and his administration had not saved the nation from assured defeat, the *Federal Republican* blared; courageous patriots like Jackson and his men had. These men had done exactly what Republicans had insisted that all noble patriots do: they had freely answered the president's call to arms.

In the wake of Jackson's victory at New Orleans, other Federalist commentaries throughout the country made this same point. The treaty at Ghent was nothing but an "armistice" that utterly abandoned the administration's rallying cry of *"free trade and sailors rights,"* a *Northern Whig* account complained. "The idiocy of our rulers has long been proverbial among the European nations, but the bravery and courage of our citizens has never been questioned."[84] The "providential" nature that Republicans attributed to the victory was also a lie, a piece in the April 1815 *Columbian Centinel* claimed. Not only had previous accounts "exaggerated" the number of men under Jackson's command, it was also trying to claim undeserved credit for protecting a city "which they knew many months previous would be attacked by at least ten thousand men."[85]

The piece echoed a point made in the *New-York Evening Post* the previous February. "On the subject of this gallant, this extraordinary defence, it is due to truth and justice to observe that on no pretence whatever, are the administration entitled to the least share of the honor attending this very brilliant affair, or to partake in the smallest of the glory acquired," the article stated. "After being three years at war with a powerful enemy, who had the means of transporting his forces to any part of our sea coast, the administration has been so utterly neglectful of this important place, the depot of immense property belonging to the trading part of the community, that it was not until his forces were actually on the point of landing, that any measure of defence were taken." Madison's administration did not even supply Jackson's men with "arms for their use, nay, not even flints for guns, nor cloathing to protect them from the cold." So derelict in its duty, so unworthy of the patriotic spirit of Americans was its negligence toward Jackson and his men, the piece concluded, that had Jackson and his men lost, "Mr. Madison would have been impeached by his own party."[86] Long disputing Republicans' contention that it was a true American's patriotic duty to fight by claiming the war was folly, Federalists now contended that the willingness of Jackson and his men to fight and win at New Orleans was all the more patriotic *because* President Madison's administration was utterly incompetent.

In Massachusetts both houses of the legislature issued formal praise for Jackson's victory. The senate thanked Jackson and his men "for his successful defence of N. Orleans," noting that "this Senate is deeply impressed with a sense of the bravery and skill, which distinguished the Officers, Soldiers and Seamen of the U[nited] States . . . and the valiant and successful defence of New-Orleans by Major General JACKSON and his brave associates, have entitled them to the high distinction of brave and honorable defenders of their country." From there, the senate's statement pivoted to address "the injustice and wantonness of this war, in its original offensive character, on the part of the United States" and stated unequivocally that its views on the war remained "unchanged." In particular, the senate singled out "the gross improvidence of the administration in conducting it," echoing the sentiment "that the Treaty of Peace between the two Countries does not secure any one of the objects for which the war was originally declared." Nonetheless, the senate concluded that it was "not disposed, from these considerations, to withhold under such circumstances due tribute to the intrepid defenders of the soil."[87]

Like the *Federal Republican*, the Massachusetts senate praised Jackson as a way to get in a final, sharp dig at Madison, heightening the praiseworthiness of Jackson's feat by laying blame for the war directly at the president's feet. Stressing that the war had been folly from the beginning, prosecuted as a foolish "offensive" war by an irresponsible administration, from Madison on down, the Massachusetts senate could then celebrate that, despite that, Jackson and his men had nonetheless agreed to serve when called, and their valor on the battlefield spoke for itself. From this perspective the obligations of citizens to the president and his administration transcended the incumbent's competence—or in this case, the lack thereof. By highlighting the bravery of Jackson and his men, the senate of Massachusetts could actually use the obligation to serve when the president called to emphasize, yet again, the foolishness of the war.[88]

The house echoed the senate's approach, damning Madison and his administration with resounding praise for Jackson and his men. "Although it has pleased the Almighty Sovereign of Nations, to put an end to the calamitous war in which, through the improvidence of the Administration, our treasures have been expended; our credit exhausted; and thousands of our lives have been destroyed; without the attainment of any of the objects for which it was declared; yet we cannot but duly appreciate the merit of those brave Officers and Men, both in our Ships and Armies, who, by the valorous exertion of their courage and skill in defence of their country, have elevated our National Character, and honoured the American Name." In the very link between presidential leadership and this "national character," Federalists believed they had found an effective means of highlighting Madison's utterly lacking presidential leadership.[89]

Maintaining that the war was foolish and reckless from the start, Federalists nonetheless echoed Republicans' insistence on an essential relationship between the president and the American people in a time of war. The American people demonstrated who they truly were—courageous, moral, and free, in stark contrast to the supine British subjects, uncivilized Indian savages, and abject slaves they fought—by voluntarily answering the president's call to war. In agreeing with the Republicans' point about the people's obligation to the president, Federalists sought to stress its corollary: that the president in a time of war was never more obligated to coordinate and support the military effectively, to fund the war effort fully, to cultivate the people's "ardor" for war, and to thus ensure victory.

In the Federalists' version, the nation had teetered on the brink of ruin, pretty much from the war's outset, because of Madison's presidential deficiencies. What ultimately saved the country was a citizenry, exemplified by Jackson and his men, who understood their obligations in spite of the president's many glaring shortcomings. Federalists now insisted that Jackson's triumph at New Orleans showed how crucial the people's obligation to answer the president's call to war truly was, especially "at a time when the General Government, disregarding the constitutional provision requiring them to 'protect each State from invasion,' had neglected the erection of works of defence; to supply the munitions of war, and to furnish the regular troops necessary for its protection," among many other oversights.[90] These citizens understood that their loyalty was to the nation and to the office charged with representing the nation's interests, not to Madison personally. Because Madison was the president, they acted when called—and saved the nation from ruin. In so doing, the people had proven their character by fulfilling their obligations to a president who fell far short of his office's demand. Madison, meanwhile, had proven himself unable to fulfill his obligation "as the father of a people, the great chief of a great nation."[91] But the people had shown up anyway.

This shift brought Federalist critics of the war in lockstep with Republicans' president-centered national narrative. As critics and supporters of the war bickered over whether or not Madison had lived up to his obligations as president, they agreed that the war had crystallized the relationship between the president and the people, defining their obligations to one another, and ultimately distinguishing the American people from un-American enemies. By 1815 whites across partisan lines agreed that the president was expected to lead the charge of independent, patriotic Americans against their nation's existential threats, to sound the call to arms that all true Americans understood was the measure of their commitment to preserving their liberty. Through leadership in war, whoever occupied the presidency was expected to bring the American people's love of liberty to a razor-sharp point, to inspire the American people to demonstrate that they were indeed an exceptional "race of men" among the people of the earth by acting decisively—and violently—against anyone who sought to pull them down to the reprehensible ranks of the savages, subjects, and slaves in their midst.[92]

8

A Violent Man for a Violent Nation

"THE DISTINGUISHED CHARACTER of *Andrew Jackson,* could not fail to attract the attention of his countrymen, in deciding on the pretensions of those who are held up as candidates to fill the office of *President* for the ensuing term of four years," a committee comprised of pro-Jackson Republicans in Hunterdon County, New Jersey, declared in a pamphlet published in 1824. Praising Jackson's "probity, honor and disinterestedness, in every private relation to society, as *citizen*: His liberal education, . . . his devoted attachment to the *rights of man,* and the liberties of his fellow citizens," Jackson's supporters in Hunterdon County were convinced that only "sectional or party prejudices" or "deception" could sway Jackson's "countrymen" to side with Jackson's rival for the presidency, John Quincy Adams. That kind of pro-Adams sentiment had provoked the Jacksonians of Hunterdon to form the committee and publicize their support in the first place. An Adams supporter, writing under the pen name The True American, had condemned Jackson's supporters in a local newspaper, as "little other than a band of conspirators or dupes, leagued together for the purpose of over-turning the republican ascendancy and character of New-Jersey," and declared John Quincy Adams to be the true Republican candidate. The Republicans of Hunterdon County called a meeting to hash it out. According to the pamphlet, the meeting sided overwhelmingly in Jackson's favor. The Jacksonians formed a committee to produce an address to the county's citizens that would set the record straight, debunking the false claims made about Jackson, "and also, to vindicate his claims to that preference which, in their minds, placed him far above all his competitors."[1]

This pamphlet is just one of the many thousands of published commentaries on the presidency generated by Americans during the turbulent decades immediately following the War of 1812. The war's end had seen even Federalists echoing the Republicans' essential talking point that taking up arms when the president called was the ultimate indicator of one's patriotism. Instead of regaining their lost political power, the Federalists continued to backslide into obscurity. The hope that an "era of good feelings" was on the horizon proved fleeting, however. The government under Madison and his successors, James Monroe and John Quincy Adams, imposed a series of tariffs on imports that enraged Southerners, especially in South Carolina. An economic depression—a "panic"—in 1819 sowed a profound sense of distrust of banks among poor laborers and yeomen farmers. Black commentators on Madison's prosecution of the War of 1812 demonstrated the capacity of nonwhites to be included fully as Americans, while news of violent slave revolts—real or imagined—circulated through the country, stoking backlash by whites from the North to the South. The Missouri Crisis further strained the relationship between Northerners, who increasingly condemned slavery as immoral, and Southern states, who stridently defended it as an essential right and held that any limits on it amounted to a violation of whites' "liberty." Political bodies mirrored this strain. In the South a white man's honor and reputation were inextricably connected to his ability to domineer over others. Any slight, real or perceived, had to be met with aggressive and even violent retribution. Southern congressmen brought this sensibility with them to Washington, and for decades after Northerners walked on eggshells around their Southern colleagues, fearful that any insult, any criticism of or perceived threat to slavery, could provoke brawls, duels, or even the beginning of an all-out civil war. The country seemed more divided than ever, the prospect of a single, harmonious American nation more fantastical than at any time in its history under the Constitution. The end of the war had not brought peace. In fact, the country seemed consumed with violence.[2]

Beginning in the 1820s, the Republican Party of Jefferson began to fracture, as some embraced Andrew Jackson, the hero of New Orleans, as their champion. Jackson's reputation as a frontier warrior and war hero, forged in multiple wars waged against Indians and, most famously, the Battle of New Orleans, was well known. The pamphlet published by the Jacksonians of Hunterdon County in 1824, the first of Jackson's campaigns for the presidency, reflects the nascent stage of the movement that would form the Jacksonian Democratic Party. In Hunterdon County in 1824, supporters of Jackson and Adams both called themselves Republicans. Yet already they were bitterly divided over Jackson, and their fundamental point of disagreement reflected a disagreement over the state of the country as a whole.

Jackson's critics had lots of reasons for hating him, but the one that consistently topped their list was Jackson's violence. They called him a murderer, a slave-trader, a renegade who abused his military authority without regard to the directives of his superiors, while demanding total obedience to his will. At times, the criticisms referenced the political acrimony that defined the political landscape of the day. A hothead like Jackson was a terrible choice for president, they claimed; to maintain the fragile union, the nation needed a leader with a much more level head. Those who endorsed Jackson, however, saw Jackson's violence as his most admirable trait. The Jacksonians of Hunterdon illustrated this by highlighting Jackson's "great and splendid *services* in the late War, when, at the call of his country, he saved the defenceless citizens, and even entire states, from savage tomahawks and British bayonets, exalting by a train of glorious victories the character of citizen-soldiers over European mercenaries, and shedding immortal lustre upon the American name, in every quarter of the world."[3]

The decades following the War of 1812 witnessed scenes of violence across the country, in the halls of government and in the streets. Jackson's rise as a presidential candidate, and then an incumbent, provoked a bitter debate over whether the violence he exemplified posed a threat to national unity or was the key to strengthening it. This exchange between Jackson's critics and his supporters reflected political developments after the war and further reinforced a belief about the relationship between the president and the people that decades of bitter public debate over previous presidential administrations had forged. It was this belief that the president was "the man of the people," the embodiment of the American people's essential dissenting spirit, that Jacksonians would brilliantly exploit in the 1820s and 1830s. For the Jacksonians of Hunterdon County, New Jersey, and for Jackson's supporters throughout the country in the 1820s and 1830s, Jackson was the perfect representative for the American people emerging from the War of 1812: a nation of dissenters who had embraced their capacity for violence in the name of asserting their liberties, who understood that those liberties were reserved for whites alone, and who now invoked the nation's Revolutionary legacy to expand westward through conquest and domination, promising swift retribution against any government attempt to deny white Americans the "rights" that distinguished them from their enemies.

JACKSONIANS' FAMILIAR MESSAGE

For all the credit that Andrew Jackson often receives for democratizing the American presidency, Jacksonians' essential message was one that Republicans and Federalists had each used for years. Jackson and his supporters argued that the national government under the current administration failed to reflect the character of the American people, and under its present leadership, even acted in ways that undermined the rights that made them Americans, thus relegating them to a position dangerously close to those who were not Americans but who sought undeserved inclusion. The government needed to be brought back under the control of "the people," starting with the presidency.

Though this message was decades old, it resonated in part due to specific measures undertaken by the Madison, Monroe, and Adams administrations, a financial collapse, and bitter division over slavery in Congress and in the streets of cities across the country in the 1820s and 1830s. After the War of 1812, the federal government prioritized a series of policies designed to improve commerce and interstate transportation. With the war at an end, calls to bear arms were no longer the means by which the government would bind the country together. Instead, "internal improvement" (public works projects, such as roads and canals) would ensure that mail, commercial goods, and people could move more effectively across the sprawling country. To this, Congress added a series of tariffs, beginning in 1816, on a variety of goods, such as wool and cotton, meant to shield American businesses from foreign competition. The Industrial Revolution came later to the United States than it did to Britain, and the tariffs were meant as a protective measure, ensuring that those American businesses thrived.[4]

Both policy measures proved controversial, provoking division that would pave the way for a split in the Republican Party. Internal improvement projects became the focus of wrangling among members of Congress, as politicians sought choice projects based on how favorable they would be to their constituents. Years of land speculation was catching up to the United States by the end of the 1810s, just as European markets began to recover from Napoleon's rampage through the continent and international demand for American food crops and cotton plummeted. As the Second Bank of the United States scaled back credit, state banks followed suit. The Panic of 1819, as it was called, was the first of several "panics" throughout the century that would be the defining feature of the nation's nascent "boom and bust" industrial economy. And as with future panics, this one fell hardest on the poor. There was little political fallout from the panic as far as the sitting president, James Monroe, was concerned, but the same could not be said for the Second Bank of the United States. The Panic of 1819 fueled suspicions that the Bank, and banks generally, could not be trusted. On the heels of the Panic, the US Congress debated

Missouri's admission as the twenty-third state in the Union, and a bitter, politically and sectionally divisive fight ensued over the fate of slavery as the nation expanded westward. Just as the Panic of 1819 sowed distrust in the nation's financial institutions, political fights over internal improvement projects, the passage of a tariff in 1816 and another, more notorious tariff in 1828, and the issue of slavery sowed distrust in the national government. Jackson and his allies would exploit these suspicions through the application of a familiar political message.[5]

At the base of Jacksonians' political messaging was white supremacy and violence. Neither of these were new in American presidential politics. But Jackson found himself the beneficiary of Republicans' pro-war propaganda, which had made explicit how foundational whiteness, manhood, and violence were to American nationhood and how crucial it was that the president uphold that foundation at all costs. By the early 1820s states were beginning to transition away from property requirements for voting, acceding to the decades-long belief among many Americans that the right to vote was an inalienable one. As technically disfranchised voters, especially white men, cast ballots in local and state elections, states that had existed since the Revolution gradually eased restrictions for white men, while most new states established before 1821 drafted their initial state constitutions based on universal white male suffrage. Other states that had allowed black men to vote if they held enough property (such as Pennsylvania) rewrote their constitutions to strip black people of the franchise. The right to vote, long reserved for the propertied elite, was becoming a rite of passage into a condition of full maturity that was reserved only for white men. This understanding of suffrage contrasted sharply with a caucus system, a key feature of the formal party system that had developed over the previous decades. The image of wealthy party insiders meeting in closed rooms to decide which candidates to support proved an effective tool for popular political mobilization—a perfect illustration of a political establishment bent on keeping political power out of the hands of ordinary (white) Americans.[6]

Even more explicitly than in the past, this political system was meant to relegate women and black people to a position of permanent subordination. So intertwined were political participation and manliness that publications later in the nineteenth century wrote of a young man's "virgin vote"—comparing the first vote he cast with his first sexual encounter. By this logic women were permanent children, and the prejudices of the day invariably emphasized their dependence on men: victims of "savage" Indian butchery and licentious black assault; paragons of virtue who lacked the mettle for the disagreeable business of politics; mistresses of home and rearers of children, made by God for the domestic sphere.[7]

So too were black people deemed permanently beneath whites, not simply as slaves in the South but as an underclass in Northern "free" states, as well. A series of broadsides, published in Boston in the 1820s, exemplify the prejudices that Northern whites harbored toward blacks who hoped to see the abolition of slavery and who sought to engage in political activity (figure 8.1). Known as the "Bobalition" broadsides, these single printed sheets were written by Northern whites in a pantomimed black language similar to that of the Quashee poem published in 1802. The Bobalition broadsides, which historian David Waldstreicher has rightly dubbed "literary blackface," were printed around the time that white performer Thomas Dartmouth Rice invented the character Jim Crow, who would be synonymous with both blackface minstrelsy and the generations-long system of segregation that would define the century following the Civil War. Both were meant to mock blacks' speech, their political understanding, and ultimately their capacity to act as full citizens—a visual and literary rebuttal to the claim that black people could ever be Americans.[8]

Whites thought such rebuttal necessary because black people had shown in both word and deed that they deserved full inclusion in an American nation that denied them liberty. The most famous of these early nineteenth-century black commentators is David Walker, a Bostonian who in 1829 published the radical abolitionist *Appeal to the Coloured Citizens of the World*. Strident and uncompromising, Walker compared white Americans' justification for fighting for liberty against Britain in the American Revolution with the oppression that blacks faced from whites: in effect claiming that black dissent against white authority was even more justified than white Americans' fight for national independence had been. "See your Declaration Americans!!! Do you understand your own language?" Walker asked white readers, quoting from the immortal statement of equality and unalienable rights in the Declaration of Independence. "Now, Americans! I ask you candidly, was your sufferings under Great Britain, one hundredth part as cruel and tyrannical as you have rendered ours under you?" Walker's *Appeal* provoked backlash from white supremacists and inspired radical abolitionists like William Lloyd Garrison, who would found the *Liberator* two years later. Yet even before David Walker's *Appeal*, black Americans had participated in the War of 1812—as combatants, as commentators, and as dissenters who laid claim to the right to participate in the public debate over "Mr. Madison's War," the president's prosecution of it, and what it portended for the nation's future. [9]

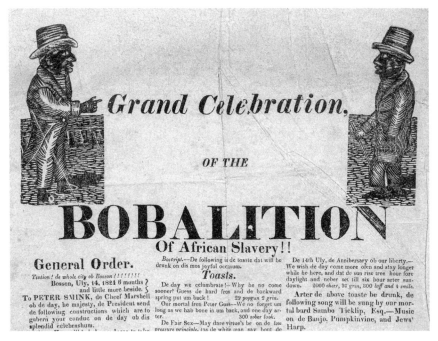

Figure 8.1: "Grand Celebration of the Bobalition of African Slavery" (1824). Detail. Courtesy of the American Antiquarian Society.

Peter Malachi Eagans, a parishioner of the African Methodist Episcopal Church, addressed the "crowded audience" before him, who had convened at the church on January 1, 1813, to hear George Lawrence's sermon, commemorating the fifth anniversary of the abolition of the transatlantic slave trade. The US Constitution stipulated that Congress could not end the slave trade until 1808. That year was indeed the end of the slave trade—but not of slavery itself. Like most black commentators during the war, and like David Walker in the years after, Eagans and Lawrence challenged the fundamental premise of the war by pointing out the hypocrisy of stating that America sought independence and freedom for its people while white Americans held black Americans in bondage. Eagans began by addressing his audience as "Citizens" and characterizing the cause of abolition as an act of dissent against tyranny—and a service to the country. Eagans declared that it was "the indispensable duty of every member of society . . . to use our utmost endeavours to detect, and having detected, strenuously to oppose every traitorous plot which [the] enemies [of abolition] may devise for its destruction." Lawrence built from Eagans's provocative introduction. "My brethren, the land in which we live gives us the opportunity rapidly to advance the prosperity of liberty. This government founded on the principles of liberty and equality, and declaring them to be the free gift of God, if not ignorant of their declaration, must enforce it; I am confident she wills it, and strong forbodings [*sic*] of it is discernable." Lawrence assured his audience that "[t]he northern sections of the union is fast conceding, and the southern must comply, although so biased by interest, that they have become callous to the voice of reason and justice." But black people, "abounding in good works, and causing our examples to shine forth as the sun at noon day," will "melt their callous hearts, and render sinewless the arm of sore oppression."[10] Eagans and Lawrence were among the many black people, free and enslaved, who challenged the white supremacist foundations of American nationalism. Some did so by fighting for Britain, who benefited from white Americans' reluctance to enlist black people for the war effort due to their own prejudicial views.[11]

Other black people fought for the United States, however, in the hopes that serving in the war would demonstrate that they deserved to be considered full-fledged American citizens alongside the whites who answered the president's call. Andrew Jackson, of all people, actually made this promise to the blacks who fought at New Orleans: "TO THE MEN OF COLOR," the address began, "*Soldiers.*—From the Shores of Mobile I collected you to arms—I invited you to share in the perils and to divide the glory of your white countrymen. I expected much from you, for I was not uninformed of those qualities which must render you so formidable to an invading foe . . . but you surpass my hopes; I have found in you, united to those qualities, that noble enthusiasm which impels to great deeds." Such words coming from a white supremacist and slave-owner are incredible. "The President of the United States shall be informed of your conduct on the present occasion," the address went on, "and the voice of the representatives of the American nation shall applaud your valor, as your general now praises your ardor."[12]

Jackson dangled in front of the black troops at New Orleans the same promise of citizenship through military service that some blacks had pursued in the Revolution by fighting for the nation's independence. Whites would make this same promise in future wars, either overtly or implicitly, and blacks would rise to take them up on it. Even after blacks in the Civil War emancipated themselves by fleeing captivity, arriving in Union camps, and forcing Union leaders—and ultimately President Lincoln—to take up the eradication of slavery as America's cause, white supremacy persisted. Following the end of slavery, blacks who endured the injustice of lynch mobs and Jim Crow legislation would seek full membership in the American nation by fighting its wars. Every time they rose, every time they sacrificed, every time they proved their courage in battle, every time they proved that they deserved to be full-fledged members of the American nation, they met more injustice: segregated units; blocked access to government programs for veterans and their families; confinement to the most arduous and low-paying jobs; redlining that banished them to the slums and ghettos of America's growing metropolises and kept them there; diminished or nonexistent educational opportunities that all but ensured their children would remain in poverty while white children benefited from better-resourced schools; the persistence of cruel and inaccurate prejudices about black laziness and criminality, fueled by both *de facto* and *de jure* segregation practices, and repeated by whites (and even many blacks) in didactic lectures that blamed deficiencies in black "culture" for the injustice. Still more lynch mobs.[13]

The sincerity of the nation's promise to blacks who fought in war can be gleaned from Jackson's decision to delegate the task of reading the address to one of his subordinates. The future seventh president of the United States could not be bothered, or was simply unwilling, to speak the words of praise and promise to black men himself. The decision gave his praise a hollowness that would prove prescient.[14]

Lemuel Haynes took a different approach. Like most black people who spoke out during the war, Haynes opposed it, pointing to the incongruity of America's claim that it fought for freedom while white Americans held black Americans as slaves. Haynes was a New Englander, born in Connecticut, who served in the American Revolution. Like Lawrence, he was a preacher, and in 1813 he gave a sermon to the Washington Benevolent Society celebrating the birthday of George Washington, using the occasion to criticize the war by laying claim to the presidential office.[15]

Haynes focused on the concept of "dissimulation," which he used synonymously with hypocrisy, and he wondered whether, given "the present convulsion of our public affairs," "we can find much of that love that is without dissimulation." "Never was there a day that men made higher pretences, and it may be there was never less to be found."[16] Like whites across political lines, Haynes asserted the right to dissent as a fundamental tenet of American citizenship. "The upright honest man will hold it as his unalienable right to examine into the measures of government," Haynes told his audience, "and bring them to the unerring standard of reason and religion, and will esteem that man unworthy the name of a republican, or

even a [C]hristian, the moment he relinquishes the sentiment." At a time
of war, such a right became even more crucial. "To suppose that we are
to obey civil magistrates, at the expence of the law of God, and a good
conscience, confronts every dictate of reason and religion. . . . When we
are called upon by civil authority to engage in war, 'tis the duty of men, if
they would not be guilty of blood, to examine the matter for themselves,
whether there be just cause for war." For Haynes, dissent was a right as
well as an obligation whose link to citizenship could not be overemphasized. "It falls within the sphere of every citizen of the United States, to
examine into the causes of the present war with Great Britain," he continued. "[I]t is a subject of strict morality."[17]

Like the leading white critics of the war, Haynes traced "the reasons for
the present war against Great Britain" to Madison. These "reasons," all
of which Haynes found wanting, "are contained in the president's manifesto, and the declaration of a committee on foreign relations, which are
before the public." In particular, Haynes highlighted the impressment of
white Americans by the British. To call impressment "slavery" and to cite
this practice as a key justification of the war, all the while keeping black
people as slaves, was the height of dissimulation. Haynes held up the president as emblematic of the American nation's profound racial hypocrisy.
"'Our president, (says one) can talk feelingly on the subject of impressment of our seamen. I am glad to have him feel for them. Yet in his own
state, Virginia, there were, in the year 1800, no less than three hundred
forty-three thousand, seven hundred ninety-six human beings holden in
bondage for life!'"[18]

If the current president's actions betrayed the dissimulation that plagued
the American nation, Haynes claimed, the first president showed that such
dissimulation did not have to be the nation's destiny. Quoting at length
from Washington's Farewell Address, Haynes credited Washington— a
Virginia slave-owner like Madison—with modeling the essential "virtue"
that all elected leaders, and all citizens, should display: "The man that
wishes well to the common wealth will love his God—will love religion,
and seek such men to guide public affairs, that have benevolence and virtue," Haynes explained. "The great inquiry will not be, who will fall in
with my party, and appoint me to office, as a reward for my services to
him; but who will promote the general good, and seek the peace and prosperity of the nation? Who has talents, knowledge and virtue, and has love
without dissimulation?"[19]

Haynes made it clear that the point was not to "idolize" Washington,
"but, by bringing his virtues into view, it may excite gratitude to God for

raising up such an instrument, and qualifying him for great usefulness to our country. That love without dissimulation directed him in the senate and in the field, we have reason to believe." In his Farewell Address, Washington had "forewarned us against foreign influence, which he saw taking place." The first president even "was an enemy to slave-holding," Haynes added, "and gave his dying testimony against, it by emancipating, and providing for those under his care." For Haynes, criticism of the current president and his war was a reassertion of—and a bid to bring the government back in line with—the core national virtues that America's citizens had adopted from their first president. Dissent from the war, Haynes argued, was a patriotic act meant to reinforce the fundamental civic values that united all American citizens and connected them to the president, thereby sustaining and strengthening the very bonds that gave the American nation meaning.[20]

Ostensibly aligning itself with the basic nationalistic premise that whites across partisan lines had come to agree upon, Haynes's address challenged that premise by radically altering who, exactly, counted as an American. Through his use of "we" and "our," Haynes, like Eagans and Lawrence, included blacks—people like himself—in the body of citizens who defined their national ideals, and suggested that the government, from the president on down, should answer to blacks as well as whites.

In laying claim to the presidency for blacks, Haynes invoked the presidency's centrality to the nation's political culture to hint at a future whose implications would be too radical for white Americans (and even most black Americans) to contemplate for generations to come. Blacks' full inclusion into the body of citizens who shared the same civic traits, and who looked to the president to exemplify and facilitate those traits in word and deed, threatened the very meaning that more than twenty years of partisan politics had given them. What did *independence* and all its ingredients—a claim to moral and civilizational superiority; the right to bear arms, own property, and extend one's dominion over inferior, "savage" people; manly firmness and masculine courage—even mean without white supremacy? What would prevent all forms of hierarchy—race, gender, class—from breaking down before the eyes of whites? What would ensure that systems of power in America remained the exclusive possession of white men?

Haynes stopped well short of fully fleshing out the future implied by his words. But for Americans during the War of 1812, and for those in the twenty-first century, Haynes's words offer a reminder that it was not inevitable that the ideals to which the United States lay claim would be defined along racial lines, nor was it impossible to redefine those ideals to bring them closer to their inclusive potential. Taking the inclusivity of the nation's ideals to its logical conclusion, Haynes critiqued Madison's presidential leadership, and in so doing, defined the contours of a national citizenry that included both black and white voices by whom the nation's democratically elected leaders—from the president on down—would be judged.

Black assertions of citizenship during and after the War of 1812 coincided with Southern opposition to the tariff, internal improvement measures, the Panic of 1819, and the contentious constitutional crisis that ensued once Congressman James Tallmadge brought a measure to the floor of Congress to include Missouri as the newest state in the Union. These seemingly disparate issues were all connected in that they all could be construed as examples of a distant and excessively powerful national government run by an entrenched political establishment attempting to strip true Americans—which most white Americans believed included only members of their race—of their political sovereignty or their financial security (or both). Southerners felt their liberty particularly threatened by the national government because its actions seemed to threaten the South's foundational financial, political, and cultural institution: slavery.

The question that drove the debate over Missouri's admission to the Union was whether Missouri would enter as a slave or a free state. Maintaining the balance between slave and free states (which had been reached, once Alabama entered the Union as the eleventh slave state in 1819) was crucial, as Southerners had already begun to fear that the tariff set a dangerous precedent for passing laws favorable to Northern states, with little to no regard for Southern interests. If Missouri was free, the scales would be tipped even further in favor of the North, potentially laying the groundwork for explicit limitations on slavery.[21]

The compromise, brokered by Kentuckian Henry Clay, left both Northerners and Southerners angry. Missouri would enter as a slave state. Maine, heretofore a part of Massachusetts, would enter as a free state to maintain the numerical balance, and—most controversially—a boundary would be fixed at Missouri's southern border, extended westward. Below that border, no free states could be established; above it, no slave states could enter. Northern opponents of slavery, like John Quincy Adams, then James Monroe's secretary of state, disliked the deal because he considered slavery to be antithetical to the Constitution's obligation to "establish justice." Slavery was "a wrongful and despotic power," Adams thought, and the Constitution empowered the Congress to limit its expanse. "What can be more needful for the establishment of justice than the interdiction of slavery where it does not exist?" John C. Calhoun disagreed. Slavery was "the best guarantee to equality among the whites," Calhoun told Adams. "It produced an unvarying level among them. It not only did not excite, but did not even admit of inequalities, by which one white man could domineer over another." To defend slavery Southerners would be willing to secede from the Union, even rejoining Britain. Southerners' willingness to leave the country—even "returning to the colonial state," as a shocked Adams put it—rather than concede any limit to slavery, testified to the fundamental nature of slavery, not only to Southern whites' economy, but to their very understanding of their freedom. It was "all perverted sentiment," Adams wrote in disgust. "The discussion of this Missouri question has betrayed the secret of their souls."[22]

Calhoun's candid admission made explicit the logic that informed Southerners' stance on every issue, even the seemingly unrelated issue of the tariff. Though the tariff was not solely responsible for the Panic of 1819, both lent themselves to a view that political and financial elites acted with total disregard for the rights or well-being of "ordinary" Americans. The racialized basis of this formulation often went unsaid, but as Calhoun explained to a bewildered Adams, slavery created a perceived sense of equality between the wealthiest Southern slave-holding aristocrat and the lowliest of white yeomen. No matter how little he owned, a poor white Southern man would never occupy the absolute bottom of society. He would always stand above both free and enslaved black people. The system gave wealthy aristocrats, poor whites, and Westerners who encroached upon indigenous American land common cause to defend slavery—even through violence—from any limits imposed on it by a distant federal government.

Though Calhoun's native state of South Carolina took the lead on the doctrine of nullification, positing that each state could declare a federal law null and void if it determined it was unconstitutional, its adherents frequently invoked "the South" as a region, arguing that its sister states would find common cause with them. The issue of "states' rights" was really foundational to protecting an interest that all Southern states had in common. That interest, as nullification advocate (and, beginning in 1832, governor of South Carolina) Robert Hayne put it, was "[t]he substantial right of property, in the plantations of the south."[23] Southerners' touchiness regarding slavery was well known in politics, even to Northerners. "[T]he slave question," Edward Cambridge Reed, a New York congressman, remarked, "is a subject upon which the Southern people are peculiarly sensitive perhaps more so than some of our Northern people are upon the Indian question."[24]

This sensitivity translated into scenes of violence, as suspicions of slave insurrections—whether genuine or simply in the minds of terrified whites—as well as evidence of black political participation provoked white mobs that tortured, maimed, and murdered at the slightest provocation. Mob violence rose in the 1830s, and scenes of mob violence were not confined to the South. One particularly reprehensible scene occurred in New York City in 1834, when white rioters attacked black-owned businesses and churches after black New Yorkers celebrated the seventh anniversary of the state's abolition of slavery. But racialized violence was especially common in the South, as Southern honor was predicated on domination through intimidation and violence. Professions that slavery was a benevolent institution, and that slaves were more or less content in slavery, ignored the lived reality of slavery's brutality and blacks' efforts to resist its dehumanizing objective. The invention of the cotton gin in the 1790s began an economic revolution that would make cotton "king" in the South. By the 1850s the Southern states were producing over one billion pounds of cotton yearly—75 percent of the world's total. Cotton production was the foundation of the Southern economy, and indeed the Northern economy as well, though Northerners did not like to admit it. Southern cotton fed Northern textile factories, linking the two regions in a market economy that belied the myth of a genteel Southern society far removed from the cold capitalism that Southern romantics equated with the North. Southerners employed a variety of torture tactics, from beating and whipping, to threats to sell slaves or their relatives further South, to wring every ounce of profit they could from black bodies. Even whites who did not own slaves expected total deference from black people, free or enslaved. Any slight, real or perceived, was grounds for swift retribution. Though most slaves strove simply to survive such horrific conditions, evidence of black resistance, in the United States and abroad, circulated widely throughout the South. The revolution that began in Saint Domingue in the early 1790s produced the independent black republic of Haiti in 1804, just a few years after Gabriel's Rebellion in Virginia. In 1822 whites suspected an insurrection plot by Denmark Vesey, resulting in the execution of Vesey and thirty-four other alleged coconspirators. Less than a decade later, Nat Turner led a violent slave revolt in Virginia, killing close to sixty white adults and children before the rebellion was foiled by the Virginia militia. Torturing and killing those involved, whites then turned on black slaves they suspected were involved, killing around 100 people in total.

Such evidence of slave resistance heightened whites' fears of blacks still further, fueling their belief that further coercive measures were necessary to maintain white mastery.[25]

The behavior of Southern representatives and senators mirrored this violent culture. Even from their white colleagues Southerners tolerated no direct challenge to the slave regime, considering any such transgression to be both a personal attack and a direct affront to their white constituents. Frequently armed, Southerners threatened virtually any Northerner who directly challenged slavery or condemned it as morally reprehensible. (The exception was John Quincy Adams, who after serving as president held a seat in Congress. Because of his advanced age—he was in his early sixties when he was elected to Congress in 1831—Southerners would not attack him, a fact he exploited with relish). But Southerners not only threatened Adams's younger colleagues, they lunged at them with blunt objects and knives; they assaulted them with their bare hands; they challenged them to duels. These verbal attacks and physical assaults accompanied Southern threats to secede from the Union at every hint of a measure or law that threatened to restrict slavery in any way. Unschooled in the language of this violent culture of honor, most Northern congressmen strained to avoid direct confrontation about slavery—compromising not only in matters of law but in their everyday interactions with their Southern colleagues—in effect, capitulating to Southerners' violent threats and actions in order to hold the fragile national union intact. In short, Congress was a perfect microcosm of a nation defined by a violent, repressive slave regime—one whose insatiable demands were pulling the nation apart.[26]

JACKSON AND HIS CRITICS

It was in this postwar political landscape that Andrew Jackson rose to prominence, ran for president in 1824, and ran again in 1828. Jackson was a polarizing figure, and no treatment of his life succeeded in maintaining neutrality, even those that claimed to be "impartial."[27] Those who opposed Jackson highlighted precisely his defiance of established authority and his propensity for violence that the sympathetic treatments of his life celebrated. As Jackson rose to prominence, critics argued that Jackson was a reckless leader, a brutal murderer, and a slave-trader. At a time when the sectional divide between North and South appeared to be widening, when violence and even bloodshed threatened to boil over into civil war, the last thing the nation needed, critics maintained, was a president who was an easily angered Southern slave-owner who disregarded any authority but his own.

Jackson's critics stressed that Jackson was at best a temperamental bully and at worst a murderer and slave-trader. Jackson's military service revealed his "martial propensities," and "[t]he egotism of his character," one wrote.[28] Jackson's actions toward Indians, his treatment of his own troops, and his wielding of authority anywhere he went, were evidence that he was the last man any sane person would want in the presidency. One often repeated story concerned Jackson's punishment, in 1814, of a half-dozen militiamen who left their posts for home after three months, thinking their term of service was over. Jackson, maintaining that their obligation was to serve for six months, had them arrested, court-martialed, and shot. The episode "furnish[es] a striking example of the cheapness in which General Jackson holds the rights and happiness, and lives of his countrymen," one pamphlet concluded. "Let every freeman, when he has candidly examined this transaction, and particularly the merciless part of General Jackson in it, ask himself whether it is desirable to have him made President of the United States, and thereby Commander in Chief of the Militia of the Union."[29]

Critics also found Jackson's treatment of Indians appalling. Commentators generally detailed the same encounters that Jackson's supporters did—Toho-peka, Talladega, Talluschatches, Emuckfau Enotichopco were mentioned, as were others—characterizing these encounters as atrocities. At Tallapoosie, Jackson engaged in wanton "slaughter" of Indian men, women, and children, one pamphleteer noted. "[T]hese wretched victims of [Jackson's] exterminating wrath . . . were immortal beings like himself—having interests at stake, as great and as precious as his own," one anti-Jackson election pamphlet wrote in 1828. "[M]oreover, they were Indians—and by a thousand considerations, having no less claims, surely on this account, to the forbearance and clemency of Americans."[30] This characterization highlighted the Indians' humanity to a greater degree than many others, even those that agreed that Jackson's "war" amounted to butchery. Other critics cast Indians as "an ignorant and superstitious race," already dying off due to the inevitable progress of more-civilized white Americans. Vastly outnumbered by Jackson's men, the Indians "had not the remotest chance of success." Jackson's massacre was not noble warfare but, quite literally, overkill. The Indians' helplessness in the face of the onslaught meant that the victory could only be a testament to Jackson's wanton cruelty. "The battles of Talledaga, Tallushatchee, Emuckfa, and Tohopeka, in which the white, was double the Indian, force, were slaughters as lamentable as inevitable," concluded another pamphlet, *The Political Mirror*, published in 1835. "The occasion called for little ability, but what it required the General possessed."[31]

This criticism took Jackson's military career as evidence of Jackson's mindless lust for violence, contrasting this with what the pamphlet described as Jackson's lack of interest in any civic obligations. "For the civil stations, whose honours he coveted, he proved incompetent," the pamphlet noted, referring to Jackson's stints as a state legislator in Tennessee, a judge, and then a member of Congress. "And after a short effort, confessing his incapacity, he renounced them." Other criticisms during the elections and Jackson's presidency drew similar conclusions. The point was not merely to depict Jackson as a serial quitter. The larger point was to use Jackson's military career to highlight his propensity for violence in every aspect of his life and career and to link that violence to Jackson's own self-interest and total disregard for the civic norms or general good that the president was tasked with upholding. Jackson was not a capable leader of free Americans. He was a tyrant, and nothing more.[32]

Jackson's propensity for violence extended beyond his military career. Jackson was a ruffian who had taken the life of Charles Dickinson in a duel that was "on a level with the worst species of assassinations," the *Character and Principles of General Andrew Jackson* informed readers. He was a slave-trader, who participated in the "odious . . . traffic" while initially denying any involvement. Astoundingly, the pamphlet claimed, Jackson claimed not to have been directly involved in the 1811 sale of an unspecified "number of negroes." Jackson initially admitted it, then changed his story, claiming "he was only a security on the transaction," an excuse that exposed him as either deceitful, incompetent, or both. "Every school-boy in the country should know, that such an instrument, both in law and equity, recognizes each of the parties as a principal," the pamphlet declared. "And yet we are told by Gen. Jackson, a judge of the Supreme Court of Tennessee, a member of the American Senate, and a candidate for the Presidency of the United States, that he was a mere security on these bonds, because his name stood last upon them, and for the idle reason that he happened to be richer than the parties who signed before him."[33] Jackson's participation in the reprehensible business of slave trafficking was another form of violence, one that exposed his roots in the slaveholding South. That Jackson tried to cover it up revealed his desire to mask his Southern interests in order to present himself as a champion of all Americans. But Jackson, opponents maintained, was not interested in advancing the cause of all Americans. He was only interested in advancing his own.

Jackson's own actions as president seemed to bear out the critics' case that his presidential leadership style was erratic, irrational, and vicious, and a threat to the fragile national union that Americans sought to preserve. On the surface Jackson might seem an ally for those who advocated nullification. Jackson was a Southerner who had been born in the Carolinas and a slave-owner whose record in Congress included votes to reduce the tariff on the goods that Southern plantation owners needed, such as wool and the clothes made from it, known as "negro cloths." Jackson's voting record was so well known that opponents used it against him in the election of 1828.[34]

Yet Jackson was no ally for nullifiers. Nullifiers invoked explosive terms, like "secession" and even "civil war." They claimed that the Southern states were simply too different from those of the North for anything like a cohesive "nation," consisting of people united by a single common interest, to exist. They argued that nullification was necessary to preserve intact the union of Southern and Northern states. Without it, Southern states would simply have to accept laws, such as the tariffs, that the federal government forced upon them—a condition that nullifiers, without a hint of irony, condemned as a state of perpetual subordination. In this way, nullifiers made an appeal that contained sectional and national components. "That the principle we contend for would, if generally recognized, promote harmony and tend to the perpetuation of the Union, is too obvious to be doubted," one proponent of nullification, William Harper, explained. "Instead of bare majorities passing sweeping laws to promote their own interests, heedless of their destructive effects on the interests of the minority, they would be under the necessity of devising measures to reconcile the interests and feelings of every section. But they would be rewarded for their toil, (if they estimate such reward) by the confidence and attachment of the whole country. Thus instead of a rope of sand, the Union would become a golden chain, which violence would not break, nor time corrode."[35]

Jackson would have none of it. "I consider, then, the power to annul a law of the United States, assumed by one State, *incompatible with the existence of the Union, contradicted expressly by the letter of the Constitution, unauthorized by its spirit, inconsistent with every principle on which It was founded, and destructive of the great object for which it was formed*," declared Jackson's December 1832 Proclamation against nullification, reflecting the legal arguments of his secretary of state, Edward Livingston, but signed by Jackson and carrying the full weight of his views. The doctrine of nullification was "absurd and dangerous." The American people were first and foremost a single nation, and the Constitution was a compact between them that superseded the states. As a testament to that, Jackson pointed to the office he currently occupied. "We are ONE PEOPLE in the choice of the President and Vice President." That same line of logic extended even to the legislative branch. For, Jackson argued, even though members of Congress were representatives of particular state interests, "their first and highest duty, as representatives of the United States, [is] to promote the general good."[36]

Jackson would be damned if any portion of the nation claimed a right to choose which federal laws to obey and which to ignore. Not on his watch. Nullification, he warned the nullifiers, was tantamount to "treason," and if they did not step back from the brink, his vengeance would be swift and decisive. "Having the fullest confidence in the justness of the legal and constitutional opinion of my duties which has been expressed, I rely with equal confidence on your undivided support in my determination to execute the laws—to preserve the Union by all constitutional means—to arrest, if possible, by moderate but firm measures, the necessity of a recourse to force," Jackson promised. "And, if it be the will of Heaven that the recurrence of its primeval curse on man for the shedding of a brother's blood should fall upon our land, that it be not called down by any offensive act on the part of the United States."[37]

Jackson's position caused a rift between him and his own vice president, John C. Calhoun, one of South Carolina's most ardent proponents of nullification and the man foremost responsible for defending and advancing nullification as a political doctrine. Jackson's proclamation warned against "disunion, by armed force," a reference to the threat of resistance issued by the convention that had been called by the nullifiers in South Carolina in response to the tariff of 1828. The convention had published its own statement on nullification that not only called the tariff repugnant to the Constitution but cribbed from the Declaration of Independence, casting Southerners' willingness to separate from the Union as a patriotic statement of dissent, in line with the nation's Revolutionary tradition. If the federal government denied the right of states to declare laws they considered unconstitutional to be "null, void, and no law," then "the people of this state . . . forthwith proceed to organize a separate government, and do all other acts and things which sovereign and independent States may of right do." Calhoun attempted to assure Jackson that it was the president, and not the people of South Carolina, who was pushing the country closer to a war. Not surprisingly, Jackson was not convinced.[38]

Jackson's other major battle as president was with the Second Bank of the United States. Originally, the Bank was the brainchild of Alexander Hamilton, as part of his ambitious financial plan during Washington's administration. Periodically, Congress needed to recertify the Bank's charter; in 1832 recertification was necessary. In the summer of 1832, just months before the nullification crisis reached its peak, Jackson vetoed Congress's bill reaffirming the Bank's charter. Not content merely to veto it, he then moved to defund the bank, bleeding it of its assets and depositing the money into state banks.[39]

Arguing that approximately a quarter of the stock was "held by foreigners," Jackson's veto message held that such a "monopoly" was antithetical to American democracy and could not be allowed to stand. By his positing that the president, Congress, and the judiciary were equally entitled to judge what was constitutionally permissible, Jackson's veto of the Bank effectively co-opted the power to interpret the Constitution on behalf of the sitting president, who then declared that the bank did not meet his standard. Crucially, Jackson claimed that the people were the basis for this broad presidential power, which paradoxically he was obligated to use to limit the power of the national government, safeguarding the liberties of hard-working Americans against government that had come to serve the interests of political and economic elites. "In the full enjoyment of the gifts of Heaven and the fruits of superior industry, economy, and virtue, every man is equally entitled to protection by law; but when the laws undertake to add to these natural and just advantages artificial distinctions, to grant titles, gratuities, and exclusive privileges, to make the rich richer and the potent more powerful, the humble members of society—the farmers, mechanics, and laborers—who have neither the time nor the means of securing like favors to themselves, have a right to complain of the injustice of their Government," Jackson concluded. "There are no necessary evils in government. Its evils exist only in its abuses. If it would confine itself to equal protection, and, as Heaven does its rains, shower its favors alike on the high and the low, the rich and the poor, it would be an unqualified blessing."[40]

Other presidential actions besides his approach to nullification and to the Bank further confirmed critics' fears. Rather than uphold the public good, Jackson installed his own cronies into choice political offices, including an informal "kitchen cabinet" of hand-picked advisors whose sole duty was to carry out tasks at Jackson's personal direction. He professed to act on behalf of the nation but really served Southern interests. To the nullifiers he talked tough about state compliance with federal law, but to the Cherokee petitioning him to uphold the law and prevent their displacement, he claimed his hands were tied and that the removal policy—resulting in the infamous "Trail of Tears"—was the result of relentless, violent white settlement, the culmination of the natural process of a superior civilization wiping out an inferior one. In short, Jackson's critics argued that the president was not the fearless defender of America's democratic ideals that he claimed to be. He cared nothing for the welfare of the nation; he and his party only cared about their own advancement. At a time when sectionalism was already pulling the nation apart, when violence and intimidation from the South fueled a toxic national landscape that threatened civil war, critics argued that Jackson's violence disqualified him from the presidency. Even during his two presidential terms, they linked his military actions to his viciousness, his selfishness, his utter disregard for the life or the liberty of anyone who stood in his way. Jackson, in short, was emblematic of exactly the kind of violence tearing the country apart.[41]

JACKSON AND HIS AMERICANS

Those who supported Jackson did so just as passionately as his detractors criticized; they celebrated his violence as his major qualification for the presidency. At a time when the nation's violence appeared to be focused inward—when Americans fought fellow Americans, dueling one another, assaulting one another, threatening one another—and civil war loomed, Jackson's supporters touted his martial skill as essential to bringing the nation back together again, revitalizing the independent, sovereign, civilized character, born in the Revolution, that distinguished Americans from their enemies. Through violence, they argued, a Jackson presidency could make America great again.

Jackson and his campaign had cast him as a champion of everyday Americans against an entrenched, power-hungry Washington elite. As president, Jackson maintained that stance, justifying his signature presidential actions—his opposition to nullification, his push to remove Indians westward to clear their land for whites, and his decision to veto, and then defund, the Second Bank of the United States—as actions on behalf of Americans against a distant national government and foreign and domestic enemies posing an existential threat to the American nation. Jackson's campaigns and subsequent presidency invited strident condemnation from his many critics. But on two key points, everyone agreed. America in the decades following the War of 1812 was a violent place. And Andrew Jackson was a violent man.

Jackson's supporters countered that Jackson's violence was quintessentially American—indicative of the defiant, pugnacious spirit of dissent that animated all liberty-loving citizens and distinguished them from entrenched government bureaucrats and nonwhite enemies. Jackson's opponent in both the 1824 and 1828 elections, John Quincy Adams, proved a perfect foil for Jackson's populist image: the son of the second president of the United States, who had served as a diplomat, a Harvard professor, and secretary of state, the more formally educated Adams was one of the "book-worms and pedants" who sneered at the rustic upbringing of most Americans, a pro-Jackson pamphlet stressed.[42] But even more than that, Jackson's political approach was unprecedented, marking a contrast with Adams that laid the groundwork for modern political campaigning. Jackson openly campaigned for president, defying a political taboo that was older than the country itself. He eschewed the standard that prospective political leaders should not openly demonstrate their desire for office—a standard to which all of Jackson's presidential predecessors, including Adams, had publicly adhered. Jackson is frequently credited with all but single-handedly transforming the presidency into the symbol of democracy that Americans recognize today.[43]

Yet the political literature produced during the presidential campaigns of 1824 and 1828 and Jackson's ensuing two presidential terms show that his political innovation was not that he invented a new way of perceiving the presidency alongside "the people." Rather, he and his supporters brilliantly exploited a vision of the presidency that was decades in the making, the product of strident and even violent debate linking what presidential incumbents and hopefuls did, and said, to whom Americans believed they were, and what threats they faced.

Jackson lost the election of 1824 to John Quincy Adams after a contentious election ended in a tie that had to be broken in the House of Representatives. Adams emerged the winner, even though Jackson had won more votes among the populace (and, thanks to the three-fifths clause) more votes in the Electoral College than any of the other four leading candidates. Henry Clay, the speaker of the House, assumed the role of Adams's secretary of state—the position that was the clear stepping-stone to the presidency—after delivering the votes in the House that made Adams the sixth president. The arrangement was clear evidence to Jackson and his supporters that a "corrupt bargain" had been struck by Adams and his allies in Congress. Jacksonians pointed to the election of 1824 as clear evidence that a distant cabal of political elites sat nestled in Washington, so determined to remain ensconced in office that the people were denied the candidate they had stated they wanted. Jackson ran again in 1828, in a campaign that was especially vicious and personal. Jackson's own relationship with his wife, Rachel, was the subject of attack, as Rachel had been married prior to meeting Jackson and was likely still married to her first husband when she and Jackson began their romantic relationship and subsequent marriage. Critics pounced, calling them both adulterers. Rachel Jackson died in December 1828, and Andrew Jackson was convinced that the slander she had endured throughout the campaign had killed her.[44]

Jackson's loss in 1824 offered an apt demonstration of a distant political establishment conspiring to rob Americans of their actual political choice. Jackson's violence, so disturbing to his critics because it deviated so strongly from political norms, appealed to his supporters for precisely the same reason. The hero of the Battle of New Orleans, Jackson was feted around the country, hailed as a hero of bravery and brilliance matched only by the likes of George Washington. John Eaton, Jackson's future secretary of war, published a biography of him in 1817 that went through multiple editions, including a third edition published in 1828, the year Jackson won election to the presidency. Eaton's biography of Jackson traced a basic narrative that campaign literature—pro- and anti-Jackson alike—would follow through the 1820s. Treatments of Jackson began by tracing his early life—including, invariably, the now famous story of his capture as a teenager by the British during the American Revolution, his refusal to clean the boots of a British officer, the officer's slashing Jackson across the face with his saber, and Jackson's attempting to parry the blow with his hand. "Thus early in life," wrote another pro-Jackson biographer, S. Putnam Waldo, in 1828, "did Jackson become a soldier of the Republic and an unalterable enemy of Britain." In short, Jackson was a quintessential dissenter: a man devoted to speaking and acting in defiance of tyranny. From there, treatments of Jackson would chronicle his legal and political career in the state of Tennessee and in the United States Congress, his battles with Indians in the Creek Wars, and invariably culminate with his actions in the War of 1812. Taken together, these biographies portrayed a man committed to resisting arbitrary authority that sought to impose itself on him, through violence if necessary. Jackson's individual exploits exemplified the nation's core political value: he would live only by laws of his own making.[45]

In supporters' versions Jackson's campaign against the Creek Indians was not a mass slaughter of a dying and helpless race, but a valiant battle against bloodthirsty "savages." Authors sprinkled descriptions of Indian butchery of white families on the frontier throughout their biographies of Jackson, in order to heighten the necessity and righteousness of his actions. Eaton himself linked the bravery of Jackson and his men directly to a kind of frontier individualism that did not need to rely on government assistance—a major theme in Jackson's populist appeal and one that Jackson would deploy in his justifications for his actions throughout his presidency. "Unassisted by the government, the settlers were forced to rely for security on their own bravery and exertions," Eaton wrote. "Although young, no person was more distinguished than Andrew Jackson, in defending the country against those predatory incursions of the savages."[46]

The 1824 pamphlet, written and published by the committee of Jacksonian supporters in Hunterdon County, New Jersey, attests to Jackson's local appeal in Northern states. The pamphlet makes clear that his supporters in Hunterdon County applied their local concerns to the national office Jackson sought. Their statements "recommending" Jackson for the American presidency were also meant to make a statement about their capacity to assess how well a presidential candidate could serve national interests. For the Republicans of Hunterdon County, Jackson's "personal qualifications," as well as his "publick services and exalted talents," were what "most deserved their gratitude and confidence." That confidence in a Southern slaveholder from a rural state, the pamphlet demonstrates, cut across simple divides between North and South, urban and rural, local and national. His Hunterdon supporters pointed out that they had "no local connection with either candidate"—Jackson or John Quincy Adams— yet they were more than qualified to evaluate how the candidates for the presidency would "promot[e] the honor and interests of the nation."[47]

They were not alone. Jackson also enjoyed support in New York and (less surprisingly) in the west, as the diary of Samuel Lord, Sr., attests. Lord kept meticulous track of electoral returns locally and throughout the country, noting that favorable returns for Jackson candidates in nearby states as far north as Pennsylvania, as far west as Ohio, and as far south as Georgia, was cause for celebration in New York City. Eighteen thirty-four was not a presidential election year, but it was the year of a contentious election for mayor and city council that provoked demonstrations and even rioting in the streets. Lord recorded that Democrats put on a "great Democratic Festival" in the city to celebrate the election to Congress of nine Jacksonians from Ohio, even before all the results were in.[48]

Crucially, Jacksonians rebutted critics' contention that Jackson's violence was evidence that he was somehow fundamentally selfish, reckless, and unfocused. To hear his opponents tell the tale, Jackson's violence revealed his lack of principles and self-control. He was a hothead, who routinely exploded into an irrational rage at the slightest provocation. Supporters countered that nothing could be farther from the truth. In fact, the *Jackson Wreath* maintained, Jackson's violence was a testament to his ability to focus his martial talents squarely in the service of the American people and against their enemies. "The impetuosity of his nature, his impatience of wrong and encroachment, his contempt for meanness, and his tenaciousness of just authority, have involved him in bitter altercations and sanguinary quarrels:—his resentments have been fiercely executed, and his censures harshly uttered," the *Wreath* admitted, "yet he cannot be accused of wanton or malicious violence—the sallies which may be deemed intemperate can be traced to strong provocations, operating, in most instances, upon his patriotic zeal and the very generosity and loftiness of his spirit. He sacrificed the enemies of his country, where he deemed that signal examples of rigor were necessary for the public welfare and the lasting suppression of murder and rapine—he was never found wanting in clemency and humanity towards those whom essential justice and paramount duty allowed him to spare and relieve." Jackson found himself the target of vicious partisan attacks—the pamphlet noted, like all "great and good" men, including George Washington. Yet through it all, Jackson's "country saw that whatever he had done against either her savage or her civilized foes, had been done, not for his own sake, but for hers."[49]

The comparison with Washington thinly veiled a crucial contrast. Those who had urged Washington's ascent to the presidency in the 1780s had celebrated Washington's military career and his virtue—themes that Jackson's supporters reprised. Yet Jackson never really gave up power. There was no grand moment where Jackson gallantly gave back his military command to a governing legislative body. The fact that he wielded all but absolute power—even over the objections of established government authorities—was precisely the point. Praise for Jackson took the form of an expression of popular dissent from politics as usual. Supporters cast Jackson's propensity for violence as a testament to his capacity to wield power decisively and bravely, rallying patriotic Americans to battle against the nation's enemies to a degree that established governmental bodies could not.

A well-circulated story in Jacksonian campaign literature involved the moments leading up to the Battle of New Orleans during which the legislature of New Orleans, as well as the judges, were powerless to stop the impending British assault; Jackson boldly stepped in to save the day. Eaton contrasted the indecisive legislature of New Orleans with Jackson's decisiveness. "The legislature of Louisiana . . . balancing in their decisions, and uncertain of the best course to be pursued to assure protection, they, as yet, had resolved upon nothing promising certainty and safety, or calculated to infuse tranquility and confidence in the public mind. The arrival of Jackson, however, produced a new aspect in affairs," Eaton wrote. "His activity and zeal in preparation, and his reputation as a brave and skillful commander, had turned all eyes towards him, and inspired even the desponding with a confidence they had not before felt."[50] So too had Jackson suspended habeas corpus in New Orleans and had a local judge arrested. After the battle the judge held Jackson in contempt and fined him $1,000. Jacksonian campaign literature cast this story as further evidence that Jackson was willing and able to act decisively when established governments had failed to do so, and he would accept the consequences. The story inevitably continued: Jackson agreed to pay the fine, but the grateful townspeople paid the fine for him.[51]

The point of stories like this was clearly to comment on how Jackson's military prowess could serve a vital civic purpose. His capacity to rally men to battle did not make him a mindless "military chieftain" but a bold leader whose decisive action could unite a motley crew of diverse people in a common cause. One Jacksonian piece blared the analogy, all but spelling out how the men that Jackson led in New Orleans were supposed to stand in for the American nation writ large. Poorly equipped, Jackson's men "composed a heterogenous mass—consisting of Creoles and Europeans, of various origin—French, Spanish and English, with a recent leaven of native-born citizens. They were as unlike and diversified in their feelings, wishes and views, as in their language, manners and birth. They were united by no general interest, and they acknowledged no common country. Spies and traitors were every where."[52]

The piece's author, Isaac Hill, credited the martial skill of Jackson and his men with saving the life and honor of white women against the brutal onslaught of British soldiers and nonwhites, particularly the ubiquitous Indian "savages." "The British commander in chief . . . had allowed himself to appeal to the very worst passions as auxiliaries to the wonted courage of his men. . . . His watchword for this battle was '*beauty and booty*,' thus fully stimulating lust and rapacity to the utmost effort for conquest, and devoting his miserable victims to penury, and to what was infinitely worse, to the unutterable horrors of 'the worst of ruins, and the worst of shames.'" Even a completed treaty, formally ending the war, "could not indemnify our plundered citizens—restore to life our slaughtered defenders, nor bring repose of mind and purity to our violated maids and matrons." But Jackson had won the day. This, too, Hill claimed, was evidence of Jackson's keen intellect, evidence that he was not the mindless barbarian that intellectual elites took him for. "*[T]he commander in chief of an army, in a difficult and complicated services, must possess a cool, calculating head, a vigorous mind, a rapidity of reasoning, with clear perceptions that will bring him at once to his conclusions,*" Hill explained. "From my experience through life I believe there *are fewer men, thus qualified* to distinguish themselves, at the head of an army, *than to fill any* OTHER STATION IN ANY GOVERNMENT. And it WOULD BE UNJUST AND ILLIBERAL TO DENY TO GENERAL JACKSON THE PROFESSION OF THESE QUALIFICATIONS."[53]

Hill joined other Jacksonians in stressing that there was a cerebral quality to Jackson's violence. It was both measured and unconstrained at the same time—not just relentless, but also focused. It was a violence that could easily be mistaken as anarchic brutishness to the established political class, who wrung their hands at Jackson's boldness and wagged their fingers at his aggressiveness. They mistook his decisiveness for mindless aggression because they could not control Jackson. But that was what the critics got wrong about Jackson. Just because elites could not understand Jackson, and more importantly could not *control* him, did not mean that Jackson was himself out of control. Jackson's violence was not evidence that he was a murderous monster. Jackson's violence was clear evidence that Jackson was in complete control: that he knew exactly who the American people were—and, crucially, who they were *not*—and how to serve the former by leading the charge against the latter.

Jackson's presidency divided the country along lines that defied easy categorization. Despite his Southern roots, Jackson found he had critics in the South and supporters in the North. Though he was a Westerner, hailed by many supporters as an exemplar of rough-and-tumble frontier individualism, he enjoyed support among Northern city folk. As with the nullification crisis, Jackson's allies described his fight with the Second Bank of the United States as an all-out battle. They registered their support by playing up his violent nature as a characteristic that connected Jackson to the Americans he represented. It was that capacity for violence that distinguished real Americans from their enemies, they argued. It was this that allowed Jackson, as president, to galvanize public support for his efforts to remake the nation's politics and government in the people's image.[54]

"Thursday 13th December 1832 . . . yesterday the important Proclamation of the President of the United States was received in this City, dated at Washington the 10th calling on the People of the United States to support him in putting down rebellion & treason in the State of South Carolina & protecting the Union & Constitution of the United States," Samuel Lord, Sr., recorded in his diary. "United States Troops have march'd to Charleston & some small Vessels of War have proceeded to that harbour." For their part, South Carolinians also braced for all-out conflict. "[W]e are on the eve of a fight," Charlestonian Charles Macbeth reported. His fellow citizens would not be "intimidated & they are preparing zealously their arms and ammunition." On January 8, Lord recorded that the people of New York City celebrated Andrew Jackson's victory at the Battle of New Orleans. Then, twelve days later, Lord wrote: "War in South Carolina is near at hand, the 1st Feb[ruar]y is the time fixed for carrying into execution their threats of Nullification & Secession from the Union—when the power of the United States will be called forth to execute the laws & to preserve the Union & the Constitution & to put down rebellion & revolution." In the end Calhoun, working alongside Kentucky senator Henry Clay, saved the day, brokering a compromise that averted war while allowing both Jackson and the nullifiers to save face. Nullifiers got a reduction of the tariff, Jackson got South Carolina's pledge to comply with the law.[55]

Lord's diary went on. On December 31, 1832, Lord wrote about the turmoil engulfing the European continent, as word of French incursion into Belgium reached New York City, while "English fleets Saild from the Dover to cooperate." War appeared to loom for "the United States so called," as Lord put it—a clear indication that the nullification crisis had forced Lord to contemplate America's crisis within a global context, and reflect on whether the country had ever been, or could ever be, one nation.[56] But all was not lost. Returns for Jacksonian candidates "from the State of New York & other states give great great & increased Majorities for the Jackson Ticket." In mid-November there had been parties in the streets "for the Success of the Democratic over the Anties."[57] In June 1833, Jackson visited New York City, drawing a crowd that Lord estimated at 200,000 people. Jackson's veto, Lord recorded, had been met with a "great Outcry,"[58] but the midterm election results for Jackson in 1834 had been spectacular. "Friends of the Administration of President Jackson" organized a massive party in the city "for the results of the elections in the states of New Jersey, Pennsylvania, Georgia, Connecticut, Ohio &c. which have recently taken place." The party took on the look of a spectacular battle: "100 guns fired from the Battery—100 from Brooklyn heights & 100 from Jersey City—Castle Garden was fill'd—congratulations, eating and drinking, Splendid fireworks in the evening, and Tammany Hall crowded.—Speeches delivered—Shouts & applauses went forth in honour of the bright prospects & maintainance [*sic*] of the great Democratic principles of the Constitution of our Country." The thunderous eruptions from the guns and fireworks likely drowned out the conversation that the small gathering of "Opposition, Bank Merchants" were having at the same time.[59]

Visual depictions of Jackson dressed in military uniform, often on horseback, already ubiquitous in hagiographies of Jackson, made a thrilling image to accompany anti-Bank sentiment. "Behold your hero, GENERAL JACKSON, protecting you and yours from British bayonets! Behold your *patriot President* assaulted by tories and traitors for defending your rights. Behold the BANK lavishing its bribes on the hirelings who vilify him. AMERICANS, Will you suffer it?" asked an 1832 broadside, published in English and German and featuring Jackson in full military splendor, saber unsheathed, leading the charge against the Bank of the United States (figures 8.2 and 8.3). "He saved your country from the blood-hounds of Britain. He saved your wives, and daughters, and sisters from pollution. He has forced all the world to respect your rights. . . . He has . . . strangled the BANK MONSTER, that would make the rich richer, and the poor poorer. Defend your hero and father from tories and traitors. Americans, to the Polls, and support the virtuous JACKSON. Read the words of the Hero and Patriot from his Veto Message."[60] "When the Creek Indians, in the late war, began to murder the women and children on our frontiers, General Jackson said VETO!—*and the murders ceased.* When the timid and the traitorous at New Orleans, 1814–15, wished to surrender the city to the British army, General Jackson said VETO!—*and the city was not surrendered,*" a piece reprinted in a Springfield, Massachusetts, paper breathlessly declared. "When a company of British Lords and gentlemen, combined with a few brokers and stockholders at home, asked the government to make them a present of some ten millions of dollars and place the currency of the country and the government itself in their power, in violation of the rights of the States and in jeopardy of the people, Gen. Jackson said, VETO!—*and our liberties and institutions are still safe.* . . . The British

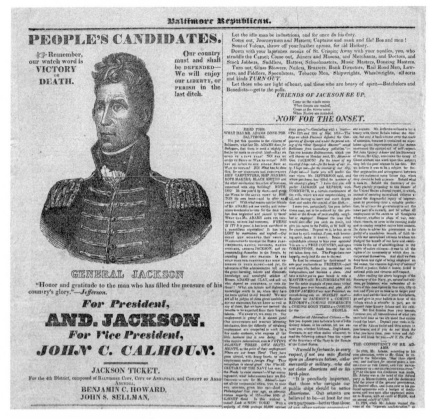

Figure 8.2: "People's Candidate," *Baltimore Republican* (November 10, 1828). Detail. Courtesy of the American Antiquarian Society.

Bank is now attempting to put its *veto* on him, and *will not the freemen of America stand by him?* We hear them say WE WILL! WE WILL!"[61]

As Jackson and his supporters saw it, the president's violence provided a contrast with the violence of the nation's enemies, most fundamentally, nonwhites. The president's actions—and by extension those of all Americans in whose name he acted—were swift, measured, and just. It was a violence that had direction and purpose. By contrast, the violence of nonwhites was anarchic and mindless—simultaneously threatening to the nation's progress yet destined to be ground down by the onslaught of the white Americans that Jackson led. So too black violence—depicted as both menacing and, increasingly, as buffoonish—provided a stark contrast with the cerebral, civilized violence that Jacksonians claimed for white Americans. A cartoon, called "Life in Philadelphia," published in

Figure 8.3: "Americans, Behold Your Hero," (1832). Detail. Courtesy of the American Antiquarian Society.

London by Edward Clay, provides an example of this and models how it could be used to attack Jackson's white political rivals. It depicts a black man admonishing a black child, who wears an issue of the pro-Jackson *Mercury* newspaper as a hat, for supporting Andrew Jackson. The man, a John Quincy Adams supporter, has grabbed the child and appears ready to strike him with a bundle of sticks. "What de debil you hurrah for General Jackson for?—you black Nigger!" the man yells to the child. "I'll larn you better.—I'm a 'ministration Man!!" (figure 8.4). The pantomimed black dialect invites comparisons with the Bobalition broadsides. But where those broadsides depict black people drinking toasts and making speeches, imitating the public civic rituals of whites, "Life in Philadelphia" hints at the propensity toward violence that whites regularly ascribed to blacks, especially black men. It depicts this violence as both misguided (directed at a black child, who wields no political power whatsoever) and comical (perpetrated by a black man who possesses the exaggerated facial features and broken English that racist whites ascribed to blacks, and who wields only a bundle of sticks). That this violence bore no resemblance to the civilized violence of American whites was exactly the point.[62]

Figure 8.4: "Life in Philadelphia," in William Joseph Snelling, *Brief and Impartial History of the Life and Actions of Andrew Jackson, President of the United States* (1831). Courtesy of the American Antiquarian Society.

The nation that emerged from the War of 1812 was in the midst of profound change. Financial panic, tariffs, partisan and sectional division over slavery, and actions by nonwhites to seek incorporation into the American nation provided evidence to Jackson and his upstart Democratic Party that the government under Republican leadership after the War of 1812 had failed to protect Americans against foreign and domestic enemies and threatened their liberties. What the nation needed was a president who could exemplify the dissenting spirit of an American people who had just concluded their second war with Britain. The hero of the Battle of New Orleans was just the man for the job.

Jackson's foes, who formed the Whig Party in 1834, condemned Jackson's violence as exemplary of a domineering Southern political culture looking to rule the political landscape. While the divide between the two parties did not split cleanly between North and South, the Democrats were understood to be the party of Southern slavery. Northerners who capitulated to the South were derisively called "doughfaces," an epithet meant to depict them as weak, softly supporting Southern interests. While Democrats praised Jacksonian democracy for governing "in accordance with just republican principles," and for "restor[ing] in practice to our beloved country that true system of democracy which the framers of our constitution intended to establish, and under which only the American people can consent to live," Whigs decried the dominance of Southern, slaveholding interests by "King Andrew," who had expanded the power of his office through a "new relation which had been created between the President and the people."[63]

So pervasive was the belief that the fate of the American people was indelibly linked to the presidency that even the Whigs adopted it as they looked to the future. While Democrats looked to continue these "principles" by advocating for the election of Martin Van Buren, Whigs claimed that Jackson and his ilk did not represent the American people but a political party that sought power for itself and subjugation for all others. "To effect this reformation we appeal to the people, the whole people, not to the portions of parties, which, in squads of some ten to fifty office-seekers, claim to be the people; but to that great mass of the community which has no interest in the Government, save in its legal and faithful administration," the *Political Mirror* concluded in 1835. "There are, and must ever be, many points of difference in a country so various and extensive as ours," the *Mirror* conceded. "But there is an interest dear to all, paramount to all, the preservation of the national freedom and integrity.

This interest must swallow up all others; in its gratification all must seek delight—to preserve it, unanimity is indispensable among all those who see and feel the dangers which threaten it. They must surrender, in the selection of a Chief Magistrate, sectional feelings and personal predilections, and unite upon some individual, who shall be the representative of the principles of all, in relation to the violations of the Constitution, by President Jackson and the party which has used him for revolution."[64]

As both a presidential candidate and a two-term incumbent, Jackson stood as the epitome of a violence that many Americans after the War of 1812 embraced as the essence of the profound link between the people and the presidency. Whigs' fears of the corrosive potential of this violence would prove prescient, as it would be that violence—promoted and defended by the seventh president and his party as the key to holding the nation together—that less than three decades hence would tear the nation apart. The only way to salvage the nation, the *Mirror* concluded, was through political dissent, to reclaim the presidency for the people once more.

Epilogue

IT HAS BEEN 183 YEARS since Andrew Jackson retired from the presidency, and 175 years since his death. In that time the United States has witnessed a cataclysmic civil war, nearly a century of Jim Crow, and multiple civil-rights movements. Slavery ended; black men, then black and white women, got the right to vote (and voted en masse); and landmark laws guaranteed access to voting and freedom from discrimination, irrespective of race or gender.

The presidency changed, too. Pushed by free and enslaved black people to make the cause of the United States the end of slavery, Abraham Lincoln wielded the powers of the presidency to turn the United States military into a force for liberation. His use of his executive authority dealt slavery its death blow—for which he was murdered, and then martyred. Every president since has lived in his shadow, and his actions during the Civil War have been credited with (or blamed for) contributing to the further expansion of executive authority. In the 1970s, Arthur M. Schlesinger, Jr., coined the term "imperial presidency," referring to an office whose powers dominate the entire federal government, rendering it dangerously unchecked by and unaccountable to the other branches of government. But the presidency's dominance does not end at the institutional level. The presidency continues to dominate our political culture, as American citizens—and people all over the world—interact with presidential personalities, real and fictitious, in ways unimaginable in the country's earliest years. America is now the world's foremost superpower, and radio, television, movies, and now social media act as vehicles by which the modern world debates the words and actions of presidents and presidential hopefuls. So much has changed since Andrew Jackson's presidency. And yet the parallels between his time and our own are unmistakable. This is why a better understanding of the office's earliest history—not simply another rehash of the actions of the first presidential incumbents—is so crucial.[1]

Yet in scholarly studies of the presidency and in American popular culture, incumbents continue to dominate the story. Even works that criticize the public's fixation on the presidency cast the public as more or less passive respondents to presidential actions, usually to argue that the more the public expects presidents to do their behalf, the less civically engaged the public becomes (thus reducing civic engagement to essentially voting in presidential elections once every four years).[2] The result is an understanding of the presidency that omits or severely downplays the public's role in defining the presidency's cultural power. Presidential incumbents become paragons of "greatness," from which the nation has declined, or paragons of the "anti-intellectual," white-supremacist, nativist nationalism that has become more overtly amplified since the election of Donald Trump in 2016. Commentators often wring their hands that the American public has become more divided and partisan than ever, a characterization that all too often reinforces the assumption that the public mainly reacts passively to the changing contours of American politics that are determined, largely if not solely, by the actions of presidential incumbents and their closest associates.[3]

Such an interpretation severely downplays the integral role the American public played in defining the contours of early national politics. Claiming that dissent against government power that threatened their liberty was a fundamental expression of every American's independent character, public defenders and critics of presidential administrations framed resistance as integral, rather than threatening, to government authority. Their focus on the presidency made the office, not simply specific incumbents, the early nation's most crucial symbol of the intimate, and innately contentious, relationship between the president and the public that fueled the office's political prestige, even as the constant criticism endemic to the office has frustrated everyone who has ever occupied it. That the public commentary on the presidency was largely white is crucial to the story. Partisan debates over how presidential actions failed or succeeded to reflect the free and independent character of the American people reinforced the underlying assumption shared by whites across partisan lines: that free or enslaved blacks, suspicious "foreigners," and Indians were not Americans. At best, they were racial or political outsiders who lacked Americans' capacity to master the civic principles of a free society. At worst, they were the nation's enemies. The racial politics of this political messaging promised to unite "the American people" by distinguishing them from their country's most existential threats, but it also reflected how openly violent and fractured the nation had become by the time Jackson occupied the office. The members of this broad political public—dominated by whites, but including nonwhite voices as well—were not passive spectators to presidential politics. On the contrary, they were active participants in it and ultimately essential co-authors of both the presidency's role as the nation's most important political symbol and the national vision that the office came to symbolize. The vitriolic and even violent debate among members of the public—each claiming to be a part of the American dissenting tradition—did not undermine the power of the presidency. In fact, it was integral to the prestige that is the key to the presidency's symbolic power. The dynamic and contentious exchanges between presidents and the American public encapsulated how divided Americans were, how elusive a single meaning of "American" remained, and yet how strongly so many yearned to achieve greater political unity in the hopes of saving the fledgling nation from irreparable political rupture. The lessons of the nation's earliest years contextualize the political turmoil surrounding the presidency today. Never in modern American history have those lessons been more badly needed.

In so many ways the particulars of our present political moment are without precedent. Before Donald Trump, no American president had ever openly solicited help from a foreign government on the campaign trail, and then again, multiple times, to multiple countries, while in office.[4] No president had ever used social media to berate his critics or the press, circulate conspiracy theories, or stoke the prejudices of his supporters with such regularity or aggressiveness. No president has seemed so impervious to political consequences for controversies or scandals that would have summarily doomed his predecessors.

Yet Trump's presidency has provoked mass opposition to his administration to a degree not seen in generations. His election has forced the United States to reckon with not only the political power of the presidency, but also his use of the office, and that of his supporters, to advance their shared vision of America—one that is avowedly nationalist and unrepentantly rooted in nativism and white supremacy.[5] Easy as it would be to attribute the ugliness of this vision, and the presidency's immense political power to reflect, promote, and reinforce it, to presidential incumbents alone, to do so would be to ignore the profound role of the American public in making the president "the man of the people" in the nation's earliest decades. This history attests to the power "the people" possess to define their nation and the cultural power of governmental institutions.

"The American people" encompasses far more people today than it did two centuries ago. The Civil War destroyed slavery officially, and out of it emerged three Constitutional amendments: ending slavery, establishing birthright citizenship and equal protection under the laws, and granting black men the right to vote. Suffrage for women took nearly another half-century, but come it did. Years of civil-rights protests pushed the nation to embrace a national vision where whites and nonwhites, women and men, native-born Americans, indigenous American Indians, and immigrants, share the nation's body politic as equals. Globalization has made Washington, DC, and the country's other major metropolises, world cities where people from around the planet live and work. To a great many, the forty-fourth president of the United States, Barack Obama, embodied this promise of a "post-racial," cosmopolitan, inclusive America, and his election to the presidency in 2008, and again in 2012, was unmistakable evidence that the American nation had finally moved beyond the prejudices at the heart of its past.

Such a context made Donald Trump's presidency all but unthinkable to most as he campaigned and all the more horrific for his many critics after he won. But to his supporters, Trump's election represented a rejection of this multicultural, inclusive national vision, and indeed a return to the American "greatness." In Trump's campaign slogan, "Make America Great Again," the word "great" receives most of the attention, for obvious reasons. But the word "again" is just as important, for Trump's presidency is making a claim about the past. Specifically, it is a national past where real Americans—white Americans—are united, prosperous, and committed to heeding the president's call to defend their nation from its "un-American" enemies beyond its borders and within.

In short, the twenty-first-century presidency stands at the center of a bitter political division over the meaning of America—a battle that began in the nation's earliest history. Current debates over whether the Electoral College preserves or undermines our democracy, whether an impeachment inquiry is a "coup" or a legitimate constitutional function, and—most fundamentally—whether Donald Trump represents the voice of the nation or poses a fundamental threat to it, attest that the presidency remains first and foremost the possession of participants in this political battle across the political spectrum.

It is tempting to view this back-and-forth as pointless argument that "divides America" and distracts from what "unites us." It is also tempting to hearken back wistfully to the nation's founding era and conjure simplistic stories of national decline from a pristine, virtuous political past, exemplified by a handful of political elites. A deeper look at our nation's earliest history, so often invoked but insufficiently understood, tells us a different story. Far from united, the early United States was divided over the question of what, if anything, actually made one an American. Claiming that their right to dissent was crucial to ensuring that the president represented them, public commentators beyond the presidency became the chief authors of the presidency's role as the symbol of the collective "We, the People," and the meaning of that "we" that predominated in the nation's earliest years. The presidency owes its cultural and symbolic power to its place at the center of strident public debate, not consensus. If anything, the bitter political division we are experiencing now is likely to enhance the presidency's prestige still further, as the president's critics and supporters alike proceed from a shared assumption that as the presidency goes, so goes the nation.

But this political struggle is not a meaningless divergence from unspoiled "founding principles." It is a testament to the capacity of public voices—political elites, along with a vast majority of people who will never personally occupy elected office—to exert phenomenal influence over the meaning of the American nation and its government institutions. The nation is in the midst of profound political change, though our political polarization makes it difficult to see what that change will ultimately look like. But whatever form that change takes, it will not be the product of a presidential incumbent—Trump or otherwise—acting in isolation. It will be the product of the political disagreement itself, of not just one but many competing national visions propagated by presidents and protestors, national politicians and local journalists, elected leaders and private citizens, native-born and immigrant Americans, of every gender, race, sexual orientation, religion, and, of course, political ideology.

As I write this in the year 2020, every occupant of the office whom the nation's earliest political commentators called "the man of the people" has been a man—and every one of those men, save one, has been white. As you read this, that may or may not still be true. Regardless of who occupies the office, presidents will almost certainly continue to dominate national politics. But they will have to contend with public commentary that continues to project onto the presidency competing visions of the nation's highest ideals. For better or for worse, the office will remain the possession of "the people": a testament to Americans' desire for national unity, the inevitable division that desire provokes, and the changing contours of that division, at the heart of American democracy.

NOTES

PROLOGUE

1. The town name is "Hoosick," but the letter spells the town name with only one "o." "Hosick, NY: Letter to Thomas Jefferson from Hoosick Republicans, 1807–08." Dated January 20, 1808. MSS Collection, Hoosick (NY) Collection, 1771–1842, AHMC-Hoosick (NY) (copy), New-York Historical Society. According to staff at the Papers of Thomas Jefferson, there is no record that Jefferson received this letter, a copy of which is housed in the Miscellaneous Manuscripts collection at the New-York Historical Society. If a version of this letter was sent to Jefferson, it is of course possible that it differs from the copy. Nonetheless, even if Jefferson never saw the original letter, the contemporaneous slash marks across "Esquire" in the copy remain evidence of the authors' attempt to grapple with Jefferson's stature as president.

2. Throughout this book I strive to follow the lead of Erica Armstrong Dunbar in referring to people in slavery as "enslaved" or "enslaved persons," rather than "slave," to emphasize their humanity in the midst of an exploitative and unjust system. I make exceptions when the word "slave" or "slaves" appears in a quote, and occasionally, as Dunbar does, "for narrative flow." This will be especially true in later chapters of the book, as I seek to capture the views held by white Americans and expressed through commentary on the presidency. See Dunbar, *Never Caught: The Washingtons' Relentless Pursuit of Their Runaway Slave, Ona Judge* (New York: Simon & Schuster, 2017), xi.

3. "Hosick, NY: Letter to Thomas Jefferson from Hoosick Republicans, 1807–08." Dated January 20, 1808. MSS Collection, Hoosick (NY) Collection, 1771–1842, AHMC-Hoosick (NY) (copy), New-York Historical Society.

4. Fisher Ames, The Republican VIII, in W. B. Allen, ed., *The Works of Fisher Ames as Published by Seth Ames*, 2 vols. (Indianapolis: Liberty Fund, 1983), 1: 329–333, quotes at 331, 332.

5. Esculapius, "A Receipt to Make a Modern Federalist," [1807?], American Historical Manuscripts Collection (formerly Miscellaneous Manuscripts), New-York Historical Society.

6. I am indebted to Peter J. Kastor for helping me find the right words to express the ideas in this paragraph.

7. The latest example of this approach is Stephen F. Knott, *The Lost Soul of the American Presidency: The Decline into Demagoguery and the Prospects for Renewal* (Lawrence: University Press of Kansas, 2019).

8. Biographies of presidential incumbents are too numerous for even a partial listing here. For a general history of the presidency, see Forrest McDonald, *The American Presidency: An Intellectual History* (Lawrence: University Press of Kansas,

1992); Knott, *Lost Soul*; and Jeremy D. Bailey, *The Idea of Presidential Representation: An Intellectual and Political History* (Lawrence: University Press of Kansas, 2019). For the early presidency (the focus of·this work), see Ralph Ketcham,
Presidents above Party: The First American Presidency, 1789–1828 (Chapel Hill:
University of North Carolina Press, 1984); Sandra Moats, *Celebrating the Republic: Presidential Ceremony and Popular Sovereignty, From Washington to Monroe*
(DeKalb: Northern Illinois University Press, 2010).

Influential examinations of early presidential elections include Richard P. McCormick, *The Presidential Game: The Origins of American Presidential Politics* (New
York: Oxford University Press, 1982); and M. J. Heale, *The Presidential Quest:
Candidates and Images in American Political Culture, 1787–1852* (New York: Longman, 1982). For a more general overview of presidential elections that goes beyond
the early republic, see Gil Troy, *See How They Ran: The Changing Role of the Presidential Candidate* (New York: The Free Press, 1991). Specific elections, especially
the elections of 1800 and 1828, have been the subject of extensive scholarly examination. For the election of 1796, see Jeffrey L. Pasley, *The First Presidential Contest: 1796 and the Founding of American Democracy* (Lawrence: University Press
of Kansas, 2013). For the election of 1800, see, for instance, Bruce Ackerman, *The
Failure of the Founding Fathers: Jefferson, Marshall, and the Rise of Presidential Democracy* (Cambridge, MA: Harvard University Press, 2005); James Horn, Jan Ellen
Lewis, and Peter S. Onuf, eds., *The Revolution of 1800: Democracy, Race, and the
New Republic* (Charlottesville: University of Virginia Press, 2002); and James Roger
Sharp, *The Deadlocked Election of 1800: Jefferson, Burr, and the Union in the Bal-
ance* (Lawrence: University Press of Kansas, 2010). For the election of 1828, see
Lynn Hudson Parsons, *The Birth of Modern Politics: Andrew Jackson, John Quincy
Adams, and the Election of 1828* (New York: Oxford University Press, 2009).

9. T. H. Breen, *George Washington's Journey: The President Forges a New Nation*
(New York: Simon & Schuster, 2015); Edward Larson, *George Washington: Nationalist* (Charlottesville: University of Virginia Press, 2016); Brian Steele, *Thomas Jefferson and American Nationhood* (Cambridge: Cambridge University Press, 2012).

10. For an overview of this historiography, see Jeffrey L. Pasley, Andrew W.
Robertson, and David Waldstreicher, "Introduction: Beyond the Founders," in Jeffrey L. Pasley, Andrew W. Robertson, and David Waldstreicher, eds., *Beyond the
Founders* (Chapel Hill: University of North Carolina Press, 2004), 1–28, esp. 3–11.
Examples of such approaches that have especially influenced my analysis are: Da-
vid Waldstreicher, *In the Midst of Perpetual Fetes: The Making of American Na-
tionalism, 1776–1820* (Chapel Hill: University of North Carolina Press, 1997); Len
Travers, *Celebrating the Fourth: Independence Day and the Rites of Nationalism in
the Early Republic* (Amherst: University of Massachusetts Press, 1997); and Carroll
Smith-Rosenberg, *This Violent Empire: The Birth of an American National Identity*
(Chapel Hill: University of North Carolina Press, 2010). Most recently, Robert G.
Parkinson has demonstrated how a nationalistic vision rooted in racial exclusion
emerged out of the American Revolution, and Jasper M. Trautsch's recent work has
explored the creation of nationalism through early US foreign policy. See Parkinson, *The Common Cause: Creating Race and Nation in the American Revolution*
(Chapel Hill: University of North Carolina Press, 2016); and Trautsch, *The Genesis
of America: U.S. Foreign Policy and the Formation of National Identity, 1793–1815*
(Cambridge: Cambridge University Press, 2018).

11. Douglas Bradburn, *The Citizenship Revolution: Politics and the Creation of the American Union, 1774–1804* (Charlottesville: University of Virginia Press, 2009); Alan Taylor, *The Civil War of 1812: American Citizens, British Subjects, Irish Rebels, & Indian Allies* (New York: Knopf, 2012), esp. 395–398; Benjamin E. Park, *American Nationalisms: Imagining Union in the Age of Revolutions* (Cambridge: Cambridge University Press, 2018); Trautsch, *Genesis of America.*

12. The effect of such narrow focus on presidential incumbents can even appear in studies that seek to situate the presidency within a broader historical context. Moats's *Celebrating the Republic* went so far as to claim that the first five presidential incumbents "invented the American political culture that endures today by employing the symbols and rituals they believed best illustrated republican principles to an American citizenry who now possessed sovereign authority over this new national government." See Moats, *Celebrating the Republic,* 3. For examples of studies of the democratization of the presidency that credit Jefferson, see Moats, *Celebrating the Republic;* and Bailey, *Jefferson and Executive Power.* For a recent study that credits Jackson, see Parsons, *Birth of Modern Politics,* esp. 190. Though not the focus of his book, political scientist Saladin M. Ambar remarks that it was not until the Progressive Era that "the *demos* somehow became embodied in the president," but that Andrew Jackson was an early innovator. His "presidency was the first to marry mass participation to primitive executive provocations." See Ambar, *How Governors Built the Modern American Presidency* (Philadelphia: University of Pennsylvania Press, 2012), 127. Dana Nelson is one scholar to mistakenly conclude that the presidency was largely inconsequential to Americans in the early republic, writing: "Citizens were not very interested in the presidency as a political office during the years of the early nation." See Nelson, *Bad for Democracy: How the Presidency Undermines the Power of the People* (Minneapolis: University of Minnesota Press, 2010), 38.

13. Ketcham, *Presidents above Party,* 4–5.

14. Benjamin H. Irvin, *Clothed in Robes of Sovereignty: The Continental Congress and the People Out of Doors* (New York: Oxford University Press, 2011). For suspicion of executive power at the state level, see Rakove, *Original Meanings: Politics and Ideas in the Making of the Constitution* (New York: Knopf, 1996), 249–250; Gordon S. Wood, *The Creation of the American Republic, 1776–1787* (Chapel Hill: University of North Carolina Press, 1969), 157; Gordon S. Wood, *The Radicalism of the American Revolution* (New York: Knopf, 1991), 187–189.

15. For the early Fourth of July, see Travers, *Celebrating the Fourth,* esp. 15–68. For the basic formula that Fourth of July rituals followed, see 41–54. Travers notes that, by the 1790s, the Fourth of July came to reflect the early nation's partisan landscape; see 69–106.

16. Parkinson, *Common Cause,* esp. 581–640. For Parkinson's discussion of the distinction between "propagation" (the word he prefers) and "propaganda," see pp. 17–18ff.

17. I have chosen not to capitalize "federalists" and "antifederalists" when discussing the public ratification debate of 1787 and 1788, to distinguish these terms from the Federalist and Republican parties that formed in the 1790s. While antifederalists in Pennsylvania during the ratification debate did embrace the term "antifederalist" and adopted the term as the name of a political party, no national federalist or antifederalist party came into existence out of the ratification debate. The terms

are best understood as Jeffrey L. Pasley characterizes them, as "temporary coalitions of like-minded politicians rather than ongoing parties." Some federalist advocates for ratification, such as James Madison, would actually become members of the opposition Republican Party in the 1790s. I therefore follow Pasley's lead in presenting "antifederalist" and "federalist" in lowercase. See Pasley, *"The Tyranny of Printers": Newspaper Politics in the Early American Republic* (Charlottesville: University of Virginia Press, 2001), xvii. See also Saul Cornell, *Other Founders: Anti-Federalism and the Dissenting Tradition in America, 1788–1828* (Chapel Hill: University of North Carolina Press, 1999); and Pauline Maier, *Ratification: The People Debate the Constitution, 1787–88* (New York: Simon and Schuster, 2010), xiv–xv.

18. Cornell, *Other Founders.* Scholars of dissent tend to emphasize resistance by those out of power to those in power, rather than explore how even those who wielded power in the early United States invoked dissent as a national value to undermine the legitimacy of their opponents. See, for example, Robert W. T. Martin, *Government by Dissent: Protest, Resistance, & Radical Democratic Thought in the Early American Republic* (New York: New York University Press, 2013).

19. As mentioned in my acknowledgments, I am deeply indebted to Jeffrey L. Pasley's *First Presidential Contest*, a debt that will be readily apparent in this chapter's footnotes.

20. Especially influential works on the intimate connection between slavery and freedom are: Edmund S. Morgan, *American Slavery, American Freedom: The Ordeal of Colonial Virginia* (New York: Norton, 1975); Waldstreicher, *Perpetual Fetes*; David Waldstreicher, *Slavery's Constitution: From Revolution to Ratification* (New York: Knopf, 2009); Carroll Smith-Rosenberg, *This Violent Empire*; Nicole Eustace, *1812: War and the Passions of Patriotism* (Philadelphia: University of Pennsylvania Press, 2012); Alan Taylor, *The Internal Enemy: Slavery and War in Virginia, 1772–1832* (New York: Norton, 2013); and Parkinson, *Common Cause.*

21. Banneker to Thomas Jefferson, August 19, 1791, Julian Boyd et al., *Papers of Thomas Jefferson*, 44 vols. to date (Princeton, NJ: Princeton University Press, 1950), 22: 49.

22. Washington to Bryan Fairfax, August 24, 1774, Abbott and Twohig, *Papers of George Washington—Colonial Series*, 10 vols. (Charlottesville: University of Virginia Press, 1983–1995), 10: 154–156.

23. For this point, I am indebted especially to Robert M. S. McDonald's *Confounding Father: Thomas Jefferson's Image in His Own Time* (Charlottesville: University of Virginia Press, 2016).

24. See, for instance, Wood, *American Republic*, 567–592; Bruce Miroff, "John Adams and the Presidency," in Thomas E. Cronin, ed., *Inventing the American Presidency* (Lawrence: University Press of Kansas, 1989), 304–325; James Grant, *John Adams: Party of One* (New York: Farrar, Straus and Giroux, 2005); Pasley, *First Presidential Contest*, esp. 277–291; Nancy Isenberg and Andrew Burstein, *The Problem of Democracy: The Presidents Adams Confront the Cult of Personality* (New York: Penguin, 2019).

25. The phrase "internal enemy" is the title of Alan Taylor's Pulitzer Prize–winning book, *The Internal Enemy*, though it also appears in primary sources from the era. For Federalist criticism of Jefferson, see Linda K. Kerber, *Federalists in Dissent: Imagery and Ideology in Jeffersonian America* (Ithaca, NY: Cornell University Press,

1970), 23–134. My analysis of the War of 1812 has been particularly influenced by Eustace, *1812*; Taylor, *Civil War of 1812*; Taylor, *Internal Enemy*; J. C. A. Stagg, *Mr. Madison's War: Politics, Diplomacy, and Warfare in the Early American Republic, 1783–1830* (Princeton: Princeton University Press, 1983); J. C. A. Stagg, *The War of 1812: Conflict for a Continent* (Cambridge: Cambridge University Press, 2012). Most recently, see also the essays in Nicole Eustace and Fredrika J. Teute, eds., *Warring for America: Cultural Contests in the Era of 1812* (Chapel Hill: University of North Carolina Press, 2017).

26. Eustace also discusses Lemuel Haynes, and her analysis has informed my own. See Eustace, *1812*, 190–193.

27. Key studies that informed my analysis in this chapter include: John Lauritz Larson, *Internal Improvement: National Public Works and the Promise of Popular Government in the United States* (Chapel Hill: University of North Carolina Press, 2001); Daniel Walker Howe, *What Hath God Wrought: The Transformation of America, 1815–1848* (New York: Oxford University Press, 2007); Parsons, *Birth of Modern Politics*; Joanne B. Freeman, *The Field of Blood: Violence in Congress and the Road to Civil War* (New York: Macmillan, 2018); and Park, *American Nationalisms*.

28. For newspaper politics in the American Revolution, see Parkinson, *Common Cause*, 10–25; and Joseph Adelman, *Revolutionary Networks: The Business and Politics of Printing the News, 1763–1789* (Baltimore: Johns Hopkins University Press, 2019). For newspaper politics in the early United States, see Seth Cotlar, *Tom Paine's America: The Rise and Fall of Transatlantic Radicalism in America* (Charlottesville: University of Virginia Press, 2011), esp. 1–10; and Pasley, *"Tyranny of Printers,"* 7–8. I am indebted to an anonymous reviewer for the article from which chapter 3 is derived and to another for pointing out that some pseudonymous writers were in fact "hired penmen" or political insiders with their own agendas to advance, pushing me to think critically about how to use these sources responsibly.

29. For an overview of these theories as they pertain to the time period discussed in this work, see the first three chapters of Bailey, *Idea of Presidential Representation*. For "patriot king," see Ketcham, *Presidents above Party*.

CHAPTER 1. RATIFICATION AND THE PROMISE
OF "THE MAN OF THE PEOPLE"

1. Archibald Stuart to John Breckenridge, October 21, 1787, in Merrill Jensen et al., *The Documentary History of the Ratification of the Constitution*, 22 vols. to date (Madison: State Historical Society of Wisconsin, 1976–), 8: 89–90. For the ratification debate as a national conversation, see Maier, *Ratification*.

2. For the United States as a union of states, see Bradburn, *Citizenship Revolution*. One of the few Americans who did have a clearer definition of the American nation was Thomas Jefferson, as Steele makes clear in *Jefferson and American Nationhood*.

3. Maier, *Ratification*, xiv–xv. For my decision to write "federalists" and "antifederalists" in lowercase, see my note in the prologue.

4. I am borrowing the phrase "friends of the Constitution" from Colleen Sheehan and Gary L. McDowell, eds., *Friends of the Constitution: Writings of the "Other"*

Federalists, 1787–1788 (Indianapolis: Liberty Fund, 1998). In making this argument, I depart significantly from Jeremy Bailey's argument that little controversy surrounded the presidency during the ratification debate. See Bailey, *Idea of Presidential Representation*, 42. For antifederalists' fears of "consolidation," see Cornell, *Other Founders*.

5. Recent studies of the Constitutional Convention are too numerous for an exhaustive list, but four that especially influenced my thinking are Mary Sarah Bilder, *Madison's Hand: Revising the Constitutional Convention* (Cambridge: Harvard University Press, 2017), (for a discussion of "leaks" during the Convention, see 55–56); Ray Raphael, *Mr. President: How and Why the Founders Created a Chief Executive* (New York: Knopf, 2012), esp. 47–125; Waldstreicher, *Slavery's Constitution*; and Richard Beeman, *Plain, Honest Men: The Making of the American Constitution* (New York: Random House, 2009).

6. Bilder, *Madison's Hand*, esp. 1–9; Raphael, *Mr. President*, 47–125.

7. For Madison's lack of interest in the executive, see Bilder, *Madison's Hand*, 134. For his "slavery strategy," see 108–109.

8. Bilder, *Madison's Hand*, 81–82. The 1790 census counted 292,627 slaves in Virginia, far more than any other state. Census data can be viewed at the "Return of the Whole Number of Persons within the Several Districts of the United States" (Philadelphia: J. Philips, 1793), https://www2.census.gov/prod2/decennial/documents /1790a.pdf.

9. July 11, 1787, in Max Farrand, *The Records of the Federal Convention of 1787*. 3 vols. (New Haven, CT: Yale University Press, 1911), 1: 581.

10. August 8, 1787, in Farrand, 2: 222.

11. Bilder, *Madison's Hand*, 82.

12. July 17, 1787, in Farrand, 2: 29; Bilder, *Madison's Hand*, 114.

13. July 17, 1787, in Farrand, 2: 30.

14. July 24, 1787, in Farrand, 2: 104–105.

15. July 24, 1787, in Farrand, 2: 104–105; Bilder, *Madison's Hand*.

16. "Great without Pomp," in John P. Kaminski and Jill Adair McCaughan, *A Great and Good Man: George Washington in the Eyes of His Contemporaries*, 1989 (reprinted New York: Rowman & Littlefield, 2007), 140. For descriptions of Washington as "godlike," see 131, 160, 161, 164. For disinterestedness, see Wood, *Radicalism*, 104–106.

17. For federalists' advantage in the press, see Pasley, *"Tyranny of Printers,"* 43–47.

18. Archibald Stuart to John Breckenridge, October 21, 1787, Jensen et al., *Ratification of the Constitution*, 8: 89–90. Cornell, *Other Founders*; Kenneth Lockridge, *Literacy in Colonial New England: An Enquiry into the Social Context of Literacy in the Early Modern West* (New York: W. W. Norton, 1974), 18–21; Cotlar, *Tom Paine's America*, 9–10; Maier, *Ratification*, xi, 334. For an example of a newspaper essay imploring women's participation in the ratification debate, see *Philadelphia Independent Gazetteer*, June 5, 1787, in Jensen et al., *Ratification of the Constitution*, 13: 126–127. Jan Ellen Lewis has argued that this inclusion of women into "We, the People" in the Constitution's preamble can be traced back to the Philadelphia Convention. See Jan Ellen Lewis, "Of Every Age Sex & Condition: The Representation of Women in the Constitution," *Journal of the Early Republic* 15, no. 3 (Autumn 1995): 359–387.

19. The "Dissent of the Minority" can be found in Jensen et al., *Ratification of the Constitution*, 15: 7–35. The editorial introduction (at 7–13) contains information about the document's circulation and Samuel Bryan's identity. For circulation of Centinel I, see Jensen et al., 13: 327–328. See also Maier, *Ratification*.

20. See, for instance, *Connecticut Journal* (New Haven), October 17, 1787.

21. *New-Jersey Journal* (Elizabethtown), December 5, 1787.

22. E. Larson, *George Washington, Nationalist*, 76–77.

23. [Virginia State Ratifying Convention] Debates, in Jensen et al., *Ratification of the Constitution*, 10: 1371, 1365.

24. Saul Cornell interprets these grievances slightly differently, including "consolidation" among the critics' list of objections to the Constitution. I think it is more useful to consider "consolidation" as a single, umbrella criticism that critics perceived, manifested in different ways, throughout the document. See Cornell, *Other Founders*. For the list of common antifederalist grievances, see 30–31.

25. "Federal Farmer," No. 3, *Poughkeepsie Country Journal* (Poughkeepsie, NY), October 10, 1787 in Jensen et al., *Ratification of the Constitution*, 19: 225; "John De Witt," Letter 2, October 29, 1787, in Jensen et al., *Ratification of the Constitution*, 4: 157. Ralph Ketcham, *The Anti-Federalist Papers* (New York: Signet, 1986), 189; Bernard Bailyn, *Ideological Origins of the American Revolution* (Cambridge: Harvard University Press, 1968), 346–349.

26. Brutus, [Robert Yates?], No. 1, *New York Journal* (New York), October 18, 1787, in Jensen et al., *Ratification of the Constitution*, 14: 113.

27. Bailyn, *Ideological Origins*, 346–349.

28. For a discussion of the relationship between power and liberty in the eighteenth century, see Bailyn, *Ideological Origins*, 55–93.

29. Elbridge Gerry to the General Court, October 18, 1787, in Jensen et al., *Ratification of the Constitution*, 4: 99; Cornell, *Other Founders*, 309.

30. "Centinel," No. 1, *Independent Gazetteer* (Philadelphia), October 5, 1787, in Jensen et al., *Ratification of the Constitution*, 13: 334; Cornell, *Other Founders*, 309.

31. "The Address and Reasons of Dissent of the Minority of the Convention of Pennsylvania to Their Constituents," *Pennsylvania Packet* (Philadelphia, PA), December 18, 1787, in Jensen et al., *Ratification of the Constitution*, 15: 21; Cornell, *Other Founders*, 309.

32. Elbridge Gerry to the General Court, October 18, 1787, in Jensen et al., *Ratification of the Constitution*, 4: 99.

33. Cornell, *Other Founders*, 30–31.

34. "An Old Whig," Letter No. 5, *Independent Gazetteer* (Philadelphia), November 1, 1787, in Jensen et al., *Ratification of the Constitution*, 13: 541–542.

35. "The Dissent of the Minority of the Pennsylvania Convention," *Pennsylvania Packet* (Philadelphia, PA), December 18, 1787, in Jensen et al., 15: 33.

36. For predictions that the president would be a king, see An Old Whig, in Jensen et al., 13: 541–542; "The Impartial Examiner," *Virginia Independent Chronicle* (Richmond), June 11, 1788, in Jensen et al., *Ratification of the Constitution*, 10: 1611–1612; Cato, No. 4, *New York Journal* (New York), November 8, 1787, in Jensen et al., 14: 7–11; and Patrick Henry, June 5, 1788, in Murray Dry and Herbert Storing, eds., *The Anti-Federalist: Writings by the Opponents of the Constitution*

(Chicago: The University of Chicago Press, 1981), 308. For commentary on the presidency as a "tool of the Senate," see John Smilie, Pennsylvania State Constitutional Convention, December 12, 1787, in Jensen et al., *Ratification of the Constitution*, 2: 566; "John De Witt," Letter No. 3, "To the Free Citizens of the Commonwealth of Massachusetts," *American Herald* (Boston), November 5, 1787, in Jensen et al., 4: 194–199. "The Address of the Seceding Assemblymen" argued that the Senate was "the most powerful" of the three "branches" of government. ("The Address of the Seceding Assemblymen," formally called "An Address of the Subscribers, Members of the Late House of Representatives of the Commonwealth of Pennsylvania, to Their Constituents," was reprinted thirty times. See Cornell, *Other Founders*, 309. For quote, see Jensen et al., *Ratification of the Constitution*, 2: 116).

37. An Old Whig, Letter No. 5 in Jensen et al., *Ratification of the Constitution*, 13: 541–542.

38. Cato, Letter No. 4 *New York Journal* (New York), November 8, 1787, in Jensen et al., *Ratification of the Constitution*, 14: 10. For the dispute over the identity of Cato, see Jensen et al., 13: 255.

39. "Cato," Letter No. 4, in Jensen et al., 14: 8–9. Irvin, *Robes of Sovereignty*; Willi Paul Adams, *The First American Constitutions: Republican Ideology and the Making of the State Constitutions in the Revolutionary Era* (Chapel Hill: University of North Carolina Press, 1980); Bailyn, *Ideological Origins*, 122–130; Parsons, *Birth of Modern Politics*, 190.

40. See "John DeWitt," Letter No. 3: "To the Free Citizens of the Commonwealth of Massachusetts," *American Herald* (Boston), November 5, 1787, in Jensen et al., *Ratification of the Constitution*, 4:194–199, quote at 196–197.

41. Mason, "Objections to the Constitution," October 7, 1787, in Jensen et al., 8: 45.

42. An Old Whig, Letter No. 5, in Jensen et al., 13: 542.

43. Brutus, Letter No. 3, *New York Journal*, November 15, 1787, and Brutus, Letter No. 10, *New York Journal*, January 24, 1788, in Jensen et al., 14: 120 and 15: 463.

44. Brutus, Letter No. 3, in Jensen et al., 14: 121.

45. Brutus, Letter No. 3, in Jensen et al., 14: 120, 121.

46. Centinel, Letter No. 1, in Jensen et al., 13: 330.

47. Quoted in Storing, *Anti-Federalist*, 21.

48. James Wilson: Speech at a Public Meeting in Philadelphia, October 6, 1787, in Jensen et al., *Ratification of the Constitution*, 13: 339; Maier, *Ratification*, 77–82.

49. Wilson: Speech at a Public Meeting, in Jensen et al., *Ratification of the Constitution*, 13: 344.

50. "A Democratic Federalist," *Independent Gazetteer* (Philadelphia), November 26, 1787, in Jensen et al., 2: 298; Wood, *American Republic*.

51. "Common Sense," *Massachusetts Gazette* (Boston), January 11, 1788, in Jensen et al., *Ratification of the Constitution*, 2: 694.

52. Williamson, "Remarks on the New Plan of Government," *Daily Advertiser* (New York), February 25–27, 1788, in Jensen et al., 16: 205–206; Sheehan and McDowell, *Friends of the Constitution*, 278.

53. A Citizen of New York, [John Jay], April 15, 1788, in Jensen et al., *Ratification of the Constitution*, 20: 928–929.

54. Livingston, quoted in Rakove, *Original Meanings*, 250.

55. Benjamin Rush, "Address to the People of the United States," [n.d.] in Jensen et al., *Ratification of the Constitution*, 13: 46.

56. Wilson, "Speech, December 4, 1787," in Jensen et al., 2: 477.

57. *Poughkeepsie Country Journal* (Poughkeepsie, NY), October 3, 1787, in Jensen et al., 19: 72.

58. "An American Citizen" [Tench Coxe], Letter No. 3, *Philadelphia Independent Gazetteer*, September 29, 1787, in Jensen et al., 13: 272.

59. Edmund Pendleton to James Madison, October 8, 1787, in Jensen et al., 13: 355.

60. Cassius, Letter No. 6, *Massachusetts Gazette* (Boston), December 21, 1787, in Jensen et al., 5: 500–501.

61. "A Foreign Spectator" (Nicholas Collin), "An Essay on the Means of Promoting Federal Sentiments in the United States," Letter No. 25, *Independent Gazetteer* (Philadelphia), September 21, 1787, in Sheehan and McDowell, *Friends of the Constitution*, 49–51.

62. "Americanus I," *Virginia Independent Chronicle* (Richmond), December 5, 1787, in Jensen et al., *Ratification of the Constitution*, 8: 203–204.

63. A Landholder [Oliver Ellsworth], Letter No. 3, *Connecticut Courant* (Hartford), November 19, 1787, in Jensen et al., 3: 463. This essay was reprinted, with minor changes, in the *Massachusetts Gazette* (Boston), December 21, 1787.

64. Ellsworth, "A Landholder," Letter No. 5, *Connecticut Courant* (Hartford), December 3, 1787, in Jensen et al., 14: 337, 339; reprinted in the *Massachusetts Gazette* (Boston), December 15, 1787.

65. Americanus, Letter No. 1, *Virginia Independent Chronicle* (Richmond), December 5, 1787, in Jensen et al., 8: 203.

66. Fabius, [John Dickinson], Letter No. 2, *Pennsylvania Mercury* (Philadelphia), April 15, 1788, in Jensen et al., 17: 124.

67. For an analysis of the role of language in shaping the competing arguments among participants in the ratification debate, see John Howe, *Language and Political Meaning in Revolutionary America* (Amherst: University of Massachusetts Press, 2004), 199–225. I am indebted to Howe's insights for my own analysis of the federalists' treatment of the language of the Constitution. For examples of appeals to the Constitution's "plain" wording, see A Landholder, Letter No. 5, *Connecticut Courant* (Hartford), December 3, 1787, in Jensen et al., *Ratification of the Constitution*, 14: 335; Americanus, Letter No. 1, *New York Daily Advertiser*, November 2, 1787, in Jensen et al., 19: 172; *New York Daily Advertiser*, February 20, 1788, in Jensen et al., 21: 1469.

68. I have chosen to use the Terence Ball edition of *The Federalist* (*The Federalist, With Letters of "Brutus"* [Cambridge, 2003]), and my citations of specific essays will list the essay number and the page number corresponding to this volume. See the editorial note, Ball, *Federalist*, xlvii.

69. Hamilton wrote the majority (fifty-one) of the *Federalist* papers. Publius devoted ten essays to addressing the House of Representatives (*Federalist* 52–61, seven written by Madison, three by Hamilton), five focused on the Senate (*Federalist* 62–66, two each written by Madison and Hamilton, and one written by Jay), and six assessing the judiciary (*Federalist* 78–83, all written by Hamilton).

70. Elaine F. Crane, "Publius in the Provinces: Where was *The Federalist* Reprinted Outside of New York City?" *The William and Mary Quarterly* 3rd Series,

21, no. 4 (October 1964): 589–592; Robert A. Rutland, "The First Great Newspaper Debate: The Constitutional Crisis of 1787–88," *Proceedings of the American Antiquarian Society*, 97, pt. 1 (1987): 53; James Ducayet, "Publius and Federalism: On the Use and Abuse of *The Federalist* in Constitutional Interpretation," *New York University Law Review* 68 (October 1993): 821–869; Bernard Bailyn, *To Begin the World Anew: The Genius and Ambiguities of the American Founders* (New York: Vintage, 2003), 101–125; Trish Loughran, *The Republic in Print: Print Culture in the Era of U.S. Nation Building, 1770–1870* (New York: Columbia University Press, 2007), 105–160; Maier, *Ratification*, 83–85.

71. Hamilton, New York ratifying convention, June 21, 1788, in Harold C. Syrett, et al., *The Papers of Alexander Hamilton*, 27 vols. (New York: Columbia University Press, 1961–87) 1: 37, 38, 39, 40. For Hamilton's intellectual influences, see Ketcham, *Presidents above Party*, 193–198. For other scholarly examinations of Hamilton and the president's role as the people's representative, see Wood, *American Republic*, 547 (who also quotes from Hamilton's New York ratifying convention speech); Gary L. Gregg II, *The Presidential Republic: Executive Representation and Deliberative Democracy* (New York: Rowman & Littlefield, 1997); Raphael, *Mr. President*, 146–149, 150–151.

72. *Federalist 67*: 327, 330.

73. *Federalist 70*: 342.

74. *Federalist 69*: 334; *Federalist 70*: 341, 340–341; *Federalist 77*: 376; *Federalist 67*: 327.

75. *Federalist 70*: 341–342, 343–344.

76. *Federalist 70*: 342; *Federalist 68*: 332.

77. *Federalist 70*: 344, 346.

78. *Federalist 71*: 349.

79. *Federalist 71*: 350.

80. *Federalist 72*: 354.

81. *Federalist 71*: 351.

82. *Federalist 72*: 352.

83. *Federalist 68*: 331, 332, 333; Raphael, *Mr. President*, 146–147.

84. *Federalist 72*: 356.

85. *Federalist 73*: 357, 356.

86. *Federalist 73*: 359.

87. *Federalist 72*: 356; *Federalist 73*: 358.

88. *Federalist 74*: 362, 363–364.

89. *Federalist 75*: 365, 366–367.

90. *Federalist 76*: 370, 371.

91. *Federalist 77*: 376; *Federalist 70*: 347; *Federalist 75*: 366.

92. Wilson, "Convention Debates," in Jensen et al., *Ratification of the Constitution*, 2: 448, 452.

CHAPTER 2. WASHINGTON'S ASCENT AND THE PEOPLE'S ASSENT

1. "The Vice-President," *Gazette of the United States* (New York) April 18–April 22, 1789.

2. Washington to Catharine Sawbridge Macaulay Graham, January 9, 1790, in Dorothy Twohig et al., *The Papers of George Washington—Presidential Series*, 19 vols. to date (Charlottesville: University of Virginia Press, 1987–), 4: 552.

3. For discussion of the eighteenth-century definition of "virtue," see Wood, *Radicalism*, esp. 104–106.

4. "Baltimore, February 13, 1789," *Pennsylvania Mercury and Universal Advertiser* (Philadelphia), February 19, 1789. Reprinted in the *Federal Herald* (Troy, NY), March 2, 1789; *Salem Mercury* (Salem, MA), March 3, 1789; *Massachusetts Spy, or, the Worcester Gazette* (Worcester), March 5, 1789.

5. "United States of America . . . Extract of a Letter from a Gentleman of Good Observation . . . ," *Country Journal* (Poughkeepsie, NY), March 3, 1789.

6. "New-Hampshire. Portsmouth, March 6," *Osborne's New-Hampshire Spy* (Portsmouth), March 6, 1789.

7. "*Extract of a Letter* . . . ," *Boston Gazette*, February 16, 1789.

8. "Philadelphia, February 9," *New-York Daily Gazette* (New York), February 12, 1789. Printed also in the *Federal Gazette and Philadelphia Evening Post*, February 9, 1789.

9. "Extract of a Letter from Lisbon . . ." *Pennsylvania Mercury* (Philadelphia), January 17, 1789; "Philadelphia, 9th February," *Federal Gazette and Philadelphia Evening Post*, February 9, 1789.

10. "The Day," *Massachusetts Centinel* (Boston), March 4, 1789.

11. "Philadelphia, April 28," *Pennsylvania Packet, and Daily Advertiser* (Philadelphia), April 28, 1789.

12. Kaminski and McCaughan, *Great and Good Man*, 108–109, 127.

13. Charles Thomson to Washington, April 14, 1789, in John P. Kaminski and Jill Adair McCaughan, eds., *A Great and Good Man: George Washington in the Eyes of His Contemporaries* (New York: Rowman & Littlefield, 2007), 102; Thomson, and Washington's reply, also quoted in E. Larson, *George Washington*, 88.

14. "Pennsylvania. Philadelphia, March 25," *Massachusetts Spy* (Worcester), April 9, 1789.

15. Census data can be viewed at the "Return of the Whole Number of Persons within the Several Districts of the United States" (Philadelphia: J. Philips, 1793), https://www2.census.gov/prod2/decennial/documents/1790a.pdf. I am including New York's population of white males over sixteen in the total, even though New York did not cast any electoral votes in the election of 1789. It had ratified the Constitution by the time of Washington's election, and even briefly served as the seat of government and the site where Washington took the oath of office. I am also including white males over sixteen in Kentucky (which was part of Virginia until it became a state in 1792) and Maine (which was part of Massachusetts until it became a state in 1820). Without these populations, the total would fall even more woefully short of the "millions" touted in publications celebrating Washington's election. See the electoral map at https://www.presidency.ucsb.edu/statistics/elections/1789.

My total ignores the fact that the "all other free persons" column includes free black women, and both the "free white females" column and the "all other free persons" column would include children, who were not eligible to vote. That is the point. Even including juvenile white females from states that enfranchised women, and "all other free persons"—including black women, and black men who lacked the property requirements to vote—from states that enfranchised free black men, the total still falls well short of the "millions" celebrated in public accounts of the election. Because Kentucky was a part of Virginia, and Virginia explicitly disfranchised free black men, I am also excluding all 114 "other free persons" in Kentucky from the total. For an analysis of voting restrictions state by state, see Donald Ratcliffe, "The Right to Vote and the Rise of Democracy, 1787–1828," *Journal of the Early Republic* 33 (Summer 2013): 219–254.

16. Washington to John Adams, May 10, 1789, in Twohig et al., *Papers of Washington—Presidential Series*, 2: 245, 246.

17. For a recent analysis of these tours, see Breen, *George Washington's Journey.*

18. This description of Washington's tours has become standard fare in scholarly analysis. See, for example, Waldstreicher, *Perpetual Fetes*, 121; Kaminski and McCaughan, *Great and Good Man*, 145–151, esp. 146; and Moats, *Celebrating the Republic*, 35–62, esp. 51–54.

19. Breen, *George Washington's Journey*, 1–12, quote at 2.

20. "Beyond Raphael's Description," *Gazette of the United States* (Philadelphia), April 25–29, 1789, in Kaminski and McCaughan, *Great and Good Man*, 116.

21. For examples, see "Welcome to Newburyport" and "Hantonia Hosts the President," in Kaminski and McCaughan, *Great and Good Man*, 168–169, 169–171.

22. "Columbia's Favourite Son," in Kaminski and McCaughan, *Great and Good Man*, 155.

23. "A 'Sensation Better Felt Than Expressed,'" in Kaminski and McCaughan, 196.

24. "Hantonia Hosts the President," *New Hampshire Gazette*, November 5, 1789 (reprinted in the Boston *Independent Chronicle*, November 12, 1789, and the *Gazette of the United States*, November 14, 1789), "Anticipating the Celebration," *Massachusetts Centinel*, October 21, 1789, and "The Chieftan Comes," *Massachusetts Centinel*, November 7, 1789, in Kaminski and McCoughan, *Great and Good Man*, 171, 152, 174.

25. Kenneth R. Bowling, "A Tub to the Whale: The Founding Fathers and the Adoption of the Federal Bill of Rights" *Journal of the Early Republic* 8, no. 3 (Autumn 1988): 223–251.

26. "Philadelphia, April 22," *Independent Gazetteer* (Philadelphia), April 22, 1789.

27. "To His Excellency," *Federal Gazette and Philadelphia Evening Post*, April 23, 1789.

28. "Philadelphia, April 28," *Pennsylvania Packet, and Daily Advertiser* (Philadelphia), April 28, 1789.

29. "Savannah, June 11. The Address of the Senate to the President of the United States," *Georgia Gazette* (Savannah), June 11, 1789.

30. "To His Excellency George Washington, Esq. . . . Sir, We, the Judges of the Supreme Court of the State of Pennsylvania . . ." and "His Excellency's Answer," *Federal Gazette and Philadelphia Evening Post*, April 23, 1789.

31. "To His Excellency George Washington, Esquire . . ." and "To Which his Excellency was pleased to make the following reply," *Freeman's Journal; or, North-American Intelligencer* (Philadelphia), April 22, 1789.

32. "April 16, 1789. His Excellency's Answer," *Pennsylvania Packet, and Daily Advertiser*, April 28, 1789.

33. "To the President of the United States," *Freeman's Journal, or the North-American Intelligencer* (Philadelphia), July 15, 1789.

34. For this insight, I am indebted to Moats, *Celebrating the Republic*, esp. 35–62; and Brendan McConville, *The King's Three Faces: The Rise and Fall of Royal America, 1688–1776* (Chapel Hill: University of North Carolina Press, 2006).

35. "Never To Be Outshone," in Kaminski and McCaughan, *Great and Good Man*, 135; Moats, *Celebrating the Republic*, 25, 55; Brendan McConville, *The King's Three Faces: The Rise and Fall of Royal America, 1688–1776* (Chapel Hill: University of North Carolina Press, 2006).

36. "No Need for Titles," *New Hampshire Spy*, October 31, 1789 (reprinted in the *New York Journal*, November 19; and the Philadelphia *American Museum*), in Kaminski and McCaughan, *Great and Good Man*, 167.

37. *Gazette of the United States*, November 18, 1789, in Kaminski and McCaughan, 178; Moats, *Celebrating the Republic*, 35–62.

38. "Answer to Gov.'s Message," *Salem Mercury* (Salem, MA), June 30, 1789.

39. *Daily Advertiser* (New York), August 5, 1789.

40. "To George Washington, President of the United States of America," *Connecticut Journal* (New Haven), October 21, 1789. Reprinted in the *New-York Daily Gazette* (New York), October 26, 1789.

41. Waldstreicher, *Perpetual Fetes*, 119–123, quote at 123.

42. "A Second Time Called Upon," *Philadelphia Federal Gazette*, April 23, 1789 (reprinted, *New York Daily Gazette*, April 30, 1789), in Kaminski and McCaughan, *Great and Good Man*, 108; "Alexis," (Philadelphia, April 6, 1787), in Jensen et al., *Ratification of the Constitution*, 13: 78.

43. Dunbar, *Never Caught*; Breen, *George Washington's Journey*, 237–239; Mary V. Thompson, *"The Only Unavoidable Subject of Regret": George Washington, Slavery, and the Enslaved Community at Mount Vernon* (Charlottesville: University of Virginia Press, 2019), 275.

44. The foundational study of this process remains Edmund S. Morgan's *American Slavery*.

45. Jefferson's *Notes on the State of Virginia* can be accessed at https://avalon.law.yale.edu/18th_century/jeffvir.asp. Banneker to Jefferson, August 19, 1791, in Boyd et al., *Papers of Thomas Jefferson*, 22: 49, 50. For background on Banneker, see Ibram X. Kendi, *Stamped From the Beginning: The Definitive History of Racist Ideas in America* (New York: Nation Books, 2016), 120–123.

46. "Philadelphia, April 22," *New-York Daily Gazette* (New York), April 27, 1789.

47. "Philadelphia, April 28," *Pennsylvania Packet, and Daily Advertiser*, April 28, 1789.

48. See "Return of the Whole Number of Persons within the Several Districts of the United States" (Philadelphia: J. Philips, 1793), found at https://www2.census.gov/prod2/decennial/documents/1790a.pdf.

49. Washington to John Adams, May 10, 1789, in Twohig et al., *Papers of Washington—Presidential Series*, 2: 245, 246.

50. Washington to John Adams, May 10, 1789, in Twohig et al., 2: 246, 247.

51. Washington to David Stuart, June 15, 1790, in Twohig et al., 5: 523–527.

52. Washington to John Adams, May 10, 1789, in Twohig et al., 2: 245.

53. May 9, 1789, in Kenneth R. Bowling and Helen E. Veit, eds., *The Diary of William Maclay and Other Notes on Senate Debates* (Baltimore: Johns Hopkins University Press, 1988), 31. The "harrange" comment is at 30. The best book-length scholarly analysis of the title controversy is Kathleen Bartoloni-Tuazon's *For Fear of an Elective King: George Washington and the Presidential Title Controversy of 1789* (Ithaca, NY: Cornell University Press, 2014).

54. Fisher Ames to George Richards Minot, May 14, 1789, in Allen, *Works of Fisher Ames*, 1: 582.

55. May 9, 1789, in Bowling and Veit, *Diary of William Maclay*, 30, 31. For Maclay's morose personality, and his "acid" writing style, see Freeman, *Affairs of Honor*, 12–13.

56. May 9, 1789, in Bowling and Veit, *Diary of William Maclay*, 31–32.

57. For discussion of Genet, see Harry Ammon, *The Genet Mission:* (New York: W. W. Norton, 1973); Freeman, *Affairs of Honor*, 91–98; Pasley, *First Presidential Contest*, 72–82; Philip S. Foner, *The Democratic-Republican Societies: A Documentary Sourcebook of Constitutions, Declarations, Resolutions, and Toasts* (Westport, CT: Greenwood Press, 1976), 1–51; Cotlar, *Tom Paine's America*; Max Edling, *A Revolution in Favor of Government: Origins of the U.S. Constitution and the Making of the American State* (New York: Oxford University Press, 2003).

58. Robert J. Spitzer, "The President's Veto Power," in Cronin, *Inventing the American Presidency*, 172–173; Raphael, *Mr. President*, 175–176; Steele, *Jefferson and American Nationhood*, 203–206; Elkins and McKitrick, *The Age of Federalism: The Early American Republic, 1788–1800* (New York: Oxford University Press, 1995), 223–244. For Hamilton's role as a proponent of a powerful state, see Edling, *Revolution in Favor*.

59. Rush, "Address to the People of the United States," in Jensen et al., *Ratification of the Constitution*, 13: 47.

60. See Jensen et al., 13: 45–46.

61. January 14, 1790, in Bowling and Veit, *Diary of William Maclay*, 183; Wood, *Empire of Liberty*, 94; Raphael, *Mr. President*, 177.

62. Lisle A. Rose, *Prologue to Democracy: The Federalists in the South, 1789–1800* (Lexington: University of Kentucky Press, 1968), 32–47. See also James H. Broussard, *The Southern Federalists, 1800–1816* (Baton Rouge: Louisiana State University Press, 1978).

63. "Opinion on the Constitutionality of a National Bank," February 15, 1791, in Boyd et al., *Papers of Thomas Jefferson*, 19: 279, 280, 277. On the early use of the veto, see Spitzer, "President's Veto Power," in Cronin, *Inventing the American Presidency*, 172–173.

64. Jefferson, "Anas," in Merrill D. Peterson, ed., *Thomas Jefferson: Writings* (New York: Library of America, 1984), 670.

65. Jefferson to George Washington, September 9, 1792, in Boyd et al., *Papers of Thomas Jefferson*, 24: 353; Leonard D. White, *The Federalists: A Study in Administrative History* (New York: Macmillan, 1956), 50–66, 116–127, 67.

66. Steele, *Jefferson and American Nationhood*, 203–206; Elkins and McKitrick, *Age of Federalism*, 236–237; Fred I. Greenstein, *Inventing the Job of President: Leadership Style from George Washington to Andrew Jackson* (Princeton, NJ: Princeton University Press, 2009), 19.

67. Pasley, *"Tyranny of Printers,"* 66–73.

68. On Madison's *National Gazette* essays, see Cornell, *Other Founders*; and Colleen Sheehan, *James Madison and the Spirit of Republican Self-Government* (New York: Cambridge University Press, 2009).

69. "Spirit of Governments"; "A Candid State of Parties," "Republican Distribution of Citizens," February 18, 1792, September 26, 1792, March 3, 1792, in William T. Hutchinson et al., *Papers of James Madison—Congressional Series*, 1st ser., Chicago, 1962–1977 (vols. 1–10), 2nd ser., Charlottesville, VA, 1977–1991 (vols. 11–17), 14: 233–234, 371, 372, 246.

70. "New-York. Friday, January 21, 1791. In the House of Delegates," *Daily Advertiser* (New York, NY), January 21, 1791. Reprinted in the *Gazette of the United States*, January 26, 1791.

71. Washington, First Annual Message, January 8, 1790, in Twohig et al., *Papers of Washington—Presidential Series*, 4: 544. For newspaper coverage of the administration's interaction with Indian tribes and congressional debates over military, see, for example, the *National Gazette* (Philadelphia), April 5 and April 9, 1792; and the *Potowmack Guardian* (Martinsburg, VA), January 14, 21, and 28, 1793. For the size of the military, see L. White, *Federalists*, 146.

72. For Washington's career with, and views toward, Indians, see Colin G. Calloway, *The Indian World of George Washington: The First President, the First Americans, and the Birth of the Nation* (New York: Oxford University Press, 2018). For the Congressional debate, see *Potowmack Guardian* (Martinsburg, VA), January 14, 21, 28, and February 4, 1793.

73. "Congress. House of Representatives," *Potowmack Guardian* (Martinsburg, VA), January 7, 1793.

74. "United States. Congress," and "Martinsburg, Feb. 4," *"Potowmack Guardian,"* February 4, 1793.

75. Hutchinson et al., *Papers of James Madison—Congressional Series*, 14: 233–234, 371, 372, 246; Calloway, *Indian World*. For military "ardor" during the War of 1812, see Eustace, *1812*.

76. Jefferson to James Madison, July 7, 1793, quoted in Michael Lienesch, "Thomas Jefferson and the Democratic Experience: The Origins of the Partisan Press, Popular Political Parties, and Public Opinion," in Onuf, *Jeffersonian Legacies* (Charlottesville: University Press of Virginia, 1993), 334. "Introduction," in Foner, *Democratic-Republican Societies*, 23. Ammon, *Genet Mission*; Freeman, *Affairs of Honor*, 91–98; Pasley, *First Presidential Contest*, 72–82. For Genet quote, see Waldstreicher, *Perpetual Fetes*, 134. The text of the Neutrality Proclamation, as well as Hamilton's ensuing "Pacificus" essays defending it, and Madison's "Helvidius" essays criticizing it, have been conveniently collected from the *Papers of Alexander Hamilton* and the *Papers of James Madison* respectively into one slim volume, edited by Morton J. Frisch, *The Pacificus-Helvidius Debates of 1793–1794: Toward the Completion of the American Founding* (Indianapolis: Liberty Fund, 2007). My citations correspond to this volume. For background on the controversy and an overview of the documents, see the introduction, vii–xv. For the proclamation, see p. 1.

77. Jefferson to James Madison, July 7, 1793, quoted in Michael Lienesch, "Thomas Jefferson and the Democratic Experience: The Origins of the Partisan Press, Popular Political Parties, and Public Opinion," in Onuf, *Jeffersonian Legacies*,

334; "Introduction," in Foner, *Democratic-Republican Societies*, 23; Freeman, *Affairs of Honor*, 91–98.

78. "Pacificus No. 1," June 29, 1793, in Frisch, *Pacificus-Helvidius Debates*, 13.

79. For Hamilton quotes, see "Defense of the President's Neutrality Proclamation," in Frisch, 3, 4–5. For Hamilton's argument that the president's authority was limited only by what was "expressed" in the Constitution, see Frisch, 13.

80. Hamilton, "Defense of the President's Neutrality Proclamation," in Frisch, 3.

81. Pasley, *First Presidential Contest*, 72–82.

82. Twohig et al., *Papers of Washington—Presidential Series*, 12: 648; Elkins and McKitrick, *Age of Federalism*, 821n157.

83. Twohig et al., *Papers of Washington—Presidential Series*, 12: 647, 648; 13: 17, 34.

84. Twohig et al., *Papers of Washington—Presidential Series*, 13: 19; Elkins and McKitrick, *Age of Federalism*, 236–237, 817n117.

85. Twohig et al., *Papers of Washington—Presidential Series*, 13: 34; 12: 647–648; 13: 18.

86. Twohig et al., 13: 18, 19.

87. Philip S. Foner, "The Democratic-Republican Societies: An Introduction," in Foner, *Democratic-Republican Societies*, 3–51. See also 439–441 for a list of members' occupations. Analyses of the Democratic-Republican societies, and voluntary associations in general, that have particularly influenced my interpretation include Cornell, *Other Founders*, esp. 195–200, 217–218; "Introduction," in Foner, *Democratic-Republican Societies*, 3–51; Neem, *Creating a Nation of Joiners: Democracy and Civil Society in Early National Massachusetts* (Cambridge: Harvard University Press, 2008); and Kevin Butterfield, "Unbound By Law: Association and Autonomy in the Early American Republic," PhD Dissertation, Washington University in St. Louis, 2010. See Eugene P. Link, *The Democratic-Republican Societies, 1770–1800* (Columbia University Press, 1942), 13–15, for a list of known societies begun between 1793 and 1800.

88. Link, *Democratic-Republican Societies*, 13–15. "Introduction," in Foner, *Democratic-Republican Societies*, xi–xii, 3–51, esp. 30–31; Pasley, "*Tyranny of Printers*," 90–92, quote at 88.

89. "Thursday the 9th of January, 1794," in Foner, *Democratic-Republican Societies*, 69. For further examples of the use of "firmness," "energy," and "union," see 77, 85, 93, 96.

90. See, for example, "Democratic Society of Canaan, Columbia County, New York," March 8, 1794, *New York Journal* (New York), March 8, 1794, in Foner, *Democratic-Republican Societies*, 238.

91. "At a meeting of a number of citizens of the county of Ulster, in the state of New-York," *New York Journal* (New York), January 18, 1794, in Foner, *Democratic-Republican Societies*, 236.

92. Neem, *Nation of Joiners*, 45–46, 47–48; "To Friends and Fellow Citizens, April 11, 1793," *National Gazette* (Philadelphia), April 13, 1793, in Foner, *Democratic-Republican Societies*, 53.

93. "Toasts Drunk at a Celebration on the Recapture of Toulon, March 20, 1794," *New York Journal* (New York), March 25, 1794, in Foner, *Democratic-Republican Societies*, 168.

94. Washington to Burgess Ball, Sept. 25, 1794, in Twohig et al., *Papers of Washington—Presidential Series*, 16: 723.

95. Washington to Burgess Ball, Sept. 25, 1794, in Twohig et al., 16: 722, 723; Foner, *Democratic-Republican Societies*, 3–51. For an overview of the "whiskey rebellion," see Slaughter, *Whiskey Rebellion*.

96. "Introduction," in Foner, *Democratic-Republican Societies*, 3–51; Martin, *Government by Dissent*, esp. 88–89. See also Pasley, *First Presidential Contest*, 82–100.

97. Richard Hofstadter, *The Idea of a Party System: The Rise of a Legitimate Opposition in the United States, 1780–1840* (Berkeley: University of California Press, 1969).

CHAPTER 3. CLAIMING THE PRESIDENCY FOR THE PEOPLE IN THE JAY TREATY CONTROVERSY

1. Jerald A. Combs, *The Jay Treaty: Political Background of the Founding Fathers* (Berkeley: University of California Press, 19700, 24–25, 26–27, 40–41, 47, 76, 114–115, 122, 128; Todd Estes, *The Jay Treaty Debate, Public Opinion, and the Evolution of American Political Culture* (Amherst: University of Massachusetts Press, 2008), 23–24. I refer to supporters and critics of the treaty by the respective party affiliations Federalist and Republican, using the terms interchangeably with "supporters" (for Federalists) and "critics" (for Republicans) and their synonyms, despite the fact that variation existed within each party regarding a host of political issues. The debate over the Jay treaty revealed a partisan divide that was years in the making.

2. The text of the treaty can be found at http://avalon.law.yale.edu/18th_century /jay.asp. Hamilton, "The Defence No. 1, [July 22, 1795]," in Syrett, *Papers of Alexander Hamilton*, 18: 481–482; Elkins and McKitrick, *Age of Federalism*, 236–237; Todd Estes, "'The Most Bewitching Piece of Parliamentary Oratory': Fisher Ames's Jay Treaty Speech Reconsidered," *Historical Journal of Massachusetts* 28, no. 1 (Winter 2000): 3–4; Estes, *Jay Treaty Debate*, esp. 24–32, 84, 85; Combs, *Jay Treaty*, 128, 134. Estes also cites Combs, *Jay Treaty*, 151–160; and Elkins and McKitrick, *Age of Federalism*, 409–415. See also Donald M. Golove, "Treaty-Making and the Nation: The Historical Foundations of the Nationalist Conception of the Treaty Power," *Michigan Law Review* 98, no. 5 (March 2000): 1075–1319.

3. Washington to Alexander Hamilton, July 29, 1795, in Twohig et al., *Papers of Washington—Presidential Series*, 18: 459; Washington to John Adams, August 20, 1795, in Twohig et al., 18: 566; Combs, *Jay Treaty*, 165–67, 177.

4. Belisarius, No. 3, *Aurora General Advertiser* (Philadelphia) September 22, 1795; "Massachusetts. Boston, July 13: Town-Meeting, on the Treaty," *Political Gazette* (Newburyport, MA), July 16, 1795; Hancock, No. 2, *Argus, & Greenleaf's New Daily Advertiser* (New York), August 29, 1795; Combs, *Jay Treaty*, 161–162; Estes, *Jay Treaty Debate*, 33–34. For an example of a claim of "almost unanimous" opposition to the treaty, see Pittachus, No. 4, *Aurora General Advertiser* (Philadelphia), September 26, 1795. For a rebuttal to such claims, see "Dissent," *Albany Register* (Albany, NY), August 28, 1795.

5. The best study to date of the political importance of newspapers in the early United States is Pasley, "*Tyranny of Printers.*"

6. See the letter "From Boston Citizen," in Twohig et al., *Papers of Washington— Presidential Series*, 18: 327–333, quote at 327, reprinted in *The Courier* (Boston) 1, no. 15: 18–19, July 15, 1795; and "From Fredericksburg, Va., Citizens," in Twohig et al., 18: 560. Estes, "Most Bewitching Piece," 3–4.

7. "Dissent," *Albany Register* (Albany, NY), August 28, 1795. See also "From the New York Journal, &c.," *Richmond Chronicle* (Richmond, VA), July 25, 1795; "Extract of a Letter," *Greenleaf's New York Journal and Patriotic Register* (New York), August 1, 1795. On Washington's decision, see Estes, *Jay Treaty Debate*, 96–103.

8. "From the New York Journal, &c.," *Richmond Chronicle* (Richmond, VA), July 25, 1795; Portius 1, *Aurora General Advertiser* (Philadelphia), September 24, 1795. For Washington's efforts to cultivate a strong national union through his presidential actions, see Moats, *Celebrating the Republic*, and, more recently, Breen, *George Washington's Journey*.

9. "From the Aurora," *Argus, & Greenleaf's New Daily Advertiser* (New York), August 29, 1795; Portius, No. 1, *Aurora General Advertiser* (Philadelphia), September 24, 1795.

10. *American Remembrancer; or, an Impartial Collection of ESSAYS, RESOLVES, SPEECHES, &c. Relative, or Having Affinity, to the TREATY With GREAT BRITAIN.* 3 vols. (Philadelphia, PA, 1795), 133, 113. Estes, "Most Bewitching Piece," esp. 19–22; Estes, *Jay Treaty Debate*, 29, 178–179; Pasley, *First Presidential Contest*, 108, 150–151.

11. "Massachusetts. Boston, July 13: Town-Meeting, on the Treaty," *Political Gazette* (Newburyport, MA), July 16, 1795; Pasley, *First Presidential Contest*, 123, 124.

12. Atticus, No. 9, *Aurora General Advertiser* (Philadelphia), October 22, 1795; Estes, *Jay Treaty Debate*, 84.

13. Atticus, No. 9, *Aurora General Advertiser* (Philadelphia), October 22, 1795; Pittachus, No. 2, *Aurora General Advertiser*, September 18, 1795; Belisarius, No. 2, *Aurora General Advertiser*, September 15, 1795.

14. "To the President of the United States" Portius, [No. 2?], *Aurora General Advertiser*, October 12, 1795; "From the (Boston) Chronicle: An Essay on Jacobinical Thinkers," in *American Remembrancer; or, an Impartial Collection of ESSAYS, RESOLVES, SPEECHES, &c. Relative, or Having Affinity, to the TREATY With GREAT BRITAIN*, 3 vols. (Philadelphia, 1795), 2: 141.

15. "From the Boston Gazette, &c.," *Aurora General Advertiser* (Philadelphia), September 7, 1795; Valerius No. 1, *Greenleaf's New York Journal and Patriotic Register* (New York), August 25, 1795; Valerius No. 8, *Aurora General Advertiser*, October 29, 1795.

16. Washington's address to the Boston selectmen can be found in Twohig et al., *Papers of Washington—Presidential Series*, 18: 441–443. The introduction to this piece notes that Washington used this answer as a template for subsequent responses. The *Centinel* piece, quoted here, is located at the Fred W. Smith National Library for the Study of George Washington at Mount Vernon, August 19, 1795.

17. Belisarius, No. 3, *Aurora General Advertiser* (Philadelphia), September 22,

1795; Pittachus, No. 21, *Aurora General Advertiser*, November 26, 1795; Pittachus, No. 2, *Aurora General Advertiser*, September 18, 1795; Valerius, No. 6, *Aurora General Advertiser*, October 8, 1795. Pittachus even used the word "aloof" to describe Washington's comportment. See Pittachus, No. 20, *Aurora General Advertiser*, November 23, 1795. For a more sympathetic reading of Washington's public addresses to treaty critics, see Todd Estes, "The Art of Presidential Leadership: George Washington and the Jay Treaty," *Virginia Magazine of History and Biography* 109, no. 2 (2001): 127–158, esp. 135–138.

18. Pittachus, No. 4, *Aurora General Advertiser* (Philadelphia), September, 26, 1795; Pittachus, No. 21, *Aurora General Advertiser*, November 26, 1795.

19. Pittachus, No. 18, *Aurora General Advertiser* (Philadelphia), November 18, 1795; Atticus, No. 2, *Aurora General Advertiser* (Philadelphia), July 23, 1795; Valerius, No. 5, *Aurora General Advertiser* (Philadelphia), September 25, 1795; Hancock, No. 2, *Argus, & Greenleaf's New Daily Advertiser* (New York), August 29, 1795.

20. *Greenleaf's New York Journal* (New York), August 1, 1795; Franklin, *Letters of Franklin*, 42–43, 38–39; Pittachus, No. 2, *Aurora General Advertiser* (Philadelphia), September 18, 1795; Valerius, No. 8, *Aurora General Advertiser*, October 29, 1795. For the Federalist use of the phrase "man of the people" in praise of Washington's endorsement of the treaty, see "Lansingburgh, August 25," *Potowmack Guardian* (Martinsville, VA), September 12, 1795. The letters of Franklin are sometimes attributed to Alexander James Dallas, though questions remain about the authorship. See Elkins and McKitrick, *Age of Federalism*, 833–834n112; Pasley, *First Presidential Contest*, 110.

21. Pittachus, No. 2, *Aurora General Advertiser* (Philadelphia), September 18, 1795; Belisarius, No. 5, *Aurora General Advertiser*, October 14, 1795.

22. Atticus, No. 2, *Aurora General Advertiser* (Philadelphia), July 23, 1795; "Massachusetts. Boston, July 13: Town-Meeting, on the Treaty," *Political Gazette* (Newburyport, MA), July 16, 1795; Hancock, No. 2, *Argus, & Greenleaf's New Daily Advertiser* (New York), August 29, 1795.

23. See the text of the treaty at http://avalon.law.yale.edu/18th_century/jay.asp; "From the Chronicle. To the Yeomanry of the United States," *American Mercury* (Hartford, CT), August 17, 1795.

24. "For the New-York Journal, & C. Correspondence Concluded from September 19," *Greenleaf's New York Journal*, September 26, 1795; "From the Argus, A New-York Paper," *Philadelphia Gazette*, July 29, 1795.

25. "For the Vermont Gazette," *Vermont Gazette* (Bennington), August 28, 1795; "From the (Phi.) Aurora," *Rural Repository* (Leominster, MA), November 5, 1795; Elkins and McKitrick, *Age of Federalism*, 236–237, 817n117, 821n157; Steele, *Jefferson and American Nationhood*, 203–206.

26. Ames to Wolcott, July 9, 1795, in Allen, *Works of Fisher Ames*, 2: 1107. For an account of a crowd burning Jay in effigy, see Estes, *Jay Treaty Debate*, 75. The story of Jay's remark is mentioned in numerous accounts of the Jay treaty. See, for example, James MacGregor Burns and Susan Dunn, *George Washington* (New York: Times Books, 2004), 111; and Ralph Ketcham, *James Madison: A Biography* (Charlottesville: University Press of Virginia, 1990), 357.

27. Valerius, No. 8, *Aurora General Advertiser* Philadelphia), October 29, 1795;

"Extract of a Letter from Philadelphia, July 29," *Greenleaf's New York Journal* (New York), August 1, 1795. Pasley, *First Presidential Contest*, 129, 114.

28. "To the Editors of the Baltimore Telegraphe," *Aurora General Advertiser* (Philadelphia), May 4, 1796. For the account of the meeting in which Hamilton was struck, see "July 20. Town Meeting," *New Hampshire and Vermont Journal* (Walpole, NH), August 4, 1795. Joanne Freeman notes that the story of Hamilton's encounter might be fictitious. But even if untrue, it exemplifies the very real capacity for violence that groups critical of the treaty possessed. See Freeman, *Affairs of Honor*, xiii, 295n1.

29. "For the New-York Journal, & C. Correspondence Concluded from September 19," *Greenleaf's New York Journal* (New York), September 26, 1795 (quote); "New-York, July 15," *Richmond Chronicle* (VA), July 25, 1795; "From the Chronicle. To the Yeomanry of the United States," *American Mercury* (Hartford, CT), August 17, 1795.

30. "Philadelphia, July 15," *Richmond Chronicle* (VA), July 25, 1795.

31. Franklin, *Letters of Franklin, on the Conduct of the Executive, and the Treaty Negociated, by the Chief Justice of the United States with the Court of Great Britain* (Philadelphia, [1795]), Letter 9, 31–32.

32. "For the New-York Journal, & C. Correspondence Concluded from September 19," *Greenleaf's New York Journal and Patriotic Register* (New York), September 26, 1795.

33. Franklin, *Letters of Franklin*, Letter 8, 28; Valerius, No. 6, *Aurora General Advertiser* (Philadelphia), October 8, 1795.

34. Pittachus, 21, *Aurora General Advertiser*, November 26, 1795.

35. Beckley's Calm Observer essays can be found in Gerard W. Gawalt, ed., *Justifying Jefferson: The Political Writings of John James Beckley* (Washington, DC: Library of Congress, 1995), 93–95, 102–113. The first appeared in the New York *Minerva*, in mid-July, 1795. The rest were first printed in the *Aurora* in late October and early November. The essay quoted here first appeared in the *Aurora* on October 23, 1795, and can be found in *Justifying Jefferson*, 102–105. It was reprinted under the headline "From the Aurora, to Oliver Wolcott" in the *Argus, & Greenleaf's New Daily Advertiser* (New York), October 26, 1795; Pasley, *First Presidential Contest*, 141–143.

36. Atticus, No. 9, *Aurora General Advertiser* (Philadelphia) October 22, 1795; Valerius, No. 7, *Aurora General Advertiser*, October 21, 1795.

37. Ames, "Speech on the Jay Treaty," April 28, 1796, in Allen, *Works of Fisher Ames*, 2: 1152.

38. Ames, "Speech on the Jay Treaty," April 28, 1796, in Allen, *Works of Fisher Ames*, 2: 1173, 1174. Estes, "Most Bewitching Piece," 1–22. For Ames's physical description, see 8n11, and Sandra M. Gustafson, *Eloquence Is Power: Oratory and Performance in Early America* (Chapel Hill: University of North Carolina Press, 2000), 236–246. See also Estes, "Art of Presidential Leadership," 127–158; and Pasley, *First Presidential Contest*, 162–172.

39. Ames, "Speech on the Jay Treaty," April 28, 1796, in Allen, *Works of Fisher Ames*, 2: 1174–1175.

40. Estes, "Most Bewitching Piece," 1–22; Gustafson, *Eloquence Is Power*, 236–246; Pasley, *First Presidential Contest*, 168–172, 271–272, 331–335.

CHAPTER 4. JEFFERSON'S "WANT OF FIRMNESS"

1. Washington to David Humphreys, June 12, 1796 (copy), Manuscript Collection, courtesy of Fred W. Smith National Library for the Study of George Washington at Mount Vernon, and the Mount Vernon Ladies' Association. Original at Library of Congress. This letter should not be confused with a similar letter, attributed to Washington, dated June 1, 1796. The June 1 letter is a suspected forgery. I am thankful to the staff at the Washington Library, especially Michele Lee, former special collections librarian at the Washington Library, and Neal Millikan, former assistant editor of the George Washington Papers, Presidential Series, for making me aware of the dubious nature of this letter, and for providing me with the library's copy of the genuine letter.

2. For my indebtedness to Jeffrey L. Pasley's marvelous book *First Presidential Contest*, see my acknowledgments.

3. See Pasley, especially 225, 268–273, 331–333. For public perceptions of Jefferson during the election of 1796, see also R. McDonald, *Confounding Father*, 43–64.

4. Bradburn, *Citizenship Revolution*; Steele, *Jefferson and American Nationhood*; Parkinson, *Common Cause*; Smith-Rosenberg, *This Violent Empire*; Nancy Isenberg, *White Trash: The 400-Year Untold History of Class in America* (New York: Penguin, 2017); Calloway, *Indian World*; Morgan, *American Slavery, American Freedom*.

5. Bradford and Keith, *Christian faith of the people of God, called in scorn, Quakers in Rhode-Island (who are in unity with all faithfull brethren of the same profession in all parts of the world) vindicated from the calumnies of Christian Lodowick, that formerly was of that profession, but is lately fallen there-from. And also from the base forgeries, and wicked slanders of Cotton Mather, called a Minister, at Boston . . . To which is added, some testimonies of our antient Friends to the true Christ of God; collected out of their printed books, for the further convincing of our opposers, that it is (and hath been) our constant and firm belief to expect salvation by the man Christ Jesus that was outwardly crucified without the gates of Jerusalem.* (Philadelphia, 1692); Philadelphia Council of Safety, *In Council of Safety, Philadelphia, December 7, 1776. Whereas the safety and security of every state depends on the virtuous exertions of individuals in its defence . . . Therefore resolved, that no excuse ought to be admitted or deemed sufficient against marching with the militia at this time, except sickness, infirmity of body . . .* (Philadelphia, 1776); Hunter, *By His Excellency Robert Hunter, Esq; captain general and governour in chief of the provinces of New-York, New-Jersey . . . a proclamation. Considering that true religion and piety are the only firm foundations of the prosperity of any people, and irreligion, immorality and prophaneness the causes of their misery and destruction, are truths attested by the Holy Scriptures, and confirmed by the suffrages of all ages. . . . Given under my hand and seal at Fort Anne in New-York this twelfth day of January . . . annoq; Dom. 1711* (New York: William Bradford), 1711.

6. Samuel Johnson, Jr., *A School Dictionary, Being a Compendium of the Latest and Most Improved Dictionaries. . . .* (New Haven, 1797), 73, 99; Thomas Sheridan, *A Complete Dictionary of the English Language* (Philadelphia, 1789) [entry pages unnumbered].

7. Declaration of Independence (1776); Travers, *Celebrating the Fourth*, 139.

8. François Furstenberg, *In the Name of the Father: Washington's Legacy, Slavery,*

and the Making of a Nation (New York: Penguin, 2006), 207–208; Morgan, *American Slavery, American Freedom.* For a more in-depth analysis of the gendered and racialized dimensions of American nationhood, see Smith-Rosenberg, *This Violent Empire.*

9. Washington to James Madison, May 20, 1792, in Kaminski and McCaughan, *Great and Good Man,* 208–209; Pasley, *First Presidential Contest,* 183.

10. "The Farewell," in Kaminski and McCaughan, *Great and Good Man,* 218, 233, 220–221.

11. "The Farewell," in Kaminski and McCoughan, *Great and Good Man,* 223; Pasley, *First Presidential Contest.*

12. Pasley, *First Presidential Contest,* 12–13.

13. *Gazette of the United States* (Philadelphia, PA), December 4, 1795.

14. *Gazette of the United States,* September 23, 1796.

15. *Gazette of the United States,* January 22, 1796.

16. *Gazette of the United States,* November 21, 1796.

17. *Gazette of the United States,* December 5, 1796.

18. Pasley, *First Presidential Contest,* 2, 17, 19–20; Ketcham, *Presidents above Party,* 4–5.

19. "It requires no talent at divination to decide who will be candidates for the chair," the *Argus, Greenleaf's New Daily Advertiser* announced on September 13. "THOMAS JEFFERSON and JOHN ADAMS will be the men." Kaminski and McCaughan, *Great and Good Man,* 198–199; *Argus, Greenleaf's New Daily Advertiser* (New York, NY), September 13, 1796.

20. Gordon S. Wood, "Interests and Disinterestedness in the Making of the Constitution," in Richard Beeman, Stephen Botein, and Edward C. Carter II, eds., *Beyond Confederation: Origins of the American Constitution and American National Identity* (Chapel Hill: University of North Carolina Press, 1987), 69–110; Wood, *Radicalism,* 292–96; Pasley, *First Presidential Contest,* 182–223, 316–317.

21. Pasley, *First Presidential Contest,* 316–324, 360–362. Eighteen thousand electoral votes for Georgia's four victorious electors is a deliberately conservative count, because there is some variance in the numbers available. Data on Georgia electors can be found at the New Nation Votes website through Tufts University and the American Antiquarian Society: http://elections.lib.tufts.edu/catalog/tufts:ga .electors.1796#note_1. According to the 1790 census, the free white population of Georgia was 53,284. See census data at http://www.census.gov/prod/www/decennial .html.

22. *The Weekly Advertiser* (Reading, PA), September 17, 1796.

23. *Argus, Greenleaf's New Daily Advertiser* (New York), October 24, 1796.

24. "To the Free and Independent Citizens of America," *Gazette of the United States* (Philadelphia, PA), November 16, 1796; Richard P. McCormick, *Presidential Game,* 46.

25. Pasley, *First Presidential Contest,* 267–269.

26. *Gazette of the United States,* October 6, 1796; Pasley, *First Presidential Contest,* 267–269.

27. Pasley, *First Presidential Contest,* 268–271.

28. George C. Rogers, Jr., *Evolution of a Federalist: William Loughton Smith of Charleston, (1758–1812)* (Columbia, SC: University of South Carolina Press,

1962), vii, 12–16, 27; Pasley, *First Presidential Contest*, 231; Phocion [William Loughton Smith], *The Pretensions of Thomas Jefferson to the Presidency Examined; and the Charges Against John Adams Refuted. Addressed to the Citizens of America in General; and Particularly to the Electors of the President*, 2 vols. (Philadelphia, 1796).

29. Phocion [Smith], *Pretensions of Thomas Jefferson*, 3.

30. Phocion; for his reference to Simms, Jefferson's retreat from the British, and his retirement from Washington's cabinet, see 33–35.

31. Phocion, 34, 36, 38, 64, 8, 50.

32. See Pasley, *First Presidential Contest*, 255, 254, 256. For Jefferson's personality quirks and how they were attacked throughout his career by Federalists, see Kerber, *Federalists in Dissent*, and more recently R. McDonald, *Confounding Father*. For Jefferson's mockingbird, see Thomas Jefferson's Monticello site: https://www.monticello.org/site/research-and-collections/mockingbirds.

33. Phocion [Smith], *Pretensions of Thomas Jefferson*, 4, 51; Pasley, *First Presidential Contest*, 254–256.

34. Quotes from this paragraph are from Jefferson's *Notes*, quoted in Phocion [Smith], *Pretensions of Thomas Jefferson*, 7, 5–6, emphasis Smith's.

35. Jefferson to Banneker, August 30, 1791, in Boyd, et al., *Papers of Thomas Jefferson*, 22: 97–98; Phocion [Smith], *Pretensions of Thomas Jefferson*, 8, 9, 10.

36. See Jefferson's *Notes on the State of Virginia*, Query 18, http://avalon.law.yale.edu/18th_century/jeffvir.asp.

37. Phocion [Smith], *Pretensions of Thomas Jefferson*, 8, 10, 29; Rogers, *Evolution of a Federalist*, vii, 12–16, 27; Pasley, *First Presidential Contest*, 231.

38. Phocion [Smith], *Pretensions of Thomas Jefferson*, 39.

39. Phocion, 37.

40. Gary Scott Smith, *Faith and the Presidency: From George Washington to George W. Bush* (New York: Oxford University Press, 2006), 21–52, esp. 25–26. For Washington's sporadic church attendance, see 27–28.

41. Phocion [Smith], *Pretensions of Thomas Jefferson*, 37.

42. Phocion, 51, 57; Pasley, *First Presidential Contest*. For a deeper investigation of the xenophobic and exceptionalist dimensions of early national identity, see Smith-Rosenberg, *This Violent Empire*.

43. Phocion [Smith], *Pretensions of Thomas Jefferson*, Part 2: 7, 39.

44. Pasley, *First Presidential Contest*, 240–248.

45. "Mr. Jungmann," *Weekly Advertiser* (Reading, PA), October 29, 1796; *Gazette of the United States*, October 26, 1796.

46. "American Crisis," No. 1, quoted in Mark Philip, ed., *Thomas Paine, Rights of Man, Common Sense, & Other Political Writings* (New York: Oxford University Press, 1998), 63.

47. For Paine's known association with French democracy, see Cotlar, *Tom Paine's America*.

48. Aurelius [John Gardner], *A Brief Consideration of the Important Services, and Distinguished Virtues and Talents, Which Recommend Mr. Adams for the Presidency of the United States* (Boston: Manning & Loring, 1796), 9.

49. Aurelius [John Gardner], *A Brief Consideration of the Important Services, and Distinguished Virtues and Talents, Which Recommend Mr. Adams for the*

Presidency of the United States (Boston: Manning & Loring, 1796), 27; "Mr. Jungmann," *Weekly Advertiser* (Reading, PA), October 29, 1796; *Boston Gazette, and Weekly Republican Journal*, October 31, 1796.

50. Aurelius, *Brief Consideration*, 9.

51. *Gazette of the United States* (Philadelphia), November 25, 1796.

52. *Gazette of the United States*, September 8, 1796.

53. A Subscriber [John Beckley], October 26, 1796, in Gawalt, *Justifying Jefferson*, 130–131.

54. Beckley to James Madison, October 15, 1796, in Gawalt, 127.

55. Beckley to William Irvine, November 2 and December 16, 1796, in Gawalt, 133, 134.

56. For news of Jefferson's authorship of the Declaration of Independence, see Pauline Maier, *American Scripture*; and more recently, R. McDonald, *Confounding Father*, esp. 7–14.

57. *New Jersey Journal* (Elizabethtown), November 2, 1796.

58. *To the Freeholders of Prince William, Stafford, and Fairfax. Fellow Citizens* ... (Fredericksburg? 1796), 3.

59. *Greenleaf's New York Journal*, November 29 and November 1, 1796; Tench Coxe, *The Federalist, Containing Some Strictures Upon a Pamphlet, Entitled, "The Pretensions of THOMAS JEFFERSON to the Presidency, examined, and the Charges against JOHN ADAMS, refuted." Which Pamphlet was first published in the Gazette of the United States, in a Series of Essays, under the Signature of PHOCION* (Philadelphia, PA: Matthew Carey, November, 1796), 39.

60. Pasley, *First Presidential Contest*, 277–295, esp. 277–278.

61. As one preface to a list of choice passages from the *Defence* put it: "The following maxims and opinions are taken from Mr. Adams's defence of the American Constitutions, and by them you will be able to judge for yourselves whether the man that holds such doctrines is a fit person to be elected President of the United States." *Argus, Greenleaf's New Daily Advertiser* (New York), October 31, 1796.

62. *Minerva* (New York), October 29, 1796. This same issue ran an essay from an Adams supporter systematically rebutting every paraphrase as an inaccurate smear.

63. *Argus, Greenleaf's New Daily Advertiser* (New York), November 22, 1796.

64. Coxe, *Federalist*, 39.

65. *Argus, Greenleaf's New Daily Advertiser* (New York), October 24, 1796; Miroff, "John Adams and the Presidency," in Cronin, *Inventing the American Presidency*, esp. 308–311.

66. "A Plebeian," *Virginia Gazette and General Advertiser* (Richmond), November 9, 1796.

67. *President II*, 13, 15.

68. *President II*, 8, 10, 11, 9; "Pittsburgh, Oct. 29. Successor as President of the United States. Thomas Jefferson," *Argus, Greenleaf's New Daily Advertiser* (New York), November 8, 1796.

69. *To the Freeholders*, 3.

70. *President II*, 15.

71. "Pittsburgh, Oct. 29. Successor as President of the United States. Thomas Jefferson," *Argus, Greenleaf's New Daily Advertiser* (New York), November 8, 1796.

72. *President II*, 15, 16.

73. Beckley to William Irvine, October 4, 1796, in Gawalt, *Justifying Jefferson*, 125.

74. Beckley to James Monroe, October 17, 1796, in Gawalt, 129.

CHAPTER 5. JOHN ADAMS'S PRESIDENCY AND
THE MORAL FATE OF THE NATION

1. Adams to John Quincy Adams, November 3, 1797, Lyman Henry Butterfield, et al., eds, *Adams Family Correspondence*, 13 vols. (Cambridge: Harvard University Press, 1963), 12: 281.

2. See Andrew S. Trees, *The Founding Fathers and the Politics of Character* (Princeton: Princeton University Press, 2004), 75–106; Freeman, *Affairs of Honor*, 105–107.

3. Alan Taylor, "John Adams," in Alan Brinkley and Davis Dyer, eds., *The American Presidency* (New York: Houghton Mifflin, 2004), 32.

4. Adams letter to John Quincy Adams, November 3, 1797, in L. Butterfield et al., *Adams Family Correspondence*, 12: 280, 281.

5. Butterfield et al., 12: 281.

6. Wood, *American Republic*, 567–592; Pasley, *Tyranny of Printers*, 117–126; Miroff, "John Adams and the Presidency," in Cronin, *Inventing the American Presidency*, 304–325; Pasley, *First Presidential Contest*, 49, 275–306.

7. John Adams to William Tudor, Sr., February 25, 1800, in Gordon S. Wood, ed., *John Adams: Writings from the New Nation, 1784–1826* (New York: Library of America, 2016), 388–389. Quoted also in Gordon S. Wood, *Friends Divided: John Adams and Thomas Jefferson* (New York: Penguin, 2018), 429–430.

8. Trees, *Founding Fathers*, 75–106.

9. "To the Citizens of Richmond, Virginia," June 10, 1798, in Wood, *John Adams*, 368.

10. "To the Grand Jury for Plymouth County, Massachusetts," May 28, 1798, and "To the Second Battalion of Militia of Prince George County, Virginia," June 6, 1798, in Wood, *John Adams*, 366, 367.

11. "To the Citizens of Concord, Massachusetts" June 25, 1798, in Wood, *John Adams*, 369.

12. Adams to Henry Knox, March 30, 1797, in Wood, *John Adams*, 336–337.

13. Adams to Henry Knox, March 30, 1787, in Wood, *John Adams*, 336

14. Adams to Elbridge Gerry, May 30, 1797, in Wood, *John Adams*, 349.

15. "To the Citizens of Concord, Massachusetts," June 25, 1798, in Wood, *John Adams*, 369.

16. To the Citizens Committee of Boston and Vicinity, August 7, 1797, in Wood, *John Adams*.

17. "From a Correspondent," *Aurora General Advertiser* (Philadelphia), March 17, 1797.

18. Alexander De Conde, *The Quasi-War: The Politics and Diplomacy of the Undeclared War With France, 1797–1801* (New York: Charles, Scribner's & Sons, 1966), 16. For analysis of the Jay treaty, see Estes, *Jay Treaty Debate*; Estes, "Most Bewitching Piece," 1–21.

19. DeConde, *Quasi-War*, 16, 8–10.

20. Adams to John Quincy Adams, March 31, 1797, L. Butterfield et al., *Adams Family Correspondence*, 12: 56.

21. De Conde, *Quasi-War*, 37–39, 45–47, 53; Wood, *Empire of Liberty, A History of the Early Republic, 1789–1815* (New York: Oxford University Press, 2009), 239–243.

22. James Morton Smith, *Freedom's Fetters: The Alien and Sedition Laws and American Civil Liberties* (Ithaca: Cornell University Press, 1956), 435–442, quote at 438. Steele, *Jefferson and American Nationhood*, 241–265; Elkins and McKitrick, *Age of Federalism*, 590–593; Wood, *Empire of Liberty*, 247–260, especially 249, 259.

23. "To the Citizens of Harrison County, Virginia," August 13, 1798, and "To the Greens & Whites Cavalry Troop of the Virginia Militia," August 15, 1798, in Wood, *John Adams*, 371 and 372.

24. For accounts of the prosecution of Lyon and Bache, see Pasley, "*Tyranny of Printers*," 79–104, 125.

25. The text of the state resolutions supporting the Alien and Sedition Acts can be found in Jonathan Elliot, ed., *The Debates in the Several State Conventions on the Adoption of the Federal Constitution, as Recommended by the General convention at Philadelphia, in 1787. Together with the Journal of the Federal Convention, Luther Martin's Letter, Yates's Minutes, Congressional Opinions, The Virginia and Kentucky Resolutions of '98–'99. And Other Illustrations of the Constitution, in Five Volumes*, 5 vols. (Philadelphia: J. B. Lippincott, 1876), 4: 532–539, quote at 539.

26. Jefferson to Mazzei, April 24, 1796, in Peterson, *Thomas Jefferson*, 1036–1037; Wood, *Empire of Liberty*, 235; R. McDonald, *Confounding Father*, 66–67.

27. "The following Address was handed to us at a late hour by a gentleman from Philadelphia . . . To the President of the United States." *Commercial Advertiser* (New York), April 24, 1798.

28. "Boston, Thursday, April 26. The Spirit of the Times!" *Boston Price-Current and Marine Intelligencer* (Boston), April 26, 1798.

29. See, for example, *Boston Price-Current and Marine Intelligencer* (Boston), April 26, 1798; *Commercial Advertiser* (New York), June 21, 1798.

30. "From the Inhabitants of the Townships of Windsor and Montgomery . . . to the President, the Senate, and House of Representatives of the United States," in *A Selection of Patriotic Addresses, to the President of the United States. Together with the President's Answers. Presented in the Year One Thousand Seven Hundred and Ninety-Eight, and the Twenty-Second of the Independence of America* (Boston: John W. Folsom, 1798), 172–176, quotes on 174–175, 176.

31. "Address from Salem to the President." *Massachusetts Mercury* (Boston), May 25, 1798.

32. Grant, *John Adams*, 380, 396.

33. "Newark, July 31." *Carey's United States Recorder* (Philadelphia), August 2, 1798.

34. For pledges of youth, see *Greenfield Gazette* (Greenfield, MA), June 25, 1798; *Gazette of the United States*, June 4, 1798. For the account of Rev. Chalmers, see "Eminent Patriotism." *Observatory* (Richmond, VA), July 19, 1798, courtesy Library of Virginia.

35. "To the Committee Composed of a Deputation From Each Militia Company of the Forty-Eighth Regiment, in the County of Botetourt, Virginia," [n.d.]; "To the Inhabitants of Accomac County, Virginia," [n.d.], in Charles Francis Adams, ed., *The Works of John Adams*, 10 vols. (Boston: Little, Brown, and Company, 1850–1856), 9: 215, 218, 219.

36. "To the Inhabitants of Chester county in [the] state of Pennsylvania," *New-York Gazette* (New York), May 26, 1798.

37. "To the Young Men of Boston, Massachusetts," May 22, 1798, in Charles Francis Adams, ed., *The Works of John Adams, Second President of the United States: With a Life of the Author, Notes and Illustrations, by His Grandson, Charles Francis Adams* (Boston: Little, Brown, 1850–1856), 9: 194–195.

38. Adams to George Washington, July 7, 1798, in Wood, *John Adams*, 370.

39. "Boston, July 25. General Washington," *Observatory* (Richmond, VA), August 9, 1798. See also July 26 and July 30 issues of the *Observatory*.

40. "Poets Corner. For the Herald of Liberty. A Parody," *Herald of Liberty* (Washington, PA), March 4, 1799.

41. "Philadelphia, July 18. An Address of the Ladies of Potts-Town, (Penn.) . . ." and "The Ladies of Deerfield," in *Observatory* (Richmond, VA), July 30, 1798, courtesy Library of Virginia.

42. "Toasts," *Commercial Advertiser* (New York), April 26, 1798.

43. "To the Grand Jury for Plymouth County, Massachusetts," May 28, 1798, in Wood, *John Adams*, 366.

44. For a reprint of the letter to Bache, see "From the Aurora. Friend Bache," *Observatory* (Richmond, VA), August 30, 1798, courtesy Library of Virginia.

45. Timothy Pickering to Washington, October 27, 1798, in W. W. Abbott and Edward G. Lengel, eds., *The Papers of George Washington—Retirement Series*, 4 vols. (Charlottesville: University of Virginia Press, 1998–1999), 3: 150–151.

46. I am relying on Pasley's calculation of fifty-one "Republican-leaning newspapers in the country" as of the previous spring, "out of a total newspaper population of 185." See Pasley, *"Tyranny of Printers,"* 117, 126.

47. Gallatin quoted in Wood, *Empire of Liberty*, 246; Jefferson to Edmund Pendleton, April 22, 1799, in Boyd et al., *Papers of Thomas Jefferson*, 31: 97.

48. "From the Aurora. The Spirit of the Press," *Observatory* (Richmond, VA), July 30, 1798, courtesy Library of Virginia.

49. Beckley to Coxe, October 25, 1798, and Beckley to Coxe, November 12, 1798, in Gawalt, *Justifying Jefferson*, 152, 154.

50. "Alien Bill," *New York Journal* (New York), July 4, 1798.

51. The text of the resolutions as adopted by the Kentucky General Assembly can be found at Boyd et al., *Papers of Thomas Jefferson*, 30: 550–556, quote at 550. For context on both the Kentucky and the Virginia Resolutions, see editorial note, in Hutchinson et al., *Papers of James Madison, Congressional Series*, 17: 185–188. I have accessed the digital version of the *Papers of James Madison—Congressional Series*, edited by J. C. A. Stagg, https://rotunda.upress.virginia.edu/founders/default .xqy?keys=JSMN-print-01&mode=TOC. Volume 17, cited in this chapter, was edited by David B. Mattern, J. C. A. Stagg, Jeanne K. Cross, and Susan Holbrook. Subsequent citations of volume 17 credit Mattern et al., but it is part of the *Congressional Series* initially edited by Hutchinson. Recently, Brian Steele has offered a

novel reading of the Kentucky Resolutions as a statement of nationalism. See Steele, *Jefferson and American Nationhood*, 265.

52. "Resolutions Adopted by the Kentucky General Assembly," November 10, 1798, in Boyd et al., *Papers of Thomas Jefferson*: 30: 551.

53. Editorial note, in Mattern, et al., *Papers of James Madison—Congressional Series*, 17: 185–188; "Virginia Resolutions," in Mattern, et al., *Papers of James Madison—Congressional Series,* 17: 190; "Resolutions Adopted by the Kentucky General Assembly," in Boyd et al., *Papers of Thomas Jefferson*, 30: 554.

54. "Resolutions Adopted by the Kentucky General Assembly," in Boyd et al., *Papers of Thomas Jefferson*, 30: 554.

55. "The Virginia Resolutions," in Mattern et al., *Papers of James Madison—Congressional Series,* 17: 189. My interpretation bears some resemblance to Steele, *Jefferson and American Nationhood*. Like Steele, I interpret the Kentucky Resolutions as fundamentally a nationalistic document.

56. Nicole Eustace, *Passion is the Gale: Emotion, Power, and the Coming of the American Revolution* (Chapel Hill: University of North Carolina Press, 2008); Eustace, *1812*.

57. *Examiner* (Richmond, VA), July 30, 1799, courtesy of the Library of Virginia.

58. "Beware of the Sedition Law!" *Independent Chronicle* (Boston), November 15, 1798.

59. "From Carey's United States Recorder. Mr. Carey," *Observatory* (Richmond, VA), August 27, 1798, courtesy Library of Virginia.

60. See, for instance, an essay from a self-described "plain-lettered farmer" in *Constitutional Telegraph* (Boston), May 10, 1800.

61. "To the Public, Continued," *Examiner* (Richmond, VA), April 11, 1800, courtesy Library of Virginia.

62. "To the Public, Continued," *Examiner* (Richmond, VA), April 11, 1800, courtesy Library of Virginia; Pasley, *Tyranny of Printers*, 98–102.

63. "To the Public, Continued," *Examiner* (Richmond, VA), April 11, 1800, courtesy Library of Virginia; John Patrick Diggins, *John Adams* (New York: Henry Holt, 2013), 143. See also Ronald Angelo Johnson, *Diplomacy in Black and White: John Adams, Toussaint L'Ouverture, and Their Atlantic World Alliance* (Athens: University of Georgia Press, 2014).

64. *Alexandria Times, and District of Columbia Daily Advertiser* (Alexandria, VA), July 2, 1800; *Constitutional Telegraphe* (Boston), February 15, and December 6, 1800; *Carlisle Gazette* (Carlisle, PA), November 6, 1799.

65. *The Constitutional Telegraphe* (Boston), February 15, 1800.

66. "For the Saratoga Register, &c.: Messrs. Child," *Saratoga Register* (Ballston Spa, NY), September 5, 1798; "From the Aurora: To JOHN ADAMS, President of the United States," *Observatory* (Richmond, VA), July 23, 1798, courtesy Library of Virginia.

67. "From the Aurora: To JOHN ADAMS," courtesy Library of Virginia.

68. "The Executive Act . . ." *Observatory* (Richmond, VA), July 23, 1798, courtesy Library of Virginia; *Universal Gazette* (Philadelphia) October 4, 1798; "For the Argus," *Greenleaf's New-York Journal* (New York), August 15, 1798.

69. Adams to Oliver Wolcott, Jr., September 24, 1798, in Wood, *John Adams,* 373, 374.

70. Adams to Oliver Wolcott, Jr., September 24, 1798, in Wood, *John Adams*, 376.

71. Hamilton to Harrison Gray Otis, January 26, 1799, in Syrett et al., *Papers of Alexander Hamilton*, 22: 440–441; Elkins and McKitrick, *Age of Federalism*, 580–612, 735–736; Greenstein, *Inventing the Job*, 28–29.

72. Elkins and McKitrick, *Age of Federalism*, 612, 735–736; Adams, Third Annual Message, December 3, 1799, in C. Adams, *Works of John Adams*, 9: 137–138.

73. Elkins and McKitrick, *Age of Federalism*, 612, 735–736; Adams, Third Annual Message, December 3, 1799, in C. Adams, *Works of John Adams*, 9: 137–138.

74. James F. Simon, *What Kind of Nation: Thomas Jefferson, John Marshall, and the Epic Struggle to Create a United States* (New York: Simon & Schuster, 2002), 126; Hamilton, *Letter from Alexander Hamilton, Concerning the Public Conduct and Character of John Adams, Esq., President of the United States* (New York, 1800).

75. Hamilton, *Letter*, 22–23.

76. Hamilton, *Letter*, 23, 24, 25.

77. William North (adjutant general in New York), Printed Instructions for Funeral Procession in New York, 1799, Misc. MSS, courtesy Fred W. Smith National Library for the Study of George Washington at Mount Vernon, and the Mount Vernon Ladies' Association; Orders Regarding the Death of George Washington, December 24, 1799, Misc. MSS, courtesy Fred W. Smith National Library for the Study of George Washington at Mount Vernon, and the Mount Vernon Ladies' Association. For national mourning of Washington, see François Furstenburg, *In the Name of the Father: Washington's Legacy, Slavery, and the Making of a Nation* (New York: Penguin, 2006).

78. Ketcham, *Presidents above Party*.

79. Dwight, "The Duty of Americans at the Present Crisis" (1798), in Ellis Sandoz, ed., *Political Sermons of the American Founding Era, 1730–1805* (Indianapolis: Liberty Fund, 1991), 1363–1394, quotes at 1382–1383, 1385–1386, 1381, 1378; G. Smith, *Faith and the Presidency*, 71, 467n189.

80. *Constitutional Telegraphe* (Boston), December 6, 1800. See also Greene [Tench Coxe], *Strictures Upon the Letter Imputed to Mr. Jefferson, Addressed to Mr. Mazzei*, 3–4, quoted in R. McDonald, *Confounding Father*, 95.

81. "True Republican Society of Philadelphia: Toasts Drunk at the Anniversary Meeting, May 7, 1800," in Foner, *Democratic-Republican Societies*, 110; *Philadelphia Gazette*, July 7, 1800; *Carlisle Gazette* (Carlisle, PA), November 6, 1799.

82. *Greenleaf's New York Journal and Patriotic Register* (New York), August 22, 1798.

83. "True Republican Society," and "Toasts Drunk on the Fourth of July, 1799," in Foner, *Democratic-Republican Societies*, 111, 219.

84. *Carlisle Gazette* (Carlisle, PA), November 6, 1799; *Constitutional Telegraphe* (Boston), December 6, 1800; *American Citizen and General Advertiser* (New York), February 23, 1801.

85. For an analysis of the intrigues of Burr's allies, see T. Baker, "An Attack Well Directed: Aaron Burr Intrigues for the Presidency," *Journal of the Early Republic* 31, no. 4 (Winter 2011): 553–598; Horn, Lewis, and Onuf, *Revolution of 1800*.

CHAPTER 6. PRESIDENT JEFFERSON'S
NATION OF DISSENTERS

1. Jefferson, First Inaugural Address, March 4, 1801, Boyd et al., *Papers of Thomas Jefferson,* 33: 134, 148. R. McDonald, *Confounding Father,* 109–110, quote at 110. See also *National Intelligencer* (Washington City), March 6, 1801.

2. Jefferson, First Inaugural Address, Boyd et al., 33: 148, 149.

3. Jefferson, First Inaugural Address, Boyd et al., 33: 150, 149.

4. Jefferson, First Inaugural Address, Boyd et al., 33: 149.

5. Jefferson, First Inaugural Address, Boyd et al., 33: 149, 151.

6. "The Triumph of Democracy; A Poem," *Connecticut Courant* (Hartford), January 5, 1801.

7. "Triumph of Democracy," *Connecticut Courant* (Hartford), January 5, 1801.

8. Jefferson to Henry Knox, March 27, 1801 in Boyd et al., *Papers of Thomas Jefferson,* 33: 466.

9. "New-Jersey," *Newburyport Herald* (Newburyport, MA), July 9, 1802; Bailey, *Jefferson and Executive Power,* 160–161.

10. Jefferson to Henry Knox, March 27, 1801 in Boyd et al., *Papers of Thomas Jefferson,* 33: 466; Stephen R. Grossbart, "Abraham Bishop: Teacher, Lawyer, Orator, and Politician," in Michael A. Morrison, ed., *The Human Tradition in Antebellum America* (New York: Rowman and Littlefield, 2000), 10.

11. "One of the principal subjects," *American Citizen and General Advertiser* (New York) November 25, 1801. For an examination of the "Mammoth Cheese," see Pasley, "The Cheese and the Words: Popular Political Culture and Participatory Democracy in the Early American Republic," in Pasley, Robertson, and Waldstreicher, *Beyond the Founders,* 31–56. For examples of Republicans' defenses of Jefferson, see *Carlisle Gazette* (Carlisle, PA), June 3, 1801; *Constitutional Telegraph* (Boston), November 28, 1801; *Republican Gazetteer* (Boston), July 21, 1802; *Constitutional Telegraph* (Boston), June 24, 1801.

12. "A Candid Examination of Mr. Jefferson's Conduct," *Philadelphia Gazette,* August 7, 1801.

13. "(Inserted by particular desire.) The answer of the President . . . ," *New York Gazette* (New York), August 12, 1801.

14. "For the Centinel. To Thomas Jefferson, Esq. President of the United States," *Columbian Centinel* (Boston), August 29, 1801.

15. "For the Centinel," *Columbian Centinel,* August 29, 1801.

16. Kerber, *Federalists in Dissent,* 23–66.

17. "Politics. For the Chronicle," *Independent Chronicle* (Boston), June 1, 1807.

18. "Sketches of the Times, Addressed to the Inhabitants of New-England," *New-York Evening Post,* January 6, 1804.

19. For Callender's turn against Jefferson, see Pasley, "*Tyranny of Printers,*" 125, 255, 260. For an account that emphasizes Callender's political miscalculation, see Rothman, *Notorious in the Neighborhood,* 14–56. For background on Sally Hemings and the Hemings family, see Annette Gordon-Reed, *The Hemingses of Monticello: An American Family* (New York: W. W. Norton, 2008); for Callender, see 554–561. See also R. McDonald, *Confounding Father,* 132–152. For a first-hand account of the blame that white plantation mistresses would place on abused female

slaves, see Harriet Jacobs, *Incidents in the Life of a Slave Girl, Written by Herself* [1860] (Cambridge: Harvard University Press, 2009), 38–45.

20. *Republican, or, Anti-Democrat* (Baltimore, MD) September 6, 1802; quoted in R. McDonald, *Confounding Father*, 132; Pasley, "*Tyranny of Printers*," 125, 255, 260.

21. *Republican, or, Anti-Democrat* (Baltimore, MD) September 6, 1802; quoted in R. McDonald, *Confounding Father*, 132; *Recorder* (Richmond, VA), November 3, 1802; Gordon-Reed, *Hemingses of Monticello*, 556.

22. "Correspondence No. 1," *Recorder* (Richmond, VA), November 10, 1802.

23. "Correspondence No. 1," *Recorder* (Richmond, VA), November 10, 1802.

24. Joshua D. Rothman, *Notorious in the Neighborhood: Sex and Families Across the Color Line in Virginia* (Chapel Hill: University of North Carolina Press, 2003), 252n44; James G. Basker, ed., *Amazing Grace: An Anthology of Poems About Slavery, 1660–1810* (New Haven: Yale University Press, 2002), 569.

25. "Decere res grandes . . .," *New-York Evening Post*, September 1, 1802.

26. "Decere res grandes . . .," *New-York Evening Post*, September 1, 1802.

27. Influential studies of the Louisiana Purchase and Jeffersonian statecraft include Jon Kukla, *A Wilderness So Immense: The Louisiana Purchase and the Destiny of America* (New York: Knopf, 2003); Peter J. Kastor, *The Nation's Crucible: The Louisiana Purchase and the Creation of America* (New Haven: Yale University Press, 2004); Francis D. Cogliano, *Emperor of Liberty: Thomas Jefferson's Foreign Policy* (New Haven: Yale University Press, 2014).

28. Wood, *Empire of Liberty*, 368–369.

29. Wood, *Empire of Liberty*, 368–369. For an assessment of the Louisiana Purchase and the expansion of slavery, see Edward Baptist, *The Half Has Never Been Told: Slavery and the Making of American Capitalism* (New York, 2014).

30. "Springfield, January 21, 1807. Communication," *Hampshire Federalist* (Springfield, MA) January 21, 1807; Kastor, *Nation's Crucible*.

31. "Reflections on the Late Treaties with France," *Poulson's American Daily Advertiser* (Philadelphia), October 31, 1803.

32. "Reflections on the Late Treaties," October 31, 1803.

33. Kerber, *Federalists in Dissent*, 23–66.

34. "New Hampshire Address," *New-York Evening Post*, October 23, 1804.

35. "For the New-York Evening Post. State Governments Attacked by the Democrats," *Newburyport Herald* (Newburyport, MA), July 1, 1803.

36. Jefferson to the Danbury Baptist Association, January 1, 1802, in Boyd et al., *Papers of Thomas Jefferson* 36: 258; July 25, 1801, Diary of Thomas Rodney, Rodney Correspondence, LOC Manuscript Division, Container 2; Jefferson to Thomas Paine, March 18, 1801, in Paul Leicester Ford, ed., *The Works of Thomas Jefferson*, 12 vols. (New York: G. P. Putnam's Sons, 1904 19055), 8: 18; *Pittsburgh Gazette* (Pittsburgh, PA), August 21, 1801; Wood, *Empire of Liberty*, 199–200.

37. "From the Trenton Federalist," *Pittsburgh Gazette*, August 28, 1801.

38. Emerson, *An Oration in Commemoration of the Anniversary of American Independence* (1802), in Sandoz, *Political Sermons*, 1556, 1564, 1566.

39. Emerson, *Oration*, in Sandoz, 1562, 1566, 1568, 1569.

40. Jefferson's Second Inaugural Address, March 4, 1805, Avalon Project, Yale University, https://avalon.law.yale.edu/19th_century/jefinau2.asp. For recent

commentary on the Twelfth Amendment, see Knott, *Lost Soul*, 31–32; Bailey, *Idea of Presidential Representation*, 55–61.

41. "From the Trenton True American. TO CANDID FEDERALISTS," *Essex Register* (Salem, MA), May 7, 1808.

42. Philip J. Lampi, "The Federalist Party Resurgence, 1808–1816: Evidence from the New Nation Votes Database," *Journal of the Early Republic* 33, no. 2 (Summer 2013): 255–281.

43. Lampi, 255–281, esp. 262–265.

44. "The Address of the Society of Constitutional Republicans . . . Friends and Fellow Citizens," *Kline's Carlisle Weekly Gazette* (Carlisle, PA), July 5, 1805.

45. "Special Message on the Burr Conspiracy," January 22, 1807, in Peterson, *Thomas Jefferson*, 532, 533, 535; Wood, *Empire of Liberty*, 384–385; Steele, *Jefferson and American Nationhood*, 280–282.

46. *Washington Federalist* (Washington City), February 14, 1807; *Hampshire Federalist* (Springfield, MA), February 4, 1807; Wood, *Empire of Liberty*, 384–385.

47. The leading historian of Jeffersonian foreign policy, Francis D. Cogliano, is the latest of scholars to reach this conclusion, writing: "As policy the embargo failed. It damaged the American economy, failed as a diplomatic tool, and was politically divisive." See Cogliano, *Emperor of Liberty*, 240.

48. Cogliano, *Emperor of Liberty*, 207–242.

49. *Impartial Observer* (Richmond, VA), May 17, 1806, courtesy Library of Virginia; Wood, *Empire of Liberty*, 207–237, 647–648; Broussard, *Southern Federalists*, 73; Cogliano, *Emperor of Liberty*, 221–222, 228–230.

50. *Impartial Observer* (Richmond, VA), May 17, 1806, courtesy Library of Virginia.

51. *New-York Commercial Advertiser*, May 12, 1806.

52. "To the Electors of New-Jersey," *Evening Post* (New York, NY), September 28, 1808. For background on William Duane, see Pasley, *"Tyranny of Printers,"* 176–195.

53. "To the Electors of New-Jersey," *Evening Post* (New York), September 28, 1808.

54. "Editor's Closet," *Balance* (Hudson, NY), December 20, 1808.

55. "Remarks by the editor of the New-York Evening Post. On Giles and Gallatin's New Embargo Bill," *Newburyport Herald* (Newburyport, MA), January 13, 1809.

56. Pasley, *"Tyranny of Printers,"* 304–313, quote at 304; McCormick, *Presidential Game*, 90.

57. "To the President of the United States, No. 1," *Pittsburgh Gazette* (Pittsburgh, PA), February 16, 1810. For discussion of Randolph as Philo-Laos, see Broussard, *Southern Federalists*, 119; Broussard cites the Raleigh, North Carolina, *Minerva* and the *Charleston Courier* carrying the Republican criticism of Madison. The *Courier* carried the essays in February 1810. Broussard, *Southern Federalists*, 119n20.

58. *Hampshire Federalist* (Springfield, MA), March 9, 1809.

59. "Springfield, January 26, 1809. Town-Meeting," *Hampshire Federalist* (Springfield, MA), January 26, 1809.

60. "We recommend to Our Readers . . .," *Evening Post* (New York), September 28, 1808.

61. "Massachusetts. Worcester, March 9. The Fourth of March," *Albany Register* (New York), March 18, 1803.

62. "On Friday Evening Last . . .," *American Citizen and General Advertiser* (New York), February 23, 1801.

63. For examination of Fourth-of-March celebrations, see Waldstreicher, *Perpetual Fetes*, 187–193.

64. For quote, see "Washington, (Penn.) March 6," *Gazette of the United States* (Philadelphia), March 17, 1797. For studies of the Fourth of July and Washington's birthday, see Waldstreicher, *Perpetual Fetes*, 112–130. Waldstreicher, *Perpetual Fetes*; and Travers, *Celebrating the Fourth*.

65. "Hartford, (Con.) March 17. A Republican Festival," *Virginia Argus* (Richmond), April 2, 1803.

66. "Republican Festivity," *Centinel of Freedom* (Newark, NJ), March 24, 1801.

67. "Bloomfield, March 4, 1800 [1801]," *Centinel of Freedom*, March 17, 1801.

68. "Address of Thomas Jefferson," *National Intelligencer* (Washington City), March 6, 1801.

69. J. Horatio Nichols, *Jefferson and Liberty; or Celebration of the Fourth of March* (n.p.), 1801, 24–26.

70. "Fredericktown, March 4," *Telescope: or, American Herald* (Leominster, MA), April 30, 1801.

71. *To the Public* (Portsmouth, NH), [1808?].

72. "Communication, Sag-Harbor, March 4, 1807," *Suffolk Gazette* (Sag Harbor, NY), March 9, 1807.

73. "Jefferson Village, March 4, 1801," *Centinel of Freedom* (Newark, NJ), March 24, 1801. I am indebted to Andrew W. Robertson for his insights on this point.

74. A gathering of Waltham, Massachusetts, Republicans celebrating Jefferson's election in 1805 raised a glass to "the Fourth of March," "the United States," "the Federal Constitution," and Thomas Jefferson himself, before saluting "the Clergy," with a toast expressing the hope that spiritual leaders "may . . . never mingle their political with their religious creed, or mistake their party zeal for divine inspiration." "At Waltham," *Democrat* (Boston), March 9, 1805.

75. Stanley Griswold, *Overcoming Evil With Good*, in Sandoz, *Political Sermons*, 1529–1554, quotes at 1546, 1551.

76. "Washington City, Friday, July 8," *National Intelligencer* (Washington City), July 8, 1803; "Richmond, Va., Celebration of the 4th of March," *National Intelligencer* (Washington City), March 28, 1804.

77. "Washington City. Friday, July 6," *National Intelligencer* (Washington City), July 6, 1804; "Select Toasts," *Eastern Argus* (Portland, ME, MA), March 22, 1805; David Ramsay, "An Oration on the Cession of Louisiana to the United States," *National Aegis* (Worcester, MA), September 5, 1804. The speech was reprinted, in whole or in part, in *American Citizen* (New York), June 15, 1804; *Republican Watch-Tower* (New York) June 16, 1804; *Alexandria Expositor* (Alexandria, VA), June 23, 1804; *Weekly Wanderer* (Randolph, VT), September 3, 1804; *American Mercury* (Hartford, CT), October 4, 1804; Kastor, *Nation's Crucible*.

78. "Select Toasts," *Eastern Argus* (Portland, Maine, MA), March 22, 1805.

79. Griswold, "Overcoming Evil with Good," in Sandoz, *Political Sermons*,

1546. For an exploration into public knowledge of Jefferson's authorship of the Declaration of Independence, see especially R. McDonald, *Confounding Father.*

80. R. McDonald, *Confounding Father*, esp. 149 and 164.

81. "Republican Festivity," *Centinel of Freedom* (Newark, NJ), March 24, 1801.

82. "Select Toasts," *Eastern Argus* (Portland, ME, MA), March 22, 1805.

83. Jefferson to Spencer Roane, September 6, 1819, Library of Congress Manuscript Division, http://www.loc.gov/exhibits/jefferson/137.html.

84. Jefferson to John Garland Jefferson, January 25, 1810, J. Jefferson Looney, et al., eds., *Papers of Thomas Jefferson—Retirement Series*, 15 vols. to date (Princeton, NJ: Princeton University Press, 2005–), 2: 183. Partially quoted in Wood, *Empire of Liberty*, 283.

85. Jefferson to Volney, April 20, 1802, Boyd et al., *Papers of Thomas Jefferson*, 37: 295.

86. Jefferson to John Dickinson, March 6, 1801, Boyd et al., *Papers of Thomas Jefferson*, 33: 196–197.

87. Jefferson to Levi Lincoln, October 25, 1802, Boyd et al., 38: 565.

88. Jefferson to Walter Jones, January 2, 1814, in Looney et al., *Papers of Thomas Jefferson—Retirement Series*, 7: 100.

89. Jonathan Gross, ed., *Thomas Jefferson's Scrapbooks: Poems of Nation, Family, & Romantic Love, Collected by America's Third President* (Hanover, NH: Steerforth Press, 2006); Gordon-Reed and Onuf, *Most Blessed*, 225, 229; R. McDonald, *Confounding Father*, esp. 235–242.

90. Gordon-Reed and Onuf, *Most Blessed*, 274–275; R. McDonald, *Confounding Father*, 129, 235–242, esp. 238.

91. Jefferson's desire for control over his environment manifested itself in other ways, as well, including his display of items sent back to him from Meriwether Lewis and William Clark's odyssey into the West. Jefferson prominently showcased bones, furs, stuffed animals, and a large map from the journey in his library. This space, writes historian Lindsay Chervinsky, was intended for Jefferson's private study as well as for meetings with members of his cabinet. In effect, the objects surrounding visitors to Jefferson's library were meant to communicate the expedition's success—and thus to send a message about the nation's ability to understand and ultimately control its newly acquired territory under Jefferson's presidential leadership. Lindsay M. Chervinsky, "The President's Office: How George Washington and Thomas Jefferson Used Private Space to Shape the Cabinet," unpublished paper given at the American Historical Association Conference (Washington, DC, 2018).

92. Thomas Jefferson's Scrapbook, Small Special Collections Library, University of Virginia (4 vols.); hereafter cited as *Scrapbook*. See, for instance, *Scrapbook* 2: 36–37, and 2: 51.

93. *Scrapbook* 3: 27–28. For the political advantages given to the South, see *Scrapbook* 4: 5. For reference to Hemings in the *Courant* poem itself, see *Scrapbook* 3: 8.

94. *Scrapbook* 1: 119.

95. *Scrapbook* 1: 119.

96. "EMBARGO," *National Intelligencer* (Washington City), January 4, 1808.

97. *Salem Gazette* (Salem, MA), June 2, 1809.

98. "Domestic," *Pittsfield Sun* (Pittsfield, MA), March 24, 1806.

99. Margaret Bayard Smith's account of the inaugural ball, March 4, 1809, in Looney et al., *Papers of Jefferson—Retirement Series*, 1: 9.

100. Jefferson to William Duane, March 28, 1811, in Looney et al., 3: 508.

CHAPTER 7. TO BEAR ARMS AT THE PRESIDENT'S CALL

1. *The American Patriotic Song-Book, A Collection of Political, Descriptive, and Humorous Songs, of National Character, and the Production of American Poets Only* (Philadelphia: John Bioren, 1816), American Antiquarian Society, 37, 24–25.

2. Stagg, *Mr. Madison's War*; Stagg, *War of 1812*; Taylor, *Civil War of 1812*; Taylor, *Internal Enemy*; Saul Cornell, *A Well-Regulated Militia: The Founding Fathers and the Origins of Gun Control in America* (New York: Oxford University Press, 2008); Eustace, *1812*; Park, *American Nationalisms*.

3. Taylor, *Internal Enemy*; Taylor, *Civil War of 1812*, 325.

4. Stagg, *Mr. Madison's War*, 29, 48–118, esp. 55–59; Stagg, *War of 1812*, 37–39; Trautsch, *Genesis of America*, 215–216.

5. Taylor, *Civil War of 1812*; Trautsch, *Genesis of America*, 215–220.

6. *National Intelligencer* (Washington, DC), March 17, 1809; Trautsch, *Genesis of America*, 215–216.

7. *Boston Independent Chronicle*, March 23, 1807. For Jefferson quote and context, see Jefferson to William Duane, March 28, 1811, in Looney et al., *Papers of Jefferson—Retirement Series*, 3: 508; Peterson, *Thomas Jefferson*, 656.

8. "For the Mercury: PROGRESS OF FEDERALISM," *New-Bedford Mercury* (New Bedford, MA), May 5, 1809. See also "For the Massachusetts Spy. Essays—No. 3: PEACE WITH GREAT BRITAIN," *Massachusetts Spy* (Worcester), May 3, 1809.

9. "True Americans," *Daily Compiler* (Richmond, VA), March 9, 1815, courtesy Library of Virginia.

10. Esculapius, "A Receipt to Make a Modern Federalist," [1807?], American Historical Manuscripts Collection (formerly Miscellaneous Manuscripts), New-York Historical Society.

11. Dickinson to George Logan, January 30, 1804, Logan Collection, Historical Society of Pennsylvania. I am grateful to Jane E. Calvert, the world's foremost expert on John Dickinson, for making this letter and the materials at the John Dickinson Papers Project available to me. See also Calvert, "An Expansive Conception of Rights: The Quakerly Abolitionism of John Dickinson," in Will R. Jordan, ed., *"When in the Course of Human Events": 1776 at Home, Abroad, and in American Memory* (Macon, GA: Mercer University Press, 2018), 21–54; Jane E. Calvert, *Quaker Constitutionalism and the Political Thought of John Dickinson* (Cambridge: Cambridge University Press, 2009). For further analysis of "bearing arms," see Cornell, *Well-Regulated Militia*. For "internal enemies" and the perceived threat of Indians and free and enslaved black people, see Taylor, *Internal Enemy*; Taylor, *Civil War of 1812*.

12. "To the People of the United States," *Democratic Press* (Philadelphia), April 10, 1807.

13. "Thoughts on the Nature of the Government of the United States," *Democratic Press* (Philadelphia), April 27, 1807.

14. "American Meeting," *Statesman* (Newburyport, MA), February 13, 1809.

15. Israel, *State of the Union Messages of the Presidents, Vol. 1: 1790–1860* (New York: Chelsea House Publishers, 1967), 92, 97.

16. "At a Numerous Meeting of Republicans . . . the Following Resolutions Were Passed Unanimously," *Old Colony Gazette* (New Bedford, MA), March 24, 1809.

17. "At a Numerous Meeting of the Republicans of That Town Last Friday . . . ," *Old Colony Gazette*, May 17, 1811; republished in the *Bee* (Hudson, NY), May 24, 1811; and the *Enquirer* (Richmond, VA), May 24, 1811. For the brief easing of calls for war, see Taylor, *Civil War of 1812*, 116.

18. Taylor, *Internal Enemy*.

19. Madison quoted in Taylor, *Internal Enemy*, 131.

20. "We Are Happy to Find That the Bill for Arming the Militia Has Passed through the Popular Branch of Congress," *Republican* (Plattsburgh, NY), March 13, 1812 (reprinted in the *Yankee* (Boston), March 6, 1812); Taylor, *Civil War of 1812*, 75–119.

21. "Popular Sentiment," *Columbian* (New York), March 18, 1811.

22. Taylor, *Internal Enemy*, 131; Trautsch, *Genesis of America*, 171–172. Historian Nicole Eustace called Lowell's pamphlet "a Boston blockbuster." The publisher, Russell & Cutler, published four separate editions. See Eustace, *1812*, 175–176, 286n16. My analysis of Lowell's work is indebted to her work.

23. My quotes come from the third edition: John Lowell, *Mr. Madison's War: A Dispassionate Inquiry into the Reasons Alleged by Mr. Madison for Declaring an Offensive and Ruinous War Against Great-Britain. Together With Some Suggestions as to a Peaceable and Constitutional mode of Averting That Dreadful Calamity. By a New-England Farmer*, 3rd ed. (Boston: Russell & Cutler, 1812).

24. Lowell, vi–vii, ix.

25. Lowell, 7.

26. Lowell, 13.

27. Lowell, 12; Eustace, *1812*, 175–176.

28. Lowell, *Mr. Madison's War*, 11.

29. Lowell, 40–41.

30. Lowell, 45, 48, 49–50.

31. *Alexandria Gazette* (Alexandria, VA), July 27, 1812. See also *Statesman* (New York), August 29, 1812.

32. *Franklin Herald* (Greenfield, MA), April 3, 1813.

33. *Dedham Gazette* (Dedham, MA), March 4, 1814.

34. "The Imperial Auction," in *Madison Agonistes; or, The Agonies of Mother Goose.* (London: D. Deans, 1814), American Antiquarian Society, quotes at 71–72, 73–74, 75.

35. "The Object of the Army Continued," *Franklin Herald* (Greenfield, MA), April 3, 1813.

36. "Memorial. To James Madison, *Esq.*," *Spectator* (New York), August 15, 1812.

37. Taylor, *Civil War of 1812*, 147, 152–153.

38. "DEFERRED ARTICLES. Cincinnati, May 8, 1812: A Citizen of one of the eastern states, who has lately travelled in the state of Ohio, feels a pleasure in making the

following communication," *Northern Post* (Salem, NY), June 11, 1812 (reprinted as "Frontier News" in *Ostego Herald* (Cooperstown, NY), June 13, 1812; Taylor, *Civil War of 1812*, 161–165.

39. "ADDRESS of the Democratic-Republican Committee of the Borough of Pittsburgh, and its Vicinity, Favorable to the Election of DE WITT CLINTON, to the Presidency of the United States, at the ensuing Election," *Pittsburgh Gazette* (Pittsburgh, PA), October 23, 1812; Taylor, *Civil War of 1812*, 182; Trautsch, *Genesis of America*, 230.

40. Park, *American Nationalisms*, 115–155.

41. "From the Virginia Patriot. Extract of a Letter from Boston, dated July 20," *Alexandria Gazette* (Alexandria, VA), August 3, 1812; "For the Newburyport Herald. THE CRISIS. The Salvation of Our Country in the Hands of the People," *Alexandria Gazette* (Alexandria, VA), July 27, 1812; "Communication. NEXT PRESIDENT," *Newburyport Herald* (Newburyport, MA), September 8, 1812.

42. "ADDRESS of the Democratic-Republican Committee; McCormick, *Presidential Game*, 195.

43. Taylor, *Civil War of 1812*, 210–214, 218–220.

44. Israel, *State of the Union*, 116–117.

45. "From the *National Intelligencer*," *National Advocate* (New York), August 23, 1813.

46. "Oration," *Democratic Press* (Philadelphia), July 8, 1813.

47. See Eustace, *1812*. For captivity narratives, see 118–167.

48. "Extract of a letter from Captain Cooper to Charles K. Mallory, Esq. Lieutenant Governor of Virginia," *Democratic Press* (Philadelphia), July 9, 1813.

49. Taylor, *Civil War of 1812*, 210.

50. Letter from STA. CRUTCHFIELD to "His Exc. Gov. Barbour," *Democratic Press* (Philadelphia), July 6, 1813.

51. "ANNIVERSARY OF INDEPENDENCE," *Democratic Press* (Philadelphia), July 10, 1813.

52. On this I agree with Eustace, who notes, "In a very real sense, women's work in childbed mattered as much as men's efforts on the battlefield." See Eustace, *1812*, 136. "THE WAR," *Democratic Press* (Philadelphia), July 24, 1813.

53. Park, *American Nationalisms*, 115–155.

54. "From the Connecticut Mirror, January 16. ENLISTING MINORS." *Washingtonian* (Windsor, VT), January 23, 1815.

55. Taylor, *Civil War of 1812*, 182.

56. "From the Lancaster Intelligencer," *Democratic Press* (Philadelphia), September 2, 1812.

57. "A LITTLE TRUTH," *Democratic Press* (Philadelphia), October 30, 1812.

58. "THE WAR," *Democratic Press* (Philadelphia), July 24, 1813.

59. "*To the People of Massachusett's* [sic]," *Military Monitor, and American Register* (New York), August 9, 1813.

60. "To the Inhabitants of Niagra, Genesee and Chatauque," *Mercantile Advertiser* (New York), December 29, 1813 (republished in the *Northern Post* (Salem, NY), December 30, 1813; *Poulson's American Daily Advertiser* (Philadelphia), December 31, 1813; *National Aegis* (Worcester, MA), January 5, 1814).

61. Elizabeth Parke Custis Law to David Warden, September 8, 1814 (copy),

Manuscript Collection, courtesy Fred W. Smith National Library for the Study of George Washington at Mount Vernon, and the Mount Vernon Ladies' Association.

62. "The Late Anniversary of Our Independence," *Philadelphia Democratic Press* (Philadelphia), July 29, 1814.

63. One of the most enduring critical commentaries came from a pamphlet, "The Bladensburg Races," which ridiculed Madison as a foolish wartime president who could not even control his horse when it became spooked by the advancing British forces and fled. The poem depicts the diminutive Madison bouncing up and down atop the horse, struggling in vain to control his mount, while the scabbard of the saber at his hip swats him in the buttocks in rhythm with the horse's stride. Angela Kreider, "Spinning the Bladensburg Races: The Commander in Chief and the Burning of Washington," paper presented at the Society for Historians of the Early American Republic Conference, July 19, 2013.

64. Elizabeth Parke Custis Law to David Warden, September 8, 1814 (copy), Manuscript Collection, courtesy Fred W. Smith National Library for the Study of George Washington at Mount Vernon, and the Mount Vernon Ladies' Association.

65. "Memorandum of a Conversation with John Armstrong," August 29, 1814, in Robert A. Rutland et al., eds., *The Papers of Madison—Presidential Series*, 10 vols. to date (Charlottesville: University of Virginia Press, 1984–), 8: 153, 154, 155.

66. See Eustace, *1812*, 36–75.

67. Stagg, *War of 1812*, 154–155.

68. "While our negociations have been going on at Ghent, under the directions of Mr. Madison, every little junto circle, and every supercilious federal dictator, have considered the President of as little weight in the business, as the most insignificant person in the U[nited] States," the piece crowed. "But how have these persons been disappointed. This same Mr. Madison maintains the dignity of his own character, and vindicates the honor of his country during the whole negociation." "'Madison's Peace' Honorably Illustrated;—or, Republicanism Triumphant," *Independent Chronicle* (Boston), February 16, 1815; Taylor, *Civil War of 1812*; Stagg, *War of 1812*, 154–155.

69. "PEACE," *Daily Compiler* (Richmond, VA), February 17, 1815, courtesy Library of Virginia.

70. "General Register. Boston, Saturday, January 28, 1815," *Boston Spectator*, January 28, 1815.

71. The *Federal Republican* reported: "[A] letter from a highly respectable correspondent in Havanna . . . states, that a large British fleet, with 10,000 troops on board, were at the mouth of the Mississippi, 100 miles from New Orleans, on the 12th" of December. "IMPORTANT." *Federal Republican* (Georgetown, DC), January 6, 1815.

72. See, for instance, "New-Orleans, Dec. 21," *Commercial Advertiser* (New York), January 23, 1815, reprinted numerous places, including *Evening Post* (New York), January 23, 1815; and *American Mercury* (Hartford, CT), January 31, 1815. For Jackson and New Orleans, see D. Howe, *What Hath God Wrought*, 8–18.

73. On this point, I concur with Alan Taylor, who makes a similar point in *The Civil War of 1812*.

74. For examples of these superlatives, see *Daily Compiler* (Richmond, VA), January 21, 1815 and February 10, 1815, courtesy Library of Virginia. The February

10 issue also contains the account of the public celebration of Jackson's victory. For "we this day have" quote, see "New-Orleans," *National Aegis* (Worcester, MA), February 22, 1815.

75. "From the Richmond Enquirer. New-Orleans," *National Advocate* (New York), February 9, 1815.

76. "What Have We Gained by the Late War?" *Massachusetts Spy* (Boston), March 1, 1815.

77. "Georgetown, Wednesday, February 16," *Federal Republican for the Country* (Georgetown, DC), February 17, 1815; Taylor, *Civil War of 1812*, 180, 182, 177–178.

78. "Our Truth-Telling President," *Federal Republican for the Country* (Georgetown, DC), February 14, 1815.

79. "State Legislature," *Boston Spectator*, January 28, 1815.

80. The terms of the Hartford Convention were widely published. Quotes here come from the article "From the Eastern Argus. HARTFORD CONVENTION," in the *Daily Compiler* (Richmond, VA), January 14, 1815, courtesy Library of Virginia.

81. "Richmond, January 14 . . . the Hartford Convention," *Daily Compiler* (Richmond, VA), January 14, 1815, courtesy Library of Virginia. For analysis of the Hartford Convention, see Trautsch, *Genesis of America*, 246–251. For the comparison between Nullifiers and the Hartford Convention, see William Harper, *Political Tract No. 6, January 1832. The Remedy by State Interposition, or Nullification; Explained and Advocated by Chancellor* [William] *Harper, in his Speech at Columbia (S.C.) on the Twentieth September 1830* (Charleston, SC: State Rights and Free Trade Association, 1832), American Antiquarian Society, 22.

82. "NEW ORLEANS," *Federal Republican for the Country* (Georgetown, DC), January 31, 1815.

83. "NEW ORLEANS."

84. "Hudson . . . Tuesday, February 23. THE TREATY," *Northern Whig* (Hudson, NY), February 28, 1815.

85. "It Appears by Official Returns," *Columbian Centinel* (Boston), April 5, 1815.

86. "New-Orleans," *New-York Evening Post*, February 7, 1815.

87. "MASSACHUSETTS LEGISLATURE. SENATE," *Daily Compiler* (Richmond, VA), March 13, 1815, courtesy Library of Virginia.

88. "MASSACHUSETTS LEGISLATURE. SENATE."

89. "HOUSE OF REPRESENTATIVES. *Monday February 24.* VOTE OF THANKS," *Daily Compiler* (Richmond, VA), March 13, 1815, courtesy Library of Virginia.

90. "HOUSE OF REPRESENTATIVES."

91. "NEW ORLEANS," *Federal Republican* (Georgetown, DC), January 31, 1815.

92. "NEW ORLEANS."

CHAPTER 8. A VIOLENT MAN FOR A VIOLENT NATION

1. Address of the Committee Appointed by a Republican Meeting in the County of Hunterdon, Recommending GEN. ANDREW JACKSON OF TENNESSEE, to the People

of New-Jersey, as PRESIDENT of the UNITED STATES (Trenton, NJ, 1824), American Antiquarian Society, 3–4.

2. Park, *American Nationalisms*; Robert Pierce Forbes, *The Missouri Compromise and Its Aftermath: Slavery and the Meaning of America* (Chapel Hill: University of North Carolina Press, 2007); Howe, *What Hath God Wrought*, 142–143; Michael P. Johnson, "Denmark Vesey and His Co-Conspirators," *William & Mary Quarterly* 3rd Series 58, no. 4 (October 2001): 915–976; Joanne B. Freeman, *Field of Blood*.

3. Address of the Committee, 3.

4. J. Larson, *Internal Improvement*; Howe, *What Hath God Wrought*, 328–445; Park, *American Nationalisms*; Parsons, *Birth of Modern Politics*.

5. Larson, *Internal Improvement*; Howe, *What Hath God Wrought*, 141–147, 147–163.

6. Ratcliffe, "Right to Vote"; Jon Grinspan, *The Virgin Vote: How Young Americans Made Democracy Social, Politics Personal, and Voting Popular in the Nineteenth Century* (Chapel Hill: University of North Carolina Press, 2016); McCormick, *Presidential Game*; Parsons, *Birth of Modern Politics*.

7. Grinspan, *Virgin Vote*.

8. Waldstreicher, *Perpetual Fetes*, 337.

9. David Walker, *David Walker's Appeal to the Coloured Citizens of the World, but in particular, and very expressly, to those of the United States of America* [1829], (Baltimore, MD: Black Classics Press, 1993), 95; Howe, *What Hath God Wrought*, 423–430.

10. George Lawrence, *An Oration on the Abolition of the Slave Trade, Delivered on the First Day of January, 1813, in the African Methodist Episcopal Church* (New York: Hardcastle and Van Pelt, 1813), 3, 4, 11.

11. Taylor, *Civil War of 1812*, 327.

12. "New Orleans, Dec. 21 . . . To the Embodied Militia," *Commercial Advertiser* (New York), January 23, 1815. For more on the accounts of black courage during the Battle of New Orleans, see Eustace, *1812*, 228–231.

13. The literature on black people in America's wars is itself vast and growing. I will list only a few excellent volumes here, but there are many more. For blacks during the Revolution, see Gary B. Nash, *The Forgotten Fifth: African Americans in the Age of Revolutions* (Cambridge, MA: Harvard University Press, 2006). For race and American nationalism during and after the American Revolution, see Parkinson, *Common Cause*, and Alan Taylor, *American Revolutions: A Continental History, 1750–1804* (New York, NY: W. W. Norton, 2016). For the story of black and white soldiers during the Civil War, see Joseph T. Glatthaar, *Forged in Battle: The Civil War Alliance of Black Soldiers and White Officers* (Baton Rouge: Louisiana State University Press, 1990). For blacks' essential role in forcing the issue of emancipation, see Ira Berlin, *The Long Emancipation: The Demise of Slavery in the United States* (Cambridge, MA: Harvard University Press, 2015). For contemporary commentary on black "culture," especially from prominent black celebrities, see Ta-Nehisi Coates, "This Is How We Lost to the White Man: The Audacity of Bill Cosby's Black Conservatism," written before allegations of rape by dozens of women shattered Cosby's illustrious reputation; and "My President Was Black," a reflection on the racial politics of the nation's first black President, Barack Obama,

in Coates, *We Were Eight Years in Power: An American Tragedy* (New York: One World, 2017), esp. 5–32, 285–339. For a recent analysis of how local, state, and federal government policies conspired to segregate the United States, see Richard Rothstein, *The Color of Law: A Forgotten History of How Our Government Segregated America* (New York: Liveright Publishing, 2017). For his discussion of the use of the word "ghetto" to describe the impoverished urban communities disproportionately occupied by blacks, see Rothstein, *Color of Law*, xvi.

14. "New Orleans, Dec. 21 . . . To the Embodied Militia," *Commercial Advertiser* (New York), January 23, 1815.

15. Lemuel Haynes, *Dissimulation Illustrated: A Sermon Delivered at Brandon, Vermont, February 22, 1813* (Rutland, VT: Fay & Davidson, 1814). For background on Haynes, see Eustace, *1812*, 190.

16. Haynes, *Dissimulation Illustrated*, 6.

17. Haynes, 6, 7, 9.

18. Haynes, 10, 11. Eustace also quotes from this passage. See *1812*, 191.

19. Haynes, *Dissimulation Illustrated*, 17, 22.

20. Haynes, 17, 22.

21. Park, *American Nationalisms*; Howe, *What Hath God Wrought*, 147–160; Forbes, *Missouri Compromise*.

22. Charles Francis Adams, ed., *Memoirs of John Quincy Adams, Comprising Portions of His Diary from 1795 to 1848*, 12 vols. (Philadelphia: J. B. Lippincott, 1875–1877), 5: 6, 10; 4: 530, online through the Library of Congress, https://catalog .loc.gov/vwebv/search?searchCode=LCCN&searchArg=04020138&searchType =1&permalink=y. Images of the original book pages can be found at https://archive .org/details/memoirsofjohnquio5adam2/page/n6, and https://archive.org/details /memoirsofjohnquino2adam/page/n4; Howe, *What Hath God Wrought*, 147–160.

23. Robert Y. Hayne, et al., *To the People of South Carolina.* (Washington, DC: July 13, 1832), William C. Cook Collection Jacksonian Materials, American Antiquarian Society, 7; Park, *American Nationalisms*, 194–241.

24. Reed to Mrs. H. M. Reed, April 8, 1832, William C. Cook Collection Jacksonian Materials, American Antiquarian Society.

25. Howe, *What Hath God Wrought*, 433–439; M. Johnson, "Denmark Vesey"; Freeman, *Field of Blood*; Baptist, *Never Been Told*, 114. Baptist aptly refers to the tactics employed by plantation owners as "torture," 139–140; Park, *American Nationalisms*, 189–190; Taylor, *Internal Enemy*, 414–415.

26. Freeman, *Field of Blood*.

27. For example, see William Joseph Snelling, *A Brief and Impartial History of the Life and Actions of Andrew Jackson, President of the United States* (Boston: Stimpson and Clapp, 1831), William C. Cook Collection Jacksonian Materials, American Antiquarian Society.

28. *The Political Mirror: or Review of Jacksonism* (New York: J. P. Peaslee, 1835), William C. Cook Collection Jacksonian Materials, American Antiquarian Society, 48–49.

29. *Sketches of Character; or Facts and Arguments Relative to the Presidential Election, 1828 . . .* (Philadelphia, PA: 1828), William C. Cook Collection Jacksonian Materials, American Antiquarian Society, 2; *The Character and Principles of General Andrew Jackson, In reference to his qualifications for President of the United*

States, illustrated by FACTS, Addressed to the Independent Electors of the Cumberland and Oxford Electoral Districts (Portland, ME?: 1828), William C. Cook Collection Jacksonian Materials, American Antiquarian Society, 21.

30. *Character and Principles, of Andrew Jackson*, 20. For a list of these encounters (although a sympathetic characterization), see Isaac Hill, *Brief Sketch of the Life, Character and Services of Major Andrew Jackson, by a Citizen of New-England* (Concord, NH: Manahan, Hoag, 1828), 11; and *Political Mirror*, 48–49.

31. *Political Mirror*, 48–49.

32. *Political Mirror*, 48; Howe, *What Hath God Wrought*, 411–445.

33. *Character and Principles*, 5, 16.

34. See, for example, *Sketches of Character*, 9–11.

35. Benjamin E. Park, "The Angel of Nullification: Imagining Disunion in an Era Before Secession," *Journal of the Early Republic* 37, no. 3 (Fall 2017): 507–536. See also Park, *American Nationalisms*, 194–241. For examples of nullification literature from the period, see *Documents. Ordered by the Convention of the People of South Carolina, to be Transmitted to the President of the United States, and to the Governor of Each State* (Columbia, SC, 1832). (Park cites this piece and discusses its contents in his analyses); Harper, *Political Tract No. 6*; Hayne et al., *To the People*. Not surprisingly, not every commentary on nullification, even in South Carolina, was sympathetic. See Christopher Gustavus Memminger, *The Book of Nullification, by A Spectator of the Past* (Charleston, SC, 1830), William C. Cook Collection Jacksonian Materials, American Antiquarian Society.

36. The proclamation, dated December 10, 1832, can be found at https://avalon.law.yale.edu/19th_century/jack01.asp#1; Howe, *What Hath God Wrought*, 405.

37. Proclamation.

38. Proclamation. Brands, *Heirs to the Founders*, 197–200; convention resolution quoted on at 197–198.

39. Howe, *What Hath God Wrought*, 373–395.

40. Jackson's veto of the Bank of the United States (July 10, 1832), https://avalon.law.yale.edu/19th_century/ajveto01.asp. For discussion of Jackson's bid to expand his presidential authority in order to limit the power of the government, see Ketcham, *Presidents above Party*, 141–154.

41. See, for instance, *Political Mirror*, 16–18, 38–41. For Jackson's "kitchen cabinet," see Howe, *What Hath God Wrought*, 332–333. Andrew Jackson, Second Annual Message to Congress, December 6, 1830, can be viewed at the American Presidency Project, https://www.presidency.ucsb.edu/documents/second-annual-message-3.

42. Hill, *Brief Sketch*, 45.

43. Jackson, one pamphleteer noted, "is the first candidate for the Presidency who has ever openly taken the field and electioneered for himself." *Sketches of Character*, 1. See also Lynn Hudson Parsons, *Birth of Modern Politics*, esp. 190; Ambar, *How Governors Built*, 127.

44. Catherine Allgor, *Parlor Politics: In Which the Ladies of Washington Help Build a City and a Government* (Charlottesville: University of Virginia Press, 2000); Howe, *What Hath God Wrought*, 203–211, 275–284, 328.

45. John Henry Eaton, *The Life of Major General Andrew Jackson: Comprising a History of the War in the South; From the Commencement of the Creek Campaign to the Termination of Hostilities Before New Orleans. Addenda: Containing*

a Brief History of the Seminole War and Cession and Government of Florida, 3rd ed. (Philadelphia: McCarty & Davis, 1828), William C. Cook Collection Jacksonian Materials, American Antiquarian Society, 7–9; S. Putnam Waldo, *Memoirs of the Illustrious Citizen and Patriot, Andrew Jackson, Late Major-General in the Army o the United States; and Commander-in-Chief of the Division of the South, by a Citizen of Hagers-Town, MD* (Chambersburg, [PA], 1828), William C. Cook Collection Jacksonian Materials, American Antiquarian Society, 10.

46. Eaton, *Major General Andrew Jackson*, 9–10.

47. *Address of the Committee*, 3; Park, *American Nationalisms*.

48. October 25 [1834], diary of Samuel Lord, Sr., Lord Family Papers, 1825–1835, MSS Folio Vols/Octavo Vol. L, American Antiquarian Society; Howe, *What Hath God Wrought*, 430–432.

49. *The Jackson Wreath, or National Souvenir. A National Tribute, Commemorative of the Great Civil Victory Achieved by the People, Through the Hero of New Orleans* (Philadelphia, Jacob Maas: 1829), William C. Cook Jacksonian Era Collection, American Antiquarian Society, 53–54, 58–59.

50. Eaton, *Major General Andrew Jackson*, 161.

51. See, for instance, Eaton, 181–183, 257–263; *Jacksonian Wreath*, 31–32, 36–37.

52. Hill, *Brief Sketch*, 11, 16.

53. Hill, 28–29.

54. Park, *American Nationalisms*, 194–241.

55. December 13, 1832, January 8 and January 20, 1833, diary of Lord; Macbeth quoted in Park, *American Nationalisms*, 234. For the resolution to the nullification crisis, see Park, 237.

56. December 31, 1832, diary of Lord.

57. November 9 and November 17, 1832, diary of Lord.

58. September 25, 1833, diary of Lord.

59. June 13, 1833, October 25 and October 28, 1833, diary of Lord.

60. James Akin, "Americans, Behold Your Hero, GENERAL JACKSON . . . ," (1832), American Antiquarian Society.

61. "Gen. Jackson's Vetoes," *Hampden Whig* (Springfield, MA), October 24, 1832.

62. For context on this image, see Patrick Rael, *Black Identity and Black Protest in the Antebellum North* (Chapel Hill: University of North Carolina Press, 2002), 167–168.

63. *Proceedings of the Democratic Republican Conventions of Young Men of the State of Pennsylvania, Held at Harrisburg, July 4, 1836* ([Harrisburg, PA]: Pennsylvania Reporter & State Journal, 1836), 11–12; *Political Mirror*, 200–205. For doughfaces, see Freeman, *Field of Blood*, 62–68; Howe, *What Hath God Wrought*, 390.

64. *Political Mirror*, 314–315.

EPILOGUE

1. James M. McPherson, *Tried by War: Abraham Lincoln as Commander in Chief* (New York: Penguin Books, 2008). For the crucial role that free and enslaved blacks played in emancipation, see Berlin, *Long Emancipation*. Arthur M. Schlesinger, Jr.,

The Imperial Presidency [1973] (Reprint, Bridgewater, NJ: Replica Books, 1998). For Schlesinger's contention that the "imperial presidency" has returned in the post–9/11 United States, see Arthur M. Schlesinger, Jr., *War and the American Presidency* (New York: W. W. Norton, 2004), 45–67, esp. 56. For the presidency's place in modern movies and film, see Burton W. Peretti, *The Leading Man: Hollywood and the Presidential Image* (New Brunswick, NJ: Rutgers University Press, 2012).

2. See, for instance, Nelson, *Bad for Democracy*. For a representative conservative libertarian version of this argument, see Gene Healy, *The Cult of the Presidency: America's Dangerous Devotion to Executive Power* (Washington, DC: Cato Institute, 2008).

3. For a recent call to reevaluate "presidential greatness," see Knott, *Lost Soul*. For the presidency's "anti-intellectual" turn, see Melvin Lim, *The Anti-Intellectual Presidency: The Decline of Presidential Rhetoric from George Washington to George W. Bush* (New York: Oxford University Press, 2008).

4. In early October 2019, while answering reporters' questions about his request to Ukrainian president Volodymyr Zelensky to investigate the then-Democratic front-runner for the 2020 nomination, Joe Biden, and Biden's son, Hunter, Trump stated on camera that Ukraine and China should investigate the Bidens. *Meet the Press* host Chuck Todd did not mince words. "I don't say this lightly, but let's be frank: a national nightmare is upon us," Todd told viewers on October 3. "This moment should arguably be a national emergency. The Founding Fathers would've considered it a national emergency if the president publicly lobbied multiple foreign governments to interfere in the next election." For the story, see Jessica Campisi, "MSNBC's Chuck Todd on Trump Moves: 'A national nightmare is upon us,'" *The Hill*, October 3, 2019, https://thehill.com/media/464316-chuck-todd-on-trump-moves-a-national-nightmare-is-upon-us. For the clip, see: https://twitter.com/i/status/1179893903719354368.

5. Baker, "Use That Word!" *New York Times* online, October 23, 2018, https://www.nytimes.com/2018/10/23/us/politics/nationalist-president-trump.html.

BIBLIOGRAPHY

ARCHIVAL SOURCES

American Antiquarian Society (Worcester, MA)
   William C. Cook Jackson Materials
   Lord Family Papers
Columbia University Special Collections (New York)
   Baltimore Collector of the Port Papers
Library of Congress (Washington, DC), Manuscript Division
   Breckenridge Family Papers
   Joshua Coit Correspondence
   Thomas Jefferson Papers
   Miscellaneous Manuscripts
   Rodney Correspondence
Library of Virginia (Richmond)
   Various Virginia newspapers (accessed on microfilm): *Daily Compiler*;
     Examiner; *Impartial Observer*; *Observatory, or, a View of the Times*; *Virginia*
     Gazette and Richmond and Manchester Advertiser; *Virginia Herald*
Massachusetts Historical Society (Boston) and the University of Iowa (Iowa City)
   Adams Family Papers (accessed on microfilm)
Eric P. Newman Numismatic Education Society (St. Louis, MO)
   Continental Currency collection
New-York Historical Society (New York)
   Joshua Brookes Papers
   Peter Curtenius Papers
   Miscellaneous Manuscripts
University of Virginia—Albert and Shirley Small Special Collections Library
    (Charlottesville)
   Jefferson-Randolph Family Scrapbooks of Clippings, 1800–1808

NEWSPAPERS

Connecticut
   Connecticut Courant (Hartford)
   Connecticut Journal (New Haven)

Georgia
   Georgia Gazette (Savannah)
Maryland
   Republican, or, Anti-Democrat (Baltimore)
Massachusetts
   American Herald (Boston)
   Boston Gazette, and Weekly Republican Journal
   Boston Price-Current and Marine Intelligencer
   Columbia Centinel (Boston)
   Constitutional Telegraph (Boston)
   Dedham Gazette
   Democrat (Boston)
   Eastern Argus (Portland, Maine, MA)
   Essex Register (Salem)
   Franklin Herald (Greenfield)
   Greenfield Gazette
   Hampden Whig (Springfield)
   Hampshire Federalist (Springfield)
   Impartial Register (Salem)
   Independent Chronicle (Boston)
   Massachusetts Mercury (Boston)
   Massachusetts Spy (Worcester)
   New-Bedford Mercury
   Newburyport Herald
   New England Palladium (Boston)
   Republican Gazetteer (Boston)
   Republican Spy (Northampton)
   Salem Gazette
   Salem Mercury
   Statesman (Newburyport)
   Sun (Pittsfield)
   Telescope; or, American Herald (Leominster)
   Western Star (Stockbridge)
New Hampshire
   Merrimack Screamer (Concord [NH?])
   New Hampshire and Vermont Journal (Walpole)
   Osborne's New-Hampshire Spy (Portsmouth)
New Jersey
   Centinel of Freedom (Newark)
   New-Jersey Journal (Elizabethtown)
New York
   Albany Centinel
   Albany Register

American Citizen and General Advertiser (New York)
Argus, Greenleaf's New Daily Advertiser (New York)
Balance (Hudson)
Columbian (New York)
Columbian Gazetteer (New York)
Commercial Advertiser (New York)
Country Journal (Poughkeepsie)
Daily Advertiser (New York)
Diary (New York)
Federal Herald (Troy)
Greenleaf's New York Journal (New York)
Herald, a Gazette for the Country (New York)
Independent American (Ballston Spa)
Independent Journal (New York)
Military Monitor, and American Register (New York)
Minerva (New York)
National Advocate (New York)
New-York Commercial Advertiser
New-York Daily Gazette
New-York Evening Post
New York Gazette
New-York Packet
Northern Post (Salem)
Northern Whig (Hudson)
Otsego Herald (Cooperstown)
Republican (Plattsburgh)
Republican Watch-Tower (New York)
Saratoga Register (Ballston Spa)
Spectator (New York)
Suffolk Gazette (Sag Harbor)
Weekly Inspector (New York)
Pennsylvania
   Aurora General Advertiser (Philadelphia)
   Carey's United States Recorder (Philadelphia)
   Carlisle Gazette
   Claypoole's American Daily Advertiser (Philadelphia)
   Democratic Press (Philadelphia)
   Federal Gazette and Philadelphia Evening Post
   Freeman's Journal, or the North-American Intelligencer (Philadelphia)
   Gazette of the United States (Philadelphia)
   Herald of Liberty (Washington)
   Independent Gazetteer (Philadelphia)
   Kline's Carlisle Weekly Gazette (Carlisle)

   National Gazette (Philadelphia)
   Oracle of Dauphin and Harrisburgh Advertiser (Harrisburg)
   Pennsylvania Mercury and Universal Advertiser (Philadelphia)
   Pennsylvania Packet or General Advertiser (Philadelphia)
   Philadelphia Gazette
   Philadelphia Independent Gazetteer
   Pittsburgh Gazette
   Poulson's American Daily Advertiser (Philadelphia)
   Universal Gazette (Philadelphia)
   Weekly Advertiser (Reading)
Rhode Island
   The Phoenix (Providence)
Vermont
   The Washingtonian (Windsor)
Virginia
   Alexandria Times, and District of Columbia Daily Advertiser
   Argus (Richmond)
   Daily Compiler (Richmond)
   Examiner (Richmond)
   Impartial Observer (Richmond)
   Observatory, or, A View of the Times (Richmond)
   Petersburgh Intelligencer (Petersburg)
   Potowmac Guardian and Berkeley Advertiser (Martinsburg)
   Recorder (Richmond)
   Richmond Chronicle
   Spirit of 'Seventy-Six (Richmond)
   Virginia Federalist (Richmond)
   Virginia Gazette, and General Advertiser (Richmond)
   Virginia Gazette and Richmond and Manchester Advertiser (Richmond)
   Virginia Herald (Fredericksburg)
Washington City (Washington, DC)
   Federal Republican
   Federal Republican for the Country
   National Intelligencer
   Washington Federalist

BOOKS AND PAMPHLETS

Address of the Committee Appointed by a Republican Meeting in the County of
   Hunterdon, Recommending GEN. ANDREW JACKSON OF TENNESSEE, to the People
   of New-Jersey, as PRESIDENT of the UNITED STATES. Trenton, NJ: 1824.
Akin, James. "Americans, Behold Your Hero, GENERAL JACKSON . . ." Pennsylvania?,
   1832.

The American Patriotic Song-Book, A Collection of Political, Descriptive, and Humorous Songs, of National Character, and the Production of American Poets Only. Philadelphia: John Bioren, 1816.

American Remembrancer; or, an Impartial Collection of ESSAYS, RESOLVES, SPEECHES, &c. *Relative, or Having Affinity, to the* TREATY *With* GREAT BRITAIN. 3 vols. Philadelphia, 1795.

Aurelius [John Gardner]. *A Brief Consideration of the Important Services, and Distinguished Virtues and Talents, Which Recommend Mr. Adams for the Presidency of the United States.* Boston: Manning & Loring, 1796.

Bradford, William, and George Keith. *The Christian faith of the people of God, called in scorn, Quakers in Rhode-Island (who are in unity with all faithfull brethren of the same profession in all parts of the world) vindicated from the calumnies of Christian Lodowick, that formerly was of that profession, but is lately fallen there-from. And also from the base forgeries, and wicked slanders of Cotton Mather, called a Minister, at Boston . . . To which is added, some testimonies of our antient Friends to the true Christ of God; collected out of their printed books, for the further convincing of our opposers, that it is (and hath been) our constant and firm belief to expect salvation by the man Christ Jesus that was outwardly crucified without the gates of Jerusalem.* Philadelphia, 1692).

The Character and Principles of General Andrew Jackson, In reference to his qualifications for President of the United States, illustrated by FACTS, *Addressed to the Independent Electors of the Cumberland and Oxford Electoral Districts.* [Portland, ME?]: 1828.

Coxe, Tench. *The Federalist, Containing Some Strictures Upon a Pamphlet, Entitled, "The Pretensions of* THOMAS JEFFERSON *to the Presidency, examined, and the Charges against* JOHN ADAMS, *refuted." Which Pamphlet was first published in the Gazette of the United States, in a Series of Essays, under the Signature of* PHOCION. Philadelphia: Matthew Carey, November, 1796.

Documents. Ordered by the Convention of the People of South Carolina, to be Transmitted to the President of the United States, and to the Governor of Each State. Columbia, SC: 1832.

Eaton, John Henry. *The Life of Major General Andrew Jackson: Comprising a History of the War in the South; From the Commencement of the Creek Campaign to the Termination of Hostilities Before New Orleans. Addenda: Containing a Brief History of the Seminole War and Cession and Government of Florida.* 3rd ed. Philadelphia: McCarty & Davis, 1828.

Franklin [Alexander James Dallas]. *Letters of Franklin, on the conduct of the executive, and the treaty negociated, by the chief justice of the United States with the Court of Great Britain.* Philadelphia, 1795.

Hamilton, Alexander. *Letter from Alexander Hamilton, Concerning the Public Conduct and Character of John Adams, Esq., President of the United States.* New York, 1800.

Harper, William. *Political Tract No. 6, January 1832. The Remedy by State Interposition, or Nullification; Explained and Advocated by Chancellor* [William] *Harper, in his Speech at Columbia (S.C.) on the Twentieth September 1830.* Charleston, SC: State Rights and Free Trade Association, 1832.

Hayne, Robert Y., et al. *To the People of South Carolina.* Washington, DC: July 13, 1832.

Haynes, Lemuel. *Dissimulation Illustrated: A Sermon Delivered at Brandon, Vermont, February 22, 1813, Before the Washington Benevolent Society; It Being the Anniversary of Gen. Washington's Birth-day.* Rutland, VT: Fay & Davidson, 1814.

Hill, Isaac. *Brief Sketch of the Life, Character and Services of Major Andrew Jackson, by a Citizen of New-England.* Concord, NH: Manahan, Hoag, 1828.

Hunter, Robert. *By His Excellency Robert Hunter, Esq; captain general and governour in chief of the provinces of New-York, New-Jersey . . . a proclamation.* New York: William Bradford, 1711.

The Jackson Wreath, or National Souvenir. A National Tribute, Commemorative of the Great Civil Victory Achieved by the People, Through the Hero of New Orleans. Philadelphia, Jacob Maas, 1829.

Johnson, Samuel, Jr. *A School Dictionary, Being a Compendium of the Latest and Most Improved Dictionaries. . . .* New Haven, CT: 1797.

Lawrence, George. *An Oration on the Abolition of the Slave Trade, Delivered on the First Day of January, 1813, in the African Methodist Episcopal Church.* New York: Hardcastle & Van Pelt, 1813.

Letters of Franklin, on the Conduct of the Executive, and the Treaty Negociated, by the Chief Justice of the United States with the Court of Great Britain. Philadelphia, 1795.

Lowell, John. *Mr. Madison's War: A Dispassionate Inquiry into the Reasons Alleged by Mr. Madison for Declaring an Offensive and Ruinous War Against Great-Britain. Together With Some Suggestions as to a Peaceable and Constitutional mode of Averting That Dreadful Calamity. By a New-England Farmer.* 3rd ed. Boston: Russell & Cutler, 1812.

Madison Agonistes; or, The Agonies of Mother Goose. Fragment of a Political Burletta, as Acting or to be Acted on the American Stage. To Which Are Added, Sundry Other Monologues, Dialogues, Songs, &c. As Spoken or Sung on the Boards of the great Political Theatre of Europe. London: D. Deans, 1814.

Massachusettensis [pseud.]. *Strictures and Observations Upon the Three Executive Departments of the Government of the United States: Calculated to Shew the Necessity of Some Change Therein, That the Public May Derive That Able and Impartial Execution of the Powers Delegated, Upon which Alone Their Happiness at Home, and Their Respectability Abroad, Must Materially Depend.* N.p., 1792.

Memminger, Christopher Gustavus. *The Book of Nullification, by A Spectator of the Past.* Charleston, SC, 1830.

Nichols, J. Horatio. *Jefferson and Liberty; or Celebration of the Fourth of March. a patriotic tragedy: a picture of the perfidy of corrupt administration. In five acts.* N.p., 1801.

Philadelphia Council of Safety. *In Council of Safety, Philadelphia, December 7, 1776.* Philadelphia, 1776.

Phocion [William Loughton Smith]. *The Pretensions of Thomas Jefferson to the Presidency Examined; and the Charges Against John Adams Refuted. Addressed to the Citizens of America in General; and Particularly to the Electors of the President.* 2 vols. Philadelphia, 1796.

The Political Mirror: or Review of Jacksonism. New York: J. P. Peaslee, 1835.

President II: Being Observations on the Late Official Address of George Washington: Designed to Promote the Interest of a Certain Candidate for the Executive, and to Explode the Pretensions of Others, Addressed to the People of the United States. Philadelphia, 1796.

Proceedings of the Democratic Republican Conventions of Young Men of the State of Pennsylvania, Held at Harrisburg, July 4, 1836 ([Harrisburg]: Pennsylvania Reporter & State Journal, 1836.

A Selection of the Patriotic Addresses, to the President of the United States. Together with the President's Answers. Presented in the Year One Thousand Seven Hundred and Ninety-Eight, and the Twenty-Second of the Independence of America. Boston: John W. Folsom, 1798.

Sheridan, Thomas. *A Complete Dictionary of the English Language.* Philadelphia, 1789.

Sketches of Character; or Facts and Arguments Relative to the Presidential Election, 1828; Earnestly, and anxiously, submitted to the feelings and judgments of the People of Pennsylvania, by one of themselves, who, as a Husband, a Father, and a Citizen, has a deep stake in the Freedom and Happiness of his Country. Philadelphia, 1828.

Snelling, William Joseph. *A Brief and Impartial History of the Life and Actions of Andrew Jackson, President of the United States.* Boston: Stimpson & Clapp, 1831.

To the Freeholders of Prince William, Stafford, and Fairfax.[Fredericksburg?], VA, 1796.

Waldo, S. Putnam. *Memoirs of the Illustrious Citizen and Patriot, Andrew Jackson, Late Major-General in the Army of the United States; and Commander-in-Chief of the Division of the South, by a Citizen of Hagers-Town, MD.* Chambersburg, PA, 1828.

Wharton, Charles Henry. *A Poetical Epistle to His Excellency George Washington, Esq., Commander in Chief of the Armies of the United States of America, From an Inhabitant of the State of Maryland.* Philadelphia, PA: George Kline, 1781.

PUBLISHED PRIMARY SOURCES

Abbott, W. W., et al., eds., *The Papers of George Washington.* 63 vols. to date. Charlottesville: University of Virginia Press, 1968–.

Abbott, W. W., and Edward G. Lengel, eds., *The Papers of George Washington— Retirement Series*. 4 vols. Charlottesville: University of Virginia Press, 1998– 1999.

Abbot, W. W., and Dorothy Twohig, eds., Papers of George Washington—Colonial Series, 10 vols. Charlottesville: University of Virginia Press, 1983–1995.

Adams, Charles Francis, ed. *Memoirs of John Quincy Adams, Comprising Portions of His Diary from 1795 to 1848*, Vol. 5. Philadelphia: J. B. Lippincott, 1875.

———. *The Works of John Adams, Second President of the United States: With a Life of the Author, Notes and Illustrations, by His Grandson, Charles Francis Adams*. Boston: Little, Brown, 1850–1856.

Allen, W. B., ed. *Works of Fisher Ames as Published by Seth Ames*. 2 vols. Indianapolis, IN: Liberty Fund, 1983.

Annual Report of the American Historical Association for the Year 1896. Washington, DC, 1897.

Ball, Terence, ed., *The Federalist with Letters of "Brutus."* Cambridge: Cambridge University Press, 2003.

Bowling, Kenneth R., and Helen E. Veit, eds. *The Diary of William Maclay, and Other Notes on Senate Debates, March 4, 1789–March 3, 1791*. Baltimore, MD: Johns Hopkins University Press, 1988.

Boyd, Julian, et al., eds. *The Papers of Thomas Jefferson*. 44 vols. to date. Princeton, NJ: Princeton University Press, 1950–.

Butterfield, Lyman Henry, et al., eds. *Adams Family Correspondence*. 13 vols. Cambridge: Harvard University Press, 1963–.

Diggins, John Patrick, ed. *The Portable John Adams*. New York: Penguin, 2004.

Dry, Murray, and Herbert Storing, eds. *The Anti-Federalist: Writings by the Opponents of the Constitution*. Chicago: University of Chicago Press, 1981.

Elliot, Jonathan, ed. *The Debates in the Several State Conventions on the Adoption of the Federal Constitution, as Recommended by the General convention at Philadelphia, in 1787. Together with the Journal of the Federal Convention, Luther Martin's Letter, Yates's Minutes, Congressional Opinions, The Virginia and Kentucky Resolutions of '98–'99. And Other Illustrations of the Constitution, in Five Volumes*. Philadelphia: J. B. Lippincott, 1876.

Farrand, Max, ed., *The Records of the Federal Convention of 1787*. 3 vols. New Haven, CT: Yale University Press, 1911.

Foner, Philip S., ed. *The Democratic-Republican Societies: A Documentary Sourcebook of Constitutions, Declarations, Addresses, Resolutions, and Toasts*. Westport, CT: Greenwood Press, 1976.

Ford, Paul Leicester. *The Works of Thomas Jefferson*. 10 vols. New York: G. P. Putnam's, 1892–1899.

Frisch, Morton J. *The Pacificus-Helvidius Debates of 1793–1794: Toward the Completion of the American Founding*. Indianapolis, IN: Liberty Fund, 2007.

Gawalt, Gerard W., ed. *Justifying Jefferson: The Political Writings of John James Beckley*. Washington, DC: Library of Congress, 1995.

Hunt, Gaillard, ed. *The Writings of James Madison.* 9 vols. New York: G. P. Putnam's Sons, 1900–1910.

Hutchinson, William T., et al., eds., *Papers of James Madison, Congressional Series.* 1st ser., Chicago, 1962–1977 (vols. 1–10), 2nd ser., Charlottesville, VA, 1977–1991 (vols. 11–17).

Israel, Fred L., ed. *State of the Union Messages of the Presidents.* Vol. 1, 1790–1860. New York: Chelsea House Publishers, 1967.

Jensen, Merrill, John P. Kaminski, Gaspare J. Saladino, et al., eds. *The Documentary History of the Ratification of the Constitution.* 22 vols. to date. Madison: State Historical Society of Wisconsin, 1976–. Digital ed. edited by John P. Kaminski, Gaspare J. Saladino, et al. Charlottesville: University of Virginia Press Rotunda project, http://rotunda.upress.virginia.edu/founders/RNCN.html.

Kaminski, John P., and Jill Adair McCaughan, eds. *A Great and Good Man: George Washington in the Eyes of His Contemporaries.* 1989. Reprinted, New York: Rowman & Littlefield, 2007.

Koch, Adrienne, ed. *Notes of Debates in the Federal Convention of 1787 Reported by James Madison.* New York: W. W. Norton, 1987.

Looney, J. Jefferson, et al., eds. *The Papers of Thomas Jefferson—Retirement Series.* 15 vols. to date. Princeton, NJ: Princeton University Press, 2005–.

A New Nation Votes: American Election Returns 1787–1825. http://elections.lib.tufts.edu/.

Niles's Weekly Register. Baltimore, 1825.

Peterson, Merrill D., ed. *Thomas Jefferson: Writings.* New York: Library of America, 1984.

Philip, Mark, ed., *Thomas Paine, Rights of Man, Common Sense, & Other Political Writings.* New York: Oxford University Press, 1998.

Rhodehamel, John, ed., *George Washington: Writings.* New York: Library of America, 1997.

Rutland, Robert A., et al., eds. *The Papers of James Madison—Presidential Series.* 10 vols. to date. Charlottesville: University of Virginia Press, 1984–.

Sandoz, Ellis, ed. *Political Sermons of the American Founding Era, 1730–1805.* Indianapolis, IN: Liberty Fund, 1991.

Sheehan, Colleen, and Gary L. McDowell, eds. *Friends of the Constitution: Writings of the "Other" Federalists, 1787–1788.* Indianapolis, IN: Liberty Fund, 1998.

Syrett, Harold C., et al., eds. *The Papers of Alexander Hamilton.* 27 vols. New York: Columbia University Press, 1961–1987.

Twohig, Dorothy, et al., eds. *The Papers of George Washington—Presidential Series.* 19 vols. to date. Charlottesville: University of Virginia Press, 1987–.

United States Census Bureau. "Census of Population and Housing." http://www.census.gov/prod/www/decennial.html.

Walker, David. *David Walker's Appeal to the Coloured Citizens of the World, but in particular, and very expressly, to those of the United States of America.* 1829. Baltimore, MD: Black Classics Press, 1993.

SECONDARY SOURCES

Ackerman, Bruce. *The Failure of the Founding Fathers: Jefferson, Marshall, and the Rise of Presidential Democracy*. Cambridge, MA: Harvard University Press, 2005.

Acosta, Katie L. "Lesbians in the Borderlands: Shifting Identities and Imagined Communities," *Gender and Society* 22, no. 5 (October 2008): 639–659.

Adams, Willi Paul. *The First American Constitutions: Republican Ideology and the Making of the State Constitutions in the Revolutionary Era*. Chapel Hill: University of North Carolina Press, 1980.

Adelman, Joseph. *Revolutionary Networks: The Business and Politics of Printing the News, 1763–1789*. Baltimore, MD: Johns Hopkins University Press, 2019.

Allgor, Catherine. *Parlor Politics: In Which the Ladies of Washington Help Build a City and a Government*. Charlottesville: University Press of Virginia, 2000.

Ambar, Saladin M. *How Governors Built the Modern American Presidency*. Philadelphia: University of Pennsylvania Press, 2012.

Ammon, Harry. *The Genet Mission*. New York: W. W. Norton, 1973.

Anderson, Benedict. *Imagined Communities: Reflections on the Origin and Spread of Nationalism*. 2nd ed. London: Verso Press, 1991.

Bailey, Jeremy D. *The Idea of Presidential Representation: An Intellectual and Political History*. Lawrence: University Press of Kansas, 2019.

———."The New Unitary Executive and Democratic Theory: The Problem of Alexander Hamilton," *American Political Science Review* 102, no. 4 (November 2008): 453–465.

———. *Thomas Jefferson and Executive Power*. Cambridge: Cambridge University Press, 2007.

Bailyn, Bernard. *Ideological Origins of the American Revolution*. Cambridge: Harvard University Press, 1967.

———. *Origins of American Politics*. New York: Knopf, 1967.

———. *To Begin the World Anew: The Genius and Ambiguities of the Founders*. New York: Knopf, 2003.

Baker, Peter. "'Use That Word!': Trump Embraces the 'Nationalist' Label." *New York Times* online, October 23, 2018. https://www.nytimes.com/2018/10/23/us/politics/nationalist-president-trump.html.

Baker, Thomas N. "An Attack Well-Directed: Aaron Burr Intrigues for the Presidency." *Journal of the Early Republic* 31, no. 4 (Winter 2011): 553–598.

Balogh, Brian. *A Government out of Sight: The Mystery of National Authority in Nineteenth-Century America*. Cambridge: Cambridge University Press, 2009.

Banning, Lance. *The Jeffersonian Persuasion: The Evolution of a Party Ideology*. Ithaca, NY: Cornell University Press, 1978.

Baptist, Edward. *The Half Has Never Been Told: Slavery and the Making of American Capitalism*. New York: Basic Books, 2014.

Bartoloni-Tuazon, Kathleen. *For Fear of an Elective King: George Washington and the Presidential Title Controversy of 1789.* Ithaca, NY: Cornell University Press, 2014.

Basker, James G., ed. *Amazing Grace: An Anthology of Poems About Slavery, 1660–1810.* New Haven, CT: Yale University Press, 2002.

Beeman, Richard. *Plain, Honest Men: The Making of the American Constitution.* New York: Random House, 2009.

Beeman, Richard, Stephen Botein, and Edward C. Carter, II, eds. *Beyond Confederation.* Chapel Hill: University of North Carolina Press, 1987.

Berlin, Ira. *The Long Emancipation: The Demise of Slavery in the United States.* Cambridge, MA: Harvard University Press, 2015.

Bilder, Mary Sarah. *Madison's Hand: Revising the Constitutional Convention.* Cambridge, MA: Harvard University Press, 2017.

Bowling, Kenneth R. "A Tub to the Whale: The Founding Fathers and the Adoption of the Federal Bill of Rights." *Journal of the Early Republic* 8, no. 3 (Autumn 1988): 223–251.

Bradburn, Douglas. *The Citizenship Revolution: Politics and the Creation of the American Union, 1774–1804.* Charlottesville: University of Virginia Press, 2009.

Brands, H. W. *Heirs to the Founders: The Epic Rivalry of Henry Clay, John Calhoun, and Daniel Webster, the Second Generation of American Giants.* New York: Knopf, 2018.

Breen, T. H. *George Washington's Journey: The President Forges a New Nation.* New York: Simon & Schuster, 2015.

Brooke, John L. "'King George Has Issued Too Many Pattents for Us': Property and Democracy in Jeffersonian New York." *Journal of the Early Republic* 33, no. 2 (Summer 2013): 187–217.

Broussard, James H. *The Southern Federalists, 1800–1816.* Baton Rouge: Louisiana State University Press, 1978.

Browne, Stephen Howard. *Jefferson's Call for Nationhood: The First Inaugural Address.* College Station: Texas A&M University Press, 2003.

Buel, Richard. *America on the Brink: How the Political Struggle over the War of 1812 Almost Destroyed the Young Republic.* New York: Palgrave Macmillan, 2005.

Burns, James MacGregor, and Susan Dunn. *George Washington.* New York: Times Books, 2004.

Butterfield, Kevin. "Unbound By Law: Association and Autonomy in the Early American Republic." PhD diss., Washington University, St. Louis, 2010.

Calloway, Colin G. *The Indian World of George Washington: The First President, the First Americans, and the Birth of the Nation.* New York: Oxford University Press, 2018.

Calvert, Jane E. "An Expansive Conception of Rights: The Quakerly Abolitionism of John Dickinson." In *"When in the Course of Human Events": 1776 at Home,*

Abroad, and in American Memory, edited by Will R. Jordan, 21–54. Macon, GA: Mercer University Press, 2018.

———. *Quaker Constitutionalism and the Political Thought of John Dickinson.* Cambridge: Cambridge University Press, 2009.

Campisi, Jessica. "MSNBC's Chuck Todd on Trump Moves: 'A National Nightmare Is upon Us,'" *The Hill*, October 3, 2019, https://thehill.com/media/464316 -chuck-todd-on-trump-moves-a-national-nightmare-is-upon-us.

Chervinsky, Lindsay M. *The Cabinet: George Washington and the Creation of an American Institution.* Cambridge, MA: Harvard University Press, 2020.

———. "The President's Office: How George Washington and Thomas Jefferson Used Private Space to Shape the Cabinet." Paper presented at the American Historical Association Conference, Washington, DC, 2018.

Coates, Ta-Nehisi. *We Were Eight Years in Power: An American Tragedy.* New York: One World, 2017.

Cogliano, Francis D. *Emperor of Liberty: Thomas Jefferson's Foreign Policy.* New Haven, CT: Yale University Press, 2014.

Combs, Jerald A. *The Jay Treaty: Political Battleground of the Founding Fathers.* Berkeley: University of California Press, 1970.

Connor, Walker. "A Nation Is a Nation, Is a State, Is an Ethnic Group Is a . . ." *Ethnic and Racial Studies* 1 (October, 1978): 377–400.

Cornell, Saul. *The Other Founders: Anti-Federalism and the Dissenting Tradition in America, 1788–1828.* Chapel Hill: University of North Carolina Press, 1999.

———. *A Well-Regulated Militia: The Founding Fathers and the Origins of Gun Control in America.* New York: Oxford University Press, 2008.

Cotlar, Seth. *Tom Paine's America: The Rise and Fall of Transatlantic Radicalism in the Early Republic.* Charlottesville: University of Virginia Press, 2011.

Crane, Elaine F. "Publius in the Provinces: Where was *The Federalist* Reprinted outside of New York City?" *William and Mary Quarterly*, 3rd series, 21, no. 4 (October 1964): 589–592.

Cronin, Thomas E., ed. *Inventing the American Presidency.* Lawrence: University Press of Kansas, 1989.

De Conde, Alexander. *The Quasi-War: The Politics and Diplomacy of the Undeclared War with France, 1797–1801.* New York: Charles Scribner's & Sons, 1966.

Diggins, John Patrick. *John Adams.* New York: Henry Holt, 2013.

Dinkin, Robert J. *Voting in Revolutionary America: A Study of Election in the Original Thirteen States, 1776–1789.* Westport, CT: Prager, 1982.

Ducayet, James. "Publius and Federalism: On the Use and Abuse of *The Federalist* in Constitutional Interpretation." *New York University Law Review* 68 (October 1993): 821–869.

Dunbar, Erica Armstrong. *Never Caught: The Washingtons' Relentless Pursuit of Their Runaway Slave, Ona Judge.* New York: Simon & Schuster, 2017.

Edling, Max. *A Revolution in Favor of Government: Origins of the U.S. Constitution and the Making of the American State.* New York: Oxford University Press, 2003.

Einhorn, Robin. *American Taxation, American Slavery.* Chicago: University of Chicago Press, 2006.

Elkins, Stanley, and Erick McKitrick. *The Age of Federalism: The Early American Republic, 1788–1800.* New York: Oxford University Press, 1995.

Ellis, Joseph J. *Founding Brothers: The Revolutionary Generation.* New York: Knopf, 2000.

Estes, Todd. "The Art of Presidential Leadership: George Washington and the Jay Treaty." *Virginia Magazine of History and Biography* 109, no. 2 (2001): 127–158.

——. *The Jay Treaty Debate, Public Opinion, and the Evolution of American Political Culture.* Amherst: University of Massachusetts Press, 2008.

——. "'The Most Bewitching Piece of Parliamentary Oratory': Fisher Ames's Jay Treaty Speech Reconsidered," *Historical Journal of Massachusetts* 28, no. 1 (Winter 2000): 1–21.

Eustace, Nicole. *1812: War and the Passions of Patriotism.* Philadelphia: University of Pennsylvania Press, 2012.

——. *Passion is the Gale: Emotion, Power, and the Coming of the American Revolution.* Chapel Hill: University of North Carolina Press, 2008.

Eustace, Nicole, and Fredrika J. Teute, eds. *Warring for America: Cultural Contests in the Era of 1812.* Chapel Hill: University of North Carolina Press, 2017.

Fischer, David Hackett. *The Revolution of American Conservatism: The Federalist Party in the Era of Jeffersonian Democracy.* New York: Harper & Row, 1965.

Forbes, Robert Pierce. *The Missouri Compromise and Its Aftermath: Slavery and the Meaning of America.* Chapel Hill: University of North Carolina Press, 2007.

Freeman, Joanne B. *Affairs of Honor: National Politics in the New Republic.* New Haven, CT: Yale University Press, 2001.

——. *The Field of Blood: Violence in Congress and the Road to Civil War.* New York: Farrar, Straus & Giroux, 2018.

Fritz, Christian G. *American Sovereigns: The People and America's Constitutional Tradition before the Civil War.* Cambridge: Cambridge University Press, 2008.

Furstenberg, François. *In the Name of the Father: Washington's Legacy, Slavery, and the Making of a Nation.* New York: Penguin, 2006.

Genovese, Michael A. *The Power of the American Presidency, 1789–2000.* New York: Oxford University Press, 2001.

Glatthaar, Joseph T. *Forged in Battle: The Civil War Alliance of Black Soldiers and White Officers.* Baton Rouge: Louisiana State University Press, 1990.

Golove, Donald M. "Treaty-Making and the Nation: The Historical Foundations of the Nationalist Conception of the Treaty Power." *Michigan Law Review* 98, no. 5 (March 2000): 1075–1319.

Gordon-Reed, Annette. *The Hemingses of Monticello: An American Family.* New York: Norton, 2008.

Gordon-Reed, Annette, and Peter S. Onuf. *"Most Blessed of the Patriarchs": Thomas Jefferson and the Empire of the Imagination.* New York: Norton, 2016.

Grant, James. *John Adams: Party of One.* New York: Farrar, Straus & Giroux, 2005.

Greenstein, Fred I. *Inventing the Job of President: Leadership Style from George Washington to Andrew Jackson*. Princeton, NJ: Princeton University Press, 2009.

Gregg, Gary L., II. *The Presidential Republic: Executive Representation and Deliberative Democracy*. New York: Rowman & Littlefield, 1997.

Grinspan, Jon. *The Virgin Vote: How Young Americans Made Democracy Social, Politics Personal, and Voting Popular in the Nineteenth Century*. Chapel Hill: University of North Carolina Press, 2016.

Gross, Jonathan, ed. *Thomas Jefferson's Scrapbooks: Poems of Nation, Family, & Romantic Love, Collected by America's Third President*. Hanover, NH: Steerforth Press, 2006.

Gustafson, Sandra M. *Eloquence Is Power: Oratory and Performance in Early America*. Chapel Hill: University of North Carolina Press, 2000.

Heale, M. J. *The Presidential Quest: Candidates and Images in American Political Culture, 1787–1852*. London: Longman, 1982.

Healy, Gene. *The Cult of the Presidency: America's Dangerous Devotion to Executive Power*. Washington, DC: Cato Institute, 2008.

Hofstadter, Richard. *The Idea of a Party System: The Rise of a Legitimate Opposition in the United States, 1780–1840*. Berkeley: University of California Press, 1970.

Horn, James, Jan Ellen Lewis, and Peter S. Onuf, eds. *The Revolution of 1800: Democracy, Race, and the New Republic*. Charlottesville: University of Virginia Press, 2002.

Howe, Daniel Walker. "The Political Psychology of *The Federalist*," *William & Mary Quarterly* 3rd series, 44, no. 3 (July 1987): 485–509.

———. *What Hath God Wrought: The Transformation of America, 1815–1848*. New York: Oxford University Press, 2007.

Howe, John. *Language and Political Meaning in Revolutionary America*. Amherst: University of Massachusetts Press, 2004.

Irvin, Benjamin. *Clothed in Robes of Sovereignty: The Continental Congress and the People out of Doors*. New York: Oxford University Press, 2011.

Isenberg, Nancy. *White Trash: The 400-Year Untold History of Class in America*. New York: Penguin, 2017.

Isenberg, Nancy, and Andrew Burstein. *The Problem of Democracy: The Presidents Adams Confront the Cult of Personality*. New York: Penguin, 2019.

Jacobs, Harriet. *Incidents in the Life of a Slave Girl, Written by Herself*. 1860. Cambridge, MA: Harvard University Press, 2009.

Johnson, Michael P. "Denmark Vesey and His Co-Conspirators," *William & Mary Quarterly* 3rd series, 58, no. 4 (October 2001): 915–976.

Johnson, Ronald Angelo. *Diplomacy in Black and White: John Adams, Toussaint L'Ouverture, and Their Atlantic World Alliance*. Athens: University of Georgia Press, 2014.

Kastor, Peter J. *The Nation's Crucible: The Louisiana Purchase and the Creation of America*. New Haven, CT: Yale University Press, 2004.

Kelly, Christopher S., ed., *Executing the Constitution: Putting the President Back into the Constitution.* Albany: SUNY Press, 2006.

Kendi, Ibram X. *Stamped from the Beginning: The Definitive History of Racist Ideas in America.* New York: Nation Books, 2016.

Kenyon, Cecilia M. "Men of Little Faith: The Anti-Federalists on the Nature of Representative Government," William and Mary Quarterly, 3rd series, 12, no. 1 (January 1955): 3–43.

Kerber, Linda K. *Federalists in Dissent: Imagery and Ideology in Jeffersonian America.* Ithaca, NY: Cornell University Press, 1970.

Ketcham, Ralph. *The Anti-Federalist Papers.* New York: Signet, 1986.

———. *James Madison: A Biography.* Charlottesville: University Press of Virginia, 1990.

———. *Presidents above Party: The First American Presidency, 1789–1829.* Chapel Hill: University of North Carolina Press, 1984.

Knott, Stephen F. *The Lost Soul of the American Presidency: The Decline into Demagoguery and the Prospects for Renewal.* Lawrence: University Press of Kansas, 2019.

Kreider, Angela. "Spinning the Bladensburg Races: The Commander in Chief and the Burning of Washington." Paper presented at the Society for Historians of the Early American Republic Conference, July 19, 2013.

Kukla, Jon. *A Wilderness So Immense: The Louisiana Purchase and the Destiny of America.* New York: Knopf, 2003.

Lainer-Vos, Dan. "Manufacturing National Attachments: Gift-Giving, Market Exchange and the Construction of Irish and Zionist Diaspora Bonds. *Theory and Society* 41 (2012): 73–106.

Lampi, Philip J. "The Federalist Party Resurgence, 1808–1816: Evidence From the New Nation Votes Database," *Journal of the Early Republic* Vol. 33, No. 2 (Summer 2013): 255–281.

Larson, Edward. *George Washington: Nationalist.* Charlottesville: University of Virginia Press, 2016.

Larson, John Lauritz. *Internal Improvement: National Public Works and the Promise of Popular Government in the United States.* Chapel Hill: University of North Carolina Press, 2001.

Lewis, Jan Ellen. "Of Every Age Sex & Condition: The Representation of Women in the Constitution." *Journal of the Early Republic* 15, no. 3 (Autumn 1995): 359–387.

Lim, Melvin. *The Anti-Intellectual Presidency: The Decline of Presidential Rhetoric from George Washington to George W. Bush.* New York: Oxford University Press, 2008.

Link, Eugene P. *The Democratic-Republican Societies, 1770–1800.* New York: Columbia University Press, 1942.

Lockridge, Kenneth. *Literacy in Colonial New England: An Enquiry into the Social Context of Literacy in the Early Modern West.* New York: W. W. Norton, 1974.

Loughran, Trish. *The Republic in Print: Print Culture in the Age of U.S. Nation Building, 1770–1870*. New York: Columbia University Press, 2007.

Maier, Pauline. *American Scripture: Making the Declaration of Independence*. New York, 1997.

———. *From Resistance to Revolution: Colonial Radicals and the Development of American Opposition to Britain, 1765–1776*. 1972. Reprinted, New York: W. W. Norton, 1991.

———. *Ratification: The People Debate the Constitution, 1787–1788*. New York: Simon & Schuster, 2011.

Malone, Dumas. *Jefferson the President, First Term*. New York: Little, Brown, 1970.

Mansfield, Harvey C., Jr. *Taming the Prince: The Ambivalence of Modern Executive Power*. New York: Free Press, 1989.

Marsten, Jerrilyn Greene. *King and Congress: The Transfer of Political Legitimacy, 1774–1776*. Princeton, NJ: Princeton University Press, 1987.

Martin, Robert W. T. *Government by Dissent: Protest, Resistance, and Radical Democratic Thought in the Early American Republic*. New York: New York University Press, 2013.

McConville, Brendan. *The King's Three Faces: The Rise and Fall of Royal America, 1688–1776*. Chapel Hill: University of North Carolina Press, 2006.

McCormick, Richard P. *The Presidential Game: The Origins of American Presidential Politics*. New York: Oxford University Press, 1982.

McDonald, Forrest. *The American Presidency: An Intellectual History*. Lawrence: University Press of Kansas, 1994.

McDonald, Robert M. S. *Confounding Father: Thomas Jefferson's Image in His Own Time*. Charlottesville: University of Virginia Press, 2016.

McPherson, James M. *Tried by War: Abraham Lincoln as Commander in Chief*. New York: Penguin Books, 2008.

Moats, Sandra. *Celebrating the Republic: Presidential Ceremony and Popular Sovereignty, From Washington to Monroe*. DeKalb: Northern Illinois University Press, 2010.

Morgan, Edmund S. *American Slavery, American Freedom: The Ordeal of Colonial Virginia*. New York: W. W. Norton, 1975.

Morrison, Michael A., ed. *The Human Tradition in Antebellum America*. New York: Rowman & Littlefield, 2000.

Nash, Gary B. *The Forgotten Fifth: African Americans in the Age of Revolutions*. Cambridge, MA: Harvard University Press, 2006.

Neem, Johann N. "American History in a Global Age." *History and Theory* 50 (February 2011): 1–70.

———. *Creating a Nation of Joiners: Democracy and Civil Society in Early National Massachusetts*. Cambridge, MA: Harvard University Press, 2008.

Nelson, Dana. *Bad for Democracy: How the Presidency Undermines the Power of the People*. Minneapolis: University of Minnesota Press, 2008.

Nichols, David K. *The Myth of the Modern Presidency*. University Park: Pennsylvania State University Press, 1994.

Onuf, Peter, ed. *Jeffersonian Legacies*. Charlottesville: University Press of Virginia, 1993.

———. *Jefferson's Empire: The Language of American Nationhood*. Charlottesville: University of Virginia Press, 2000.

Park, Benjamin E. *American Nationalisms: Imagining Union in the Age of Revolutions*. Cambridge: Cambridge University Press, 2018.

———. "The Angel of Nullification: Imagining Disunion in an Era Before Secession." *Journal of the Early Republic* 37, no. 3 (Fall 2017): 507–536.

Parkinson, Robert G. *The Common Cause: Creating Race and Nation in the American Revolution*. Chapel Hill: University of North Carolina Press, 2016.

Parsons, Lynn Hudson. *The Birth of Modern Politics: Andrew Jackson, John Quincy Adams, and the Election of 1828*. New York: Oxford University Press, 2009.

Pasley, Jeffrey L. *The First Presidential Contest: 1796 and the Founding of American Democracy*. Lawrence: University Press of Kansas, 2013.

———. *"The Tyranny of Printers": Newspaper Politics in the Early American Republic*. Charlottesville: University of Virginia Press, 2001.

Pasley, Jeffrey L., Andrew Robertson, and David Waldstreicher, eds., *Beyond the Founders: New Approaches to the Political History of the Early American Republic*. Chapel Hill: University of North Carolina Press, 2004.

Peretti, Burton W. *The Leading Man: Hollywood and the Presidential Image*. New Brunswick, NJ: Rutgers University Press, 2012.

Peterson, Merrill D. *Thomas Jefferson and the New Nation: A Biography*. New York: Oxford University Press, 1970.

Polsky, Andrew J. *Elusive Victories: The American Presidency at War*. New York: Oxford University Press, 2012.

Posner, Eric A., and Adrian Vermeule. *The Executive Unbound: After the Madisonian Republic*. New York: Oxford University Press, 2010.

Rael, Patrick. *Black Identity and Black Protest in the Antebellum North*. Chapel Hill: University of North Carolina Press, 2002.

Rakove, Jack N. *Original Meanings: Politics and Ideas in the Making of the Constitution*. New York: Vintage, 1996.

Raphael, Ray. *Mr. President: How and Why the Founders Created a Chief Executive*. New York: Knopf, 2012.

Ratcliffe, Donald. "The Right to Vote and the Rise of Democracy, 1787–1828." *Journal of the Early Republic* 33, no. 2 (Summer 2013): 219–254.

Riccards, Michael P. *A Republic, If You Can Keep It: The Foundation of the American Presidency: 1700–1800*. Westport, CT: Greenwood Press, 1987.

Rogers, George C., Jr. *Evolution of a Federalist: William Loughton Smith of Charleston (1758–1812)*. Columbia: University of South Carolina Press, 1962.

Rose, Lisle A. *Prologue to Democracy: The Federalists in the South, 1789–1800*. Lexington: University of Kentucky Press, 1968.

Rothman, Joshua. *Notorious in the Neighborhood: Sex and Families across the Color Line in Virginia, 1787–1861*. Chapel Hill: University of North Carolina Press, 2003.

Rothstein, Richard. *The Color of Law: A Forgotten History of How Our Government Segregated America*. New York: Liveright Publishing, 2017.

Rudalevige, Andrew. *The New Imperial Presidency*. Ann Arbor: University of Michigan Press, 2005.

Rutland, Robert A. "The First Great Newspaper Debate: The Constitutional Crisis of 1787–88," *Proceedings of the American Antiquarian Society* 97, pt. 1 (1987): 43–58.

Schlesinger, Arthur M., Jr., ed., *The History of American Presidential Elections*. 4 vols. New York: Chelsea House, 1971.

———. *The Imperial Presidency*. 1973. New York: Houghton Mifflin, 2004.

———. *War and the American Presidency*. New York: W. W. Norton, 2004.

Scofield, Merry Ellen. "The Fatigues of His Table: The Politics of Presidential Dining during the Jefferson Administration." *Journal of the Early Republic* 26, no. 3 (Fall 2006): 449–469.

Shane, Peter M. *Madison's Nightmare: How Executive Power Threatens American Democracy*. Chicago: University of Chicago Press, 2009.

Sharp, James Roger. *American Politics in the New Republic: The New Nation in Crisis*. New Haven, CT: Yale University Press, 1993.

———. *The Deadlocked Election of 1800: Jefferson, Burr, and the Union in the Balance*. Lawrence: University Press of Kansas, 2010.

Sheehan, Colleen. *James Madison and the Spirit of Republican Self-Government*. New York: Cambridge University Press, 2009.

Simon, James F. *What Kind of Nation: Thomas Jefferson, John Marshall, and the Epic Struggle to Create a United States*. New York: Simon & Schuster, 2002.

Skowronek, Stephen. *The Politics Presidents Make: Leadership from John Adams to George Bush*. Cambridge, MA: Harvard University Press, 1993.

———. *Presidential Leadership in Political Time: Reprise and Reappraisal*. Lawrence: University Press of Kansas, 2008.

Slaughter, Thomas P. *The Whiskey Rebellion: Frontier Epilogue to the American Revolution*. New York: Oxford University Press, 1988.

Smith, Gary Scott. *Faith and the Presidency: From George Washington to George W. Bush*. New York: Oxford University Press, 2006.

Smith, James Morton. *Freedom's Fetters: The Alien and Sedition Laws and American Civil Liberties*. Ithaca, NY: Cornell University Press, 1956.

Smith-Rosenberg, Carroll. *This Violent Empire: The Birth of an American National Identity*. Chapel Hill: University of North Carolina Press, 2011.

Stagg, J. C. A. *Mr. Madison's War: Politics, Diplomacy, and Warfare in the Early American Republic, 1783–1830*. Princeton, NJ: Princeton University Press, 1983.

———. *The War of 1812: Conflict for a Continent*. Cambridge: Cambridge University Press, 2012.

Steele, Brian. *Thomas Jefferson and American Nationhood*. Cambridge: Cambridge University Press, 2012.

Storing, Herbert J., ed. *The Anti-Federalist: Writings by the Opponents of the Constitution*. Chicago: University of Chicago Press, 1981.

Taylor, Alan. *American Revolutions: A Continental History, 1750–1804*. New York: W. W. Norton, 2016.

———. *The Civil War of 1812: American Citizens, British Subjects, Irish Rebels, and Indian Allies*. New York: Knopf, 2010.

———. *The Internal Enemy: Slavery and War in Virginia, 1772–1832*. New York: Norton, 2013.

———. "John Adams." In *The American Presidency*, edited by Alan Brinkley and Davis Dyer, 20–32. New York: Houghton Mifflin, 2004.

Thompson, Mary. *"The Only Unavoidable Subject of Regret": George Washington, Slavery, and the Enslaved Community at Mount Vernon*. Charlottesville: University of Virginia Press, 2019.

Trautsch, Jasper M. *The Genesis of America: U.S. Foreign Policy and the Formation of National Identity, 1793–1815*. Cambridge: Cambridge University Press, 2018.

Travers, Len. *Celebrating the Fourth: Independence Day and the Rites of Nationalism in the Early Republic*. Amherst: University of Massachusetts Press, 1997.

Trees, Andrew S. *The Founding Fathers and the Politics of Character*. Princeton, NJ: Princeton University Press, 2004.

Troy, Gil. *See How They Ran: The Changing Role of the Presidential Candidate*. New York: Free Press, 1991.

Waldstreicher, David. *In the Midst of Perpetual Fetes: The Making of American Nationalism, 1776–1820*. Chapel Hill: University of North Carolina Press, 1997.

———. *Slavery's Constitution: From Revolution to Ratification*. New York: Hill & Wang, 2010.

White, Ed. "Early American Nations as Imagined Communities," *American Quarterly* 56, no. 1 (March 2004): 49–81.

White, Leonard D. *The Federalists: A Study in Administrative History*. New York: MacMillan, 1956.

———. *The Jeffersonians: A Study in Administrative History, 1801–1829*. New York: MacMillan, 1951.

Wilentz, Sean. *The Rise of American Democracy: Jefferson to Lincoln*. New York: W. W. Norton, 2008.

Wood, Gordon S. *Creation of the American Republic, 1776–1787*. Chapel Hill: University of North Carolina Press, 1969.

———. *Empire of Liberty: A History of the Early Republic, 1789–1815*. New York: Oxford University Press, 2009.

———. *Friends Divided: John Adams and Thomas Jefferson*. New York: Penguin, 2018.

———. *The Radicalism of the American Revolution*. New York: Knopf, 1991.

————, ed. *John Adams: Writings from the New Nation, 1784–1826.* New York: Library of America, 2016.

Yokota, Kariann Akemi. *Unbecoming British: How Revolutionary America Became a Postcolonial Nation.* New York: Oxford University Press, 2011.

Young, James Sterling. *The Washington Community, 1800–1828.* New York: Columbia University Press, 1966.

Zelizer, Julian. *Governing America: The Revival of Political History.* Princeton, NJ: Princeton University Press, 2012.

INDEX

abolitionism: black, white opposition to, 254, 255 (fig.), 262; Dickinson and, 216; Eagans on, 255

Adams, John
on American character: decline of, indicated in 1796 election, 137; destructive effect of dissent on, 141; as masculine, vs. French effeminacy, 135–136; presidents' responsibility to guard and develop, xxvi, 133, 134–135, 138, 143, 145
bluntness of, 132
correspondence with John Quincy Adams, 132–133, 159
criticisms of monarchist views, 61–62, 125–127, 132, 149
Defence of the Constitutions, 125–126, 134
Discourses on Davila, 134
election as vice president, 44–45
and election of 1796, 109–110
on election of 1796 as evidence of American decline, 137
on executive's power to balance competing interests, 134
and foreign influence, opposition to, 138
on French character, 135–137
on French influence, dangers of, 137
and French Revolution, opposition to excesses of, 125
and grandiose title for President, 60–62
and Hamilton, dislike of, 159–160
insecurities of, 131–132
on Jefferson, poor character of, 137
and Knox, dislike of, 159
legacy of, 131

as more relatable that other founders, 132
as nativist, 160
personal offense at criticism, 131, 134
as political theorist, xxvi
Republican dissent against, xxvi–xxvii
as spirit of selfishness infesting US, 137
trust of British, 137
on virtue as byproduct of morality, 135
Washington's queries to, 58, 60
See also election of 1796

Adams, John, as president, xxvi
and Alien and Sedition Acts, xxvi, 133, 139–140
Annual Message of 1799, 160–161
conflation of support for US and for president, 136, 143
desire to unite Americans with common values, 134–135, 138, 144
on dissent as destructive and un-American, 129, 132, 133, 136, 138
firmness of, 145
Hamilton's attack on, 161–162
immigration restrictions, 156
on importance of national unity, 136
Republican dissent against, 129, 134, 150–159
and Saint Domingue slave rebellion, 156–157
and theory of representative government vs. practical need for strong executive, 135

353

revolution, in Jefferson's view, 202; as tie in Electoral College, 165
election of 1804, 184
election of 1808, 213, 219
election of 1812, War of 1812 and, 221, 227
election of 1824: candidates in, 249, 250, 269; and fracturing of Republican Party, 250; resolution of, in Congress, 270; as stolen by Washington elites, in Jackson's view, 270–271
election of 1828: candidates in, 269; vicious campaign in, 271
election of 1832, Jackson victory in, 276–277
elections, local, Republican focus on, 151
Electoral College: current debates on, 285; and election of 1800, 165; and election of Washington as president, 44–45, 47; federalists on, as check of presidential power, 28; indirect selection of electors, 165; and people's indirect selection of President, 35
Elkins, Stanley, 66
Ellsworth, Oliver, 27
Embargo Act of 1807
  burden on New England states, 215
  Federalist criticism of, 189–193; as abuse of power, 193; as exposure of Jefferson's military impotence, 189–192, 206–207; for foreign influence in Jefferson administration, 191; as indicative of general decline under Jefferson, 191; in Jefferson's scrapbook, 206–207; as reckless tyranny, 215
  as foreign policy blunder, 189
  Jefferson's reasons for imposing, 189
  Republican defense of, 207, 218
Emerson, William, 183–184
enslaved blacks: defining of freedom in opposition to, xxv, xxvii, 57, 104; exclusion from American

unity, 56–58; exclusion from voting in Washington's election, 47, 299–300n15; masters' sexual relations with, as well known but not discussed, 174–175; number of attempted escapes from George Washington, 57; and War of 1812, 211
Esculapius, xv
executive: responsibility for public acceptance of Constitution, 7; responsibility for shaping American identity, 7

Fabius, 28
factions, Hamilton on presidential power as antidote to, 31–33, 36
federal government: overreach, turbulent decades following War of 1812 and, 260; stronger, Hamilton's support for, 63
Federalist criticisms of Jefferson, 116–118, 168–193
  for arbitrary and secretive rule, 192
  as beginning of end for US, 169, 207–208
  for Burr conspiracy, 188–189
  as conduit of French radicalism, 112, 114, 115, 120, 121, 183–184
  for disingenuousness, 169
  for divisive partisanship, 172–173, 174
  for Hemings, Sally, 156, 174–178, 191–192
  for insufficient support of white supremacy, 174, 175–179
  as power-hungry absolutist, 171
  for pushing Southern slaveholders' interests, 169
  for radical democratization leading to chaos, 169, 177–179
  as reflection of pervasive racism, 184
  for religious views, 122, 182–183
  for replacing Adams' appointees with his own, 170–174
  as slaveholder seeking enslavement of opponents, 173–174, 179, 192

Valerius, 86, 89, 90, 94, 95, 97

Van Buren, Martin, 281

Veritas, 73–74, 77, 83

Vesey, Denmark, 262

veto power of president, as type of dissent, 27

"Vice-President" (1789), 39

Virginia: Constitution ratification, 11, 38; Constitution ratifying convention, 12; and debate on 3/5ths rule, 5, 6, 8, 9; and War of 1812, 230–231

Virginia general assembly, criticism of National Bank plan, 67–68

Virginia Resolutions, 152–153

voting rights; adoption of universal white male suffrage, 253; exclusion of women and black people from, 253

Waldo, S. Putnam, 271

Waldstreicher, David, 55, 254

Walker, David, 254

Walpole, Robert, 64–65

Warden, David, 235–237

War of 1812
  American victories in, 228
  Armstrong as scapegoat for failures of, 236–238
  Battle of Sacketts Harbor, 228
  black commentators on, 250, 254, 257–258, 260
  black soldiers in, xxvii, 254, 256
  British attacks on Southern plantations, 230
  British/Indian/black barbarity in: as point of agreement across party lines, 235; as racist and sexist narrative, 230; in US war Patriot Rebellion, 236, 237 (fig.); in US war propaganda, 228–232
  British satire on US motives in, 224–225
  and burning of Washington, 211, 235–236
  criticism of: as attempt by Southern slave owners to enslave North,

224, 225; growth in, with military defeats, 228; for insufficient cause for war, 222–223, 226; for likely devastating effects, 221; for Madison's lack of firmness and military skill, 236, 241–242, 326n63; for Madison's manipulation by French, 212, 221–222, 223–225; for plans to take Canada, 223–224; for Southern interests' control of war, 222, 224–225, 242; tensions between sectional and national rhetoric in, 227; turn from war itself to Madison's leadership, after Jackson's victory, 238, 241–242, 243–246, 247
  critics of: as complicit in losses, 229, 234; as unmanly, slave-like, and un-American, 232, 233–235; on war's costs without any gain, 241–242, 245, 246
  declaration of war, 220
  early US losses in, 226
  and election of 1812, 221, 227
  end of, 212
  enemy in, as foreign and nonwhite, 211
  and enslaved blacks, 211
  events leading to, 208–209, 212
  Federalist resistance to, 211–212, 221–223, 225–227
  Federalist states refusing to participate in, 226–227, 232–233, 241
  Fort Detroit, British capture of, 226, 227–228, 229
  Fort Michilimackinac, British capture of, 226, 227–228
  Hartford Convention and, 243
  impact on presidential politics, 211
  and invasion of Canada, 223, 224, 226
  and Jackson, rise of, 253, 281
  Jefferson's preparations for, 218–219
  Madison on necessity of, 220